Heath's Modern Language Series

Goethes Faust

EDITED BY

CALVIN THOMAS

VOLUME II: THE SECOND PART

D. C. HEATH & CO., PUBLISHERS
BOSTON NEW YORK CHICAGO

3 A 6

Printed in U. S. A.

PREFACE.

THE guiding principles of this edition of *Faust* are sufficiently explained in the preface to the First Part. In this volume, as in the first, I have given much space to genetic considerations, my conviction being that these studies, far from being a hindrance, are the greatest of helps toward the right understanding and the full enjoyment of the poem as a work of art; and that they are also the best of safeguards against subjective vagaries of interpretation. One who regards *Faust* as if it had come into the world ready-made, who looks at it always from the logical point of view and is over-anxious about its philosophic unity, will invariably miss its poetic *Eigenart* and end by giving us himself instead of Goethe. One may learn much, I have myself learned much, from the philosophic expounders; but they need to be taken cautiously, with the antidote ever at hand. I fear it does not strengthen the case for the Second Part to 'claim for it,' as did Bayard Taylor, 'a higher intellectual character, if a lower dramatic and poetical value, than the First Part.' Both parts must stand or fall as poetry. And they are going to stand. There is no longer room for doubt on that point.

In editing the Second Part I have wished to make friends for it, but I have thought that I could do this best not by praising it or arguing for it, but simply by showing how it came to be what it is, giving necessary explanations and leaving the rest to the reader's poetic sense. The *quam pulchre* of an editor or a guide can not give sight to the blind, but it may easily bore those that have eyes to see. With critical questions I have tried to deal in a spirit remote alike from the 'toothless piety' which Vischer deprecated and from the unteachable rigor which he exemplified. One should indeed be inexorable with a great poet, as Lessing says; but one should never forget that the initial presumption is always in the great poet's favor.

In my commentary I have tried to be useful and to meet every genuine difficulty, but not, like some of my German predecessors, to supply a manual of general intelligence. For example: One who does not know the rudiments of the Greek and Roman mythology will not find them in my notes. The Second Part of *Faust* is not for analphabetics of any kind. As in the First Part, I have avoided the extended discussion of conflicting opinions, preferring that the learned should accuse me of dogmatism rather than that the student should find me prolix. To illustrate the necessity of conciseness: Had I quoted and discussed the pros and cons of all the interpretations of the line

Das Unerhörte hört sich nicht,

I should have needed several pages. For a similar reason I have foreborne to cite parallel passages save where they are unusually illuminative.

Following the Weimar text, as I have done, I have felt exempt from the necessity of dealing much with textual questions or of quoting paralipomena and variant readings, except where they are clearly and highly important for the understanding of the text in its final form. The most of the variant readings published in Vol. 15 of the Weimar Goethe are mere chips from the poet's workshop. Scholarship owes a lasting debt of gratitude to Prof.

Erich Schmidt for the skill and care with which this mass of material has been edited; for among it is much that is valuable. But the mass is very great and the bulk of it has only a curious interest.

Finally, I wish to express my thanks to Prof. Suphan, of Weimar, who kindly gave me access to the manuscripts of the Goethe-Schiller archives and to the library of the Goethe-Gesellschaft; also to the able corps of scholars who are engaged under his general supervision in preparing the monumental Weimar edition of Goethe's works. To Dr. Wahle, Dr. Fresenius, Dr. Steiner and Dr. Leitzmann I often had occasion to go for help, and was met always with the most obliging courtesy. I am also under great obligation to the genial Dr. Ruland, who permitted me to make use of Goethe's private library, to examine his collection of engravings, and to make photographs at my pleasure. The inspiration of working with these gentlemen for half a year in the quiet city of the muses — Weimar with the 'peculiar lot' — will always remain in my memory as the pleasantest part of a task which has been throughout a labor of love.

CALVIN THOMAS.

NEW YORK, August, 1897.

INTRODUCTION.

I.

THE GENESIS OF THE SECOND PART.

1. The Bipartition of the Poem.

THE earliest datable reference to a Second Part of *Faust* is found in a letter of Schiller to Goethe, written Sept. 13, 1800.* By this time, that is, some eight years before the publication of the First Part, the plan of dividing the poem into two parts was a fully settled matter, and numerous passages intended for the Second Part had been written down.† That the idea of bipartition was conceived prior to the year 1797 is hardly probable, though a recently published document seems to afford some ground for assuming an earlier date. This document, found

* Cf. Intr. to Part I, p. lvii.

† On May 5, 1798, Goethe wrote to Schiller that he had 'copied his old and exceedingly confused MS. of *Faust* and distributed it in fascicles numbered according to a complete scheme.' This 'complete scheme,' as we learn from his diary, was made June 23, 1797. Papers found in the archives at Weimar show numbers running up to 30, those from 20 on having to do with Part II. One of them, bearing the number 20, exhibits Faust at the Emperor's court with Mephistopheles as 'physicus.' No. 22 is of uncertain reference. In No. 24 Faust is disconsolate over the death of Helena. No. 27 relates to his last hours and death (song of the Lemurs). No. 30 contains a 'Parting Announcement' and a 'Farewell,' which were to close the entire poem and correspond to the 'Prelude' and 'Dedication' at the beginning. But these verses, except the song of the Lemurs, were rejected. Of the text as it stands there is pretty good evidence that the following portions were written prior to 1800: Faust's monologue in *terza rima*, ll. 4679–4727, the Baccalaureus-scene, and the death-scene in the 5th act. When we add to these the '*Helena* of 1800,' embracing 265 lines, we see that Part II had really received a large amount of attention before Part I was completed.

among the papers of Goethe at Weimar, consists of a hastily written and curiously abstract outline of the play couched in the following language:

'Ideal striving for influence over and sympathetic communion with the whole of Nature. Appearance of the Spirit as genius of the world and of deeds. Conflict between form and the formless. Preference for formless content over empty form. Content brings form with it. Form is never without content. These antitheses, instead of reconciling them, to be made more disparate. Clear, cold, scientific endeavor, Wagner. Vague, warm, scientific endeavor, Student. Personal enjoyment of life seen from without. In vagueness (*Dumpfheit*) passion. First Part. Enjoyment of deeds looking without and enjoyment with consciousness. Beauty. Second Part. Enjoyment of deeds from within. Epilogue in chaos on the way to hell.'

We see here at first a clear reference to the opening monologue and the Earth-Spirit. The 'conflict between form and the formless' alludes to Faust and Wagner; the 'personal enjoyment of life seen from without' is obscure, but seems to point to 'Auerbach's Cellar' and the 'Witch's Kitchen'; while the 'passion in vagueness' (i.e. confusion, lack of mental clearness) means the love-tragedy. The 'enjoyment of deeds looking outward' refers to Faust's beneficent activity in his old age, and the 'beauty' to Helena. The sketch bears no date, and the paper and handwriting are such as might belong to any period of Goethe's work upon *Faust*, except indeed the last. Some are inclined, accordingly, to date it back to his youth and to see in the proposed 'epilogue' the evidence of an original intention to dispose of Faust in accordance with the legend.* Against this it must be urged, however, that the style of the paper is quite out of tune with the

* See, e.g., G.-J., XVII, 209, where E. W. Manning publishes the paralipomenon in facsimile and contends for the date 1773. Harnack, V. L. IV, 169, argues for 1788; Pniower, V. L. V, 408, for 1795 or 1797; Graffunder, in *Preussische Jahrbücher* 68, 709, for 1797. Lack of space prevents a review of arguments pro and con, or a detailed defence of the conclusion recorded in the text above.

poetic method of the youthful Goethe, who saw with vivid directness and wrote in pictures. It is not easy to think of him in his pre-Weimarian period as trying to help his imagination by laying out his work in such a clumsy jargon of analytical abstractions. On the contrary, the language suggests a poet who has become estranged from his theme and is trying to return to it by ratiocination; who is recapitulating as philosopher what he has already written as seer, in order that he may fit it to what he purposes to write, and make the whole cohere in accordance with an 'idea.' We know that such was the mood of Goethe and such his occupation in 1788 and again in 1797; and while there is no conclusive evidence for either date, there seems a slight balance of probability in favor of the later.

What then of the proposed 'epilogue in chaos'? Nothing in the 'Fragment,' and nothing in the Göchhausen *Faust*, requires us to suppose that the hero is on the way to perdition; and there are good reasons for thinking that no such ending was ever planned.* The probability is, as we have already observed, that the youthful Goethe did not concern himself very much over the ultimate fate of his hero after death. He simply paid no attention to the theology or the mythology of the legend, but invented a devil of his own and assigned an important role to the Earth-Spirit, who is not in the legend at all. The play was to be, indeed, a tragedy; and this meant that its hero would succumb to a higher power. But his defeat was to be only the shipwreck of his titanic idealism; the ending in death of his aspirations for superhuman power and experience. He was to engage in battle with the nature of things, and the nature of things would of course prove too strong for him. But that he was to be morally van-

* Cf. what is said on the subject in Intr. to Part I, p. xxxvi ff. In his old age Goethe insisted repeatedly that, in completing *Faust* as he did complete it, he was but working out the conception of his youth. It was the same *Faust*. But would it have been if, midway in his life, he had made the most radical change in his plan which it would be possible to make or to imagine?

quished — lost for sins that were not sins of the will, or damned for an intellectual presumption which, however foolish it might be, was not ignoble, — this we can not easily suppose. Such an ending would have run counter to Goethe's own most cherished convictions and to all the tendencies of the time in which he lived. The moral superiority of Faust to the devil is a vital postulate of the plot, and is patent enough even in the Göchhausen scenes.

What then can have lain in Goethe's mind when he penned the words 'epilogue in chaos on the way to hell'? The most plausible answer seems to be the following: The idea of the epilogue grew out of the requirements of the legend. Inasmuch as the climax of the old popular drama was the final scene, in which the wicked Dr. Faustus is carried off by devils, any Faust who should escape that fate would be, one may say, no Faust at all. And so, although Goethe's hero was to be saved, it was necessary that he go, at the close of his earthly days, or at least seem to go, the way of his legendary prototype. Afterwards it would be for divine grace to rescue him. This led to the idea of an epilogue in which Mephistopheles, carrying off his prey in seeming triumph, would pass through 'chaos' (conceived as an abysmal void situate between earth and hell) and there perhaps boast of his victory over the Lord.* Then, before the gates of hell, good angels would appear and claim their own.†

It would appear then that the bipartition of *Faust* was not foreseen in Goethe's early scheme, but grew partly out of the mere magnitude of the subject as it developed on his hands, and partly out of the poetic requirements of the theme, as they presented themselves to his mind after the enlargement of his plan in 1797.‡

---

* In fulfillment of ll. 332–3.

† I owe to Prof. Witkowski, of Leipzig, the suggestion that Goethe's imagination may have been influenced at this point by the church legend of Christ's descent into hell, — an awful descent as the forerunner of a glorious apotheosis.

‡ Cf. Intr. to Part I, pp. lx, lxi.

Originally, it is to be presumed, he had had in view a play of ordinary length, though he did not trouble himself greatly about stage requirements. He did not dream that his work was to become the poetic mirror of a lifetime, and much that was destined to go into it he could not possibly foresee. What he very certainly did contemplate from the outset, however, was a complete reproduction of the legend in its essential features. Of this there can no longer be any doubt whatever. Now the matter of the legend, considered as a dramatic theme, groups itself about three main centers of interest: first, Faust's discontent, leading up to his compact with the devil; secondly, his exploits and experiences in the course of twenty-four years passed in the devil's company; and thirdly, his last hours and fate after death. In dealing with this material the prose narratives lead quickly up to the compact, and are mainly occupied with the exploits and experiences. And the same is true of the puppet-plays. On the other hand, Goethe, working in a desultory way and letting his imagination play freely upon the pictures that presented themselves to his mind's eye, had led slowly up to the compact, and then intercalated not a little matter that does not belong to the legend.* And thus he found, when he had filled in to his satisfaction those portions of the work that were to precede the death of Gretchen, that he had written verses enough for a play of ordinary length and had hardly crossed the threshold of the legend. The real Faust-story was yet to come.

It is perfectly certain, therefore, that from the first moment after his resumption of work in 1797, he must have had in view, if not a Second Part under that name, at least an indefinite extension of his plot beyond the close of the love-tragedy. The

* The Student-scene, the 'Witch's Kitchen,' and the entire love-tragedy. Leaving out the three preliminary poems, some 1500 verses are occupied with the exposition of Faust's *Weltschmerz* before the compact is reached. The love-tragedy, minus the 'Walpurgis-Night' and the 'Intermezzo,' take as many more.

Prelude and the Prologue are a prelude and a prologue not to the First Part, but to a much more comprehensive work. The Prologue promises that Faust, hitherto a wanderer in the dark, shall be led into the light; and this has reference, as we see from the metaphor of the growing tree,* not to any sudden interposition of divine power, but to the slow-acting operation of time and experience. Mephistopheles is to be discomfited in the end.† Lines 1765–1775 foretell a long and wide acquaintance with life in all its phases, and the compact provides for a service on the part of Mephistopheles, which is to last until Faust shall say: It is enough; I am content.‡ Finally, Faust is to see the 'great world' as well as the 'small.' § — All these passages point clearly to a dramatic action which has only begun when Faust emerges from the prison-cell of the dead Gretchen.

And then as to the poetic requirements of the theme. The mind of Faust was to be 'cleared up'; i.e., he was to outgrow his hypochondria and his pessimism, and rise to a saner, serener view of human existence. Enlarged experience was to reconcile him to life. He was to find ideals the pursuit of which should seem worthy and dignified. Above all he was to find a sphere of activity capable of affording him solid satisfaction; not indeed the placid contentment stipulated in the compact, but the higher gratification of having lived to some purpose. All this required that there should be a Second Part and that this Second Part should open upon a new world.

2. *The Helena of 1800.*

But how was this redemption of Faust to be connected with the data of tradition? What the legend gives in describing his experience of 'life' is a medley of sensual gratifications, travels,

---

* Ll. 308–11.

† L. 327.

‡ Ll. 1692 ff.

§ L. 2052.

tricks, magical exploits, etc., which are for the most part ridiculous in themselves, without any organic connection, and without any lasting effect upon his character. Among them, however, is the incident of Helena. In the original Faust-book we read of a revel held one evening by a company of jolly students at the house of Dr. Faust.* The conversation turns upon beautiful women, and one of the students declares that, of all the women that ever lived, he would like best to see 'the fair Helena of Greece,' on whose account the goodly city of Troy was destroyed. Dr. Faust promises to produce her 'spirit,' in form and appearance just as she was on earth. First enjoining upon his guests to remain perfectly still, he leaves the room, and when he returns Helena follows him, a vision of ravishing beauty. Later, at the end of his career, Faust demands of the devil that this selfsame Helena be given him for a paramour. Mephistopheles complies, and Faust becomes by Helena the father of a son, Justus Faustus, who has prophetic powers and disappears forever, together with his mother, on the day of Faust's death.

In the Christlich Meynenden Faust-book the episode is somewhat differently motivated. Faust desires to marry, but the devil objects on the ground that marriage is a Christian ordinance. He first terrifies Faust into submission and then gives him Helena as a substitute for a lawful wife.

In the puppet-plays the story appears in a still different setting. At the end of his twenty-four years Faust becomes penitent and endeavors by prayer to make his peace with God so as to escape the consequences of his folly. The devil comes and finds him on his knees, expostulates with him and denounces him as a weakling. Finally, when nothing else will avail, he brings in Helena. Faust is entranced by her beauty and goes away with her saying: 'I will be thy Paris.' Thus he falls again and fin-

* Cap. L.

ally into the devil's clutches. In several of the plays, when Faust attempts to embrace her, she vanishes into nothing, or else turns into a hideous dragon, thus evincing her true character as a diabolical illusion — a *Teufelinne* — produced for the purpose of ensnaring Faust's soul and diverting his mind from holy thoughts.

From the first, as we have seen, Goethe planned to make use of this episode; but his early intention bore little resemblance to the elaborate play-within-a-play that finally came from his hand under the name of *Helena: A Classico-Romantic Phantasmagoria*. Like *Faust* itself, the *Helena* was the work of a lifetime, which grew with its author's growth and changed with his changes.* Extant paralipomena tell us in part the story of its evolution.

As at first conceived, the episode was to be entirely medieval. Helena was to be conjured up and to make her appearance at once in Faust's magic castle on the Rhine. Here she was to fall in with an old 'Egyptian' stewardess (Mephistopheles as Gypsy pander), who would introduce her to Faust. At first she was to think him 'abominable' (in his costume of medieval knight) and to pine for 'her own people.' On being told that these were 'all gone' and that she herself was a shade called up from Orcus, she was to complain that 'Venus had again deceived her,' and then, without much need of persuasion, to accept the situation and take Faust as her liege lord. The whole scene was pitched in the key of the legend, — grotesque, fantastic supernaturalism. The characters were to speak in rimed octosyllabic verse. Helena was not a stately antique heroine, but the seductive *Buhlerin* of the

* On the 14th of November, 1827, a few months after the appearance of the *Helena*, Goethe wrote a letter to his friend Knebel, in which he speaks of the work as 'a product of many years that seems to me now as wonderful as the high trees in my garden which, in fact younger than the conception of the *Helena*, have grown to such a height that a reality which I myself called into being seems like something miraculous, incredible, and beyond experience.' — Goethe's diary shows that the trees were planted Nov. 1, 1776.

Faust-tradition. What the higher poetic import of the scene was to have been can not be guessed with any approach to certainty.

With this conception in his mind Goethe arrived at that period of his life in which he was to complete the First Part of *Faust.* It was the time of his most enthusiastic Hellenism. He had become estranged from the literary ideals of his youth and looked upon them as barbarous. Greek forms, the Greek spirit, were now, to his mind, synonymous with perfection. He began studying the Greek poets and discussing them with Schiller and other friends. He founded the *Propylæa* to further the knowledge of classical art, and he even tried to vie with Homer by making an *Achilleid* in hexameters.

No wonder, then, when the ardent classicist of 1797 resumed his musings upon the Faust-theme with a view to converting the old theological legend of sin and damnation into a modern drama of mental clearing-up, — no wonder that the Helena-episode soon began to take on a new meaning and to open before him a vista of richest poetic possibilities. He saw in the infatuation of the German magician for an ancient Greek ideal of womanly beauty the key to his dramatic problem. Faust should be made heroic by his union with Helena. Just as he himself, Goethe, dated a new epoch in his own life, an epoch of clearer ideas and of larger effort, from his acquaintance with classical forms in Italy; and just as modern Europe owed its intellectual renaissance to the rediscovery of Hellas in the 15th century, being led thereby to put away the crotchets of medieval scholasticism and to enter upon a new era of aspiration and achievement, — so Faust should be lifted out of himself, his hypochondria cured, and his nature attuned to deeds of high emprise, by his marriage to the antique Queen of Beauty.

But if all this was to be made dramatically plausible the first requirement of art was that the character of Helena herself be ennobled. If Faust was to be redeemed by the 'glory that was

Greece,' it must be the genuine glory, and not a grotesque medieval counterfeit of it. It would not do to bring Helena to a German castle and let her *suppose* herself in Sparta; for a phantom-heroine endowed, by poetic fiat, with sufficient life-likeness to work the regeneration of Faust would not be so easily deceived. She must actually *be* in Sparta and must appear in a Spartan environment. She must speak the language of a Greek tragic heroine, i.e., the iambic trimeter. And then, of course, there must be a chorus.

Such a poetic project for bringing the antique into sharp contrast with the modern by means of a severely classical introduction to be followed by a magic shifting of the scene to a German castle, where all should be romantic, grew naturally out of the living issues of the day. Schiller had recently published his famous essay *Upon Naive and Sentimental Poetry*, in which he attempts to define in general terms the characteristic differences between ancient and modern poetry and to claim for the modern its rights as 'art of the infinite.'* Tieck and Novalis and the Schlegels had but lately begun to put forth the efforts which were to result in the so-called 'Romantic School.' The Middle Ages, which the eighteenth century had for the most part serenely ignored as 'dark,' were just beginning to be interesting and to reveal to searching eyes their own peculiar greatness. And the brooding-place of all these new ideas was the little city of Jena, where Goethe was as much at home as in Weimar, and with whose leading spirits he stood in constant and intimate association. Of course he could not fail to be affected. His sympathies were classical, but the man who had kindled to enthusiasm in his youth over Gothic architecture and had immortalized 'the rude self-helper Götz von Berlichingen,' could never be-

* "Jener (der alte Dichter) ist mächtig durch die Kunst der Begrenzung, dieser ist es durch die Kunst des Unendlichen." — *Schillers Werke,* X, 454.

come totally insensible to the poetic glamour of the medieval epoch.

And so we find our poet addressing himself in the summer of 1800 to the elaboration of a Faust-episode to be known as *Helena in the Middle Ages. A Satyr-Drama.** Sept. 12 he writes to Schiller: 'Luckily I have been able these last eight days to hold fast the beautiful situations of which you know and my Helena has actually appeared on the stage. Now, however, I am so attracted by the beauty of my heroine's situation that I am sorry to think of converting her into a specter (*Fratze*). Really I feel no small inclination to make my beginning the basis of a serious tragedy.' To this Schiller replies the next day congratulating his friend on the progress of the new work and urging him not to be troubled over the necessity of 'barbarizing the beautiful forms and situations.' The 'barbarism' that is imposed by the nature of the subject will not destroy the higher import of the work, nor neutralize its beauty, but will rather give it a unique charm of its own. Sept. 23 Goethe reports further progress upon the *Helena*, and felicitates himself upon his friend's approval. All is going well; only for the present he prefers to restrain himself and not look far ahead. He can see already, however, that from this 'peak,' and from this alone, will a right view of the whole work be obtainable. Schiller replies encouragingly respecting the 'synthesis of the noble and the barbarous,' and then the correspondence becomes silent respecting the *Helena*, save that a letter of Goethe, written Nov. 18, notes that 'some good motives have lately suggested themselves.' We must suppose that leisure failed, or else that our poet lost interest in his theme as he drew

---

* So the MSS. of 1800. A later MS. has 'Satyroma' pasted over the title 'Satyr-Drama.' Both titles were meant simply to call attention to the element of grotesqueness and fantastic unreality in the proposed work. It was neither tragedy nor comedy, and so there was nothing left, in view of its antique character, but to call it a satyr-drama, though there were no satyrs in it.

nearer to the necessity of 'barbarizing' his antique heroine, i.e., of disclosing her real character as a phantom-puppet moved at will by Mephistopheles, and of whisking her away from her Spartan home to a medieval German castle. At any rate he presently turned his attention to the completion of the First Part and decided to publish that alone provisionally and let the completion of the work take its chances in the future.

The *Helena* of 1800 has been preserved.* It comprises 265 lines and coincides substantially in form and substance with lines 8488–8802 of the final version, save that several choruses are lacking † and that the meter has been retouched in many places. The conception of Helena as antique heroine is already fully developed, and Phorkyas ‡ is there in all her hideousness. Both are conceived less grossly than the *Buhlerin* and *Kupplerin* of the earlier plan. Instead of taking up with Faust through a desire of male society and under the sensual promptings of the stewardess, Helena is made to dread death § at the hands of her husband Menelaus. For the rest there is no suggestion that Helena and the chorus of Trojan maidens are phantoms. The lines might in very truth be taken as the beginning of a serious antique trag-

---

* It is published in *Werke* XV, 2, p. 72 ff.

† Namely, ll. 8516–23, 8560–7, 8591–8603, 8610–37.

‡ One wonders how Goethe came to give his devil this particular name and disguise at a time when the Classical Walpurgis-Night had not yet been dreamed of. The explanation is probably something like this: From the first his fancy had been attracted by the simple *motif:* beauty in visible contrast with ugliness; and he had embodied the latter in the form of a Gypsy hag. But with the transference of the scene to Sparta the stewardess had of course to be Hellenized. Moreover, to accord with the canons of Greek tragedy the scene had to take place *in the open air*. Hence came the happy thought of letting Helena first enter the palace and then be frightened back into the sunlight by the portentous ugliness of the stewardess, who would then follow her and form a picturesque figure standing in the doorway during the following chorus and colloquy. But if the daughter of Zeus was to be stampeded by vulgar fear, the cause must be equal to the effect. An ordinarily ugly old woman would not do. So the choice fell upon Enyo, daughter of Phorkys, the very acme of female hideousness. (Cf. n. to l. 7967.)

§ This motive was borrowed by Goethe from Euripides; cf. the *Troades*, l. 876.

edy. In other words, we see that the fragment of 1800 stopped short, after all, of the deprecated 'barbarization.'

3. The Prose Sketch of 1816.

After the year 1808, in which the First Part was published, it would seem that the problem of completing the drama received no further attention and was gradually lost sight of.* For this neglect no other reason can be assigned than that our poet had again fallen out of sympathy with his theme. The mood was lacking; he was more interested in other matters. Of one thing, however, we may be sure: The neglect was not due to any feeling that the First Part was after all sufficiently complete in itself. In Goethe's autobiographical 'Annals' for the year 1806 (the passage was probably written in 1823) we read: 'The two divisions of the *Elegies*, as they now stand, were arranged, and *Faust*, in its present form, given the character of a fragment (fragmentarisch behandelt).' This shows clearly enough, if any proof were needed beyond the mere form of publication,† how the author himself

* Goethe's diary for May 13, 1808, contains, in Riemer's handwriting, the words: *De Fausti dramatis parte secunda et quae in ea continebuntur.*

† In the first edition, of 1808, we find, first, the full-page title, *Faust, Eine Tragödie;* after this, each with full-page titles: *Zueignung*, *Vorspiel auf dem Theater*, and *Prolog im Himmel.* After this comes the title: *Der Tragödie, Erster Theil.* When, therefore, Carlyle 'questioned,' in 1828, 'whether it had ever occurred to any English reader of *Faust* that the work needed a continuation or even admitted one,' he imputed to English readers a large measure of obtuseness. But the error appears also in more recent writings. For example, the late Prof. Blackie wrote in the *Nineteenth Century* for April, 1886: "There certainly was not to be looked for (namely in Goethe's old age) a consistent continuation of what had been for thirty years before the public as a 'tragedy,' — for a tragedy certainly it is, as the title-page bears, in the main; a very human tragedy, in which a dreamy, vague speculation, joined to a monstrous intellectual ambition, plunging for relief of its overstrain into a current of sentimental sensuality, lands all concerned, as it always must do, in ruin. — In this last scene and with these last words ('hither to me') the tragedy is both dramatically and morally wound up. No continuation is required." Still grosser, if possible, is the error of Gwinner, *Goethe's Faustidee nach der ursprünglichen Conception*, u.s.w., Frankfurt, 1892, p. 15: "Erst viele Jahre nach der Vollendung dieser 'Tragödie,' die ja nicht als ein erster Theil sondern als ein abgeschlossenes Werk erschien," u.s.w.

continued to regard that portion of the play which was already in print. He recognized that it was an unfinished work which could give but an imperfect idea of his poetic intention, but he had not the courage to attack the gigantic task of further elaboration. Under these circumstances he decided, in the year 1816,* to take the public into his confidence and make known what his original intention had been. In other words, he decided to incorporate in the eighteenth book of his autobiography, the book which was to tell the story of the year 1775, a sketch of his plot as it then lay in his mind. The sketch was prepared, but better things were in store for *Faust*, and it was never used. It was luckily preserved, however, and has lately been published.†

The sketch of 1816 deals, naturally enough, only with that portion of the plot which was not then familiar to the public, i.e., the Second Part; wherefore the allusion to the Second Part in the first sentence can not be taken as evidence that the bipartition of the poem had itself been a part of the original plan. With reference to the substance of the plot, it is reasonable to suppose that the poet of 1816 may no longer have been able to distinguish sharply at every point between original elements of 1775 and later accretions of 1797–1800. On the other hand, there is no reason to doubt that the outline is, in a general way, just what it purports to be; and one can only regret that it breaks off before the conclusion of the drama is reached. The substance of the sketch is as follows:

At the beginning of the Second Part Faust is seen asleep. Spirits sing to him alluring songs of glory and power, and he wakens, cured of his sensuality and in an exalted mood. Mephistopheles comes and tells him that his presence is desired at the court of Emperor Maximilian in Augsburg. The pair go to Augsburg and are well received by the Emperor. The talk turns

* *Tagebuch*, 16. Dec. 1816: "Meine Biographie. Schema des 2. Theils von Faust."
† *Werke*, XV, II, p. 173 ff. See also Eckermann, I, 112 (Aug. 10, 1824).

on magic, and his Majesty calls for spirit-manifestations. Faust goes out to get ready and Mephistopheles prescribes as court-doctor. In the evening a magic theater builds itself. The shades of Helena and Paris appear and are commented on by the spectators. Confusion arises, the spirits vanish suddenly and Faust is left in a swoon. When he comes to himself he is madly in love with Helena and insists on following her. Mephistopheles tells of great difficulties in the way: she belongs to Orcus, can be conjured up but not retained, etc. Faust insists and Mephistopheles finally consents. A castle on the Rhine is chosen as the future home of Helena and Faust. The owner is a crusader absent in Palestine, the castellan a magician. Helena appears with a corporeal being given her by means of a magic ring which she wears on her finger. She thinks she is just coming home from Troy to Sparta, feels lonely and pines for society, especially for that of men. Faust appears as medieval German knight. At first she does not like him, but presently yields to his suit and becomes queen of the castle. The pair have a son who, from the moment of his birth, sings, dances, and beats the air. The boy is petted and given full liberty, save that he is forbidden to cross a certain line which bounds the magic precinct of the castle. But one day he hears music and sees soldiers; crosses the line out of curiosity, gets into a quarrel with the soldiers and is killed. The mother wrings her hands in grief, and in so doing pulls off her ring. She falls back into the arms of Faust, who finds that he has only her dress in his embrace. Mephistopheles, who has seen all this in the capacity of an old stewardess, tries to comfort Faust by directing his attention to the charms of wealth and power. The owner of the castle has been killed in Palestine and greedy monks try to get possession of the place. Faust fights with them, aided by three mighty men, whom Mephistopheles gives him as allies, comes off victorious, avenges the death of his son and wins a great estate. Meanwhile he grows old, and what happens to him later will appear when we gather together at some future time the fragments, or rather the sporadic passages of the Second Part which have already been worked out, and thus rescue some things that will be of interest to the reader.

It is unnecessary to compare this sketch in detail with the final version. One sees at a glance the general resemblance and the radical differences. The chief value of the document is to prove beyond a doubt that an elaborate Helena-episode in the *Märchen* style was part of Goethe's original Faust-plan. For the rest it stops just short of the interesting point and leaves one to speculate in vain concerning the reasons which induced its author, in the year 1816, to withhold the conclusion of his plot. Was it that the dramatic details just before and just after his hero's death were not now sufficiently clear in his own mind to admit of succinct recital? Was it that the gap between the fantastic *Märchen* and the lofty seriousness of the conclusion was not yet bridged over in thought to his satisfaction? Or was it that he did not wish to divulge the momentous secret of his intended departure from the legend in the matter of Faust's salvation? One can see at this date no very good ground for such reluctance, but we know from another source that it was felt by the author of *Faust*. Under date of August 3, 1815, Boisserée reports the following dialogue with Goethe:

"Then he came to talk of *Faust*, remarking that the First Part ends with the death of Gretchen, and now it must be begun anew *par ricochet*. That, he says, is difficult, since the painter has now another hand, another brush. What he could do now would not go together with the earlier matter. I (Boisserée) replied that he should have no scruples on that account; one man can transport himself into another, how much more the master into his earlier works. Goethe: 'Very true; and besides much is already done.' I asked about the conclusion. Goethe: 'That I will not say, must not say; but it also is already finished, and very well done too, in the grandiose style of my best period.'"

The 'conclusion' here referred to is not the apotheosis of Faust, but the scenes depicting his last hours and death.

4. The Helena of 1827, i.e., the Third Act.

After the year 1816 we hear no more of *Faust* for another period of eight years. That part of *Dichtung und Wahrheit* which was to contain the sketch just spoken of did not get itself written until long afterward, and the sketch itself remained unpublished. In the summer of 1824, as Goethe was occupied, with the advice and assistance of Eckermann, in preparing for the final edition of his works, the momentous question arose, What to do with *Faust?* On being shown the sketch of 1816 Eckermann advised against the publication of it in the hope that he might yet see the completion of the poem itself. And so it was to be. The following winter our poet, now in the seventy-sixth year of his age, but with the vigor of his genius all unharmed by time, returned once more to the long-neglected project of his youth; and although even now, for the time being, his intentions did not go further than the completion of the *Helena*, he kept returning to his task at the friendly instigation of Eckermann,* and finally, in the summer of 1831, was able to pronounce his great life-work finished.

We have now to study the genesis of the Second Part somewhat in detail; for the manner of its completion throws light upon its character as an artistic whole. As in the case of the First Part, we have to do not with an orderly procedure from the beginning to the end, but with a desultory process of filling-in and rounding-out here and there. Speaking roughly, the third act was written first, and after that the first and second. Next came the completion of the already half-finished fifth, and last of all the fourth.†

---

* 'You may take the credit for it,' said Goethe to Eckermann, March 7, 1830, 'if I finish the Second Part of *Faust*. I have often told you so before, but I must repeat it in order that you may know it.'

† The authorities for the genesis of Part II are (1) Goethe's diary, the data of which, so far as they relate to *Faust*, are given by Erich Schmidt in an appendix to his edition of the Göchhausen *Faust;* (2) Eckermann's *Gespräche mit Goethe;* (3) Goethe's letters; and (4) a mass of dated paralipomena, i.e. 'schemes,' first drafts, etc. that chanced to get written down on envelopes, play-bills, freight-bills, or other such scraps of paper bearing a definite date. For these consult the *Lesarten* in vol. XV of the Weimar *Goethe*. Cf. also Düntzer in *Zeitschrift für deutsche Philologie* XXIII, 67 ff. and the same author's *Zur Goethe-Forschung* (Stuttgart, 1891), p. 246 ff.; also Niejahr in the *Euphorion*, vol. I, p. 81 ff.

The records show that Goethe took up *Faust* Feb. 25, 1825, and 'held it fast' about six weeks. At first he seems to have turned his thoughts to the very end of the drama: The poet who was now beginning to think of his own legacy to the after-world, and who knew that 'the traces of *his* earthly days would not perish in æons,' felt drawn to the close of Faust's career.* Very soon, however, it was the *Helena* that claimed his attention; and if this project had interested him in the year 1800, how much more must it interest him now!

For since 1800 he had lived through one of the most thrilling and fateful epochs in modern history. He had seen the great events of 1806, the ruinous defeat of Prussia, and the final collapse of the Holy Roman Empire. He had seen Napoleon dictate European politics from Berlin and Vienna, had shared in the humiliation of Germany, and had himself fallen a prey, perhaps somewhat too easily, to the illusion that the Corsican was invincible. And then came the great days of the liberation-period. He saw the German heart take fire, and the love of country become, in particular cases, a very ecstasy of devotion. He saw the new romanticism in literature ally itself with the patriot cause and illustrate with sword and pen the terrible poetry of the soldier passion. He saw a gifted young poet leave home and love and art and career, and take the field to die, with song on his lips, for the fatherland.

And after this the Greek Revolution and the Quixotic enterprise of Lord Byron, ending in his untimely death at Missolonghi on the 19th of April, 1824.

For years Goethe had watched the career of Byron with interest, admiring the eminence of his personality and the power of his writings. A friendly intercourse had sprung up between the two

* The Diary for Mar. 13, 1825, contains the entry: 'An *Faust* den Schluss fernerhin redigirt.' Besides this, ll. 11424–36 and ll. 11519–26 have been found, the one on a *Brief-concept*, the other on an inquiry to the library, of March, 1825.

poets through exchange of letters.* In March, 1823, Goethe sent to Byron through Sterling an assurance of 'the inexhaustible reverence, admiration and love that we cherish for him.' Byron answered from Leghorn in July, being then already on his way to Greece to 'see if he could be of any little use there,' and promising that if he ever came back he would 'pay a visit to Weimar to offer the sincere homage of one of the many millions of admirers' of the 'undisputed sovereign of European literature.' After Byron's death his character continued for years to be a favorite subject of Goethe's conversation. He saw here a shining example of genius unable to tame itself or to make its peace with the world of commonplace fact; a gifted nature dowered with titanic passion, a superb gift of song, and the reasoning powers of a child; † an embodied wilfulness spurning the ties of family and country, making a law unto itself, and finally lured on to death by a dazzling dream of impossible military achievement.

The recent death of Byron, and the prominence of the Greek war in the public interest, led Goethe, in the spring of 1825, to turn his attention to the history and geography of Greece. He began reading on the subject,‡ and ere long a new design had taken shape in his mind for the second, or romantic, part of the *Helena*.§ The Rhine-castle of the earlier plan was transferred to the heart of the Peloponnesus — to Arcadia. Here Faust should

---

* Cf. E. Schmidt, *Helena und Euphorion* (Strassburg, 1889), p. 170.

† 'Lord Byron is great only as a poet; as soon as he reflects, he is a child.' — Goethe to Eckermann, Jan. 18, 1825.

‡ Among the books drawn by Goethe from the Court Library at Weimar in 1825 were: Luden, (history of Greece in) *Allgemeine Geschichte der Völker und Staaten;* Gell, *Journey in the Morea;* Stanhope, *Greece in 1823-4;* Blacquière, *Die griechische Revolution;* Dodwell, *Travels in Greece;* Williams, *Select Views in Greece;* Castellan, *Briefe über Morea;* Depping, *La Grèce;* Stanhope, *Olympia;* Spon and Wheeler, *Reise nach Griechenland.*

§ How this part of the episode had been imagined in 1800, — what name had been thought of for the child of Helena and Faust, how his character was conceived, what his fate was to symbolize, — we do not know; we only know that all was different from what

rule for a brief season over the fabled land of love and poetry, with the Queen of Beauty for a consort. The situation should body forth poetically the Germanic conquest of classic soil, the relation of a feudal prince to his vassals, the chivalrous devotion of a medieval knight to his lady-love. The child should be called Euphorion, 'the lightly borne,' — a name which ancient Greek legend had already given to the son borne by Helena to Achilles after their return to earth from Hades. His character should be that of an earth-spurning genius of poesy, becoming intoxicate at the last with martial frenzy, and ending his career, like the fabled Icarus, in an impotent attempt to fly. And since Euphorion was to express, in his very personality, the infectious spell of song, his part should be given the form of opera, in order that the power of music might appear wedded to the power of words. For music, as 'art of the infinite,' the art which aims to express that which lies too deep for words, is pre-eminently *the* romantic art. Finally, the magic ring of Helena, as being at best but a rather cheap device for connecting her 'death' with that of her son, should be given up, and the connection simply taken for granted; the magic bond of life should break with the magic bond of love.*

How much of the new *Helena* was actually worked out in the spring of 1825 does not appear: probably but little, since the poet's attention was soon diverted to other subjects. From April 5 the records are silent for nearly a year, save for an isolated indication that the end of the episode was under consideration in October.† Feb. 11, 1826, the 'main business' was once more in hand. March 12 some scenes of the 'new Faust' were read to Eckermann, and from April 1 on there is evidence of unintermit-

---

we actually have in the final version. In July, 1827, Goethe said to Eckermann: 'At an earlier date I had thought out the conclusion altogether differently, and once right well; but I will not tell you what it was. Then time brought me this of Lord Byron and Missolonghi and I willingly dropped everything else.'

* L. 9941. Scherer's speculations, *Aufsätze über Goethe*, p. 341, are wrong.

† A *brouillon* of ll. 9958–61 has been found on a 'letter-concept' of Oct. 26, 1825.

ted progress for some three months. Before the end of June the *Helena*, which it was purposed to publish separately as an 'interlude to *Faust*,' had been completed, copied, and provided with a short prose introduction explanatory of the antecedent action. In this introduction the poet set forth in a few words that the marriage of Faust to Helena was an important part of the legend which it was not for him to ignore. The marriage could not be brought about by 'Blocksberg confederates, nor by the hideous Enyo,* who is akin to northern witches and vampyres.' In the Second Part everything was to move on a 'higher and nobler plane.' It was necessary, therefore, to take Faust to the mountain-gorges of Thessaly and have him consult an ancient sibyl, who would show him the way to Hades. Here he would entreat Persephone, like a second Orpheus, to permit the return of Helena to the upper air. Persephone would grant the prayer on condition that Helena should not be taken from Spartan territory, and that 'everything else, including the winning of her love, should take place in human fashion.'

We see that Goethe, who had poetic reasons of his own for locating his love-idyl in Arcadia, is here concerned to invent a plausible explanation of the fact that Faust, whom the legend does not connect with Greece, would appear in the 'interlude' as ruler of the Peloponnesus. We see, too, the germ of the Classical Walpurgis-Night. Faust was to be given the rôle of an ancient hero. Just as Æneas consults the Cumæan sibyl and enters the lower world from her cave, so Faust was to get help from a Thessalian sibyl; for Thessaly was famed in ancient times as the home of witches. On the other hand we can also see why Goethe presently discarded the introduction he had written and set about the preparation of a much longer one. For, in the first place, the reader of the 'interlude' would want to know how Faust came to

* That is, Phorkyas. Cf. n. to l. 7967.

be so madly enamored of Helena. And then, if it was to be a part of the fiction that the northern devil had no relations with classical witches, and no authority in the Greek Hades, then who was to escort Faust to Thessaly and recommend him to the right quarter? Again, if it was to be assumed that 'the hideous Enyo' could not mediate between romantic love and antique beauty, then one would wish to know why Mephistopheles should appear in the interlude in the precise guise of Enyo, and not only appear, but manage the whole fantastic business, and finally 'comment on the piece'* in an epilogue, as if it were all a thing of his contriving.

Thus it was that Goethe, after reading his interlude to various friends and making some corrections, set about the writing of a better introduction. The result was a somewhat detailed account † of the 'antecedents' of the *Helena* as they lay in his mind at the close of the year 1826. In large part the details are identical with those which were subsequently elaborated in verse, but the differences are numerous and instructive. The substance of the plot here outlined is as follows:

At a great court-festival apparitions of Paris and Helena are produced to amuse the Emperor. Faust becoming jealous, lays hands upon Paris. There is an explosion, the phantoms vanish, Faust lies in a swoon. Recovering after a long time, he imperiously demands Helena for a wife. Mephistopheles, not wishing to confess his impotence in the Greek Hades, beats about the bush and recommends a visit to the learned Dr. Wagner. They find that Wagner has just succeeded in producing, by chemical synthesis, a wonderful 'little man,' who bursts his glass house and forthwith evinces an astonishing knowledge of occult history. He declares that the present night is an anniversary of the battle of Pharsalia. Mephistopheles disputes this, whereat the clever Lilliputian asserts further that it is

* L. 10038 +.

† It was finished Dec. 21, 1826, and can now be read in the Weimar *Goethe,* XV, 2, pp. 198–212.

just now the time for the Classical Walpurgis-Night, which has been celebrated annually in Thessaly since the beginning of the mythic age, and was really, in the occult connection of events, the cause of the great battle between Cæsar and Pompey. The four now decide to go to Thessaly at once. Wagner puts the dwarf in one pocket, and in the other a fresh bottle in which to collect the ingredients for a female mate to the little man, and then they all ride to Thessaly in Faust's magic mantle. Here they first encounter the witch Erichtho, who is still eagerly sniffing the scent of blood from the battle. They then go their several ways. The dwarf, intent upon having a mate, scrapes up a handful of shining atoms from the ground and gives them to Wagner, who puts them in his bottle. But no sooner does he shake the bottle than he is beset by a myriad ghosts of Roman soldiers who angrily protest against this violent interference with their hoped-for resurrection of the body. Then the four winds come to Wagner's rescue and he is permitted to retain the atoms, though we hear nothing more of him or of the dwarf. Faust makes the acquaintance of divers sphinxes, griffins, etc., and then of the centaur Chiron, who takes him to the sibyl Manto, who escorts him through a dark subterranean passage to the throne of Persephone, where he makes a successful plea for the return of Helena to earth. Mephistopheles, after various other adventures, comes upon the Phorkyads. He is charmed by their superlative hideousness, borrows their form and becomes one of the sisterhood.

Looking at this sketch, we see how the Classical Walpurgis-Night, as a pendant to the northern Walpurgis-Night of the First Part, has grown out of the germ-idea to which attention was drawn above. The evolution may be described thus: Faust must consult an ancient Thessalian sibyl. But are ancient Thessalian sibyls still alive and doing business? Yes; they have an annual convention similar to that of their northern 'colleagues' on the Brocken. When is it held? On the anniversary of the battle of Pharsalia. Where? On the battle-ground. Who knows all this, if not Mephistopheles? The chemical homunculus. Why should *he* know it? Because such knowledge belongs to his specialty.* — But when we reach this point we see that the journey to Thessaly is still somewhat awkwardly motivated. We are not told why the four set out, nor who is in charge of the expedition. And why should Wagner be taken along to no purpose and then left to his fate among the spooks? The sketch makes an attempt to meet this query with the problem of a female mate for Homunculus. But why should Wagner, fresh from a great triumph in his laboratory, care to go to Thessaly for such a purpose?

It is not unlikely that Goethe himself felt these defects and lent for that reason a more willing ear to those friends who advised him not to publish the scheme, lest its publication should act as a bar to further poetic effort. At any rate such advice was given and followed. In January, 1827, the *Helena* was sent to the printer with no Introduction whatever. It appeared a few months later, in volume 4 of the new *Works*, with the sub-titles: *A Classico-Romantic Phantasmagoria. Interlude to Faust.* This 'Interlude,' conceived from the first as a semi-independent drama in itself, was in due time to be known as the third act of the Second Part. The problem of completion was henceforward the problem of filling-in before and after the *Helena*.

5. The First and Second Acts.

As might have been expected, the separate publication of the *Helena* in 1827 attracted but little attention from the literary world. It was not a production to captivate readers instantly, either for its own sake or for the sake of its connection with the fragmentary *Faust* which was already known and had come to be very generally admired. The style of the new work bore no re-

* Father Wagner is fond of old parchments and an expert in *real* history and chronology (ll. 560–73, 1105–9); naturally, therefore, a marvellous product of his laboratory, his son-by-chemical-synthesis, would be an expert in *marvellous* history and chronology Cf., further, the general note introductory to the scene 'Laboratorium.'

semblance to that of the old and appealed to a different order of feelings. Nor was its relation to the Faust-story very obvious. The all-important Phorkyas did not belong to the legend at all, and was not even a familiar figure of Greek mythology; hence it was not easy to see why the poet had given his devil this particular disguise. The action seemed to move in a world of fantastic unrealities quite remote from the living interests of living men. The real merits of the poem, the superb workmanship of the classical part, and the rich symbolism and magic melodies of the romantic part, were not of a kind to make a quick conquest of the casual reader. But Goethe had long ago learned to bide his time. For the present, the cordial praise and sympathetic interest with which his new work was greeted by the select few who stood nearest to him, were a sufficient reward and a sufficient spur to further endeavor.

And so we find him, in the summer of 1827, beginning to cherish in a somewhat more definite way the purpose of completing *Faust*. As early as May 18 he 'attacked the main business' in earnest. His diary for June and July contains sporadic indications that work was proceeding; after that it shows pretty constant progress to the end of the year. On the 14th of January, 1828, the first three scenes and a little more (ll. 4613–6036) were sent to the printer for publication. Shortly after this *Faust* seems to have been laid aside until autumn. From October, 1828, until February, 1829, it was again in hand, the poet being now occupied with the last four scenes of the first act and the first two of the second. During the remainder of the year 1829 there are no indications of further progress until December. At this time Goethe read to Eckermann the scenes just mentioned, and began the 'Classical Walpurgis-Night,' which then occupied him almost continuously until it was finished.

With the completion of the 'Walpurgis-Night,' in the summer of 1830, the octogenarian poet had accomplished the larger and more difficult part of his great task. Let us now take the dramaturgic point of view and consider the make-up of the first two acts.

The idea of the first scene, as a symbolical transition-scene, appears in the prose sketch of 1816. Faust was to be cured of his 'sensuality' and his 'dependence upon passion,' and to be strengthened for a new and higher life; and this process was to be represented as the work of spirits singing to him in 'melodious' but 'ironical' and 'deceptive' strains of the charms of honor, fame, and power. The spirits were at first conceived apparently as malicious, lying minions of Mephistopheles, but were later converted into good fairies in order that Faust's regeneration might appear as a solid reality and not as a trick of the devil. Some such scene was evidently required at the point of division between the two Parts. For the Second Part as a whole was to move on a 'higher and nobler plane.' The slave of passion was to be set free and become the votary of ideas and at last the apostle of action. It would not do, therefore, to take him directly with his sorrow and his sense of guilt, from the prison-cell of Gretchen to the court of the Emperor. In some way it had to be indicated that old things had passed away and all become new. But how was this to be managed unless by the help of symbolism? Most readers probably feel, upon first acquaintance with *Faust*, that its hero should be made to suffer for his wrong-doing. An average judge upon the bench would no doubt wish to punish him, and the churchman would insist that he at least do penance for his sins before talking of a 'higher life.' But punishment and penance were alike unavailable in a dramatic action dominated throughout by magic, — in other words, were foreign to the tone of the legend. Moreover it must not be forgotten that Faust does suffer like a man; and also that his conduct is portrayed as due to evil guidance for a brief period and not to any atrophy of conscience. His heart and his will are still sound. — Here then was a clear case for the healing touch of time. It is true that in real life Mother Nature repairs her ravages slowly, taking not one night only, but a thousand, in which to 'withdraw the bitter, burning arrows of remorse' and bathe the sick heart in Lethean dews. But the drama cannot utilize this silent lapse of years, and in a symbolic drama like *Faust*, which all along sets at nought the bonds of time and space, it is easy to think of the healing and restoring process as concentrated into a single night; as a work performed in a few hours by the soothing, refreshing genii of sleep.

But another element was needed in the symbolism: Faust was to be not only cured, but uplifted; and for this our poet had recourse to the Alpine sunrise. We need not stop to inquire how it has come about that this particular phenomenon appeals so powerfully to the soul of the modern man. Enough that the magic is real; and that it *is* real any one knows who has ever *seen* the day break in the Alps and felt his own nature touched to finer issues under the spell of that 'most solemn hour.'

We come now to the second scene. In the puppet-plays Faust always appears at a court (usually that of the Duke of Parma) where he exhibits his magic powers by conjuring up spirits (generally those of Alexander the Great and his wife), and thus incurs the enmity of the clergy. From the first this situation appealed to Goethe's dramatic instinct, and with the growth of his plan it acquired fundamental importance. By making the prince ask to see Helena, instead of Alexander the Great, it became possible to develop the whole action out of Faust's relation to the court. And as to the court to be represented, no other could compare in poetic interest for Goethe with that of the Holy Roman Empire, whose elaborate ceremonial had excited his boyish curiosity, whose laws and customs he had studied as a young lawyer, and whose political incohesiveness had been a by-word in his youth. At first he thought of Maximilian and his court at Augsburg, but so definite a localization of the scene did not commend itself to his maturer thought. He did not wish to be hampered by any requirements of local color or historical fact. He wished to depict not Maximilian, but a 'prince possessed of every possible capacity for losing his kingdom.'* And so instead of a particular place and man, we have simply 'Imperial Court' and 'the Emperor.'

According to the original plan Faust and Mephistopheles were to appear at court simultaneously. The devil was to break in upon Faust's sublime communings with nature (just as in the scene 'Forest and Cavern' and again in Act 4) and draw him away to Augsburg on the pretext that the Emperor wished to see him. Once there they were to proceed at once to the spirit-manifestations for the amusement of his Majesty. In the final elaboration, however, a new motive was introduced — that of 'first making him rich' by means of paper money issued against metallic treasures not yet dug up from the ground. This was clearly a field for the devil, and not for a man who had lately been talking in lofty strains of 'striving ever onward to the highest existence.' So Mephistopheles was sent ahead alone to ingratiate himself with the Emperor as court-fool, attend a cabinet-meeting in that capacity, and propound *his* remedy for the troubles of the state; incidentally also, to prepare the way for the appearance of Faust in a rôle befitting his dignity of character.

This preparation is effected by the 'Carnival Masquerade.' The scene furnishes an excellent occasion for exhibitions of the black art, and Mephistopheles takes advantage of it in order to accredit himself and Faust at court as magicians and also to procure the Emperor's signature for an issue of fiat money. Dramatically this is all that the nine hundred verses of the *Mummenschanz* signify; otherwise it is simply a picture painted with

---

* Eckermann, Oct. 1, 1827.

reference to spectacular effect. To impute to it as a whole any profound allegorical or 'philosophical' meaning, as was done by some of the early commentators, is simply to mistake the character of Goethe's art.

The following scene, which exhibits Mephisto's financial triumph, calls for no special comment at this point. Not so, however, with Faust's journey to the realm of the Mothers. This invention greatly mystified Eckermann and has perplexed others since. But the difficulties are not very serious if we first realize clearly the exact nature of the dramatic problem presented and then remember that the scene is *meant* to mystify; that is, that it is not an embodiment of owlish wisdom, but a bit of solemn fooling. The Emperor has demanded of the two wonder-workers, now officially installed as purveyors of entertainment, that they produce the shades of Helena and Paris. This desire must be gratified, and Faust must fall in love with Helena. But the 'real' shade lives in the Greek Hades, and there he is presently to go in search of her. As such a journey can not be undertaken twice, and as Mephistopheles, by hypothesis, has no relations with the Greeks, the Emperor must be cheated by an illusion, just as happens in the legend. But now Faust must be cheated also. He must not know that what he sees is a mere air-phantom that will vanish into nothing if he touches it. So the devil, knowing his man, resorts to a piece of deep-diving humbug: He has not the key to Hades, but he *has* a key which will guide one to the realm of the Mothers.

Helena and Paris are Greek ideals of beauty. But 'ideal' is derived from ἰδέα, which means, as nearly as one can express it in English, 'mental picture,' 'form seen by the mind's eye.' According to Plato's well-known doctrine 'ideas' were real, in fact were the only reality: all that 'appears' to the senses being a transitory and more or less imperfect embodiment of an eternal archetype, or 'idea,' existing in the mind of creative intelligence

Goethe's humor simply plays upon the 'reality of ideas,' by perverting the meaning of 'reality' from its philosophical sense of 'noumenal' to its ordinary meaning of 'apparent to the senses.' So he imagines a realm of 'ideas,' or *Urbilder*, that exist in the form of cloud-like wraiths. This realm, naturally enough, he locates outside of time and space. No way leads to it; it is neither up nor down, but simply 'aloof from all that exists.' And having read in Plutarch of mysterious goddesses worshiped in ancient Sicily under the name of 'the Mothers,' he appropriates the horrific name for his own purposes; gives to 'the Mothers' a home in the Absolute Void (so the realm of 'ideas' would naturally appear to the devil) and makes them the creators and guardians of his nebulous *Urbilder*. Here — we must imagine — the ideal archetypes of all things that ever were exist eternally. Of their own will the Mothers may send them forth for temporary embodiment on earth, but only the bold magician can steal away the unincarnate archetype itself. Even for him the danger is great. This 'danger,' of which Mephistopheles gives due warning, is meant to prepare us for the final explosion which takes place when Faust tries to seize and hold the apparition that he has evoked. The explosion is simply a part of the folk-lore pertaining to the production of phantom 'spirits' by the devil.* It is always stipulated that they must simply be looked at; if touched they explode and vanish into nothing, or perhaps undergo some hideous metamorphosis. The paralytic shock, with resulting trance, is, indeed, an invention of Goethe; but it is no very far cry from the conception of a man infatuated with an ideal of beauty to that of a man lying in a trance and dead to all things but his inner vision. 'Enraptured' means 'carried away' from one's self. So Faust's body remains where it was, but his mind, his soul, is in Greece, and thither his body must be taken to restore the broken connection.

---

* Cf. the note introductory to the scene 'Knights' Hall.'

At the beginning of Act 2 we find that Goethe's first thought with regard to the motivation of the journey to Greece has given way to a new and better one. According to the sketch of 1826 Faust was to recover spontaneously from his swoon and demand Helena for a wife. Mephistopheles, as a makeshift for gaining time, was to bring him to Wagner's laboratory, where they were to find the homunculus ready made. But this was not very plausible, because Wagner was no wonder-worker, but simply a man of learning. He might *try* to produce a man by chemical synthesis, but that he should actually succeed without supernatural aid was carrying the joke too far. Nor would it be very clear why Mephistopheles with his well-known opinions of learning and 'speculation,' should go for help to Faust's old famulus. Hence came the thought of prolonging Faust's swoon into a mesmeric trance that would at least *seem* to bring Mephistopheles to his wits' end and make it necessary for him to call to his aid a superior 'cousin,' who, as mind-reader, would instantly comprehend Faust's case and prescribe the right remedy, namely, that he be taken to the land of his dreams. This meant that the wonderful dwarf would be only nominally the product of Wagner's science.

The idea of the laboratory-scene is, then (what precedes is quite episodical), simply to provide in Homunculus a competent guide to Greece; one who, wiser in ancient matters than the medieval devil, knows all about the Classical Walpurgis-Night and the possibility of turning it to advantage for an interesting tour as well as for the benefit of Faust.

Coming now to the Walpurgis-Night itself, we see that it has three centers of interest: first, the doings of Faust up to the time when he is taken in charge by the priestess Manto; secondly, the adventures of Mephistopheles, ending with his metamorphosis into a Phorkyad; and, thirdly, the efforts of Homunculus to find the right medium in which to 'commence existence.' According to Goethe's first intention there was to have been a scene in Hades.

Faust was to appear, with Manto as his advocate, before the throne of Queen Persephone, and secure by his (or Manto's) pathetic eloquence the release of Helena to the upper air. But this scene was finally left to the imagination; probably because, in addition to the intrinsic difficulties of the theme, Goethe perceived that it would not really render the fiction of the third act any more intelligible. For, the decree of Persephone once secured, Helena could hardly be supposed to follow Faust as Eurydice follows Orpheus. She would have no motive for doing so: Faust would be a stranger to her, and Hades was no place for love-making, even if the love-making had not already been provided for in the third act. And even if she were to be represented as following him back to earth on some pretext (as, for instance, the natural love of life), there would still remain the problem of conveying her to Sparta and investing her with the necessary illusions in respect to time, place, and her own personality. In the end, therefore, she would simply have to be conjured back to Sparta by magic; and this being so the formal consent of Persephone might be dispensed with.

For the conjuring a classical witch would be needed, since by hypothesis Mephistopheles could not manage it in his own proper person. There was nothing left for him then but to merge his own being temporarily in that of some kindred spirit of antique mold and feminine gender. Ostensibly it is only his cynical humor that leads him to become one of the daughters of Phorkys, they being the most superlatively hideous creatures he has been able to find in the land of beauty. *We* know, however, the occasion of his metamorphosis. — It appears, then, that the limitation of Mephisto's powers is not in the end taken very seriously, since he can accomplish by an easy transformation what he could not do in his ordinary character.

It now remains to follow the fortunes of Homunculus, whose character appears altogether different from that originally given him. According to the prose sketch of 1826 he was to burst his bottle and 'commence existence' in the laboratory; then he was to ride, in Wagner's pocket, to Thessaly, where he would try to find the chemical ingredients for a female mate. At that time Goethe evidently took the joke of the 'chemical man' rather lightly and had not given himself the trouble to think it out to any sort of conclusion. For the prose sketch does not tell us whether the homuncula was to be found or not, nor how Wagner and Homunculus were to get back home from Thessaly; it simply drops the jest as something not worth carrying further. But when the poet came to the final elaboration of the scene in verse, he saw that this would not do. Such a gifted and useful creature as Homunculus could not be treated so shabbily. He must have an errand of his own in Thessaly and he must accomplish it. And as to this errand: Why should a being who had himself come into the world without parents, in defiance of 'the usual mode of propagation,' be looking about for a wife? Evidently he must be given a more plausible mission. And what should a homunculus naturally desire if not to become a *homo*, i.e., to get a body befitting his brilliant mental powers? But if his errand in Thessaly was to be the getting of a body, then he must have no body on arriving there. This led to the conceit of keeping him for a while in his bottle in the form of an imponderable luminosity, and representing him as mere mind and aspiration, but without any physical substratum. Thus his case would reverse the creation-myth of Genesis, according to which Adam 'begins' as a complete body made out of the dust of the ground, and has his soul superadded afterwards, it being 'breathed into' him by the Creator. Homunculus would begin as soul and get his body afterwards; but there being nothing of him to feed he could not get it in a short time like an ordinary infant by the ordinary process of nutrition. It would be necessary for him to begin at the beginning and travel the road of evolution. — In giving this turn to his whimsical conception Goethe no doubt intended a fanciful adumbration of scientific views which he actually held; but we must beware of taking his 'science' too seriously. The 'Walpurgis-Night' is not science, nor allegory, nor philosophy, but the poetic revivification of legend. Incidentally it contains enough of 'wisdom,' of symbolism, and of covert satire; but taken as a whole it is not didactic. From the dramatic point of view it is quite episodical, save that it prepares us for the appearance of Mephistopheles as Phorkyas and for that of Helena as a Greek shade dismissed for a season from Hades.

6. The Fourth and Fifth Acts.

The puppet-plays end with a midnight-scene in Faust's house. A watchman calls out the hours as the twenty-four years draw to a close, and when the stroke of twelve is reached Faust is carried off by devils. As this was the climax of the old popular tragedy it is not improbable that Goethe's early plan provided for a corresponding midnight-scene with ominous foreshadowings of Faust's death, although *his* hero was not to die violently at the end of a specified time, but to finish the whole banquet of life and die naturally in the fulness of years. How the last hours and the death of Faust may have been conceived by Goethe in his youth we do not know; but there are certain recently discovered paralipomena which reveal at least in dim outline the picture which lay in his mind at the close of the eighteenth century. It was something like this:

Faust would appear at the last as a very old man, blind and decrepit, but with his energy of character still unabated. Mephistopheles would come to him one night at the stroke of twelve and say ominously: 'That stroke betokens the midnight hour.' 'What fable is this?' Faust would reply. 'It is high noon; I can feel the warm sun in these old limbs of mine. Come with me.' After this was to come the death-scene substantially as we know it from the final version. That is, Faust would die victorious in reality, but with words upon his lips which would give Mephistopheles the semblance of a valid claim to his soul. The devil would accordingly have a grave dug by Lemurs and order his minions to take possession of the dead man's immortal part. After this was to come, according to the poet's first shadowy intention, an 'epilogue in chaos on the way to hell.' How this was conceived we can only guess, and what seems the most plausible guess has already been given (see above, p. viii). In any event the idea of an 'epilogue in chaos' was quite ephemeral. It probably antedated that of the 'Prologue in Heaven,' and when the latter was written in 1797 the conclusion of the poem took a different shape in its author's mind. First came the thought of letting Mephistopheles leave the body of Faust before the escape of the soul, and rush away to heaven to boast there of his triumph over the Lord. But this soon gave way to a different idea according to which Mephistopheles, while watching for the escape of Faust's soul, should be attacked by good angels, emissaries of Christ in heaven, who would beat back the devils and bear away the soul in triumph. The devil, feeling that he had been cheated, would then appeal his case to the court of heaven. There would be a formal trial and a decision, of course in Faust's favor. After this was to come a 'parting announcement,' corresponding to the 'Prelude in the Theater.' Here the Manager would reappear, comment on the piece, decline to repeat it, and bespeak the plaudits of the house. Finally, to complete the symmetry, there was to be a 'farewell' corresponding to the 'Dedication,' in which the Poet would felicitate himself upon having reached the end of his barbarous composition.*

* The early paralipomena from which the above-sketched outline has been deduced are Nos. 92–98. They contain (1) a fragment of the midnight dialogue between Faust and Mephistopheles; (2) the song of the Lemurs; (3) several lines of a boastful soliloquy of Mephistopheles over the dead body of Faust; (4) several lines of a soliloquy of Mephistopheles upon the appearance and character of the angels; (5) the 'announcement' (Abkündigung); and (6) the 'farewell' (Abschied). The death-scene is not found in any

We have already seen that when Goethe resumed work upon *Faust*, in 1825, he occupied himself for a short time with the conclusion of the poem. It was at this time, probably, that the scene 'Midnight' received its final form.* The old idea was dropped, and in place of Mephistopheles, whose appearance as monitor of death had not been clearly motivated, came the allegorical Frau Sorge, Dame Worry, whom Goethe had come to look upon as man's, but especially the old man's, direst enemy. The idea of the scene was to exhibit Faust at the very end of his days as still full of energy and eagerness for further achievement; as a man who had outgrown the hypochondria of his youth and learned not to fret over the nature of things, but to accept life, with all its woes and limitations, as a boon worth having if rightly used. And how better give expression to this philosophy of resignation without apathy than by means of a dialogue with the old hag whose office it is to torment us with harrowing solicitudes, unnerve us with care, and befool us with vain imaginings? As to the antecedents of the scene, they were probably somewhat nebulous. Faust had been thought of as the owner of a princely estate on the seashore, and the acquisition of this estate had of course been provided for in thought. But the details were still indefinite. It should be remembered, too, that in 1825 the *Helena* was still a project, and the plan of dividing the Second Part into five acts, approximately equal in length and each a little drama in itself, had not yet been formed.

We are now prepared to understand how Goethe could say to Eckermann,† in the spring of 1830, that the end of *Faust* was

---

old paralipomenon, but its antiquity is vouched for by the statement of Goethe to Boisserée, in 1815. The trial of Faust in heaven, on Mephisto's appeal, is to be sure not found in any early scheme; but it appears in three later ones (see Paralipomena, Nos. 194-5) which only resume and record old thoughts.

* Cf. foot-note on p. xxii above.

† *Gespräche mit Goethe*, II, 155. Eckermann left Weimar in April for a tour in Italy. In September he wrote to Goethe from Geneva: 'To my great delight I have

already finished. By the 'end' he meant the two scenes, 'Midnight' and 'Large Forecourt of the Palace,' in which the mundane action ends and the ethical import of the whole is clearly brought to view. The acquisition of the estate had now been set apart as the theme of the fourth act, but meanwhile the fifth was still far from complete. In the first place there was the 'end of the end,' that is, Faust's fate after death; and to this subject the poet next addressed himself, in the last weeks of the year 1830.

According to the plan outlined above, there was to have been at the last a '*da capo*' in heaven; that is, a scene representing the formal trial of Faust in the presence of 'Christ, the Holy Virgin, the evangelists, and all the saints.' The locus of the scene as originally imagined was probably the remote inter-spheral heaven of the Prologue; but when it came to the final elaboration the idea of the trial was dropped and a different conception of heaven adopted; that, namely, of a holy mountain reaching up from earth to the abode of the blest and peopled by anchorites and penitents in different stages of devotional ecstasy. Hints for the scenery and the characterization were drawn from many and in part from recondite sources — the biblical Zion, Montserrat in Spain, the visions of Swedenborg, the hagiology of the medieval church, the lives of the mystics, the frescoes of the Campo Santo in Pisa, and perhaps other pictorial representations. The result is a scene very different in kind from the 'Prologue,' not quite so near perhaps to the sympathies of most readers, especially Protestant readers, but no less admirable as a specimen of poetic workmanship. It is a wonderful tribute to its author's power of realizing vividly in

learned from one of your latest letters that the lacunae and the end of the Classical Walpurgis-Night are conquered. It appears then that the first three acts are finished, the *Helena* connected, and the hardest part therefore over. The end is, as you told me, already done; and so I hope that the fourth act will soon have surrendered and a great work have been created in which coming centuries will find edification and food for thought.' The same statement that the 'end' was already finished can be found in a letter of Goethe to Zelter, written May 24, 1827, and also in a letter of July 19, 1829.

extreme old age, a world of thought and feeling that had never been in a marked degree *his* world. Well might he say to Eckermann that 'the conclusion was very difficult, and that in dealing with such supersensuous, well-nigh unimaginable things, he might easily have lost himself in the vague, had he not given his poetic intentions an agreeable definiteness and substantiality by means of the clear-cut forms and conceptions of the Christian church.' *

On the 4th of January, 1831, Goethe was able to write to his friend Zelter that 'the fifth act was on paper to the end of the end' and he only wished the gods would help him with the fourth. Feb. 9 he told Eckermann that he had now begun the fourth act and three days later we find him felicitating himself that the difficult beginning of this act had at last been worked out to his satisfaction. '*What* was to happen,' he remarked, 'I have long known, but I was not quite satisfied with the *how*; and so it is gratifying that good thoughts have come to me.'† It appears, however, that the fifth act was not complete after all; for on April 9 he wrote in his diary: 'Philemon and Baucis and kindred matters very satisfactory.' This tallies with Eckermann's record of May 2, to the effect that the hitherto existing gap at the beginning of the fifth act had lately been filled up. If this seems inconsistent with previous assurances we have to remember that in his earlier musings Goethe had been occupied with the plot of *Faust*, but not with the division of it into acts. He had probably,—for he assured Eckermann that 'the intention of these scenes was also more than thirty years old,'—conceived simply of a pious old couple whose peaceful existence would be disturbed by the unhallowed operations of Faust; but he had not found a name for them, and their episode had been connected in his mind with the acquisition of the estate, that is, with the general theme of the fourth act. Now, however, he determined to place the dividing

* *Gespräche mit Goethe,* II, 237 (May 29, 1831).

† *Gespräche mit Goethe,* II, 178.

line further forward, to call the aged pair by the familiar classical names of Philemon and Baucis and to let the picture of their idyllic life and the rude destruction of it open the last act and motivate the midnight visit of Dame Worry.

As to the fourth act, the archives at Weimar contain a complete scheme dated May 16, 1831, and a number of partial schemes, mostly of later origin. These papers, taken in connection with what we already know, tell us pretty clearly how the act grew into its final shape. The germ-idea is contained in the prose sketch of 1816, in which Faust, after the loss of Helena, turns for comfort at the suggestion of Mephistopheles to the acquisition of wealth and power. In a battle with hostile monks he avenges the death of his son and wins large estates. One sees that these ideas date from an early period, when the Helena-episode had not yet been invested in Goethe's mind with any serious ethical import. The later conception required a nobler motive for Faust's conduct than the desire of vengeance or the mere lust of gain. Such a motive was provided by imputing to him a sort of abstract *Thatenlust;* that is, a will to do great things for the simple sake of doing. It is not the desire of glory which engages Faust's mind, nor the utility of the thing to be acquired; it is only a question of self-expression, of living himself out; whence the significant words:

Die That ist alles, nicht der Ruhm.

As a field for the putting forth of his powers he chooses a battle with the sea. On his aerial journey from Arcadia he has observed the waves beating on the shore and suddenly conceived a wish to curb this aimless violence and rescue a tract of land from the power of the blind element. One is surprised at first to find such a quixotic incentive assigned for an eminently practical undertaking. There is nothing in the third act which seems calculated to convert Faust suddenly into a dyke-builder *à la hollan-*

daise, nor is it clear that familiarity with the Greek spirit, whatever else it may do, especially disposes the mind to large works of engineering. Nevertheless this bit of motivation is an important part of Goethe's plot and must be taken for what it is worth. His thought was, no doubt, that the Greek joy of life and love of beauty were the best of antidotes for morbid preoccupation with one's self; and so Helena might properly enough be made the instrument of Faust's redemption through the turning of his mind away from himself in the direction of some large and useful activity. But it was not necessary that the specific form of this activity should itself grow out of his relation to the Greek heroine.

As a matter of fact it seems to have grown out of Goethe's interest in the stone dykes of Venice. In his *Italian Journey*, under date of Oct. 9, 1786, we read:

'A precious day from morning till night! I rode as far as Palestrina, in the direction of Chiozza, past the great works which the republic is erecting against the sea. They are made of hewn stone and are intended to protect the tongue of land which separates the lagoons from the sea against the wild element. The lagoons are an ancient product of nature. First the tide and the earth, working against each other, and then the gradual subsidence of the primeval waters, brought it about that at the upper end of the Adriatic there is a considerable expanse of swamp which is visited by the flood-tide but left partly to itself at low water. Art has taken possession of the highest points, and thus Venice lies there, composed of a hundred islands grouped together and surrounded by yet other hundreds. At the same time, with incredible effort and expense, deep canals have been furrowed in the swamp, so that war-ships can reach the principal points even at low tide. What human wit and industry devised and executed ages ago, shrewdness and industry are now compelled to preserve.'

We have here the essential features of Faust's domain. What impressed the northern traveler and lingered in his memory was the picture of an energetic community that had wrested a dwelling-place from the sea and was then compelled to maintain itself by eternal vigilance against the invading water. Interested as he was, to the end of his days, in great works of practical enterprise, it was only natural that Goethe should see in such a battle with the sea an ideal sphere of activity for his aspiring hero.* For here was a nobler kind of enterprise than any conquest of the sword; the opportunity for a bloodless battle that should leave no sting of defeat in a conquered population; a chance to bring order and beauty out of ugly desolation and create a home for millions yet to come. It is the lure of this prospect which leads Faust to take part, with Mephisto's aid, in the battle between the imperial factions. By putting the Emperor under obligations he hopes to secure the swampy sea-shore as his fief.

The scheme of May 16, 1831, and also a later one (No. 182), provide for the formal enfeoffment of the magician, and the verses were actually written which were to fulfil the promise of the lines:

So kniest du nieder und empfängst
Die Lehn von gränzenlosem Strande.

At the very last, however, Goethe decided to conclude the act with a satirical picture of imperial incapacity and ecclesiastical greed. The Emperor solemnly rewards the worthless princes who have done nothing for him, and atones by rich gifts to the church for profiting by agencies which the church condemns. The real author of the victory, the magician Faust, does not appear, and we are left to imagine the enfeoffment.

In this scene, which comprises some two hundred Alexandrine

---

* Cf. Eckermann, III, 83, where Goethe is reported as expressing a wish that he might live to see a canal across the Isthmus of Suez, another from the Gulf of Mexico to the Pacific, and a third connecting the Rhine with the Danube. It is worth noting that Goethe was interested in American canal projects in the spring of 1825. But the attempt of Henning in V. L., I, 246, to find American scenery in *Faust*, must be pronounced a failure.

verses, the poet returned to the meter in which he had written his first dramatic attempts more than sixty years before. It fills out the fourth act to an approximate equality with the fifth, but it lacks movement and is undeniably somewhat labored. More than any other portion of the great work which it finally brought to an end, it tells of the failing hand of age. It was finished in midsummer, 1831. In the following January Goethe read the entire Second Part to his daughter Ottilie, made some slight corrections, and was minded at one time to elaborate further certain portions which he felt that he had treated too briefly. But it was not done, and in a few weeks more the aged poet had gone where *Faust* could no longer tease him.

II.

THE COMPLETED SECOND PART.

It is now in order to consider the Second Part as a finished work, and the first thing needful is to get a clear idea of what may be called its more obvious poetic import. This can be done best by means of a simple analysis of the argument. Ignoring for the present all difficult questions of criticism or interpretation and passing over side-issues of every kind, let us see what the work offers at first glance, so to speak, to the spectator and to the intelligent lover of poetry.

Not long after the sad ending of the First Part the curtain rises upon a noble Alpine landscape, and Faust reappears, still bearing his burden of woe. The symbolism presents him as a weary traveller seeking rest at nightfall. Good fairies that personify the soothing and invigorating power of sleep sing their magic lullaby and watch over his slumbers during the night, bestowing oblivion of the past and courage for the future. At dawn he awakens in a mood of high aspiration and drinks in with solemn joy the glories of the Alpine sunrise. [Imagine that he is joined by Mephistopheles, against whom, of course, his fierce wrath has now subsided. Mindful of his promise regarding the 'great world' (l. 2052) the devil proposes a visit to the Emperor's court. Faust assents to the journey].

The next scene opens upon an imperial cabinet-meeting held in presence of the assembled court. It is Shrove Tuesday, and the people are in gala-dress in anticipation of a grand carnival masquerade. By the Emperor's order the festival is to be celebrated in the Italian style. There are to be various groups and processions of masqueraders representing southern life, either real or fictitious; e.g., Florentine flower-girls, Neapolitan Pulcinelli, woodcutters, parasites, a drunken man, a mother with a marriageable daughter. After this are to come impersonations from Greek mythology, the Graces, the Fates, the Furies; then an allegorical procession with an elephant as central figure; and finally a grand entry of the Emperor himself in the character of Pan, with attendant chorus of satyrs, fauns, etc. All this has been planned in advance, and planned, of course, without thought of magic interference. Meanwhile public affairs are in a deplorable condition, and the frivolous young Emperor has been constrained to call a hurried meeting of his state council. Into this meeting Mephistopheles makes his way by a trick, ingratiates himself with the Emperor as candidate for the vacant position of court-fool, and listens to the proceedings. One after another the ministers of state take the floor and portray the desperate condition of affairs in their several departments. Things have come to a terrible pass and something must be done. The Emperor, always impatient of serious business, jocosely invites a suggestion from the new fool, who at once diagnoses the malady of the state as due to a lack of money. And yet, he observes, there is wealth enough in the empire, consisting of treasure buried in the ground at one time and another by owners fleeing from some invading enemy. All this boundless wealth belongs to the Emperor. The only problem is to get it up, and that, Mephistopheles hints, is only a matter of knowing how. The half-credulous Emperor wants to begin digging at once, but is told that the time is not favorable. They must first sharpen their faith by religious penance. So the digging is postponed (Mephistopheles having another and easier plan of financial relief) and they all proceed to celebrate the Carnival as if no clouds lowered o'er the state.

At first the festival proceeds according to previous calculations. The various groups appear and speak, or rather sing, verses descriptive of their several characters. But meanwhile the new fool, having got a foothold at court and being entitled to take part in the proceedings, devises for himself and Faust rôles which were not on the program. *His* contribution is all that part which has to do with magic — the two-headed monster Zoilo-Thersites, the chariot of Poesy, with its wonderful box of gems, the kneading of the liquid gold, and finally the sham conflagration which seems about to end the festival with an awful calamity, but is checked by a mimic shower of mist, leaving everybody unhurt and in good humor. Before the grand *finale*, however, a bit of serious business has been transacted. As the Emperor in the mask of Pan stands gazing at a stream of molten treasure to which the gnomes have called his attention, the Chancellor approaches and obtains the Emperor's signature to a paper, the exact nature of which his Majesty does not stop to inquire into. Enough for him that it is represented as 'for the good of the people.' The paper is in reality a note drawn against the buried treasure yet to be dug up.

The next scene is irradiated by the glory of the greenback. On the morning after the masquerade the Emperor thanks the two magicians for their fine work of the night before, and, in order to have them always at hand, appoints them custodians of his subterraneous treasure, and directors of the digging. But there is no need to dig; for at this point the ministers come rushing in excitedly and we learn that the country is already saved. The Emperor's signature has been manifolded during the night and a huge issue of paper money in all denominations set afloat. Plenty reigns and everybody is deliriously happy. The Emperor can not quite approve the new régime, but makes an easy truce with his conscience and then proceeds to a general distribution of the wonder-working bits of paper. Only the old drunken fool hits upon a wise use of his sudden wealth. The sequel of it all we see in the fourth act.

Having been made rich by the magicians, the Emperor next demands that they amuse him by conjuring up the shades of Paris and Helena. Faust promises readily, but upon presenting the problem to Mephistopheles is told that there are enormous difficulties in the way. It will be necessary to undertake an awful journey to Nowhere — to the realm of the Mothers. Faust is awestruck but not frightened, and sets out alone in high hope, after having been duly coached as to what he must do. While he is absent Mephistopheles prescribes remedies for the ills of the court-people. At nightfall they all assemble in the Knights' Hall, eager for the promised show. The room is first converted by magic into an antique theater, and Faust emerges upon the stage with the tripod which he has purloined from the mysterious Mothers. From the smoke of the tripod he proceeds, with priestly hocus-pocus, to evoke the apparition of Paris, who appears as a cloudlike form moving rhythmically in the air to the strains of a supernatural music. The women are delighted with him, but the men think him effeminate. Then Helena comes into view and the men are pleased while the women have much fault to find. Meanwhile Faust has fallen madly in love with Helena and forgets that what he sees is only a phantom that he has himself conjured up with Mephisto's aid, and that he has been warned not to touch. The amorous pantomime of the two figures excites his jealousy, and when the phantom man clasps the woman in his arms as if about to carry her away, the infatuate magician can endure it no longer. He grasps at Helena in order to retain her, and touches Paris with his magic key. There is an explosion and Faust lies on the floor in a trance.

The second act is occupied with the quest of Helena. With the swooning Faust on his hands, Mephistopheles pretends to be nonplussed. He does not comprehend the sleeper's malady and can not deal with it alone, but he knows where to get help. So he repairs with his patient to the laboratory of the renowned Doctor Wagner, who still occupies the old quarters. While waiting to be ushered into the great man's presence he indulges in reminiscences of the time when he coached a timid freshman with regard to the four faculties. Presently this selfsame youth, now become a Bachelor of Arts, arrives on the scene, though he has no obvious errand except to air his greatness and claim the earth. He is a personification of youthful conceit and extravagance.

Admitted to the laboratory, Mephistopheles finds a great experiment in progress. Wagner has long been trying to produce a human being by chemical synthesis and is now sure that a glorious success is just ahead. Mephistopheles slyly furthers the grand work, and a luminous manikin appears in Wagner's bottle. But the little fellow is as yet by no means a *Mensch*. Intellectually he is full grown and even more, but, alas, he has no body. He would like to 'commence existence,' that is, to break out of his glass prison, as the chick bursts its shell, and 'stand forth' (*entstehen*, *existere*) as a physical entity, an incipient *Mensch*. But he does not like the ugly locality in which he finds himself. So he decides to remain for the present in the glass house, which gives him 'weight' and a local being (though this being comes painfully short of 'existence'), and meanwhile to investigate the conditions of life and find out where he can 'begin' with the best hope and promise. With his clairvoyant mind he sees that Faust is wrapt in a voluptuous vision of Leda and the Swan, and that he must be taken for recovery to the land of his dreams. Luckily it is just the time of the Classical Walpurgis-Night, a grand conclave of classical spooks which is held annually in Thessaly on the site of the battle between Cæsar and Pompey. Mephistopheles is not averse to making the acquaintance of some of those antique witches for which Thessaly was famous, and so the trio set out together, leaving poor Wagner to pursue his momentous researches alone.

Arrived above the Pharsalian plain, they find it covered with an apparition of spectral tents, as if the ghosts of the two great Roman armies were bivouacking on the field in anticipation of the morrow's battle. Bluish watch-fires glow here and there in the dim moonlight, and the soil emits a phosphorescent reflection of shed blood. The witch Erichtho, whom Sextus Pompey consulted with regard to the outcome of the battle, appears first, soliloquizing upon the ghostly anniversary, but retreats in haste when she sees above her the luminous bottle of Homunculus and scents the approach of flesh and blood (Faust). The three voyagers now alight upon the ground — Faust recovering his senses instantly as soon as his feet touch classic soil — and soon separate, each pursuing his own errand. That of Faust is of course to find Helena. He inquires first of the Sphinxes, who direct him to the wise Centaur Chiron. Chiron, in noble compassion for his mental affliction, takes him to Manto, daughter of the great physician Asklepias. With the sibyl Manto he disappears down a dark passage leading to Hades, and we see no more of him until he emerges in the third act as medieval knight and Prince of Arcadia. That is, the manner of his procuring the release of Helena and the conditions on which his request is granted by Persephone are left to the imagination.

The errand of Mephistopheles is ostensibly to reconnoitre strange ground and amuse himself. He falls in with various denizens of the ancient land of fable, converses with them, observes their ways, and makes comparisons with what he has seen at home. Being fond of dancing, he essays a waltz with a group of Lamiæ, but they make sport of him in all sorts of ways until he is glad to retreat. Finally he descries a triad of old hags crouching in a dark cave — the three daughters of Phorkys, who have gray hair and one eye and one tooth in common. They are so superlatively hideous that he is captivated and gets permission — as if it were a mere lark of his — to become for a short time one of the sisterhood. In this disguise he will presently reappear as the stewardess of Menelaus and the general manager of the 'phantasmagory' which forms the third act.

The concern of Homunculus, as we have seen, is to find a place in which he can 'commence existence,' with the hope of becoming human. Feeling the need of counsel from some one who is wise in the ways of nature, he looks up the two philosophers Anaxagoras and Thales, of whom the former is a Plutonist, believing in the igneous, eruptive origin of rocks, and the latter a Neptunist, who puts his faith in the action of water. Anaxagoras tries to win the manikin for a glorious career on land, by offering to make him king of a volcanic mountain that has just been heaved up and is already peopled with warring tribes. Thales points out the dangers of such an existence and draws him away to see the beauty of life in the water. Arrived in the blue Ægean, Homunculus is charmed with the loveliness of the scene, and with a wise instinct (for the evolution of life began in the water) feels that he has found his element. When the beautiful nymph Galatea approaches in her chariot of shell, his delight rises to ecstasy and he dashes his bottle in pieces against her throne, thus merging his being with the minute forms of aquatic life. Thus his 'commencement of existence' is an act of delirious homage to the Universal Love, for Galatea here represents the Paphian Aphrodite, Goddess of Reproduction. It will be long indeed ere he reaches the physical estate of the *genus homo*, but he has time enough. He has begun well, and his patron deity will watch over each step of his ascent from amœba to man.

As we read it in its final form, the presuppositions of the third act are as follows: Helena is a shade conjured up from Hades and invested by magic with a semblance of life. But only a semblance: There is no blood in her veins, and the life that is restored to her is a sort of dream-life. She has a dim, shadowy memory, and is all along half-conscious that she herself and the Trojan girls who accompany her are nothing but phantoms that belong in the kingdom of Persephone and are back on earth playing a rôle imposed upon them by the constraints of magic. The time is of course that of Doctor Faust. Mephistopheles as Phorkyas has called into quasi-being two phantasmal palaces, the one representing the ancient house of Tyndareus with appropriate Spartan surroundings, the other a medieval castle seeming to be located in the center of the Peloponnesus. The whole action, be it remembered, is a 'phantasmagoria.'

At the beginning Helena appears with her maids before the steps of her ancestral home, under the illusion that she is just coming from Troy. Her husband, Menelaus, has remained on the sea-shore to muster his men, and has sent her ahead to make preparations for a thank-offering to the gods. She enters the palace for this purpose, but is straightway frightened back by the horrible figure of Phorkyas crouching near the hearth. Phorkyas follows her to the door and, after a long altercation with the chorus and a reminiscent review of Helena's life, informs her that she herself and her maids are the victims selected for sacrifice. But a means of rescue is at hand. During her long absence a northern prince has established himself near the head waters of the Eurotas and built a strange palace there. If Helena will but say the word she shall be transferred with her maids to this palace. The word is spoken and the transition made by magic to the inner court of a medieval castle. As Helena enters, a procession of pages marches down the castle-steps bearing a throne, on which she seats herself. Faust advances slowly, leading in chains the warder Lynceus, who has failed to announce the approach of strangers. His life is forfeit, but Faust permits him to lay his case before Helena. Lynceus excuses himself in rimed stanzas which sound strange to the ears of his judge: He was so dazzled by the glorious vision — the sun rising in the south — that he forgot to blow his horn. Helena pardons him — it is her fate to bewitch the minds of men — and he rushes away to get his boxes of treasure and lay them at her feet. But Faust declares that particular gifts are unnecessary, since the whole castle and its owner are henceforth hers. She calls her new protector to the throne at her side, and receives from him a lesson in riming. Their love-making is rudely interrupted by Phorkyas, who announces that Menelaus is on the march for the recovery of his again recreant wife. Faust orders out his troops and harangues them on their past achievements. Then he parcels out the Peloponnesus in fiefs to his generals and leaves the campaign in their hands, while he himself remains in his Arcadian home, to live for love and beauty.

The scene now changes again to an idyllic Arcadian landscape. The Trojan girls are asleep in the shade, Faust and Helena invisible in a grotto. Phorkyas, who has been peeping, wakes the chorus to tell them about the appearance and precocious antics of the new crown-prince. The girls refuse to be astonished, for they know of a still more wonderful child, the infant Hermes. But Phorkyas bids them forget such fables — the day of the old gods and the old poetry is past. At this moment enchanting music is heard from the grotto, and soon Euphorion appears as Genius of Poesy — in form a little Phœbus with halo and golden lyre. The delirious operatic scene which follows does not lend itself readily to analysis in plain prose. Beginning as an embodiment of buoyant, bounding, childish caprice, Euphorion becomes more and more vehement, more and more reckless. Presently he begins to climb a high rock from which he sees that he is in the midst of Pelops' land and hears the roar of battle — the war between Menelaus and the vassals of Faust. A martial frenzy seizes him: He too will face death and win glory. Climbing still higher he appears now as a young man in armor. In his mad longing to be at the scene of battle he dreams that he can fly. Casting himself upon the air he falls at the feet of Helena and Faust. For a moment his appearance suggests 'a familiar form' (that of Byron), but the corporeal illusion quickly vanishes, the aureole mounts skyward and the voice of Euphorion is heard from below imploring his mother not to leave him alone in the 'dismal realm.' With the death of Euphorion the magic spell that holds Helena to earth is broken and she follows her son, leaving her dress and veil in the embrace of Faust. By advice of Phorkyas he clings to these mementoes, and they presently become a vehicle of cloud which envelops him and bears him away through the air. Panthalis, the leader of the chorus, follows her mistress; but the unnamed choretids, eager to escape the ignominy of an anonymous existence in Hades, divide into four groups and remain on earth as spirits of trees, echoes, brooks and vines. The curtain now falls upon the phantasmagoria. Phorkyas throws off her antique mask and appears as Mephistopheles, who delivers an epilogue, if any is needed, and then follows Faust upon seven-league boots.

The fourth act opens in a wild mountain-region and discloses Faust just alighting from the vehicle of cloud which has borne him over land and sea, 'far above all that is vulgar,' — back from Arcadia. His supreme desire, or what he lately thought to be his supreme desire, has been gratified in a way by a pleasing illusion; but now the illusion is vanished. Helena, like Gretchen, is but a memory, and he is ready for something new. For life has not become insipid; on the contrary it has acquired fresh zest, for the antique heroine has bequeathed to him the spirit of heroic enterprise.

As his chariot of cloud floats away it parts in twain, the one half taking for an instant the semblance of Helena, the other that of Gretchen; the one betokening the 'large import' of the recent past, the other the long-vanished sweetness of youthful love. But this brief 'time for memory and for tears' is soon cut short by Mephistopheles, who provokes a geological discussion anent the circumjacent rocks. The devil argues as Plutonist, that the rocks were brought to their present position by a primitive eruption; but being unable to convince his opponent, who is a bit-by-bit geologist, he changes the subject and inquires if Faust has not some further project suggested during his recent voyage through the air. Faust answers affirmatively and sets his servitor a-guessing; but Mephistopheles guesses wide of the mark, and has to be told finally that the new scheme is nothing less than a battle with the sea for the purpose of gaining property and power. That is, a large estate is to be won by draining a swampy tract along the shore and shutting out the insolent tide by means of dykes. For once Mephistopheles makes no objection, but declares that the thing is easy and the needed opportunity right at hand. He explains that their friend the Emperor is in trouble: The paper-money debauch led quickly to anarchy; the clamor then arose for a strong ruler, a rival claimant to the throne appeared, and even now the two armies are drawn up for a decisive battle. It is only necessary to take a hand in the struggle, help the legitimate Emperor to victory, and then claim the sea-shore as a guerdon. Faust pleads his lack of military knowledge, but Mephistopheles promises efficient help and forthwith calls up three allegorical 'mighty men,' Fighthard, Getquick, and Holdfast.

Then comes the battle. The Emperor and his Generalissimo observe and discuss the position of the loyal troops and listen to the reports of spies. In a sudden burst of valor the Emperor despatches a herald and challenges his rival to a settlement by personal combat. Faust now appears with his 'mighty men' and offers the further aid of the mountain-folk. He explains that he has come at the behest of an Italian wizard whom the Emperor had once saved from burning at the stake. The Emperor does not reject the proffered help, but thinks it would become him to fight in person for his crown. Faust protests against the risking of so precious a life, and just at this juncture the herald returns and reports that his challenge had been contemptuously rejected. The Generalissimo now orders an assault, and Faust by permission sends Fighthard with the right wing, Getquick with the center, and Holdfast with the left. At the same time Mephistopheles strengthens the rear with a noisy phantom-army consisting really of empty suits of armor borrowed from the neighboring collections. The battle now proceeds amid all sorts of magic manifestations. The right wing holds its own, but the left is driven back and the Emperor loses heart. Mephistopheles tries to reassure him and asks to be given command. Seeing his sovereign in conference with a magician, the Generalissimo throws up his command and retires to his tent in a huff, followed by the Emperor himself. Mephistopheles, now having full swing, sends his courier-ravens to a neighboring lake and borrows from the undines the *appearance* of water. Very soon the hostile column is floundering in imaginary floods. Then the appearance of flame is borrowed from the mountain-folk, and bursting fire-balls, blinding flashes, etc., complete the demoralization of the enemy. They break and flee, and the fight is won. Getquick and Speedbooty now plunder the Pretender's tent, but retire when the legitimate sovereign arrives with his officers. His Majesty now assumes the pompous tone of one who has won a great battle solely through the skill and fidelity of his generals — there was magic involved, but that was a mere incident. So he proceeds to reward the 'victorious' princes with court-titles and with the confiscated lands and prerogatives of those who have fought against him. The Archbishop-Chancellor is ordered to prepare charters confirming these new arrangements. The wily prelate promises obedience and then, when the secular princes have retired, takes occasion to do a stroke of work for the church. He has seen with pain how the young Emperor has been willing to profit by the help of magic. Such a grievous sin must be atoned for by handsome gifts to the church if he would escape the ban of Rome. The frightened Emperor consents ruefully to the priest's exactions, which finally culminate in the demand that even the watery domain which has been given to the accursed magician shall pay tithes to Holy Church.

The fifth act follows after a long interval of time. With the the aid of Mephisto's devices Faust has drained his wet fief, shut out the sea and become the feudal lord of a fertile paradise. But he is not content even now, for one little spot in his vast domain is not his. This is the hillock owned by an aged couple, Philemon and Baucis, who live in their little hut, worshiping 'the old God' in the neighboring chapel, and refusing the offers of the new magnate, who would like their land for a building-site. Faust — no saint even in his old age — is angered at their obstinacy, and feels that all he has is worthless, since he has not everything in sight. The one little check to his imperious will renders life unbearable. Mephistopheles, who has now become a pirate skipper in the service of Faust, though the latter does not approve the piracy, advises that Philemon and Baucis be removed by force to another home. Faust is weak enough to consent, and to entrust the business to his servitor, whose brutal conduct results in the death of the pious old couple and the burning of their cottage. The warder Lynceus sees the fire from his tower, and as he is mourning the destruction of the ancient and beautiful landmark, Faust appears on the balcony of his palace and descries the smouldering ruin. Not yet knowing all that has happened he tries to soothe his conscience with the thought of the better house he will provide for the old people in another place. A moment later he learns the truth from Mephisto's report, and then he 'curses' the lawless, unintended deed. But the curse does not lift the burden from his soul. As he gazes at the ruin the smoke is wafted toward him by the breeze and takes the form of four grey old women, Want, Debt, Distress, and Worry. The first three soon go away, being unable to get into the rich man's house; but Worry slips through the keyhole, croons in his ear her dismal litany of care, and answers his defiant declaration of independence by breathing on his eyelids and blinding him.

This last scene gives expression to the creed at which Faust has arrived in extreme old age, for he is now to be thought of as having lived a hundred years. The mental clearing-up which was promised in the Prologue is here well-nigh an accomplished fact, and what we hear is a sweeping recantation of the old pessimism. Magic has proved a delusion: Instead of solving the hard problems it only darkens the life of its votary with all sorts of silly superstitions. He to whom life had seemed so pitifully mean because of its galling limitations, who had pined to be an elemental spirit, to 'flow through the veins' of nature like a god, to soar away in pursuit of the sun, now wishes for nothing better than to 'stand before nature as a man alone.' He is quite content to let his vision be bounded by the horizon of this earth, incurious of what is beyond. The riddle of life is no riddle for one who is good for something. What knowledge man needs is within his reach. Let him therefore go on his way with firm step and open eyes, untroubled by any spooks that may beset his path. And as to happiness, let him not expect to find it unmixed with pain, but let him accept his lot as it befalls, content to be discontented every moment of his life.

Returning to the argument, we see that Faust's will to live is not subdued by the visit of the four weird sisters with their dismal forewarning of death. Though old and blind, the inner light of his forward-ranging idealism still burns brightly. He has yet a great work to do, and time being now precious he forthwith orders out an army of workmen with tools for the digging of a ditch (*Graben*). Mephistopheles, as overseer, perceiving that the end is at hand and that it will be a question of a *Grab* rather than a *Graben*, calls up the Lemurs and orders them to dig a grave. The blind old Faust now gropes his way out of the palace and expresses his delight in the music of pick and spade. We learn what the new project is. With all its great possibilities his domain is still badly damaged by a miasmatic swamp running along the distant foothills. The draining of this swamp is to be the crowning achievement of his life and the basis of a deathless fame; for by that means he will create a home for millions of happy and industrious burghers, 'to dwell not in secure idleness but in free activity.' The ever present danger of the sea will be a blessing, for it will form an incentive to public spirit and be a constant reminder that vigilance must be the price of safety. Thus the population will feel that their welfare depends upon themselves and will learn the priceless lesson, 'the highest conclusion of wisdom,' that happiness must be earned from day to day; that it is a matter of winning rather than of enjoying passively what has already been won. Could all this be realized and he himself stand with such a people on a free soil, Faust thinks he *might* say to the passing moment, 'Pray tarry, thou art so fair.' Absorbed in his dream of the future, of the good he will yet do, and the immortal name he will leave behind, he speaks the words: 'In the anticipation of such high happiness I enjoy now the supreme moment.' Then he falls back dead — victorious under the spirit of the compact, though Mephistopheles, relying upon the letter, regards himself as the winner.

For Faust has never wished to delay the passing moment;

he has merely imagined that he *might wish* to delay it, if his great plan were realized. He has not proclaimed himself satisfied, nor 'stretched himself upon a bed of ease.' And if he has at last found a happy moment he has found it not in the passive enjoyment of any sensual pleasure purveyed by the devil, but in an altruistic dream of a great work yet to be done for others. In fact so clear is the case that even the devil can not take himself very seriously with his *prima facie* claim to the dead man's soul. He must of course play out his part, but he does it in the manner of a jovial old cynic who sees the humorous rather than the solemn aspect of the business. Indeed, it is unthinkable that such a mellow and amiable devil should wish to consign a human soul to endless suffering. He would be ashamed of himself. There is nothing left for him, therefore, but to make a show of standing upon his legal rights, and then, when the battle inevitably goes against him, to — laugh himself off the field. He orders up a cohort of devils to watch the body and seize the soul upon its escape, and himself grumbles the while over the increasing hardness of the modern devil's lot. For views have changed as to the time, place, and manner of the soul's final exit, and the signs of death once relied upon with confidence are no longer regarded as trustworthy. As he is scolding vociferously about these things a chorus of angels appears, scattering roses — the symbol of divine love. He orders his minions to puff and blow, but their breath converts the flowers into scorching flames, before which the devils weaken and retreat precipitately. He resolves to hold his ground in spite of the intolerable fire, but allows his attention to be diverted for an instant to the sensuous beauty of the angels, and, before he is aware of it, they have taken possession of the soul and carried it away. Thus he is left alone and discomfited, and makes his final exit chiding himself for an old fool.

The last scene, which takes the place of an epilogue, discloses a sacred mountain reaching from earth to heaven. Holy anchorites, whom love has made physically buoyant, hover in the air and give expression to their inner ecstasy. The angels who have rescued the soul of Faust arrive with their precious burden, and since it is not yet fully purged of earthly dross, they surrender it to a band of 'blessed boys' — child-angels who died before they had known sin. In their charge the soul quickly develops a new and radiant spiritual body and is borne aloft to where a band of penitent women are chanting the praise of the Glorified Mother. One of the penitents, known on earth as Gretchen, seeing her former lover approach, asks permission to take him in her charge and give him his first instruction in the ways of the new life. The Holy Mother grants the prayer, saying: 'Come, rise to higher spheres! If he divines thy presence he will follow thee.' Thus the new-born Faust mounts upward to the perfect light, drawn on by the mystic attraction of the 'eternal womanly,' that is, of redeeming love.

III.

CRITICAL OBSERVATIONS.

1. The Second Part and the Critics.

The history of opinion concerning the Second Part of *Faust* is a large subject, to which we can here devote but few words. If told fully the story would begin with a record of extreme opinions, some praising the work as a monument of wonderful wisdom, and others denouncing it as a monument of senile folly, and both based upon a somewhat radical misconception of Goethe's art. In its later chapters the story would tell of a better understanding, a more reasonable criticism, and an ever-growing appreciation.

The first interpreters * regarded the poem as didactic through

* The most important are Deycks and Löwe, 1834; Weber, Rosenkranz and Düntzer, 1836; Weisse, 1837; Leutbecher, 1838; Rötscher, 1840; Meyer, 1847; Düntzer.

and through. Assuming, rightly enough, the presence of an underlying 'idea,' they treated this idea as all-in-all and tried to find philosophy everywhere. Their problem was to explain the logical relation of the two Parts to each other and of each scene to the ground-plan of the whole. And since there are many scenes and characters which, in a natural reading of the text, show little trace of any didactic purpose, there was no recourse but to ascribe to these an allegorical meaning. The masquerade was an allegory of 'society,' the sham fire at the end denoting 'revolution.' Helena was Greek art; Euphorion the logical offspring of classicism and romanticism; Mephisto's insects the 'whims, crotchets and theories of mechanical scholarship,' and so forth. Or, if not allegory, the text was veiled biography. Goethe had everywhere represented himself, his personal experiences, his relation to his friends, his views of literature, science, and art.

Thus, in a well-meant attempt to explain *Faust* for the reading public, the poetry of it was resolved into a mass of prosaic abstractions and egotistic puerilities. The poet's symbolism was confounded with allegory. His humor, his pictures, his legendary hocus-pocus, his bits of solemn fun at the expense of the learned (as, for example, the incident of the Kabiri), were expounded at tedious length, paraphrased and schematized for the philosophic intellect, and made to yield all sorts of owlish lessons. Worst of all, hardly two interpreters agreed in any matter of detail.

All this being so, it is little wonder that the poem got, at first, a very dubious reputation. The critics assumed that it was what its friends said it was, namely, a mass of oracular wisdom, to be comprehended with the philosophic organ by the help of abstract analysis; and finding that they could not comprehend it in this

---

1850; Hartung, 1855; and Schnetger, 1858. For exact titles and a full list (down to 1850 the curious reader is referred to the first edition of Düntzer's larger commentary, which is still valuable for philological material.

way, and that the 'wisdom,' as set forth by the expounders, was no reward for the trouble required to get at it, they concluded, not unnaturally, that the whole affair was not worth bothering over. This opinion was of course cheerfully concurred in and handed on by all those writers who disliked Goethe on religious or political grounds. And so it became a widely-accepted dogma in the literary world, that the Second Part of *Faust* was a colossal failure. Some said it never ought to have been written. It was not really a continuation of the First Part, and was very much inferior both in artistic power and in human interest. It was an exasperating production, which kept the reader forever wondering, speculating, guessing, and finally left his curiosity unsatisfied. It could give pleasure to no one except the philologist in search of hard nuts to crack. It was a product of decadent powers, labored, incoherent, without plan and without action, and loaded down with an old man's crotchets. It was marred by annoying mannerisms of style. In fine, it was the work of a man who had forgotten both the German language and the art of poetry.*

Thus the criticism of *Faust* ranged between extremes of misjudgment, both parties failing to comprehend in its full import the simple fact that Goethe is the poet of the concrete, not of the abstract. The first thing needful was to get rid of the allegorical nonsense. A mild protest was entered in 1860 by Köstlin, and a still more effective one two years later by Vischer in his amusing satire of *Mystifizinski*, though Vischer hated the Second Part, and meant his fire to rake the poem no less than its expounders.

---

* What can be urged against the Second Part is best stated by Fr. Vischer; see especially his *Neue Beiträge zur Kritik des Gedichts*, 1875, *passim*. Cf. further, R. von Raumer, *Vom deutschen Geist*, 1850, p. 167; Gruppe, *Geschichte der deutschen Poesie*, 1868, IV, p. 411; R. Gottschall, *Literaturgeschichte*, I, p. 123. Of more recent implacables let it suffice to mention Gwinner, *Goethe's Faustidee* u. s. w., 1892, and Weitbrecht, *Diesseits von Weimar*, 1895.

The great merit of first showing how *Faust* ought to be read belongs to Von Loeper, whose first edition, of the year 1870, marks an epoch in the study of the poem. In a short introduction Von Loeper drew attention to the two fundamental vices of the interpreters, — their habit of reading particular experiences of Goethe into the text, and their habit of allegorizing. In a convincing argument he showed the groundlessness and absurdity of these practices. What had been mistaken for didactic allegory was in each case simply what it purports to be in the text, and must be laid hold of with the imagination and the fancy. The prime requisite therefore was constant attention to the legendary basis of Goethe's fantastic creations.*

Thus the way was prepared both for a more fruitful study of the text by the philologists and for a more enjoyable reading of it by educated persons in general. It was a relief to many to find that they could, if they chose, read the Second Part of *Faust* like other poetry, without continually going in search of a philosophic abstraction or a bit of personal history behind every play of the poet's fancy; and that, when so read, it could really be enjoyed and did not seem so very hard to understand; not harder, for example, than the bulk of the First Part. Indeed, for the purposes of critical scholarship, if not for those of a first reading, the First Part is the more difficult of the two, and it is with that that recent Faust-literature has been chiefly concerned. The writings of Scherer and Fischer † calling attention to incongruities of plan and character-drawing, opened a field of study and discussion that was quickly occupied by numerous writers, and

---

* One can only regret that Loeper's work did not appear in time to be of use to Bayard Taylor, whose Notes, consisting largely of quotations from the early didactic commentators, have probably neutralized, for a large number of persons, the pleasure derived from his excellent translation.

† The reader is referred to the bibliographic list contained in an Appendix to Vol I of this edition.

these genetic studies were then greatly stimulated by the discovery of the Göchhausen MS. in 1887.

Meanwhile the Second Part has not been neglected, though it has received less attention. The edition by Schröer, with its excellent introduction and copious commentary, though open to the charge of explaining more than enough, has done good service in the Socratic work of bringing philosophy down from the clouds. The opening of the archives at Weimar brought to light a mass of material which, while mostly of little value, at any rate makes it forevermore impossible to speak of the Second Part as an afterthought, or even to speak of it as the work of Goethe's old age without duly qualifying the statement. Recent years have shown an increasing volume of notes and short articles devoted to the elucidation of particular points; while quotations and allusions in all sorts of journals testify to the fact that a very large number of Germans have now appropriated *Faust* in its entirety. As this process has gone on it has become apparent that the most of the very harsh criticisms which gained currency a generation ago rested upon misapprehension of one kind or another. Very many, though not indeed all, of the far-famed faults of diction can either be defended on philological grounds or paralleled with others equally 'bad' from the poet's early writings. That is, they are not senile vagaries. One who knows what the German language owes to Goethe will not be inclined to break the rod of the schoolmaster over him for these eccentricities. 'Nice customs curtesy to great kings.'

But the most important agency for bringing about a better understanding of *Faust* has been, it is safe to say, the stage. The first attempt to represent the entire drama in a spirit of decent loyalty to the author's plan was made at Weimar, in 1875, by the late Otto Devrient, who arranged the text for two evenings under the name of 'A Mystery in two Days' Works.' The success of the Weimar performance was such that the staging of the complete *Faust* soon became a practical problem for the German theaters. Devrient's arrangement was tried in many places, and is still used as the basis of the annual performances at Weimar and Leipzig. In 1883 a new adaptation, extending over three evenings, was brought out by Wilbrandt at the Burg Theater in Vienna, with never-to-be-forgotten success, so its author testifies. It has since been frequently repeated and has now appeared in print. There are, however, some rather cogent objections both to the mystery-stage and to the three evenings; wherefore there was room enough for the latest adaptation by Possart, which achieved a great triumph at Munich in 1894, and has become a permanent attraction of the Court Theater in that city. These performances, witnessed now every year in several different cities by crowded houses that are innocent of philosophy and know nothing of the critic's small perplexities, are rapidly familiarizing the German people with the real *Faust*. As one sees the Second Part on the stage, the cobwebs with which it has been invested by prejudice and misapplied learning fall away, and one is left face to face with the visions of Goethe as he saw them.

To sum up: Blemishes in the Second Part there undoubtedly are. One may say that there is too much of it. It is occasionally prolix. We could easily spare several figures from the 'Masquerade' and get along with shorter speeches from the rest. And the same is true of the 'Walpurgis-Night' and the third act. The erudition is sometimes too recondite. Now and then the symbolism is a little tantalizing. There are obvious faults of style and of dramatic construction. But all these defects can be found in the First Part also. On the other hand it remains true that the separate scenes of the Second Part were very vividly realized and were portrayed with what deserves to be called, speaking broadly, superb art. Quite apart from its didactic element it presents a series of fascinating pictures, matchless in variety of interest and in many-sided suggestiveness. It contains some of the noblest poetry in the world. While it sets at nought some of the ordinary conventions of dramatic art (as does the First Part likewise), it is not incoherent, nor planless, nor devoid of action. On the contrary, it is all action, and the general plan and connection are perfectly clear. And as to the 'wisdom,' it is at any rate the matured wisdom of Goethe; a man not infallible, a man with his hobbies and vagaries and prejudices, like other men, but upon the whole the broadest, the sanest, and the most helpful among the great critics of modern life.

2. *The Didactic Element.*

Nothing is more characteristic of Goethe's poetic genius from youth to age than its objectivity. His starting-point is always the mental image. He does not first conceive an abstract idea and then search in the realm of fact (nature, history, legend) for a suitable embodiment of his thought, but he sees the fact first and then looks at it intently until it yields up its 'philosophy.' To a degree this is true of all the greatest poets, but it is preeminently true of Goethe, although he, more than any other perhaps, has been mistaken for a metaphysician. His plays and novels all illustrate this fundamental quality of his mind, which also dominates his scientific thinking. In a suggestive essay of the year 1822 he writes of his poetic method: 'Certain large *motifs*, legends, ancient traditions, impressed themselves so deeply upon my mind that I kept them alive and effective within me for forty or fifty years. It seemed to me the most beautiful of possessions to see such dear pictures frequently renewed in my imagination as they kept ever transforming themselves, but without changing their character, and ripening toward a clearer shape, a more definite representation.'* Further on in the same essay he observes that his poetic procedure is a matter of induction. He

---

* *Bedeutendes Förderniss durch ein einziges geistreiches Wort, Werke, H.* 27, 350.

does not rest until he finds 'a pregnant point from which much can be derived.'

This seeking after a 'pregnant point' gives rise to symbolism, which is the opposite of allegory, since it begins with the concrete. Take for illustration the incident of Helena. The essentials of the story are given by the legend. Goethe does not invent them, nor change their fundamental character, but takes them as they are and turns them over in his mind until he finds the 'pregnant point,' namely, the effect on Faust's character of his infatuation for an ancient Greek ideal of womanly beauty. From this 'much can be derived,'—much that is not really in the story, but can easily be got out of it when one has the right point of view. *What* one is to get out of it will depend very largely, however, upon one's own culture. The 'meaning' is not something that can be formulated in exact terms like the answer to a conundrum. Helena is not Greek art, nor an embodiment of any other abstraction whatever, but a legendary personage. The symbolism is not to be grasped by the help of a 'key' or of logical analysis, but by the poetic imagination; and it will suggest more or less to the reader according to his familiarity with the underlying legend, with Greek poetry, with medieval life and history, with the great classico-romantic controversy. One who knows or cares little about these things will not find the *Helena* very interesting.

Or take Homunculus. The imponderable transparent manikin, produced by chemical synthesis and endowed with wonderful knowledge, is a datum of learned superstition. Goethe takes him as a fact, just as Shakspere takes Ariel and Puck, uses him for his own dramatic purposes, and finds the 'pregnant point' of the little man's life-history in an imputed yearning for a corporeal existence. From this, again, much can be derived; among other things a whimsical application of the poet's theory concerning the evolution of organic forms. But what then does Homunculus 'mean'? The question is absurd. As well ask what Puck means, or Robin Goodfellow, or Jack-the-Giant-Killer. In other words: One must accept Goethe's fantastic creations naively, for what they are and what they suggest, without trying to rationalize them for the logical understanding.

And if this is true of particular characters and scenes, it is no less true of the poem as a whole. *Faust* is not a didactic treatise, though it has a didactic element. It is not there for the purpose of enforcing an opinion or systematically developing a philosophic idea. On this point nothing so good has been said by any critic as what Goethe himself said to Eckermann in 1827:

"People come to me and ask what idea I have tried to embody in my *Faust*. As if I myself knew and could express it! 'From heaven through the world to hell' — one might get along with that, only that is no idea, but the course of the action. And further, that the devil loses the wager, and that a man who ever strives upward out of grievous errors toward that which is better is to be saved — that is surely a good thought, which is effective and explains much; but it is not an idea which underlies the whole and every individual scene. Really it would have been a fine business if I had tried to string such a rich, varied, and many-sided life as I have exhibited in *Faust* upon the thread of a single pervading idea. Speaking broadly, it was never my way as poet to attempt the embodiment of any abstraction. I received *impressions*, — impressions of a sensuous, life-like, winsome, motley, manifold character, such as an active imagination offered; and I had nothing further to do as poet than to round out and perfect such visions and impressions inwardly, and then portray them vividly, so that others might receive the same impressions when they heard or read my representation. If ever I wished to represent an idea, I did it in short poems which could readily be seen through and might be dominated by a rigorous unity."

In the same conversation the poet expressed with emphasis the opinion that 'the more incommensurable, the more incomprehensible, a poetic production is for the understanding, the better.' *

* *Gespräche mit Goethe,* III, 118 (May 6, 1827).

Surely these words from the highest possible authority are a sufficient warning against every attempt to read into *Faust* an all-pervading unity of purpose. It was not written to point a moral or expound a thesis, and one should beware of treating it as if it were a kind of high-class Sunday-school book. The name of 'secular Bible,' which has often been applied to it, is perhaps not altogether a misnomer, since the Bible is also a collection of very heterogeneous documents separated from one another in their origin by long periods of time. Like the Bible, too, *Faust* is instructive and often quoted; but one should not take its multifarious scenes for a series of moral texts converging with strenuous logic to a plan of salvation. On this point, again, we have a good word from Goethe himself. 'All poetry,' he wrote in 1825, 'should be instructive, but unnoticeably so. It should draw one's attention to that whereof instruction might appear desirable. One should then extract the doctrine for himself, just as from life.' *

Only in the sense here implied, that is, just as history or biography is didactic, can *Faust* be called a didactic poem. The teaching is to be found in the totality of what happens, and not in any pivotal doctrine. We hear, to be sure, from the angels in heaven, that they have been able to save Faust because he has always 'striven'. But this is too general to be of much use as an all-explaining formula, and too vague, we may add, to satisfy a sterner theologian than Goethe. Striven for what? one naturally asks. For what was he striving in the 'Witches' Kitchen,' as lover of Gretchen, at the Masquerade, or in his attempted deportation of Philemon and Baucis? Evidently his 'striving' must be understood in a rather abstract way of his idealism, which is indeed the dominant trait of his character, but not the mainspring of all that he does. Nevertheless, that he should be saved in vir-

---

* *Über das Lehrgedicht, Werke, H.* 29, 226.

tue of this quality, rather than by faith or good works, accords with the deepest convictions of our poet. To live one's life in a large and eager way, with joy for its joys and pain for its pains, without stagnation or embitterment, with mind and soul unsated and insatiable, 'still achieving, still pursuing' to the end, — this seemed to him worth while for its own sake. This is the sense of one of his favorite mottoes: Über Gräber vorwärts.* He did not deem it necessary to ground the goodness of life upon issues that are beyond the grave — to live being the all-sufficient end and aim of living. Nevertheless he believed in immortality; so that it would be a great mistake to regard Faust's salvation as a mere concession to conventional ideas. 'The conviction of our continued existence,' he said to Eckermann in an oft-quoted conversation of the year 1829, 'arises to my mind from the idea of activity. If I exert myself restlessly to the end, nature is bound to provide me another form of existence when this present one can no longer suffice for my spirit.' † This gives us the logic of Faust's salvation. He wins heaven not as a reward of any specific merit (not, for example, because he becomes an altruist in his old age), but because, by the central rightness of things, a soul constituted like his is entitled to a further chance of growth. If it be asked who would go to hell according to such a system, the answer would have to be, apparently: Those who do not strive with good will. Such persons do not really *live* on earth. Their hell is the

* Cf. the noble verses which stand as a motto to the collection of poems entitled *Gott und Welt*:

'Weite Welt und breites Leben,
Langer Jahre redlich Streben,
Stets geforscht und stets gegründet,
Nie geschlossen, oft geründet,
Ältestes bewahrt mit Treue,
Freundlich aufgefasstes Neue,
Heitern Sinn und reine Zwecke:
Nun, man kommt wohl eine Strecke.'

† *Gespräche mit Goethe*, II, 40 (Feb. 4, 1829).

prolongation of their worthlessness amid the society of their kind.

But if Faust's final conversion to altruism is not the key which unlocks paradise, it is still a matter of importance. He finds the supreme moment of his life in anticipating the joy of completing a great work for the benefit of those who are to come. Nothing turns here upon the nature of the work to be done, everything upon the self-surrender of the individual. He finds his best self only when he loses sight of himself in the feeling of large helpfulness, in the thought that he is contributing toward a better hereafter. The theme of *Faust*, on its purely ethical side, is the redemption of a self-centered and self-tormenting pessimist through enlarged experience of life, culminating in self-forgetful activity. Its philosophy is the cheerful, practical philosophy of meliorism. It says, in effect, that we need no abstract *summum bonum* in order to live. We are born into life and endowed with various instincts, passions, desires, which impel us this way and that in the assertion of self. The world is not ordered with reference to man's happiness, but it offers him a boundless field in which to exert his powers for the accomplishment of definite aims. Incidentally he has a right to such happiness as he can get, and a noble nature secures his share best by ceasing to think of his own personal satisfaction as an end itself, and becoming an energetic worker in the cause of making a better future for better men. Thus the highest realization of self culminates in self-surrender.

Aside from the doctrine of 'striving' and the tardy altruism which evolves at last somewhat unexpectedly out of a selfish pursuit of 'experience,' the ethical message of our poem must be sought in the change which takes place in Faust's general attitude toward life. The later attitude, as evinced in the dialogue with Dame Worry, is not optimism, but resignation without apathy. It presents activity, the finding of something to do and the doing of it with energy, as the best cure for *Weltschmerz*. This doctrine is the corner-stone of Goethe's ethics and accounts in large measure for his powerful influence over Carlyle. Instead of quarreling with the conditions of existence, a man is to make the most of them as they are. Instead of crying 'Behind the veil! Behind the veil!' he is to turn resolutely to the things he can do and know this side of the veil. This prescription, it is true, can not satisfy the mind of the pessimist, for it makes no pretense of meeting his argument; but practically it is the best nepenthe for the griefs of which the pessimist complains. If not a profound philosophy, it suffices for the great mass of practical men everywhere, and squares well with the energetic spirit of western civilization. In its essence, too, it comes close to the saying of Jesus: 'If any man will *do* his will, he shall know of the doctrine.' One who is exerting himself vigorously for the achievement of definite ends which he believes to be good usually finds the business so interesting that he has no time or mood for prolonged misgivings over the constitution of the world. He gets his reward as he goes along in the satisfaction of *doing*, and does not feel the need of a constantly renewed proof that the Builder of the universe was wise. His attitude is like that of the great American preacher who remarked once concerning the slow progress of the mighty up-hill battle against wrong of every sort: 'What fun it is, though!'

From the ethical point of view, then, we can heartily accept Faust's 'final conclusion of wisdom,' that 'he only deserves freedom and life who is daily compelled to conquer them.' At the same time the literary critic has a right to urge that this conclusion is reached in our drama *per saltum*. That is to say, the philosophy of Faust as he appears at the last is not very clearly the logical outcome of anything that precedes. In the beginning of the Second Part we find him resolved to 'strive ever onward to the highest existence.' Here we are distinctly in the ethical sphere, and one is led to expect a progressive development toward an ideal of noble living. What follows, however, is his appearance as magician at the Emperor's court, his infatuation for and brief union with the fair shade Helena, then a victory won for the worthless Emperor by means of magic, and finally a large engineering project, also carried through by magic. What is there here to prepare us for the lofty altruism of the dying hour? It was Goethe's thought, as we have seen, to effect this preparation through the incident of Helena, and so the play must be understood. But when one reads the third act as finally completed, one finds very little of ethical suggestion. We are there in a different sphere. Nowhere is there any hint that the phantasmagory is designed to ripen any particular ethical convictions in the mind of Faust, nor does one see how the episode — a kind of daydream managed by Mephistopheles, and known by Faust to be so managed — can have the effect under consideration. Now this would be undeniably a very grave defect if *Faust* were a rigorous philosophic poem. But, let it be said again, such is not its nature. What fascinated Goethe at the outset was not a thesis in ethics, but a picture — the picture of a life-history. Fancying that he saw some resemblance between his own experiences and those of Doctor Faust, he transformed the wicked magician of the legend into a good man of high aspirations. Looking ahead, he saw the whole career of this man, and very naturally conceived him as arriving finally at that philosophy which he himself, Goethe, had arrived at after the subsidence of his youthful storm and stress. So he depicted his *Faustus moriturus* as a dreamer of the dream of human betterment, a believer in the goodness of life, an exemplar of the blessedness of devotion to Man. The picture lay finished in his mind at a comparatively early date. And then, when he came to fill in the preceding matter that should lead up to this philosophy, he found himself absorbed more and more in fantastic data of the legend, which were indeed rich enough in poetic possibilities, but did not belong to the ethical sphere of interest. The result is a certain lack of logical coherence, — a lack with which the reader must make his peace as best he can, but the existence of which it is folly to deny.

Is the poem then the worse for this quality? We have seen that its author did not think so. He had a poor opinion of logical poetry. And surely it must be admitted as antecedently probable that a mind like Goethe's, occupied for sixty years with the Faust-legend, would be a better judge of its poetic capabilities than any critic looking at the subject from a *doctrinaire* point of of view. On the whole, it is the part of wisdom to make the most of what we have rather than to carp and gird because we have not something else. There are logical poems enough in the world, but only one Goethe's *Faust*.

Der

Tragödie

Zweiter Theil

in fünf Acten.

Erster Act.

Anmuthige Gegend.

Faust
auf blumigen Rasen gebettet, ermüdet, unruhig, schlafsuchend.

Dämmerung.

Geister-Kreis
schwebend bewegt, anmuthige kleine Gestalten.

Ariel. Gesang von Äolsharfen begleitet.

Wenn der Blüthen Frühlings-Regen
Über alle schwebend sinkt,
4615 Wenn der Felder grüner Segen
Allen Erdgebornen blinkt,
Kleiner Elfen Geistergröße
Eilet wo sie helfen kann,
Ob er heilig, ob er böse,
4620 Jammert sie der Unglücksmann.

Die ihr dieß Haupt umschwebt im luft'gen Kreise,
Erzeigt euch hier nach edler Elfen Weise,
Besänftiget des Herzens grimmen Strauß,
Entfernt des Vorwurfs glühend bittre Pfeile,
4625 Sein Innres reinigt von erlebtem Graus.
Vier sind die Pausen nächtiger Weile,
Nun ohne Säumen füllt sie freundlich aus.

Erst senkt sein Haupt auf's kühle Polster nieder,
Dann badet ihn im Thau aus Lethe's Fluth;
Gelenk sind bald die krampferstarrten Glieder, 4630
Wenn er gestärkt dem Tag entgegen ruht;
Vollbringt der Elfen schönste Pflicht,
Gebt ihn zurück dem heiligen Licht.

Chor.

Einzeln, zu zweien und vielen, abwechselnd und gesammelt.

Wenn sich lau die Lüfte füllen
Um den grünumschränkten Plan, 4635
Süße Düfte, Nebelhüllen
Senkt die Dämmerung heran.
Lispelt leise süßen Frieden,
Wiegt das Herz in Kindesruh;
Und den Augen dieses Müden 4640
Schließt des Tages Pforte zu.

Nacht ist schon hereingesunken,
Schließt sich heilig Stern an Stern,
Große Lichter, kleine Funken
Glitzern nah und glänzen fern; 4645
Glitzern hier im See sich spiegelnd,
Glänzen droben klarer Nacht,
Tiefsten Ruhens Glück besiegelnd
Herrscht des Mondes volle Pracht.

Schon verloschen sind die Stunden, 4650
Hingeschwunden Schmerz und Glück;
Fühl' es vor! Du wirst gesunden;
Traue neuem Tagesblick.
Thäler grünen, Hügel schwellen,
Buschen sich zu Schatten=Ruh; 4655

Und in schwanken Silberwellen
Wogt die Saat der Ernte zu.

Wunsch um Wünsche zu erlangen
Schaue nach dem Glanze dort!
4660 Leise bist du nur umfangen,
Schlaf ist Schale, wirf sie fort!
Säume nicht dich zu erdreisten,
Wenn die Menge zaudernd schweift;
Alles kann der Edle leisten,
4665 Der versteht und rasch ergreift.

Ungeheures Getöse verkündet das Herannahen der Sonne.

Ariel.

Horchet! horcht dem Sturm der Horen!
Tönend wird für Geistes-Ohren
Schon der neue Tag geboren.
Felsenthore knarren rasselnd,
4670 Phöbus Räder rollen prasselnd,
Welch Getöse bringt das Licht!
Es trommetet, es posaunet,
Auge blinzt und Ohr erstaunet,
Unerhörtes hört sich nicht.
4675 Schlüpfet zu den Blumenkronen,
Tiefer, tiefer, still zu wohnen,
In die Felsen, unter's Laub;
Trifft es euch, so seid ihr taub.

Faust.

Des Lebens Pulse schlagen frisch lebendig,
4680 Ätherische Dämmerung milde zu begrüßen;
Du, Erde, warst auch diese Nacht beständig

Und athmest neu erquickt zu meinen Füßen,
Beginnest schon mit Lust mich zu umgeben,
Du regst und rührst ein kräftiges Beschließen,
Zum höchsten Dasein immerfort zu streben. — 4685
In Dämmerschein liegt schon die Welt erschlossen,
Der Wald ertönt von tausendstimmigem Leben,
Thal aus, Thal ein ist Nebelstreif ergossen,
Doch senkt sich Himmelsklarheit in die Tiefen,
Und Zweig' und Äste, frisch erquickt, entsprossen 4690
Dem duft'gen Abgrund wo versenkt sie schliefen;
Auch Farb' an Farbe klärt sich los vom Grunde,
Wo Blum' und Blatt von Zitterperle triefen,
Ein Paradies wird um mich her die Runde.

Hinaufgeschaut! — Der Berge Gipfelriesen 4695
Verkünden schon die feierlichste Stunde,
Sie dürfen früh des ewigen Lichts genießen
Das später sich zu uns hernieder wendet.
Jetzt zu der Alpe grüngesenkten Wiesen
Wird neuer Glanz und Deutlichkeit gespendet, 4700
Und stufenweis herab ist es gelungen; —
Sie tritt hervor! — und, leider schon geblendet,
Kehr' ich mich weg, vom Augenschmerz durchdrungen.

So ist es also, wenn ein sehnend Hoffen
Dem höchsten Wunsch sich traulich zugerungen, 4705
Erfüllungspforten findet flügeloffen;
Nun aber bricht aus jenen ewigen Gründen
Ein Flammen-Übermaß, wir stehn betroffen;
Des Lebens Fackel wollten wir entzünden,
Ein Feuermeer umschlingt uns, welch ein Feuer! 4710
Ist's Lieb'? Ist's Haß? die glühend uns umwinden,

Mit Schmerz- und Freuden wechselnd ungeheuer,
So daß wir wieder nach der Erde blicken,
Zu bergen uns in jugendlichstem Schleier.

4715 So bleibe denn die Sonne mir im Rücken!
Der Wassersturz, das Felsenriff durchbrausend,
Ihn schau' ich an mit wachsendem Entzücken.
Von Sturz zu Sturzen wälzt er jetzt in tausend
Dann abertausend Strömen sich ergießend,
4720 Hoch in die Lüfte Schaum an Schäume sausend.
Allein wie herrlich diesem Sturm ersprießend,
Wölbt sich des bunten Bogens Wechsel-Dauer,
Bald rein gezeichnet, bald in Luft zerfließend,
Umher verbreitend duftig kühle Schauer.
4725 Der spiegelt ab das menschliche Bestreben.
Ihm sinne nach und du begreifst genauer:
Am farbigen Abglanz haben wir das Leben.

Kaiserliche Pfalz.

Saal des Thrones.

Staatsrath in Erwartung des Kaisers.

Trompeten.

Hofgesinde aller Art, prächtig gekleidet, tritt vor.

Der Kaiser gelangt auf den Thron, zu seiner Rechten der Astrolog.

Kaiser.

Ich grüße die Getreuen, Lieben,
Versammelt aus der Näh und Weite; —
Den Weisen seh' ich mir zur Seite, 4730
Allein wo ist der Narr geblieben?

Junker.

Gleich hinter deiner Mantel-Schleppe
Stürzt' er zusammen auf der Treppe,
Man trug hinweg das Fett-Gewicht,
Todt oder trunken? weiß man nicht. 4735

Zweiter Junker.

Sogleich mit wunderbarer Schnelle
Drängt sich ein andrer an die Stelle.

Gar köstlich ist er aufgeputzt,
Doch fratzenhaft daß jeder stutzt;
4740 Die Wache hält ihm an der Schwelle
Kreuzweis die Hellebarden vor —
Da ist er doch der kühne Thor!

Mephistopheles am Throne knieend.

Was ist verwünscht und stets willkommen?
Was ist ersehnt und stets verjagt?
4745 Was immerfort in Schutz genommen?
Was hart gescholten und verklagt?
Wen darfst du nicht herbeiberufen?
Wen höret jeder gern genannt?
Was naht sich deines Thrones Stufen?
4750 Was hat sich selbst hinweggebannt?

Kaiser.

Für dießmal spare deine Worte!
Hier sind die Räthsel nicht am Orte,
Das ist die Sache dieser Herrn. —
Da löse du! das hört' ich gern.
4755 Mein alter Narr ging, fürcht' ich, weit in's Weite;
Nimm seinen Platz und komm an meine Seite.

Mephistopheles steigt hinauf und stellt sich zur Linken.

Gemurmel der Menge.

Ein neuer Narr — Zu neuer Pein —
Wo kommt er her — Wie kam er ein —
Der alte fiel — Der hat verthan —
4760 Es war ein Faß — Nun ist's ein Span —

Kaiser.

Und also ihr Getreuen, Lieben,
Willkommen aus der Näh und Ferne,
Ihr sammelt euch mit günstigem Sterne,
Da droben ist uns Glück und Heil geschrieben.
Doch sagt, warum in diesen Tagen, 4765
Wo wir der Sorgen uns entschlagen,
Schönbärte mummenschänzlich tragen
Und Heitres nur genießen wollten,
Warum wir uns rathschlagend quälen sollten?
Doch weil ihr meint, es ging' nicht anders an, 4770
Geschehen ist's, so sei's gethan.

Canzler.

Die höchste Tugend, wie ein Heiligen-Schein,
Umgibt des Kaisers Haupt, nur er allein
Vermag sie gültig auszuüben:
Gerechtigkeit! — Was alle Menschen lieben, 4775
Was alle fordern, wünschen, schwer entbehren,
Es liegt an ihm dem Volk es zu gewähren.
Doch ach! Was hilft dem Menschengeist Verstand,
Dem Herzen Güte, Willigkeit der Hand,
Wenn's fieberhaft durchaus im Staate wüthet, 4780
Und Übel sich in Übeln überbrütet.
Wer schaut hinab von diesem hohen Raum
In's weite Reich, ihm scheint's ein schwerer Traum,
Wo Mißgestalt in Mißgestalten schaltet,
Das Ungesetz gesetzlich überwaltet, 4785
Und eine Welt des Irrthums sich entfaltet.

Der raubt sich Heerden, der ein Weib,
Kelch, Kreuz und Leuchter vom Altare,

Berühmt sich dessen manche Jahre
4790 Mit heiler Haut, mit unverletztem Leib.
Jetzt drängen Kläger sich zur Halle,
Der Richter prunkt auf hohem Pfühl,
Indessen wogt, in grimmigem Schwalle,
Des Aufruhrs wachsendes Gewühl.
4795 Der darf auf Schand' und Frevel pochen
Der auf Mitschuldigste sich stützt,
Und: Schuldig! hörst du ausgesprochen
Wo Unschuld nur sich selber schützt.
So will sich alle Welt zerstückeln,
4800 Vernichtigen was sich gebührt;
Wie soll sich da der Sinn entwickeln
Der einzig uns zum Rechten führt?
Zuletzt ein wohlgesinnter Mann
Neigt sich dem Schmeichler, dem Bestecher,
4805 Ein Richter der nicht strafen kann
Gesellt sich endlich zum Verbrecher.
Ich mahlte schwarz, doch dichtern Flor
Zög' ich dem Bilde lieber vor.

Pause.

Entschlüsse sind nicht zu vermeiden,
4810 Wenn alle schädigen, alle leiden,
Geht selbst die Majestät zu Raub.

Heermeister.

Wie tobt's in diesen wilden Tagen!
Ein jeder schlägt und wird erschlagen
Und für's Commando bleibt man taub.
4815 Der Bürger hinter seinen Mauern,
Der Ritter auf dem Felsenneſt

Verschwuren sich uns auszudauern
Und halten ihre Kräfte fest.
Der Miethsoldat wird ungeduldig,
Mit Ungestüm verlangt er seinen Lohn, 4820
Und wären wir ihm nichts mehr schuldig,
Er liefe ganz und gar davon.
Verbiete wer was alle wollten,
Der hat in's Wespennest gestört;
Das Reich das sie beschützen sollten 4825
Es liegt geplündert und verheert.
Man läßt ihr Toben wüthend hausen,
Schon ist die halbe Welt verthan;
Es sind noch Könige da draußen,
Doch keiner denkt, es ging' ihn irgend an. 4830

Schatzmeister.

Wer wird auf Bundsgenossen pochen!
Subsidien die man uns versprochen,
Wie Röhrenwasser, bleiben aus.
Auch, Herr, in deinen weiten Staaten
An wen ist der Besitz gerathen? 4835
Wohin man kommt da hält ein Neuer Haus
Und unabhängig will er leben,
Zusehen muß man wie er's treibt;
Wir haben so viel Rechte hingegeben,
Daß uns auf nichts ein Recht mehr übrig bleibt. 4840
Auch auf Parteien, wie sie heißen,
Ist heut zu Tage kein Verlaß;
Sie mögen schelten oder preisen,
Gleichgültig wurden Lieb' und Haß.
Die Ghibellinen wie die Guelfen 4845
Verbergen sich um auszuruhn;

Wer jetzt will seinem Nachbar helfen?
Ein jeder hat für sich zu thun.
Die Goldespforten sind verrammelt,
4850 Ein jeder kratzt und scharrt und sammelt
Und unsre Cassen bleiben leer.

Marschalk.

Welch Unheil muß auch ich erfahren;
Wir wollen alle Tage sparen
Und brauchen alle Tage mehr.
4855 Und täglich wächs't mir neue Pein.
Den Köchen thut kein Mangel wehe;
Wildschweine, Hirsche, Hasen, Rehe,
Wälschhühner, Hühner, Gäns' und Enten,
Die Deputate, sichre Renten,
4860 Sie gehen noch so ziemlich ein.
Jedoch am Ende fehlt's an Wein.
Wenn sonst im Keller Faß an Faß sich häufte,
Der besten Berg' und Jahresläufte,
So schlürft unendliches Gesäufte
4865 Der edlen Herrn den letzten Tropfen aus.
Der Stadtrath muß sein Lager auch verzapfen,
Man greift zu Humpen, greift zu Napfen,
Und unter'm Tische liegt der Schmaus.
Nun soll ich zahlen, alle lohnen;
4870 Der Jude wird mich nicht verschonen,
Der schafft Anticipationen,
Die speisen Jahr um Jahr voraus.
Die Schweine kommen nicht zu Fette,
Verpfändet ist der Pfühl im Bette,
4875 Und auf den Tisch kommt vorgegessen Brot.

Kaiser nach einigem Nachdenken zu Mephistopheles.

Sag', weißt du Narr nicht auch noch eine Noth?

Mephistopheles.

Ich keineswegs. Den Glanz umher zu schauen,
Dich und die Deinen! — Mangelte Vertrauen,
Wo Majestät unweigerlich gebeut,
Bereite Macht Feindseliges zerstreut, 4880
Wo guter Wille, kräftig durch Verstand
Und Thätigkeit, vielfältige, zur Hand?
Was könnte da zum Unheil sich vereinen,
Zur Finsterniß, wo solche Sterne scheinen?

Gemurmel

Das ist ein Schalk — Der's wohl versteht — 4885
Er lügt sich ein — So lang es geht —
Ich weiß schon — Was dahinter steckt —
Und was denn weiter? — Ein Project —

Mephistopheles.

Wo fehlt's nicht irgendwo auf dieser Welt?
Dem dieß, dem das, hier aber fehlt das Geld. 4890
Vom Estrich zwar ist es nicht aufzuraffen;
Doch Weisheit weiß das Tiefste herzuschaffen.
In Bergesadern, Mauergründen
Ist Gold gemünzt und ungemünzt zu finden,
Und fragt ihr mich wer es zu Tage schafft: 4895
Begabten Manns Natur- und Geisteskraft.

Canzler.

Natur und Geist — so spricht man nicht zu Christen.
Deßhalb verbrennt man Atheisten,

Weil solche Reden höchst gefährlich sind.
4900 Natur ist Sünde, Geist ist Teufel,
Sie hegen zwischen sich den Zweifel,
Ihr mißgestaltet Zwitterkind.
Uns nicht so! — Kaisers alten Landen
Sind zwei Geschlechter nur entstanden,
4905 Sie stützen würdig seinen Thron:
Die Heiligen sind es und die Ritter;
Sie stehen jedem Ungewitter
Und nehmen Kirch' und Staat zum Lohn.
Dem Pöbelsinn verworrner Geister
4910 Entwickelt sich ein Widerstand,
Die Ketzer sind's! die Hexenmeister!
Und sie verderben Stadt und Land.
Die willst du nun mit frechen Scherzen
In diese hohen Kreise schwärzen,
4915 Ihr hegt euch an verderbtem Herzen,
Dem Narren sind sie nah verwandt.

Mephistopheles.

Daran erkenn' ich den gelehrten Herrn!
Was ihr nicht tastet steht euch meilenfern,
Was ihr nicht faßt das fehlt euch ganz und gar,
4920 Was ihr nicht rechnet glaubt ihr sei nicht wahr,
Was ihr nicht wägt hat für euch kein Gewicht,
Was ihr nicht münzt das meint ihr gelte nicht.

Kaiser.

Dadurch sind unsre Mängel nicht erledigt,
Was willst du jetzt mit deiner Fastenpredigt?
4925 Ich habe satt das ewige Wie und Wenn;
Es fehlt an Geld, nun gut so schaff' es denn.

Mephistopheles.

Ich schaffe was ihr wollt und schaffe mehr;
Zwar ist es leicht, doch ist das Leichte schwer;
Es liegt schon da, doch um es zu erlangen
Das ist die Kunst, wer weiß es anzufangen? 4930
Bedenkt doch nur: in jenen Schreckensläuften
Wo Menschenfluthen Land und Volk ersäuften,
Wie der und der, so sehr es ihn erschreckte,
Sein Liebstes da- und dortwohin versteckte.
So war's von je in mächtiger Römer Zeit, 4935
Und so fortan, bis gestern, ja bis heut.
Das alles liegt im Boden still begraben,
Der Boden ist des Kaisers, der soll's haben.

Schatzmeister.

Für einen Narren spricht er gar nicht schlecht,
Das ist fürwahr des alten Kaisers Recht. 4940

Canzler.

Der Satan legt euch goldgewirkte Schlingen:
Es geht nicht zu mit frommen rechten Dingen.

Marschalk.

Schafft' er uns nur zu Hof willkommne Gaben,
Ich wollte gern ein bißchen Unrecht haben.

Heermeister.

Der Narr ist klug, verspricht was jedem frommt; 4945
Fragt der Soldat doch nicht woher es kommt.

Mephistopheles.

Und glaubt ihr euch vielleicht durch mich betrogen;
Hier steht ein Mann! da! fragt den Astrologen,

In Kreis' um Kreise kennt er Stund' und Haus;
4950 So sage denn: wie sieht's am Himmel aus?

Gemurmel.

Zwei Schelme sind's — Verstehn sich schon —
Narr und Phantast — So nah dem Thron —
Ein mattgesungen — Alt Gedicht —
Der Thor bläs't ein — Der Weise spricht —

Astrolog spricht, Mephistopheles bläs't ein.

4955 Die Sonne selbst sie ist ein lautres Gold,
Mercur der Bote dient um Gunst und Sold,
Frau Venus hat's euch allen angethan,
So früh als spat blickt sie euch lieblich an;
Die keusche Luna launet grillenhaft,
4960 Mars, trifft er nicht, so dräut euch seine Kraft.
Und Jupiter bleibt doch der schönste Schein,
Saturn ist groß, dem Auge fern und klein.
Ihn als Metall verehren wir nicht sehr,
An Werth gering, doch im Gewichte schwer.
4965 Ja! wenn zu Sol sich Luna fein gesellt,
Zum Silber Gold, dann ist es heitre Welt,
Das Übrige ist alles zu erlangen,
Paläste, Gärten, Brüstlein, rothe Wangen,
Das alles schafft der hochgelahrte Mann
4970 Der das vermag was unser keiner kann.

Kaiser.

Ich höre doppelt was er spricht
Und dennoch überzeugt's mich nicht.

Gemurmel.

Was soll uns das — Gedroschner Spaß —
Kalenderei — Chymisterei —
Das hört ich oft — Und falsch gehofft — 4975
Und kommt er auch — So ist's ein Gauch —

Mephistopheles.

Da stehen sie umher und staunen,
Vertrauen nicht dem hohen Fund,
Der eine faselt von Alraunen
Der andre von dem schwarzen Hund. 4980
Was soll es daß der eine witzelt,
Ein andrer Zauberei verklagt,
Wenn ihm doch auch einmal die Sohle kitzelt,
Wenn ihm der sichre Schritt versagt.

Ihr alle fühlt geheimes Wirken 4985
Der ewig waltenden Natur,
Und aus den untersten Bezirken
Schmiegt sich herauf lebend'ge Spur.
Wenn es in allen Gliedern zwackt,
Wenn es unheimlich wird am Platz, 4990
Nur gleich entschlossen grabt und hackt,
Da liegt der Spielmann, liegt der Schatz!

Gemurmel.

Mir liegt's im Fuß wie Bleigewicht —
Mir krampft's im Arme — Das ist Gicht —
Mir krabbelt's an der großen Zeh — 4995
Mir thut der ganze Rücken weh —
Nach solchen Zeichen wäre hier
Das allerreichste Schatzrevier.

Kaiser.

Nur eilig! du entschlüpfst nicht wieder,
5000 Erprobe deine Lügenschäume,
Und zeig' uns gleich die edlen Räume.
Ich lege Schwert und Scepter nieder,
Und will mit eignen hohen Händen,
Wenn du nicht lügst, das Werk vollenden,
5005 Dich, wenn du lügst, zur Hölle senden!

Mephistopheles.

Den Weg dahin wüßt' allenfalls zu finden —
Doch kann ich nicht genug verkünden
Was überall besitzlos harrend liegt.
Der Bauer der die Furche pflügt
5010 Hebt einen Goldtopf mit der Scholle,
Salpeter hofft er von der Leimenwand
Und findet golden=goldne Rolle
Erschreckt, erfreut in kümmerlicher Hand.
Was für Gewölbe sind zu sprengen,
5015 In welchen Klüften, welchen Gängen
Muß sich der Schatzbewußte drängen,
Zur Nachbarschaft der Unterwelt!
In weiten altverwahrten Kellern,
Von goldnen Humpen, Schüsseln, Tellern,
5020 Sieht er sich Reihen aufgestellt.
Pokale stehen aus Rubinen
Und will er deren sich bedienen
Daneben liegt uraltes Naß.
Doch — werdet ihr dem Kundigen glauben —
5025 Verfault ist längst das Holz der Dauben,
Der Weinstein schuf dem Wein ein Faß.

Essenzen solcher edlen Weine,
Gold und Juwelen nicht alleine
Umhüllen sich mit Nacht und Graus.
Der Weise forscht hier unverdrossen; 5030
Am Tag erkennen das sind Possen,
Im Finstern sind Mysterien zu Haus.

Kaiser.

Die lass' ich dir! Was will das Düstre frommen?
Hat etwas Werth, es muß zu Tage kommen.
Wer kennt den Schelm in tiefer Nacht genau? 5035
Schwarz sind die Kühe, so die Katzen grau.
Die Töpfe drunten, voll von Goldgewicht,
Zieh deinen Pflug, und ackre sie an's Licht.

Mephistopheles.

Nimm Hack' und Spaten, grabe selber,
Die Bauernarbeit macht dich groß, 5040
Und eine Heerde goldner Kälber
Sie reißen sich vom Boden los.
Dann ohne Zaudern, mit Entzücken,
Kannst du dich selbst, wirst die Geliebte schmücken;
Ein leuchtend Farb- und Glanzgestein erhöht 5045
Die Schönheit wie die Majestät.

Kaiser.

Nur gleich, nur gleich! Wie lange soll es währen!

Astrolog wie oben.

Herr mäßige solch dringendes Begehren,
Laß erst vorbei das bunte Freudenspiel;
Zerstreutes Wesen führt uns nicht zum Ziel. 5050

Erst müssen wir in Fassung uns versühnen,
Das Untre durch das Obere verdienen.
Wer Gutes will der sei erst gut;
Wer Freude will besänftige sein Blut;
5055 Wer Wein verlangt der keltre reife Trauben;
Wer Wunder hofft der stärke seinen Glauben.

Kaiser.

So sei die Zeit in Fröhlichkeit verthan!
Und ganz erwünscht kommt Aschermittwoch an.
Indessen feiern wir, auf jeden Fall,
5060 Nur lustiger das wilde Carneval.

Trompeten, Exeunt.

Mephistopheles.

Wie sich Verdienst und Glück verketten
Das fällt den Thoren niemals ein;
Wenn sie den Stein der Weisen hätten,
Der Weise mangelte dem Stein.

Weitläufiger Saal

mit Nebengemächern, verziert und aufgeputzt zur

Mummenschanz.

Herold.

Denkt nicht ihr seid in deutschen Gränzen 5065
Von Teufels=, Narren= und Todtentänzen,
Ein heitres Fest erwartet euch.
Der Herr, auf seinen Römerzügen,
Hat, sich zu Nutz, euch zum Vergnügen,
Die hohen Alpen überstiegen, 5070
Gewonnen sich ein heitres Reich.
Der Kaiser, er, an heiligen Sohlen
Erbat sich erst das Recht zur Macht,
Und als er ging die Krone sich zu holen,
Hat er uns auch die Kappe mitgebracht. 5075
Nun sind wir alle neugeboren;
Ein jeder weltgewandte Mann
Zieht sie behaglich über Kopf und Ohren;
Sie ähnlet ihn verrückten Thoren,
Er ist darunter weise wie er kann. 5080
Ich sehe schon wie sie sich schaaren,
Sich schwankend sondern, traulich paaren;
Zudringlich schließt sich Chor an Chor.

Herein, hinaus, nur unverdrossen;
5085 Es bleibt doch endlich nach wie vor
Mit ihren hunderttausend Possen
Die Welt ein einzig großer Thor.

Gärtnerinnen.

Gesang begleitet von Mandolinen.

Euren Beifall zu gewinnen
Schmückten wir uns diese Nacht,
5090 Junge Florentinerinnen
Folgten deutschen Hofes Pracht;

Tragen wir in braunen Locken
Mancher heitern Blume Zier;
Seidenfäden, Seidenflocken
5095 Spielen ihre Rolle hier.

Denn wir halten es verdienstlich,
Lobenswürdig ganz und gar,
Unsere Blumen, glänzend künstlich,
Blühen fort das ganze Jahr.

5100 Allerlei gefärbten Schnitzeln
Ward symmetrisch Recht gethan;
Mögt ihr Stück für Stück bewitzeln,
Doch das Ganze zieht euch an.

Niedlich sind wir anzuschauen,
5105 Gärtnerinnen und galant;
Denn das Naturell der Frauen
Ist so nah mit Kunst verwandt.

Herold.

Laßt die reichen Körbe sehen
Die ihr auf den Häupten traget,
Die sich bunt am Arme blähen, 5110
Jeder wähle was behaget.
Eilig daß in Laub und Gängen
Sich ein Garten offenbare,
Würdig sind sie zu umdrängen
Krämerinnen wie die Waare. 5115

Gärtnerinnen.

Feilschet nun am heitern Orte,
Doch kein Markten findet statt!
Und mit sinnig kurzem Worte
Wisse jeder was er hat.

Olivenzweig mit Früchten.

Keinen Blumenflor beneid' ich, 5120
Allen Widerstreit vermeid' ich;
Mir ist's gegen die Natur:
Bin ich doch das Mark der Lande,
Und, zum sichern Unterpfande,
Friedenszeichen jeder Flur; 5125
Heute, hoff' ich, soll mir's glücken
Würdig schönes Haupt zu schmücken.

Ährenkranz golden.

Ceres Gaben, euch zu putzen,
Werden hold und lieblich stehn:
Das Erwünschteste dem Nutzen 5130
Sei als eure Zierde schön.

Phantasiekranz.

Bunte Blumen Malven ähnlich
Aus dem Moos ein Wunderflor!
Der Natur ist's nicht gewöhnlich,
5135 Doch die Mode bringt's hervor.

Phantasiestrauß.

Meinen Namen euch zu sagen
Würde Theophrast nicht wagen,
Und doch hoff' ich wo nicht allen,
Aber mancher zu gefallen,
5140 Der ich mich wohl eignen möchte,
Wenn sie mich in's Haar verflöchte,
Wenn sie sich entschließen könnte,
Mir am Herzen Platz vergönnte.

Ausforderung.

Mögen bunte Phantasien
5145 Für des Tages Mode blühen,
Wunderseltsam sein gestaltet
Wie Natur sich nie entfaltet;
Grüne Stiele, goldne Glocken,
Blickt hervor aus reichen Locken! —
5150 Doch wir

Rosenknospen.

halten uns versteckt,
Glücklich wer uns frisch entdeckt.

Wenn der Sommer sich verkündet,
Rosenknospe sich entzündet,
Wer mag solches Glück entbehren?
5155 Das Versprechen, das Gewähren,

Das beherrscht, in Florens Reich,
Blick und Sinn und Herz zugleich.

Unter grünen Laubgängen putzen die Gärtnerinnen zierlich ihren Kram auf.

Gärtner.

Gesang begleitet von Theorben.

Blumen sehet ruhig sprießen,
Reizend euer Haupt umzieren,
Früchte wollen nicht verführen, 5160
Kostend mag man sie genießen.

Bieten bräunliche Gesichter
Kirschen, Pfirschen, Königspflaumen,
Kauft! denn gegen Zung' und Gaumen
Hält sich Auge schlecht als Richter. 5165

Kommt von allerreifsten Früchten
Mit Geschmack und Lust zu speisen!
Über Rosen läßt sich dichten,
In die Äpfel muß man beißen.

Sei's erlaubt uns anzupaaren 5170
Eurem reichen Jugendflor,
Und wir putzen reifer Waaren
Fülle nachbarlich empor.

Unter lustigen Gewinden
In geschmückter Lauben Bucht, 5175
Alles ist zugleich zu finden:
Knospe, Blätter, Blume, Frucht.

Unter Wechselgesang, begleitet von Guitarren und Theorben, fahren beide Chöre fort ihre Waaren stufenweis in die Höhe zu schmücken und auszubieten.

Mutter und Tochter.

Mutter.

Mädchen, als du kamst an's Licht
Schmückt' ich dich im Häubchen,
5180 Warst so lieblich von Gesicht,
Und so zart am Leibchen.
Dachte dich sogleich als Braut,
Gleich dem Reichsten angetraut,
Dachte dich als Weibchen.

5185 Ach! nun ist schon manches Jahr
Ungenützt verflogen,
Der Sponsirer bunte Schaar
Schnell vorbei gezogen;
Tanztest mit dem einen flink,
5190 Gabst dem andern feinen Wink
Mit dem Ellenbogen.

Welches Fest man auch ersann,
Ward umsonst begangen,
Pfänderspiel und dritter Mann
5195 Wollten nicht verfangen;
Heute sind die Narren los,
Liebchen, öffne deinen Schoos,
Bleibt wohl einer hangen.

Gespielinnen jung und schön gesellen sich hinzu, ein vertrauliches Geplauder wird laut.

Fischer und Vogelsteller

mit Netzen, Angeln und Leimruthen, auch sonstigem Geräthe treten auf, mischen sich unter die schönen Kinder. Wechselseitige Versuche zu gewinnen, zu fangen, zu entgehen und fest zu halten geben zu den angenehmsten Dialogen Gelegenheit.

Holzhauer treten ein ungestüm und ungeschlacht.

Nur Platz! nur Blöße!
Wir brauchen Räume, 5200
Wir fällen Bäume
Die krachen, schlagen:
Und wenn wir tragen
Da gibt es Stöße.
Zu unserm Lobe 5205
Bringt dieß in's Reine;
Denn wirkten Grobe
Nicht auch im Lande,
Wie kämen Feine
Für sich zu Stande, 5210
So sehr sie witzten?
Deß seid belehret!
Denn ihr erfröret,
Wenn wir nicht schwitzten.

Pulcinelle täppisch, fast läppisch.

Ihr seid die Thoren, 5215
Gebückt geboren.
Wir sind die Klugen
Die nie was trugen;
Denn unsre Kappen,
Jacken und Lappen 5220
Sind leicht zu tragen.
Und mit Behagen
Wir immer müßig,
Pantoffelfüßig,
Durch Markt und Haufen 5225
Einher zu laufen,

Gaffend zu stehen,
Uns anzukrähen;
Auf solche Klänge
5230 Durch Drang und Menge
Aalgleich zu schlüpfen,
Gesammt zu hüpfen,
Vereint zu toben.
Ihr mögt uns loben,
5235 Ihr mögt uns schelten,
Wir lassen's gelten.

Parasiten schmeichelnd-lüstern.

Ihr wackern Träger
Und eure Schwäger,
Die Kohlenbrenner,
5240 Sind unsre Männer.
Denn alles Bücken,
Bejahndes Nicken,
Gewundne Phrasen,
Das Doppelblasen,
5245 Das wärmt und kühlet
Wie's einer fühlet,
Was könnt' es frommen?
Es möchte Feuer
Selbst ungeheuer
5250 Vom Himmel kommen,
Gäb' es nicht Scheite
Und Kohlentrachten
Die Herdesbreite
Zur Gluth entfachten.
5255 Da brät's und prudelt's,
Da kocht's und strudelt's.

Der wahre Schmecker,
Der Tellerlecker,
Er riecht den Braten,
Er ahnet Fische; 5260
Das regt zu Thaten
An Gönners Tische.

Trunkner unbewußt.

Sei mir heute nichts zuwider!
Fühle mich so frank und frei;
Frische Luft und heitre Lieder 5265
Holt' ich selbst sie doch herbei.
Und so trink' ich! Trinke, trinke.
Stoßet an ihr! Tinke, Tinke!
Du dorthinten komm heran!
Stoßet an, so ist's gethan. 5270

Schrie mein Weibchen doch entrüstet,
Rümpfte diesem bunten Rock,
Und, wie sehr ich mich gebrüstet,
Schalt mich einen Maskenstock.
Doch ich trinke! Trinke, trinke! 5275
Angeklungen! Tinke, Tinke!
Maskenstöcke, stoßet an!
Wenn es klingt, so ist's gethan.

Saget nicht daß ich verirrt bin,
Bin ich doch wo mir's behagt. 5280
Borgt der Wirth nicht, borgt die Wirthin,
Und am Ende borgt die Magd.
Immer trink' ich! Trinke, trinke!
Auf ihr andern! Tinke, Tinke!

5285 Jeder jedem! so fortan!
Dünkt mich's doch es sei gethan.

Wie und wo ich mich vergnüge
Mag es immerhin geschehn;
Laßt mich liegen wo ich liege,
5290 Denn ich mag nicht länger stehn.

Chor.

Jeder Bruder trinke, trinke!
Toastet frisch ein Tinke, Tinke!
Sitzet fest auf Bank und Span,
Unter'm Tisch Dem ist's gethan.

Der Herold

kündigt verschiedene Poeten an, Naturdichter, Hof- und Rittersänger, zärtliche so wie Enthusiasten. Im Gedräng von Mitwerbern aller Art läßt keiner den andern zum Vortrag kommen. Einer schleicht mit wenigen Worten vorüber.

Satiriker.

5295 Wißt ihr was mich Poeten
Erst recht erfreuen sollte?
Dürft ich singen und reden
Was niemand hören wollte.

Die Nacht- und Grabdichter lassen sich entschuldigen, weil sie so eben im interessantesten Gespräch mit einem frischerstandenen Vampyren begriffen seien, woraus eine neue Dichtart sich vielleicht entwickeln könnte; der Herold muß es gelten lassen und ruft indessen die griechische Mythologie hervor, die, selbst in moderner Maske, weder Charakter noch Gefälliges verliert.

Die Grazien.

Aglaia.

Anmuth bringen wir in's Leben;
Leget Anmuth in das Geben. 5300

Hegemone.

Leget Anmuth in's Empfangen,
Lieblich ist's den Wunsch erlangen.

Euphrosyne.

Und in stiller Tage Schranken
Höchst anmuthig sei das Danken.

Die Parzen.

Atropos.

Mich die älteste zum Spinnen 5305
Hat man dießmal eingeladen;
Viel zu denken, viel zu sinnen
Gibt's bei'm zarten Lebensfaden.

Daß er euch gelenk und weich sei
Wußt' ich feinsten Flachs zu sichten; 5310
Daß er glatt und schlank und gleich sei
Wird der kluge Finger schlichten.

Wolltet ihr bei Lust und Tänzen
Allzu üppig euch erweisen;
5315 Denkt an dieses Fadens Gränzen,
Hütet euch! Er möchte reißen!

Klotho.

Wißt, in diesen letzten Tagen
Ward die Schere mir vertraut;
Denn man war von dem Betragen
5320 Unsrer Alten nicht erbaut.

Zerrt unnützeste Gespinnste
Lange sie an Licht und Luft,
Hoffnung herrlichster Gewinnste
Schleppt sie schneidend zu der Gruft.

5325 Doch auch ich im Jugend-Walten
Irrte mich schon hundertmal;
Heute mich im Zaum zu halten,
Schere steckt im Futteral.

Und so bin ich gern gebunden,
5330 Blicke freundlich diesem Ort;
Ihr in diesen freien Stunden
Schwärmt nur immer fort und fort.

Lachesis.

Mir, die ich allein verständig,
Blieb das Ordnen zugetheilt;
5335 Meine Weife, stets lebendig,
Hat noch nie sich übereilt.

Fäden kommen, Fäden weifen,
Jeden lenk' ich seine Bahn,

Keinen lass' ich überschweifen,
Füg' er sich im Kreis heran. 5340

Könnt' ich einmal mich vergessen
Wär' es um die Welt mir bang,
Stunden zählen, Jahre messen
Und der Weber nimmt den Strang.

Herold.

Die jetzo kommen werdet ihr nicht kennen, 5345
Wärt ihr noch so gelehrt in alten Schriften;
Sie anzusehn die so viel Übel stiften,
Ihr würdet sie willkommne Gäste nennen.

Die Furien sind es, niemand wird uns glauben,
Hübsch, wohlgestaltet, freundlich, jung von Jahren; 5350
Laßt euch mit ihnen ein, ihr sollt erfahren
Wie schlangenhaft verletzen solche Tauben.

Zwar sind sie tückisch, doch am heutigen Tage
Wo jeder Narr sich rühmet seiner Mängel,
Auch sie verlangen nicht den Ruhm als Engel, 5355
Bekennen sich als Stadt- und Landesplage.

Die Furien.

Alekto.

Was hilft es euch, ihr werdet uns vertrauen,
Denn wir sind hübsch und jung und Schmeichelkätzchen;
Hat einer unter euch ein Liebe-Schätzchen,
Wir werden ihm so lang die Ohren krauen, 5360

Bis wir ihm sagen dürfen, Aug' in Auge:
Daß sie zugleich auch dem und jenem winke,
Im Kopfe dumm, im Rücken krumm, und hinke,
Und, wenn sie seine Braut ist, gar nichts tauge.

5365 So wissen wir die Braut auch zu bedrängen:
Es hat sogar der Freund, vor wenig Wochen,
Verächtliches von ihr zu der gesprochen! —
Versöhnt man sich, so bleibt doch etwas hängen.

Megära.

Das ist nur Spaß! denn, sind sie erst verbunden,
5370 Ich nehm' es auf, und weiß in allen Fällen
Das schönste Glück durch Grille zu vergällen;
Der Mensch ist ungleich, ungleich sind die Stunden.

Und niemand hat Erwünschtes fest in Armen,
Der sich nicht nach Erwünschterem thörig sehnte,
5375 Vom höchsten Glück, woran er sich gewöhnte;
Die Sonne flieht er, will den Frost erwarmen.

Mit diesem allen weiß ich zu gebahren,
Und führe her Asmodi den Getreuen,
Zu rechter Zeit Unseliges auszustreuen,
5380 Verderbe so das Menschenvolk in Paaren.

Tisiphone.

Gift und Dolch statt böser Zungen
Misch' ich, schärf' ich dem Verräther;
Liebst du andre, früher, später
Hat Verderben dich durchdrungen.

5385 Muß der Augenblicke Süßtes
Sich zu Gischt und Galle wandeln!

Hier kein Markten, hier kein Handeln,
Wie er es beging', er büßt es.

Singe keiner vom Vergeben!
Felsen klag' ich meine Sache, 5390
Echo! Horch! erwidert Rache;
Und wer wechselt soll nicht leben.

Herold.

Belieb' es euch zur Seite wegzuweichen,
Denn was jetzt kommt ist nicht von Euresgleichen.
Ihr seht wie sich ein Berg herangedrängt, 5395
Mit bunten Teppichen die Weichen stolz behängt,
Ein Haupt mit langen Zähnen, Schlangenrüssel,
Geheimnißvoll, doch zeig' ich euch den Schlüssel.
Im Nacken sitzt ihm zierlich-zarte Frau,
Mit feinem Stäbchen lenkt sie ihn genau, 5400
Die andre droben stehend herrlich-hehr
Umgibt ein Glanz der blendet mich zu sehr.
Zur Seite gehn gekettet edle Frauen.
Die eine bang, die andre froh zu schauen,
Die eine wünscht, die andre fühlt sich frei, 5405
Verkünde jede wer sie sei.

Furcht.

Dunstige Fackeln, Lampen, Lichter,
Dämmern durch's verworrne Fest,
Zwischen diese Truggesichter
Bannt mich ach die Kette fest. 5410

Fort, ihr lächerlichen Lacher!
Euer Grinsen gibt Verdacht;
Alle meine Widersacher
Drängen mich in dieser Nacht.

5415 Hier! ein Freund ist Feind geworden,
Seine Maske kenn' ich schon;
Jener wollte mich ermorden,
Nun entdeckt schleicht er davon.

Ach wie gern in jeder Richtung
5420 Flöh' ich zu der Welt hinaus;
Doch von drüben droht Vernichtung,
Hält mich zwischen Dunst und Graus.

Hoffnung.

Seid gegrüßt, ihr lieben Schwestern.
Habt ihr euch schon heut und gestern
5425 In Vermummungen gefallen,
Weiß ich doch gewiß von allen
Morgen wollt ihr euch enthüllen.
Und wenn wir bei Fackelscheine
Uns nicht sonderlich behagen,
5430 Werden wir in heitern Tagen,
Ganz nach unserm eignen Willen,
Bald gesellig, bald alleine
Frei durch schöne Fluren wandeln,
Nach Belieben ruhn und handeln
5435 Und in sorgenfreiem Leben
Nie entbehren, stets erstreben;
Überall willkommne Gäste
Treten wir getrost hinein:
Sicherlich es muß das Beste
5440 Irgendwo zu finden sein.

Klugheit.

Zwei der größten Menschenfeinde,
Furcht und Hoffnung angekettet,

Halt' ich ab von der Gemeinde;
Platz gemacht! ihr seid gerettet.

Den lebendigen Colossen 5445
Führ' ich, seht ihr, thurmbeladen,
Und er wandelt unverdrossen
Schritt vor Schritt auf steilen Pfaden.

Droben aber auf der Zinne
Jene Göttin mit behenden 5450
Breiten Flügeln, zum Gewinne
Allerseits sich hinzuwenden.

Rings umgibt sie Glanz und Glorie
Leuchtend fern nach allen Seiten;
Und sie nennet sich Victorie, 5455
Göttin aller Thätigkeiten.

Zoilo-Thersites.

Hu! Hu! da komm' ich eben recht,
Ich schelt' euch allzusammen schlecht!
Doch was ich mir zum Ziel ersah
Ist oben Frau Victoria, 5460
Mit ihrem weißen Flügelpaar,
Sie dünkt sich wohl sie sei ein Aar,
Und wo sie sich nur hingewandt
Gehör' ihr alles Volk und Land;
Doch, wo was Rühmliches gelingt 5465
Es mich sogleich in Harnisch bringt.
Das Tiefe hoch, das Hohe tief,
Das Schiefe g'rad, das G'rade schief,
Das ganz allein macht mich gesund,
So will ich's auf dem Erdenrund. 5470

Herold.

So treffe dich, du Lumpenhund,
Des frommen Stabes Meisterstreich,
Da krümm' und winde dich sogleich! —
Wie sich die Doppelzwerggestalt
5475 So schnell zum eklen Klumpen ballt! —
— Doch Wunder! — Klumpen wird zum Ei,
Das bläht sich auf und platzt entzwei.
Nun fällt ein Zwillingspaar heraus,
Die Otter und die Fledermaus;
5480 Die eine fort im Staube kriecht,
Die andre schwarz zur Decke fliegt.
Sie eilen draußen zum Verein;
Da möcht' ich nicht der Dritte sein.

Gemurmel.

Frisch! dahinten tanzt man schon —
5485 Nein! Ich wollt' ich wär' davon —
Fühlst du, wie uns das umflicht,
Das gespenstische Gezücht? —
Saus't es mir doch über's Haar —
Ward ich's doch am Fuß gewahr —
5490 Keiner ist von uns verletzt —
Alle doch in Furcht gesetzt —
Ganz verdorben ist der Spaß —
Und die Bestien wollten das.

Herold.

Seit mir sind bei Maskeraden
5495 Heroldspflichten aufgeladen,
Wach' ich ernstlich an der Pforte,
Daß euch hier am lustigen Orte

Nichts Verderbliches erschleiche,
Weder wanke, weder weiche.
Doch ich fürchte durch die Fenster 5500
Ziehen luftige Gespenster,
Und von Spuk und Zaubereien
Wüßt' ich euch nicht zu befreien.
Machte sich der Zwerg verdächtig,
Nun! dort hinten strömt es mächtig. 5505
Die Bedeutung der Gestalten
Möcht ich amtsgemäß entfalten.
Aber was nicht zu begreifen
Wüßt' ich auch nicht zu erklären,
Helfet alle mich belehren! — 5510
Seht ihr's durch die Menge schweifen? —
Vierbespannt ein prächtiger Wagen
Wird durch alles durchgetragen;
Doch er theilet nicht die Menge,
Nirgend seh' ich ein Gedränge. 5515
Farbig glitzert's in der Ferne,
Irrend leuchten bunte Sterne,
Wie von magischer Laterne,
Schnaubt heran mit Sturmgewalt.
Platz gemacht! Mich schaudert's! 5520

Knabe Wagenlenker.

Halt
Rosse hemmet eure Flügel,
Fühlet den gewohnten Zügel,
Meistert euch wie ich euch meistre,
Rauschet hin wenn ich begeistre —
Diese Räume laßt uns ehren! 5525
Schaut umher wie sie sich mehren

Die Bewundrer, Kreis um Kreise.
Herold auf! nach deiner Weise,
Ehe wir von euch entfliehen,
5530 Uns zu schildern uns zu nennen;
Denn wir sind Allegorien
Und so solltest du uns kennen.

Herold.

Wüßte nicht dich zu benennen,
Eher könnt' ich dich beschreiben.

Knabe Lenker.

5535 So probir's!

Herold.

Man muß gestehn:
Erstlich bist du jung und schön.
Halbwüchsiger Knabe bist du; doch die Frauen
Sie möchten dich ganz ausgewachsen schauen.
Du scheinest mir ein künftiger Sponsirer,
5540 Recht so von Haus aus ein Verführer.

Knabe Lenker.

Das läßt sich hören! fahre fort,
Erfinde dir des Räthsels heitres Wort.

Herold.

Der Augen schwarzer Blitz, die Nacht der Locken
Erheitert von juwelnem Band!
5545 Und welch ein zierliches Gewand
Fließt dir von Schultern zu den Socken,
Mit Purpursaum und Glitzertand!
Man könnte dich ein Mädchen schelten,
Doch würdest du, zu Wohl und Weh,

Auch jetzo schon bei Mädchen gelten, 5550
Sie lehrten dich das A. B. C.

Knabe Lenker.

Und dieser der als Prachtgebilde
Hier auf dem Wagenthrone prangt?

Herold.

Er scheint ein König reich und milde,
Wohl dem der seine Gunst erlangt! 5555
Er hat nichts weiter zu erstreben,
Wo's irgend fehlte späht sein Blick,
Und seine reine Lust zu geben
Ist größer als Besitz und Glück.

Knabe Lenker.

Hiebei darfst du nicht stehen bleiben, 5560
Du mußt ihn recht genau beschreiben.

Herold.

Das Würdige beschreibt sich nicht.
Doch das gesunde Mondgesicht,
Ein voller Mund, erblühte Wangen,
Die unter'm Schmuck des Turbans prangen; 5565
Im Faltenkleid ein reich Behagen!
Was soll ich von dem Anstand sagen?
Als Herrscher scheint er mir bekannt.

Knabe Lenker.

Plutus, des Reichthums Gott genannt,
Derselbe kommt in Prunk daher, 5570
Der hohe Kaiser wünscht ihn sehr.

Herold.

Sag' von dir selber auch das Was und Wie?

Knabe Lenker.

Bin die Verschwendung, bin die Poesie;
Bin der Poet, der sich vollendet
5575 Wenn er sein eigenst Gut verschwendet.
Auch ich bin unermeßlich reich
Und schätze mich dem Plutus gleich,
Beleb' und schmück' ihm Tanz und Schmaus,
Das was ihm fehlt das theil' ich aus.

Herold.

5580 Das Prahlen steht dir gar zu schön,
Doch laß uns deine Künste sehn.

Knabe Lenker.

Hier seht mich nur ein Schnippchen schlagen,
Schon glänzt's und glitzert's um den Wagen.
Da springt eine Perlenschnur hervor;

Immerfort umherschnippend.

5585 Nehmt goldne Spange für Hals und Ohr;
Auch Kamm und Krönchen ohne Fehl,
In Ringen köstliches Juwel;
Auch Flämmchen spend' ich dann und wann,
Erwartend wo es zünden kann.

Herold.

5590 Wie greift und hascht die liebe Menge!
Fast kommt der Geber in's Gedränge.
Kleinode schnippt er wie ein Traum
Und alles hascht im weiten Raum.
Doch da erleb' ich neue Pfiffe:
5595 Was einer noch so emsig griffe

Deß hat er wirklich schlechten Lohn,
Die Gabe flattert ihm davon.
Es löſ't sich auf das Perlenband,
Ihm krabbeln Käfer in der Hand,
Er wirft sie weg der arme Tropf, 5600
Und sie umsummen ihm den Kopf.
Die andern statt solider Dinge
Erhaschen frevle Schmetterlinge.
Wie doch der Schelm so viel verheißt,
Und nur verleiht was golden gleißt! 5605

Knabe Lenker.

Zwar Masken, merk' ich, weißt du zu verkünden,
Allein der Schale Wesen zu ergründen
Sind Herolds Hofgeschäfte nicht;
Das fordert schärferes Gesicht.
Doch hüt' ich mich vor jeder Fehde; 5610
An dich, Gebieter, wend' ich Frag' und Rede.

Zu Plutus gewendet.

Hast du mir nicht die Windesbraut
Des Viergespannes anvertraut?
Lenk' ich nicht glücklich wie du leiteſt?
Bin ich nicht da wohin du deuteſt? 5615
Und wußt' ich nicht auf kühnen Schwingen
Für dich die Palme zu erringen?
Wie oft ich auch für dich gefochten,
Mir ist es jederzeit geglückt,
Wenn Lorbeer deine Stirne schmückt, 5620
Hab' ich ihn nicht mit Sinn und Hand geflochten?

Plutus.

Wenn's nöthig ist daß ich dir Zeugniß leiste,
So sag' ich gern: Bist Geist von meinem Geiste.

Du handelst stets nach meinem Sinn,
5625 Bist reicher als ich selber bin.
Ich schätze, deinen Dienst zu lohnen,
Den grünen Zweig vor allen meinen Kronen.
Ein wahres Wort verkünd' ich allen:
Mein lieber Sohn, an dir hab' ich Gefallen.

Knabe Lenker zur Menge.

5630 Die größten Gaben meiner Hand
Seht! hab' ich rings umher gesandt.
Auf dem und jenem Kopfe glüht
Ein Flämmchen das ich angesprüht,
Von einem zu dem andern hüpft's,
5635 An diesem hält sich's, dem entschlüpft's,
Gar selten aber flammt's empor,
Und leuchtet rasch in kurzem Flor;
Doch vielen, eh' man's noch erkannt,
Verlischt es, traurig ausgebrannt.

Weiber-Geklatsch.

5640 Da droben auf dem Viergespann
Das ist gewiß ein Charlatan;
Gekauzt da hintendrauf Hanswurst,
Doch abgezehrt von Hunger und Durst,
Wie man ihn niemals noch erblickt;
5645 Er fühlt wohl nicht, wenn man ihn zwickt.

Der Abgemagerte.

Vom Leibe mir, ekles Weibsgeschlecht!
Ich weiß, dir komm' ich niemals recht. —
Wie noch die Frau den Herd versah,
Da hieß ich Avaritia;
5650 Da stand es gut um unser Haus:
Nur viel herein, und nichts hinaus!

Ich eiferte für Kist' und Schrein;
Das sollte wohl gar ein Laster sein.
Doch als in allerneusten Jahren
Das Weib nicht mehr gewohnt zu sparen, 5655
Und, wie ein jeder böser Zahler,
Weit mehr Begierden hat als Thaler,
Da bleibt dem Manne viel zu dulden,
Wo er nur hinsieht da sind Schulden.
Sie wendet's, kann sie was erspulen, 5660
An ihren Leib, an ihren Buhlen;
Auch speis't sie besser, trinkt noch mehr
Mit der Sponsirer leidigem Heer;
Das steigert mir des Goldes Reiz:
Bin männlichen Geschlechts, der Geiz! 5665

Hauptweib.

Mit Drachen mag der Drache geizen,
Ist's doch am Ende Lug und Trug!
Er kommt die Männer aufzureizen,
Sie sind schon unbequem genug.

Weiber in Masse.

Der Strohmann! Reich' ihm eine Schlappe! 5670
Was will das Marterholz uns dräun?
Wir sollen seine Fratze scheun!
Die Drachen sind von Holz und Pappe,
Frisch an und dringt auf ihn hinein!

Herold.

Bei meinem Stabe! Ruh gehalten! — 5675
Doch braucht es meiner Hülfe kaum,
Seht wie die grimmen Ungestalten
Bewegt im rasch gewonnenen Raum

Das Doppel-Flügelpaar entfalten.
5680 Entrüstet schütteln sich der Drachen
Umschuppte feuerspeiende Rachen;
Die Menge flieht, rein ist der Platz.

Plutus steigt vom Wagen.

Herold.

Er tritt herab, wie königlich!
Er winkt, die Drachen rühren sich,
5685 Die Kiste haben sie vom Wagen
Mit Gold und Geiz herangetragen,
Sie steht zu seinen Füßen da:
Ein Wunder ist es wie's geschah.

Plutus zum Lenker.

Nun bist du los der allzulästigen Schwere,
5690 Bist frei und frank, nun frisch zu deiner Sphäre!
Hier ist sie nicht! Verworren, schäckig, wild
Umdrängt uns hier ein fratzenhaft Gebild.
Nur wo du klar in's holde Klare schaust,
Dir angehörst und dir allein vertraust,
5695 Dorthin wo Schönes, Gutes nur gefällt,
Zur Einsamkeit! — Da schaffe deine Welt.

Knabe Lenker.

So acht' ich mich als werthen Abgesandten,
So lieb' ich dich als nächsten Anverwandten.
Wo du verweilst ist Fülle, wo ich bin
5700 Fühlt jeder sich im herrlichsten Gewinn;
Auch schwankt er oft im widersinnigen Leben:
Soll er sich dir? soll er sich mir ergeben?

Die Deinen freilich können müßig ruhn,
Doch wer mir folgt hat immer was zu thun.
Nicht in's geheim vollführ' ich meine Thaten 5705
Ich athme nur und schon bin ich verrathen.
So lebe wohl! Du gönnst mir ja mein Glück,
Doch lisple leis und gleich bin ich zurück.

Ab wie er kam.

Plutus.

Nun ist es Zeit die Schätze zu entfesseln!
Die Schlosser treff' ich mit des Herolds Ruthe. 5710
Es thut sich auf! schaut her! in ehrnen Kesseln
Entwickelt sich's und wallt von goldnem Blute,
Zunächst der Schmuck von Kronen, Ketten, Ringen;
Es schwillt und droht ihn schmelzend zu verschlingen.

Wechselgeschrei der Menge.

Seht hier, o hin! wie's reichlich quillt, 5715
Die Kiste bis zum Rande füllt. —
Gefäße, goldne, schmelzen sich,
Gemünzte Rollen wälzen sich. —
Dukaten hüpfen wie geprägt,
O wie mir das den Busen regt — 5720
Wie schau' ich alle mein Begehr!
Da kollern sie am Boden her. —
Man bietet's euch, benutzt's nur gleich
Und bückt euch nur und werdet reich. —
Wir andern, rüstig wie der Blitz, 5725
Wir nehmen den Koffer in Besitz.

Herold.

Was soll's, ihr Thoren? soll mir das?
Es ist ja nur ein Maskenspaß.

Heut Abend wird nicht mehr begehrt;
5730 Glaubt ihr man geb' euch Gold und Werth?
Sind doch für euch in diesem Spiel
Selbst Rechenpfennige zu viel.
Ihr Täppischen! ein artiger Schein
Soll gleich die plumpe Wahrheit sein.
5735 Was soll euch Wahrheit? — Dumpfen Wahn
Packt ihr an allen Zipfeln an. —
Vermummter Plutus, Maskenheld,
Schlag' dieses Volk mir aus dem Feld.

Plutus.

Dein Stab ist wohl dazu bereit,
5740 Verleih ihn mir auf kurze Zeit. —
Ich tauch' ihn rasch in Sud und Gluth. —
Nun! Masken seid auf eurer Hut.
Wie's blitzt und platzt, in Funken sprüht!
Der Stab schon ist er angeglüht.
5745 Wer sich zu nah herangedrängt
Ist unbarmherzig gleich versengt —
Jetzt fang' ich meinen Umgang an.

Geschrei und Gedräng.

O weh! Es ist um uns gethan. —
Entfliehe wer entfliehen kann! —
5750 Zurück, zurück du Hintermann! —
Mir sprüht es heiß in's Angesicht. —
Mich drückt des glühenden Stabs Gewicht —
Verloren sind wir all' und all'. —
Zurück, zurück du Maskenschwall!
5755 Zurück, zurück unsinniger Hauf!
O hätt' ich Flügel, flög' ich auf. —

Plutus.

Schon ist der Kreis zurückgedrängt
Und niemand glaub' ich ist versengt.
Die Menge weicht,
Sie ist verscheucht. — 5760
Doch solcher Ordnung Unterpfand
Zieh' ich ein unsichtbares Band.

Herold.

Du hast ein herrlich Werk vollbracht,
Wie dank' ich deiner klugen Macht!

Plutus.

Noch braucht es, edler Freund, Geduld: 5765
Es droht noch mancherlei Tumult.

Geiz.

So kann man doch, wenn es beliebt,
Vergnüglich diesen Kreis beschauen;
Denn immerfort sind vornen an die Frauen
Wo's was zu gaffen, was zu naschen gibt. 5770
Noch bin ich nicht so völlig eingerostet!
Ein schönes Weib ist immer schön;
Und heute weil es mich nichts kostet,
So wollen wir getrost sponsiren gehn.
Doch weil am überfüllten Orte 5775
Nicht jedem Ohr vernehmlich alle Worte,
Versuch' ich klug und hoff' es soll mir glücken,
Mich pantomimisch deutlich auszudrücken.
Hand, Fuß, Gebärde reicht mir da nicht hin,
Da muß ich mich um einen Schwank bemühn. 5780
Wie feuchten Thon will ich das Gold behandeln,
Denn dieß Metall läßt sich in alles wandeln.

Herold.

Was fängt der an der magre Thor!
Hat so ein Hungermann Humor?
5785 Er knetet alles Gold zu Teig,
Ihm wird es unter'n Händen weich,
Wie er es drückt und wie es ballt
Bleibt's immer doch nur ungestalt.
Er wendet sich zu den Weibern dort,
5790 Sie schreien alle, möchten fort,
Gebärden sich gar widerwärtig;
Der Schalk erweis't sich übelfertig.
Ich fürchte daß er sich ergetzt,
Wenn er die Sittlichkeit verletzt.
5795 Dazu darf ich nicht schweigsam bleiben,
Gib meinen Stab, ihn zu vertreiben.

Plutus.

Er ahnet nicht was uns von außen droht;
Laß ihn die Narrentheidung treiben,
Ihm wird kein Raum für seine Possen bleiben;
5800 Gesetz ist mächtig, mächtiger ist die Noth.

Getümmel und Gesang.

Das wilde Heer es kommt zumal
Von Bergeshöh und Waldes Thal,
Unwiderstehlich schreitet's an:
Sie feiern ihren großen Pan.
5805 Sie wissen doch was keiner weiß
Und drängen in den leeren Kreis.

Plutus.

Ich kenn' euch wohl und euren großen Pan!
Zusammen habt ihr kühnen Schritt gethan.

Ich weiß recht gut was nicht ein jeder weiß
Und öffne schuldig diesen engen Kreis. 5810
Mag sie ein gut Geschick begleiten!
Das Wunderlichste kann geschehn;
Sie wissen nicht wohin sie schreiten,
Sie haben sich nicht vorgesehn.

Wildgesang.

Geputztes Volk du, Flitterschau! 5815
Sie kommen roh, sie kommen rauh,
In hohem Sprung, in raschem Lauf,
Sie treten derb und tüchtig auf.

Faunen.

Die Faunenschaar
Im lustigen Tanz, 5820
Den Eichenkranz
Im krausen Haar,
Ein feines zugespitztes Ohr
Dringt an dem Lockenkopf hervor,
Ein stumpfes Näschen, ein breit Gesicht 5825
Das schadet alles bei Frauen nicht.
Dem Faun wenn er die Patsche reicht
Versagt die schönste den Tanz nicht leicht.

Satyr.

Der Satyr hüpft nun hinterdrein
Mit Ziegenfuß und dürrem Bein, 5830
Ihm sollen sie mager und sehnig sein,
Und gemsenartig auf Bergeshöhn
Belustigt er sich umherzusehn.
In Freiheitsluft erquickt alsdann
Verhöhnt er Kind und Weib und Mann, 5835

Die tief in Thales Dampf und Rauch
Behaglich meinen sie lebten auch,
Da ihm doch rein und ungestört
Die Welt dort oben allein gehört.

Gnomen.

5840 Da trippelt ein die kleine Schaar,
Sie hält nicht gern sich Paar und Paar;
Im moosigen Kleid mit Lämplein hell
Bewegt sich's durcheinander schnell,
Wo jedes für sich selber schafft,
5845 Wie Leuchtameisen wimmelhaft;
Und wuselt emsig hin und her,
Beschäftigt in die Kreuz und Quer.

Den frommen Gütchen nah verwandt,
Als Felschirurgen wohl bekannt;
5850 Die hohen Berge schröpfen wir,
Aus vollen Adern schöpfen wir;
Metalle stürzen wir zu Hauf,
Mit Gruß getrost: Glück auf! Glück auf!
Das ist von Grund aus wohl gemeint:
5855 Wir sind der guten Menschen Freund'.
Doch bringen wir das Gold zu Tag
Damit man stehlen und kuppeln mag,
Nicht Eisen fehle dem stolzen Mann,
Der allgemeinen Mord ersann.
5860 Und wer die drei Gebot' veracht't
Sich auch nichts aus den andern macht.
Das alles ist nicht unsre Schuld,
Drum habt sofort wie wir Geduld.

Riesen.

Die wilden Männer sind s' genannt,
Am Harzgebirge wohl bekannt, 5865
Natürlich nackt in aller Kraft,
Sie kommen sämmtlich riesenhaft.
Den Fichtenstamm in rechter Hand
Und um den Leib ein wulstig Band,
Den derbsten Schurz von Zweig und Blatt, 5870
Leibwache wie der Papst nicht hat.

Nymphen im Chor.

Sie umschließen den großen Pan.

Auch kommt er an! —
Das All der Welt
Wird vorgestellt
Im großen Pan. 5875
Ihr Heitersten umgebet ihn,
Im Gaukeltanz umschwebet ihn,
Denn weil er ernst und gut dabei,
So will er daß man fröhlich sei.
Auch unter'm blauen Wölbedach 5880
Verhielt er sich beständig wach,
Doch rieseln ihm die Bäche zu,
Und Lüftlein wiegen ihn mild in Ruh.
Und wenn er zu Mittage schläft
Sich nicht das Blatt am Zweige regt; 5885
Gesunder Pflanzen Balsamduft
Erfüllt die schweigsam stille Luft;
Die Nymphe darf nicht munter sein
Und wo sie stand da schläft sie ein.
Wenn unerwartet mit Gewalt 5890
Dann aber seine Stimm' erschallt,

Wie Blitzes Knattern, Meergebraus,
Dann niemand weiß wo ein noch aus,
Zerstreut sich tapfres Heer im Feld
5895 Und im Getümmel bebt der Held.
So Ehre dem, dem Ehre gebührt
Und Heil ihm der uns hergeführt!

Deputation der Gnomen an den großen Pan.

Wenn das glänzend reiche Gute
Fadenweis durch Klüfte streicht,
5900 Nur der klugen Wünschelruthe
Seine Labyrinthe zeigt,

Wölben wir in dunklen Grüften
Troglodytisch unser Haus,
Und an reinen Tageslüften
5905 Theilst du Schätze gnädig aus.

Nun entdecken wir hieneben
Eine Quelle wunderbar,
Die bequem verspricht zu geben
Was kaum zu erreichen war.
5910 Dieß vermagst du zu vollenden,
Nimm es Herr in deine Hut:
Jeder Schatz in deinen Händen
Kommt der ganzen Welt zu Gut.

Plutus zum Herold.

Wir müssen uns im hohen Sinne fassen
5915 Und was geschieht getrost geschehen lassen,
Du bist ja sonst des stärksten Muthes voll.
Nun wird sich gleich ein Greulichstes eräugnen,
Hartnäckig wird es Welt und Nachwelt läugnen:
Du schreib' es treulich in dein Protokoll.

Herold.

den Stab anfassend, welchen Plutus in der Hand behält.

Die Zwerge führen den großen Pan 5920
Zur Feuerquelle sacht heran,
Sie siedet auf vom tiefsten Schlund,
Dann sinkt sie wieder hinab zum Grund,
Und finster steht der offne Mund;
Wallt wieder auf in Gluth und Sud, 5925
Der große Pan steht wohlgemuth,
Freut sich des wundersamen Dings,
Und Perlenschaum sprüht rechts und links.
Wie mag er solchem Wesen traun?
Er bückt sich tief hinein zu schaun. — 5930
Nun aber fällt sein Bart hinein! —
Wer mag das glatte Kinn wohl sein?
Die Hand verbirgt es unserm Blick. —
Nun folgt ein großes Ungeschick,
Der Bart entflammt und fliegt zurück, 5935
Enzündet Kranz und Haupt und Brust,
Zu Leiden wandelt sich die Lust. —
Zu löschen läuft die Schaar herbei,
Doch keiner bleibt von Flammen frei,
Und wie es patscht und wie es schlägt 5940
Wird neues Flammen aufgeregt;
Verflochten in das Element
Ein ganzer Maskenklump verbrennt.

Was aber hör' ich wird uns kund
Von Ohr zu Ohr, von Mund zu Mund! 5945
O ewig unglücksel'ge Nacht
Was hast du uns für Leid gebracht!

Verkünden wird der nächste Tag
Was niemand willig hören mag;
5950 Doch hör' ich aller Orten schrein
„Der Kaiser" leidet solche Pein.
O wäre doch ein Andres wahr!
Der Kaiser brennt und seine Schaar.
Sie sei verflucht die ihn verführt,
5955 In harzig Reis sich eingeschnürt,
Zu toben her mit Brüll-Gesang
Zu allerseitigem Untergang.
O Jugend, Jugend wirst du nie
Der Freude reines Maß bezirken?
5960 O Hoheit, Hoheit wirst du nie
Vernünftig wie allmächtig wirken?

Schon geht der Wald in Flammen auf,
Sie züngeln leckend spitz hinauf,
Zum holzverschränkten Deckenband,
5965 Uns droht ein allgemeiner Brand.
Des Jammers Maß ist übervoll,
Ich weiß nicht wer uns retten soll.
Ein Aschenhaufen einer Nacht
Liegt morgen reiche Kaiserpracht.

Plutus.

5970 Schrecken ist genug verbreitet,
Hülfe sei nun eingeleitet! —
Schlage heil'gen Stabs Gewalt,
Daß der Boden bebt und schallt!
Du geräumig weite Luft
5975 Fülle dich mit kühlem Duft.

Zieht heran, umherzuschweifen,
Nebeldünste, schwangre Streifen,
Deckt ein flammendes Gewühl;
Rieselt, säuselt, Wölkchen kräuselt,
Schlüpfet wallend, leise dämpfet, 5980
Löschend überall bekämpfet,
Ihr, die lindernden, die feuchten,
Wandelt in ein Wetterleuchten
Solcher eitlen Flamme Spiel. —
Drohen Geister uns zu schädigen 5985
Soll sich die Magie bethätigen.

Lustgarten.

Morgensonne.

Der Kaiser, Hofleute. Faust, Mephistopheles, anständig, nicht auffallend, nach Sitte gekleidet; beide knieen.

Faust.

Verzeihst du, Herr, das Flammengaukelspiel?

Kaiser zum Aufstehn winkend.

Ich wünsche mir dergleichen Scherze viel. —
Auf einmal sah ich mich in glühnder Sphäre,
5990 Es schien mir fast als ob ich Pluto wäre.
Aus Nacht und Kohlen lag ein Felsengrund,
Von Flämmchen glühend. Dem und jenem Schlund
Aufwirbelten viel tausend wilde Flammen
Und flackerten in Ein Gewölb zusammen.
5995 Zum höchsten Dome züngelt' es empor,
Der immer ward und immer sich verlor.
Durch fernen Raum gewundner Feuersäulen
Sah ich bewegt der Völker lange Zeilen,
Sie drängten sich im weiten Kreis heran,
6000 Und huldigten, wie sie es stets gethan.
Von meinem Hof erkannt' ich ein= und andern,
Ich schien ein Fürst von tausend Salamandern.

Mephistopheles.

Das bist du, Herr! weil jedes Element
Die Majestät als unbedingt erkennt.
Gehorsam Feuer hast du nun erprobt; 6005
Wirf dich in's Meer wo es am wildsten tobt,
Und kaum betrittst du perlenreichen Grund,
So bildet wallend sich ein herrlich Rund;
Siehst auf und ab lichtgrüne schwanke Wellen,
Mit Purpursaum, zur schönsten Wohnung schwellen, 6010
Um dich, den Mittelpunct. Bei jedem Schritt,
Wohin du gehst, gehn die Paläste mit.
Die Wände selbst erfreuen sich des Lebens,
Pfeilschnellen Wimmlens, Hin= und Widerstrebens.
Meerwunder drängen sich zum neuen milden Schein, 6015
Sie schießen an, und keines darf herein.
Da spielen farbig goldbeschuppte Drachen,
Der Haifisch klafft, du lachst ihm in den Rachen.
Wie sich auch jetzt der Hof um dich entzückt,
Hast du doch nie ein solch Gedräng erblickt. 6020
Doch bleibst du nicht vom Lieblichsten geschieden:
Es nahen sich neugierige Nereiden
Der prächt'gen Wohnung in der ew'gen Frische,
Die jüngsten scheu und lüstern wie die Fische,
Die spätern klug. Schon wird es Thetis kund, 6025
Dem zweiten Peleus reicht sie Hand und Mund. —
Den Sitz alsdann auf des Olymps Revier...

Kaiser.

Die luft'gen Räume die erlass' ich dir:
Noch früh genug besteigt man jenen Thron.

Mephistopheles.

Und, höchster Herr! die Erde hast du schon. 6030

Kaiser.

Welch gut Geschick hat dich hieher gebracht,
Unmittelbar aus Tausend Einer Nacht?
Gleichst du an Fruchtbarkeit Scheherazaden,
Versichr' ich dich der höchsten aller Gnaden.
6035 Sei stets bereit, wenn eure Tageswelt,
Wie's oft geschieht, mir widerlichst mißfällt.

Marschalk tritt eilig auf.

Durchlauchtigster, ich dacht' in meinem Leben
Vom schönsten Glück Verkündung nicht zu geben
Als diese, die mich hoch beglückt,
6040 In deiner Gegenwart entzückt:
Rechnung für Rechnung ist berichtigt,
Die Wucherklauen sind beschwichtigt,
Los bin ich solcher Höllenpein;
Im Himmel kann's nicht heitrer sein.

Heermeister folgt eilig.

6045 Abschläglich ist der Sold entrichtet,
Das ganze Heer auf's neu' verpflichtet,
Der Lanzknecht fühlt sich frisches Blut,
Und Wirth und Dirnen haben's gut.

Kaiser.

Wie athmet eure Brust erweitert!
6050 Das faltige Gesicht erheitert!
Wie eilig tretet ihr heran!

Schatzmeister der sich einfindet.

Befrage diese die das Werk gethan.

Faust.

Dem Canzler ziemt's die Sache vorzutragen.

Canzler der langsam herankommt.

Beglückt genug in meinen alten Tagen. —
So hört und schaut das schicksalschwere Blatt, 6055
Das alles Weh in Wohl verwandelt hat.

Er liest.

„Zu wissen sei es jedem der's begehrt:
Der Zettel hier ist tausend Kronen werth.
Ihm liegt gesichert, als gewisses Pfand,
Unzahl vergrabnen Guts im Kaiserland. 6060
Nun ist gesorgt, damit der reiche Schatz,
Sogleich gehoben, diene zum Ersatz."

Kaiser.

Ich ahne Frevel, ungeheuren Trug!
Wer fälschte hier des Kaisers Namenszug?
Ist solch Verbrechen ungestraft geblieben? 6065

Schatzmeister.

Erinnre dich! hast selbst es unterschrieben;
Erst heute Nacht. Du standst als großer Pan,
Der Canzler sprach mit uns zu dir heran:
„Gewähre dir das hohe Festvergnügen,
Des Volkes Heil, mit wenig Federzügen." 6070
Du zogst sie rein, dann ward's in dieser Nacht
Durch Tausendkünstler schnell vertausendfacht,
Damit die Wohlthat allen gleich gedeihe,
So stempelten wir gleich die ganze Reihe,
Zehn, Dreißig, Funfzig, Hundert sind parat, 6075
Ihr denkt euch nicht wie wohl's dem Volke that.
Seht eure Stadt, sonst halb im Tod verschimmelt,
Wie alles lebt und lustgenießend wimmelt!
Obschon dein Name längst die Welt beglückt,

6080 Man hat ihn nie so freundlich angeblickt.
Das Alphabet ist nun erst überzählig,
In diesem Zeichen wird nun jeder selig.

Kaiser.

Und meinen Leuten gilt's für gutes Gold?
Dem Heer, dem Hofe g'nügt's zu vollem Sold?
6085 So sehr mich's wundert muß ich's gelten lassen.

Marschalk.

Unmöglich wär's die Flüchtigen einzufassen;
Mit Blitzeswink zerstreute sich's im Lauf.
Die Wechsler-Bänke stehen sperrig auf,
Man honorirt daselbst ein jedes Blatt
6090 Durch Gold und Silber, freilich mit Rabatt.
Nun geht's von da zum Fleischer, Bäcker, Schenken;
Die halbe Welt scheint nur an Schmaus zu denken,
Wenn sich die andre neu in Kleidern bläht.
Der Krämer schneidet aus, der Schneider näht.
6095 Bei: „Hoch dem Kaiser!“ sprudelt's in den Kellern,
Dort kocht's und brät's und klappert mit den Tellern.

Mephistopheles.

Wer die Terrassen einsam abspaziert,
Gewahrt die Schönste, herrlich aufgeziert,
Ein Aug' verdeckt vom stolzen Pfauenwedel,
6100 Sie schmunzelt uns und blickt nach solcher Schedel;
Und hurt'ger als durch Witz und Redekunst
Vermittelt sich die reichste Liebesgunst.
Man wird sich nicht mit Börs' und Beutel plagen,
Ein Blättchen ist im Busen leicht zu tragen,
6105 Mit Liebesbrieflein paart's bequem sich hier.
Der Priester trägt's andächtig im Brevier,

Und der Soldat, um rascher sich zu wenden,
Erleichtert schnell den Gürtel seiner Lenden.
Die Majestät verzeihe wenn in's Kleine
Das hohe Werk ich zu erniedern scheine. 6110

Faust.

Das Übermaß der Schätze, das, erstarrt,
In deinen Landen tief im Boden harrt,
Liegt ungenutzt. Der weiteste Gedanke
Ist solchen Reichthums kümmerlichste Schranke,
Die Phantasie, in ihrem höchsten Flug, 6115
Sie strengt sich an und thut sich nie genug.
Doch fassen Geister, würdig tief zu schauen,
Zum Gränzenlosen gränzenlos Vertrauen.

Mephistopheles.

Ein solch Papier, an Gold und Perlen Statt,
Ist so bequem, man weiß doch was man hat, 6120
Man braucht nicht erst zu markten noch zu tauschen,
Kann sich nach Lust in Lieb' und Wein berauschen;
Will man Metall, ein Wechsler ist bereit,
Und fehlt es da, so gräbt man eine Zeit.
Pokal und Kette wird verauctionirt, 6125
Und das Papier, sogleich amortisirt,
Beschämt den Zweifler der uns frech verhöhnt.
Man will nichts anders, ist daran gewöhnt.
So bleibt von nun an allen Kaiser-Landen
An Kleinod, Gold, Papier genug vorhanden. 6130

Kaiser.

Das hohe Wohl verdankt euch unser Reich,
Wo möglich sei der Lohn dem Dienste gleich.

Vertraut sei euch des Reiches innrer Boden,
Ihr seid der Schätze würdigste Custoden.
6135 Ihr kennt den weiten wohlverwahrten Hort,
Und wenn man gräbt, so sei's auf euer Wort.
Vereint euch nun, ihr Meister unsres Schatzes,
Erfüllt mit Lust die Würden eures Platzes,
Wo mit der obern sich die Unterwelt,
6140 In Einigkeit beglückt, zusammenstellt.

Schatzmeister.

Soll zwischen uns kein fernster Zwist sich regen,
Ich liebe mir den Zaubrer zum Collegen.

Ab mit Faust.

Kaiser.

Beschenk' ich nun bei Hofe Mann für Mann,
Gesteh' er mir wozu er's brauchen kann.

Page empfangend.

6145 Ich lebe lustig, heiter, guter Dinge.

Ein andrer gleichfalls.

Ich schaffe gleich dem Liebchen Kett' und Ringe.

Kämmerer annehmend.

Von nun an trink' ich doppelt bessre Flasche.

Ein andrer gleichfalls.

Die Würfel jucken mich schon in der Tasche.

Bannerherr mit Bedacht.

Mein Schloß und Feld ich mach' es schuldenfrei.

Ein andrer gleichfalls.

6150 Es ist ein Schatz, den leg' ich Schätzen bei.

Kaiser.

Ich hoffte Lust und Muth zu neuen Thaten;
Doch wer euch kennt, der wird euch leicht errathen.
Ich merk' es wohl, bei aller Schätze Flor
Wie ihr gewesen bleibt ihr nach wie vor.

Narr herbeikommend.

Ihr spendet Gnaden, gönnt auch mir davon. 6155

Kaiser.

Und lebst du wieder, du vertrinkst sie schon.

Narr.

Die Zauber-Blätter! ich versteh's nicht recht.

Kaiser.

Das glaub' ich wohl, denn du gebrauchst sie schlecht.

Narr.

Da fallen andere, weiß nicht was ich thu'.

Kaiser.

Nimm sie nur hin, sie fielen dir ja zu. 6160

Ab.

Narr.

Fünftausend Kronen wären mir zu Handen!

Mephistopheles.

Zweibeiniger Schlauch, bist wieder auferstanden?

Narr.

Geschieht mir oft, doch nicht so gut als jetzt.

Mephistopheles.

Du freust dich so, daß dich's in Schweiß versetzt.

Narr.

6165 Da seht nur her, ist das wohl Geldes wert?

Mephistopheles.

Du hast dafür was Schlund und Bauch begehrt.

Narr.

Und kaufen kann ich Acker, Haus und Vieh?

Mephistopheles.

Versteht sich! biete nur, das fehlt dir nie.

Narr.

Und Schloß, mit Wald und Jagd und Fischbach?

Mephistopheles.

Traun!

6170 Ich möchte dich gestrengen Herrn wohl schaun!

Narr.

Heut Abend wieg' ich mich im Grundbesitz! —

Ab.

Mephistopheles solus.

Wer zweifelt noch an unsres Narren Witz!

Finstere Galerie.

Faust. Mephistopheles.

Mephistopheles.

Was ziehst du mich in diese düstern Gänge?
Ist nicht da drinnen Lust genug,
Im dichten bunten Hofgedränge 6175
Gelegenheit zu Spaß und Trug?

Faust.

Sag' mir das nicht, du hast's in alten Tagen
Längst an den Sohlen abgetragen;
Doch jetzt, dein Hin- und Widergehn
Ist nur um mir nicht Wort zu stehn. 6180
Ich aber bin gequält zu thun,
Der Marschalk und der Kämmrer treibt mich nun.
Der Kaiser will, es muß sogleich geschehn,
Will Helena und Paris vor sich sehn;
Das Musterbild der Männer so der Frauen 6185
In deutlichen Gestalten will er schauen.
Geschwind an's Werk! ich darf mein Wort nicht brechen.

Mephistopheles.

Unsinnig war's leichtsinnig zu versprechen.

Faust.

Du hast, Geselle, nicht bedacht
6190 Wohin uns deine Künste führen;
Erst haben wir ihn reich gemacht,
Nun sollen wir ihn amüsiren.

Mephistopheles.

Du wähnst es füge sich sogleich;
Hier stehen wir vor steilern Stufen,
6195 Greifst in ein fremdestes Bereich,
Machst frevelhaft am Ende neue Schulden,
Denkst Helenen so leicht hervorzurufen
Wie das Papiergespenst der Gulden. —
Mit Hexen-Fexen, mit Gespenst-Gespinnsten,
6200 Kielkröpfigen Zwergen steh' ich gleich zu Diensten;
Doch Teufels-Liebchen, wenn auch nicht zu schelten,
Sie können nicht für Heroinen gelten.

Faust.

Da haben wir den alten Leierton!
Bei dir geräth man stets in's Ungewisse.
6205 Der Vater bist du aller Hindernisse,
Für jedes Mittel willst du neuen Lohn.
Mit wenig Murmeln weiß ich ist's gethan,
Wie man sich umschaut bringst du sie zur Stelle.

Mephistopheles.

Das Heidenvolk geht mich nichts an,
6210 Es haus't in seiner eignen Hölle;
Doch gibt's ein Mittel.

Faust.

Sprich, und ohne Säumniß!

Mephistopheles.

Ungern entdeck' ich höheres Geheimniß. —
Göttinnen thronen hehr in Einsamkeit,
Um sie kein Ort noch weniger eine Zeit,
Von ihnen sprechen ist Verlegenheit. 6215
Die Mütter sind es!

Faust aufgeschreckt.

Mütter!

Mephistopheles.

Schaudert's dich?

Faust.

Die Mütter! Mütter! — 's klingt so wunderlich.

Mephistopheles.

Das ist es auch. Göttinnen, ungekannt
Euch Sterblichen, von uns nicht gern genannt.
Nach ihrer Wohnung magst in's Tiefste schürfen; 6220
Du selbst bist Schuld daß ihrer wir bedürfen.

Faust.

Wohin der Weg?

Mephistopheles.

Kein Weg! In's Unbetretene,
Nicht zu Betretende; ein Weg an's Unerbetene,
Nicht zu Erbittende. Bist du bereit? —
Nicht Schlösser sind, nicht Riegel wegzuschieben, 6225
Von Einsamkeiten wirst umhergetrieben.
Hast du Begriff von Öd' und Einsamkeit?

Faust.

Du spartest dächt' ich solche Sprüche,
Hier wittert's nach der Hexenküche,
6230 Nach einer längst vergangnen Zeit.
Mußt' ich nicht mit der Welt verkehren?
Das Leere lernen, Leeres lehren? —
Sprach ich vernünftig wie ich's angeschaut,
Erklang der Widerspruch gedoppelt laut;
6235 Mußt' ich sogar vor widerwärtigen Streichen
Zur Einsamkeit, zur Wilderniß entweichen;
Und um nicht ganz versäumt, allein zu leben
Mich doch zuletzt dem Teufel übergeben.

Mephistopheles.

Und hättest du den Ocean durchschwommen,
6240 Das Gränzenlose dort geschaut,
So sähst du dort doch Well' auf Welle kommen,
Selbst wenn es dir vor'm Untergange graut.
Du sähst doch etwas. Sähst wohl in der Grüne
Gestillter Meere streichende Delphine;
6245 Sähst Wolken ziehen, Sonne, Mond und Sterne;
Nichts wirst du sehn in ewig leerer Ferne,
Den Schritt nicht hören den du thust,
Nichts Festes finden wo du ruhst.

Faust.

Du sprichst als erster aller Mystagogen,
6250 Die treue Neophyten je betrogen;
Nur umgekehrt. Du sendest mich in's Leere,
Damit ich dort so Kunst als Kraft vermehre;
Behandelst mich, daß ich, wie jene Katze,
Dir die Kastanien aus den Gluthen kratze.

Nur immer zu! wir wollen es ergründen, 6255
In deinem Nichts hoff' ich das All zu finden.

Mephistopheles.

Ich rühme dich eh' du dich von mir trennst,
Und sehe wohl, daß du den Teufel kennst;
Hier diesen Schlüssel nimm.

Faust.

Das kleine Ding!

Mephistopheles.

Erst faß ihn an und schätz' ihn nicht gering. 6260

Faust.

Er wächs't in meiner Hand! er leuchtet, blitzt!

Mephistopheles.

Merkst du nun bald was man an ihm besitzt?
Der Schlüssel wird die rechte Stelle wittern,
Folg' ihm hinab, er führt dich zu den Müttern.

Faust schaudernd.

Den Müttern! Trifft's mich immer wie ein Schlag! 6265
Was ist das Wort das ich nicht hören mag?

Mephistopheles.

Bist du beschränkt daß neues Wort dich stört?
Willst du nur hören was du schon gehört?
Dich störe nichts wie es auch weiter klinge,
Schon längst gewohnt der wunderbarsten Dinge. 6270

Faust.

Doch im Erstarren such' ich nicht mein Heil,
Das Schaudern ist der Menschheit bestes Theil;

Wie auch die Welt ihm das Gefühl vertheure,
Ergriffen, fühlt er tief das Ungeheure.

Mephistopheles.

6275 Versinke denn! Ich könnt' auch sagen: steige!
's ist einerlei. Entfliehe dem Entstandnen
In der Gebilde losgebundne Reiche!
Ergetze dich am längst nicht mehr Vorhandnen;
Wie Wolkenzüge schlingt sich das Getreibe,
6280 Den Schlüssel schwinge, halte sie vom Leibe.

Faust begeistert.

Wohl! fest ihn fassend fühl' ich neue Stärke,
Die Brust erweitert, hin zum großen Werke.

Mephistopheles.

Ein glühnder Dreifuß thut dir endlich kund
Du seist im tiefsten, allertiefsten Grund.
6285 Bei seinem Schein wirst du die Mütter sehn,
Die einen sitzen, andre stehn und gehn,
Wie's eben kommt. Gestaltung, Umgestaltung,
Des ewigen Sinnes ewige Unterhaltung,
Umschwebt von Bildern aller Creatur.
6290 Sie sehn dich nicht, denn Schemen sehn sie nur.
Da faß ein Herz, denn die Gefahr ist groß,
Und gehe g'rad' auf jenen Dreifuß los,
Berühr' ihn mit dem Schlüssel!

Faust macht eine entschieden gebietende Attitüde mit dem Schlüssel.

Mephistopheles ihn betrachtend.

So ist's recht!

Er schließt sich an, er folgt als treuer Knecht;

Gelassen steigst du, dich erhebt das Glück, 6295
Und eh' sie's merken bist mit ihm zurück.
Und hast du ihn einmal hierher gebracht,
So rufst du Held und Heldin aus der Nacht,
Der erste der sich jener That erdreistet;
Sie ist gethan und du hast es geleistet. 6300
Dann muß fortan, nach magischem Behandeln,
Der Weihrauchsnebel sich in Götter wandeln.

Faust.

Und nun was jetzt?

Mephistopheles.

Dein Wesen strebe nieder;
Versinke stampfend, stampfend steigst du wieder.

Faust stampft und versinkt.

Mephistopheles.

Wenn ihm der Schlüssel nur zum besten frommt! 6305
Neugierig bin ich ob er wieder kommt?

Hell erleuchtete Säle.

Kaiser und Fürsten, Hof in Bewegung.

Kämmerer zu Mephistopheles.

Ihr seid uns noch die Geisterscene schuldig;
Macht euch daran! der Herr ist ungeduldig.

Marschalk.

So eben fragt der Gnädigste darnach;
6310 Ihr! zaudert nicht der Majestät zur Schmach.

Mephistopheles.

Ist mein Cumpan doch deßhalb weggegangen,
Er weiß schon wie es anzufangen,
Und laborirt verschlossen still,
Muß ganz besonders sich befleißen;
6315 Denn wer den Schatz, das Schöne, heben will,
Bedarf der höchsten Kunst, Magie der Weisen.

Marschalk.

Was ihr für Künste braucht ist einerlei,
Der Kaiser will daß alles fertig sei.

Blondine zu Mephistopheles.

Ein Wort, mein Herr! Ihr seht ein klar Gesicht,
6320 Jedoch so ist's im leidigen Sommer nicht!

Da sprossen hundert bräunlich rothe Flecken,
Die zum Verdruß die weiße Haut bedecken.
Ein Mittel!

Mephistopheles.

Schade! so ein leuchtend Schätzchen,
Im Mai getupft wie eure Pantherkätzchen.
Nehmt Froschlaich, Krötenzungen, cohobirt, 6325
Im vollsten Mondlicht sorglich distillirt;
Und, wenn er abnimmt, reinlich aufgestrichen,
Der Frühling kommt, die Tupfen sind entwichen.

Braune.

Die Menge drängt heran euch zu umschranzen.
Ich bitt' um Mittel! Ein erfrorner Fuß 6330
Verhindert mich am Wandeln wie am Tanzen,
Selbst ungeschickt beweg' ich mich zum Gruß.

Mephistopheles.

Erlaubet einen Tritt von meinem Fuß.

Braune.

Nun das geschieht wohl unter Liebesleuten.

Mephistopheles.

Mein Fußtritt, Kind! hat Größres zu bedeuten, 6335
Zu Gleichem Gleiches, was auch einer litt!
Fuß heilet Fuß, so ist's mit allen Gliedern.
Heran! Gebt Acht! Ihr sollt es nicht erwidern.

Braune schreiend.

Weh! Weh! das brennt! das war ein harter Tritt,
Wie Pferdehuf. 6340

Mephistopheles.

Die Heilung nehmt ihr mit.
Du kannst nunmehr den Tanz nach Lust verüben,
Bei Tafel schwelgend füßle mit dem Lieben.

Dame herandringend.

Laßt mich hindurch! zu groß sind meine Schmerzen,
Sie wühlen siedend mir im tiefsten Herzen;
6345 Bis gestern sucht Er Heil in meinen Blicken,
Er schwatzt mit ihr und wendet mir den Rücken.

Mephistopheles.

Bedenklich ist es, aber höre mich.
An ihn heran mußt du dich leise drücken;
Nimm diese Kohle, streich' ihm einen Strich
6350 Auf Ärmel, Mantel, Schulter wie sich's macht;
Er fühlt im Herzen holden Reuestich.
Die Kohle doch mußt du sogleich verschlingen,
Nicht Wein, nicht Wasser an die Lippen bringen;
Er seufzt vor deiner Thür noch heute Nacht.

Dame.

6355 Ist doch kein Gift?

Mephistopheles entrüstet.

Respect wo sich's gebührt!
Weit müßtet ihr nach solcher Kohle laufen;
Sie kommt von einem Scheiterhaufen
Den wir sonst emsiger angeschürt.

Page.

Ich bin verliebt, man hält mich nicht für voll.

Mephistopheles bei Seite.

Ich weiß nicht mehr, wohin ich hören soll. 6360

Zum Pagen.

Müßt euer Glück nicht auf die Jüngste setzen.
Die Angejahrten wissen euch zu schätzen. —

Andere drängen sich herzu.

Schon wieder Neue! Welch ein harter Strauß!
Ich helfe mir zuletzt mit Wahrheit aus;
Der schlechteste Behelf! Die Noth ist groß. — 6365
O Mütter, Mütter! Laßt nur Fausten los!

Umherschauend.

Die Lichter brennen trübe schon im Saal,
Der ganze Hof bewegt sich auf einmal.
Anständig seh' ich sie in Folge ziehn,
Durch lange Gänge, ferne Galerien. 6370
Nun! sie versammeln sich im weiten Raum
Des alten Rittersaals, er faßt sie kaum.
Auf breite Wände Teppiche spendirt,
Mit Rüstung Eck- und Nischen ausgeziert.
Hier braucht es dächt' ich keine Zauberworte; 6375
Die Geister finden sich von selbst zum Orte.

Rittersaal.

Dämmernde Beleuchtung.

Kaiser und Hof sind eingezogen.

Herold.

Mein alt Geschäft, das Schauspiel anzukünden,
Verkümmert mir der Geister heimlich Walten;
Vergebens wagt man aus verständigen Gründen
6380 Sich zu erklären das verworrene Schalten.
Die Sessel sind, die Stühle schon zur Hand;
Den Kaiser setzt man g'rade vor die Wand;
Auf den Tapeten mag er da die Schlachten
Der großen Zeit bequemlichstens betrachten.
6385 Hier sitzt nun alles, Herr und Hof im Runde,
Die Bänke drängen sich im Hintergrunde;
Auch Liebchen hat, in düstern Geisterstunden,
Zur Seite Liebchens lieblich Raum gefunden.
Und so, da alle schicklich Platz genommen,
6390 Sind wir bereit, die Geister mögen kommen!

Posaunen.

Astrolog.

Beginne gleich das Drama seinen Lauf,
Der Herr befiehlt's, ihr Wände thut euch auf!

Nichts hindert mehr, hier ist Magie zur Hand,
Die Tepp'che schwinden, wie gerollt vom Brand;
Die Mauer spaltet sich, sie kehrt sich um, 6395
Ein tief Theater scheint sich aufzustellen,
Geheimnißvoll ein Schein uns zu erhellen,
Und ich besteige das Proscenium.

Mephistopheles aus dem Souffleurloche auftauchend.

Von hier aus hoff' ich allgemeine Gunst,
Einbläsereien sind des Teufels Redekunst. 6400

Zum Astrologen.

Du kennst den Tact, in dem die Sterne gehn,
Und wirst mein Flüstern meisterlich verstehn.

Astrolog.

Durch Wunderkraft erscheint allhier zur Schau,
Massiv genug, ein alter Tempelbau.
Dem Atlas gleich der einst den Himmel trug 6405
Stehn, reihenweis, der Säulen hier genug;
Sie mögen wohl der Felsenlast genügen,
Da zweie schon ein groß Gebäude trügen.

Architekt.

Das wär' antik! ich wüßt' es nicht zu preisen,
Es sollte plump und überlästig heißen. 6410
Roh nennt man edel, unbehülflich groß.
Schmal-Pfeiler lieb' ich, strebend, gränzenlos;
Spitzbögiger Zenith erhebt den Geist;
Solch ein Gebäu erbaut uns allermeist.

Astrolog.

Empfangt mit Ehrfurcht sterngegönnte Stunden; 6415
Durch magisch Wort sei die Vernunft gebunden;

Dagegen weit heran bewege frei
Sich herrliche verwegne Phantasei.
Mit Augen schaut nun was ihr kühn begehrt,
6420 Unmöglich ist's, drum eben glaubenswerth.

Faust steigt auf der andern Seite des Prosceniums herauf.

Astrolog.

Im Priesterkleid, bekränzt, ein Wundermann,
Der nun vollbringt was er getrost begann.
Ein Dreifuß steigt mit ihm aus hohler Gruft,
Schon ahn' ich aus der Schale Weihrauchduft.
6425 Er rüstet sich das hohe Werk zu segnen,
Es kann fortan nur Glückliches begegnen.

Faust großartig.

In eurem Namen, Mütter, die ihr thront
Im Gränzenlosen, ewig einsam wohnt,
Und doch gesellig. Euer Haupt umschweben
6430 Des Lebens Bilder, regsam, ohne Leben.
Was einmal war, in allem Glanz und Schein,
Es regt sich dort; denn es will ewig sein.
Und ihr vertheilt es, allgewaltige Mächte,
Zum Zelt des Tages, zum Gewölb der Nächte.
6435 Die einen faßt des Lebens holder Lauf,
Die andern sucht der kühne Magier auf;
In reicher Spende läßt er, voll Vertrauen,
Was jeder wünscht, das Wunderwürdige schauen.

Astrolog.

Der glühnde Schlüssel rührt die Schale kaum,
6440 Ein dunstiger Nebel deckt sogleich den Raum,

Er schleicht sich ein, er wogt nach Wolkenart,
Gedehnt, geballt, verschränkt, getheilt, gepaart.
Und nun erkennt ein Geister-Meister-Stück!
So wie sie wandeln machen sie Musik.
Aus luft'gen Tönen quillt ein Weißnichtwie, 6445
Indem sie ziehn wird alles Melodie.
Der Säulenschaft, auch die Triglyphe klingt,
Ich glaube gar der ganze Tempel singt.
Das Dunstige senkt sich; aus dem leichten Flor
Ein schöner Jüngling tritt im Tact hervor. 6450
Hier schweigt mein Amt, ich brauch' ihn nicht zu nennen,
Wer sollte nicht den holden Paris kennen!

Paris hervortretend.

Dame.

O! welch ein Glanz aufblühender Jugendkraft!

Zweite.

Wie eine Pfirsche frisch und voller Saft!

Dritte.

Die fein gezognen, süß geschwollnen Lippen! 6455

Vierte.

Du möchtest wohl an solchem Becher nippen?

Fünfte.

Er ist gar hübsch, wenn auch nicht eben fein.

Sechste.

Ein bißchen könnt' er doch gewandter sein.

Ritter.

Den Schäferknecht glaub' ich allhier zu spüren,
Vom Prinzen nichts und nichts von Hofmanieren. 6460

Andrer.

Eh nun! halb nackt ist wohl der Junge schön,
Doch müßten wir ihn erst im Harnisch sehn!

Dame.

Er setzt sich nieder, weichlich, angenehm.

Ritter.

Auf seinem Schoose wär' euch wohl bequem?

Andre.

6465 Er lehnt den Arm so zierlich über's Haupt.

Kämmerer.

Die Flegelei! Das find' ich unerlaubt!

Dame.

Ihr Herren wißt an allem was zu mäkeln.

Derselbe.

In Kaisers Gegenwart sich hinzuräkeln!

Dame.

Er stellt's nur vor! Er glaubt sich ganz allein.

Derselbe.

6470 Das Schauspiel selbst, hier sollt' es höflich sein.

Dame.

Sanft hat der Schlaf den Holden übernommen.

Derselbe.

Er schnarcht nun gleich, natürlich ist's, vollkommen!

Junge Dame entzückt.

Zum Weihrauchsdampf was duftet so gemischt?
Das mir das Herz zum innigsten erfrischt.

Ältere.

Fürwahr! Es dringt ein Hauch tief in's Gemüthe, 6475
Er kommt von ihm!

Älteste.

Es ist des Wachsthums Blüthe,
Im Jüngling als Ambrosia bereitet,
Und atmosphärisch rings umher verbreitet.

Helena hervortretend.

Mephistopheles.

Das wär' sie denn! Vor dieser hätt' ich Ruh;
Hübsch ist sie wohl, doch sagt sie mir nicht zu. 6480

Astrolog.

Für mich ist dießmal weiter nichts zu thun,
Als Ehrenmann gesteh', bekenn' ich's nun.
Die Schöne kommt, und hätt' ich Feuerzungen!
Von Schönheit ward von jeher viel gesungen;
Wem sie erscheint wird aus sich selbst entrückt, 6485
Wem sie gehörte ward zu hoch beglückt.

Faust.

Hab' ich noch Augen? Zeigt sich tief im Sinn
Der Schönheit Quelle reichlichstens ergossen?
Mein Schreckensgang bringt seligsten Gewinn,
Wie war die Welt mir nichtig, unerschlossen! 6490
Was ist sie nun seit meiner Priesterschaft?

Diane et Endimion

D'après le dessein de Sébastien Conca, gravé par Nicolas le Sueur, Sous la Conduite de M.[le] Basseporte 134

Erst wünschenswerth, gegründet, dauerhaft!
Verschwinde mir des Lebens Athemkraft,
Wenn ich mich je von dir zurückgewöhne! —
6495 Die Wohlgestalt die mich voreinst entzückte,
In Zauberspiegelung beglückte,
War nur ein Schaumbild solcher Schöne! —
Du bist's der ich die Regung aller Kraft,
Den Inbegriff der Leidenschaft,
6500 Dir Neigung, Lieb', Anbetung, Wahnsinn zolle.

Mephistopheles aus dem Kasten.

So faßt euch doch, und fallt nicht aus der Rolle!

Ältere Dame.

Groß, wohlgestaltet, nur der Kopf zu klein.

Jüngere.

Seht nur den Fuß! Wie könnt' er plumper sein!

Diplomat.

Fürstinnen hab' ich dieser Art gesehn,
6505 Mich däucht sie ist vom Kopf zum Fuße schön.

Hofmann.

Sie nähert sich dem Schläfer listig mild.

Dame.

Wie häßlich neben jugendreinem Bild!

Poet.

Von ihrer Schönheit ist er angestrahlt.

Dame.

Endymion und Luna! wie gemahlt!

Derselbe.

Ganz recht! Die Göttin scheint herabzusinken, 6510
Sie neigt sich über, seinen Hauch zu trinken;
Beneidenswerth! — Ein Kuß! — Das Maß ist voll.

Duenna.

Vor allen Leuten! Das ist doch zu toll!

Faust.

Furchtbare Gunst dem Knaben! —

Mephistopheles.

Ruhig! still!
Laß das Gespenst doch machen was es will. 6515

Hofmann.

Sie schleicht sich weg, leichtfüßig; er erwacht.

Dame.

Sie sieht sich um! Das hab' ich wohl gedacht.

Hofmann.

Er staunt! Ein Wunder ist's was ihm geschieht.

Dame.

Ihr ist kein Wunder was sie vor sich sieht.

Hofmann.

Mit Anstand kehrt sie sich zu ihm herum. 6520

Dame.

Ich merke schon sie nimmt ihn in die Lehre;
In solchem Fall sind alle Männer dumm,
Er glaubt wohl auch daß er der erste wäre.

Ritter.

Laßt mir sie gelten! Majestätisch fein! —

Dame.

6525 Die Buhlerin! Das nenn' ich doch gemein!

Page.

Ich möchte wohl an seiner Stelle sein!

Hofmann.

Wer würde nicht in solchem Netz gefangen?

Dame.

Das Kleinod ist durch manche Hand gegangen,
Auch die Verguldung ziemlich abgebraucht.

Andre.

6530 Vom zehnten Jahr an hat sie nichts getaugt.

Ritter.

Gelegentlich nimmt jeder sich das Beste;
Ich hielte mich an diese schönen Reste.

Gelahrter.

Ich seh' sie deutlich, doch gesteh' ich frei,
Zu zweiflen ist, ob sie die rechte sei.
6535 Die Gegenwart verführt in's Übertriebne,
Ich halte mich vor allem an's Geschriebne.
Da les' ich denn: sie habe wirklich allen
Graubärten Troja's sonderlich gefallen;
Und, wie mich dünkt, vollkommen paßt das hier,
6540 Ich bin nicht jung und doch gefällt sie mir.

Astrolog.

Nicht Knabe mehr! Ein kühner Heldenmann
Umfaßt er sie, die kaum sich wehren kann.
Gestärkten Arms hebt er sie hoch empor,
Entführt er sie wohl gar?

Faust.

Verwegner Thor!
Du wagst! Du hörst nicht! halt! das ist zu viel! 6545

Mephistopheles

Machst du's doch selbst das Fratzengeisterspiel!

Astrolog.

Nur noch ein Wort! Nach allem was geschah
Nenn ich das Stück den Raub der Helena.

Faust.

Was Raub! Bin ich für nichts an dieser Stelle!
Ist dieser Schlüssel nicht in meiner Hand! 6550
Er führte mich, durch Graus und Wog' und Welle
Der Einsamkeiten, her zum festen Strand.
Hier fass' ich Fuß! Hier sind es Wirklichkeiten,
Von hier aus darf der Geist mit Geistern streiten,
Das Doppelreich, das große, sich bereiten. 6555
So fern sie war, wie kann sie näher sein!
Ich rette sie und sie ist doppelt mein.
Gewagt! Ihr Mütter! Mütter! müßt's gewähren!
Wer sie erkannt der darf sie nicht entbehren.

Astrolog.

Was thust du, Fauste! Fauste! — Mit Gewalt 6560
Faßt er sie an, schon trübt sich die Gestalt.

Den Schlüssel kehrt er nach dem Jüngling zu,
Berührt ihn! — Weh uns, Wehe! Nu! im Nu!

Explosion, Faust liegt am Boden. Die Geister gehen in Dunst auf.

Mephistopheles der Fausten auf die Schulter nimmt.

Da habt ihr's nun! mit Narren sich beladen
6565 Das kommt zuletzt dem Teufel selbst zu Schaden.

Finsterniß, Tumult.

Zweiter Act.

Hochgewölbtes enges gothisches Zimmer,

ehemals Faustens, unverändert.

Mephistopheles

hinter einem Vorhang hervortretend. Indem er ihn aufhebt und zurücksieht, erblickt man Fausten hingestreckt auf einem altväterischen Bette.

Hier lieg', Unseliger! verführt
Zu schwergelöst'tem Liebesbande!
Wen Helena paralysirt
Der kommt so leicht nicht zu Verstande.

Sich umschauend.

Blick' ich hinauf, hierher, hinüber, 6570
Allunverändert ist es, unversehrt;
Die bunten Scheiben sind, so dünkt mich, trüber,
Die Spinneweben haben sich vermehrt;
Die Tinte starrt, vergilbt ist das Papier;
Doch alles ist am Platz geblieben; 6575
Sogar die Feder liegt noch hier,
Mit welcher Faust dem Teufel sich verschrieben.
Ja! tiefer in dem Rohre stockt
Ein Tröpflein Blut, wie ich's ihm abgelockt.
Zu einem solchen einzigen Stück 6580
Wünscht' ich dem größten Sammler Glück.

Auch hängt der alte Pelz am alten Haken,
Erinnert mich an jene Schnaken
Wie ich den Knaben einst belehrt,
6585 Woran er noch vielleicht als Jüngling zehrt.
Es kommt mir wahrlich das Gelüsten,
Rauchwarme Hülle, dir vereint,
Mich als Docent noch einmal zu erbrüsten,
Wie man so völlig Recht zu haben meint.
6590 Gelehrte wissen's zu erlangen,
Dem Teufel ist es längst vergangen.

Er schüttelt den herabgenommenen Pelz, Cicaden, Käfer und Farfarellen fahren heraus.

Chor der Insecten.

Willkommen! willkommen,
Du alter Patron,
Wir schweben und summen
6595 Und kennen dich schon.
Nur einzeln im Stillen
Du hast uns gepflanzt,
Zu Tausenden kommen wir,
Vater, getanzt.
6600 Der Schalk in dem Busen
Verbirgt sich so sehr,
Vom Pelze die Läuschen
Enthüllen sich eh'r.

Mephistopheles.

Wie überraschend mich die junge Schöpfung freut!
6605 Man säe nur, man erntet mit der Zeit.
Ich schüttle noch einmal den alten Flaus,
Noch eines flattert hier und dort hinaus. —

Hinauf! umher! in hunderttausend Ecken
Eilt euch, ihr Liebchen, zu verstecken.
Dort wo die alten Schachteln stehn, 6610
Hier im bebräunten Pergamen,
In staubigen Scherben alter Töpfe,
Dem Hohlaug' jener Todtenköpfe.
In solchem Wust und Moderleben
Muß es für ewig Grillen geben. 6615

Schlüpft in den Pelz.

Komm, decke mir die Schultern noch einmal!
Heut bin ich wieder Principal.
Doch hilft es nichts mich so zu nennen,
Wo sind die Leute die mich anerkennen!

Er zieht die Glocke die einen gellenden durchdringenden Ton erschallen läßt; wovon die Hallen erbeben und die Thüren aufspringen.

Famulus den langen finstern Gang herwankend.

Welch ein Tönen! welch ein Schauer! 6620
Treppe schwankt, es bebt die Mauer;
Durch der Fenster buntes Zittern
Seh' ich wetterleuchtend Wittern.
Springt das Estrich, und von oben
Rieselt Kalk und Schutt verschoben. 6625
Und die Thüre, fest verriegelt,
Ist durch Wunderkraft entsiegelt. —
Dort! Wie fürchterlich! Ein Riese
Steht in Faustens altem Vließe!
Seinen Blicken, seinem Winken 6630
Möcht' ich in die Kniee sinken.
Soll ich fliehen? Soll ich stehn?
Ach wie wird es mir ergehn!

Mephistopheles winkend.

Heran, mein Freund! — Ihr heißet Nicodemus.

Famulus.

6635 Hochwürdiger Herr! so ist mein Nam' — Oremus.

Mephistopheles.

Das lassen wir!

Famulus.

Wie froh! daß ihr mich kennt.

Mephistopheles.

Ich weiß es wohl, bejahrt und noch Student,
Bemoos'ter Herr! Auch ein gelehrter Mann
Studirt so fort, weil er nicht anders kann.
6640 So baut man sich ein mäßig Kartenhaus,
Der größte Geist baut's doch nicht völlig aus.
Doch euer Meister das ist ein Beschlagner:
Wer kennt ihn nicht den edlen Doctor Wagner,
Den Ersten jetzt in der gelehrten Welt!
6645 Er ist's allein der sie zusammenhält,
Der Weisheit täglicher Vermehrer.
Allwißbegierige Horcher, Hörer
Versammeln sich um ihn zu Hauf.
Er leuchtet einzig vom Katheder;
6650 Die Schlüssel übt er wie Sanct Peter,
Das Untre so das Obre schließt er auf.
Wie er vor allen glüht und funkelt,
Kein Ruf, kein Ruhm hält weiter Stand;
Selbst Faustus Name wird verdunkelt,
6655 Er ist es, der allein erfand.

Famulus.

Verzeiht! Hochwürdiger Herr! wenn ich euch sage,
Wenn ich zu widersprechen wage:
Von allem dem ist nicht die Frage,
Bescheidenheit ist sein beschieden Theil.
In's unbegreifliche Verschwinden 6660
Des hohen Manns weiß er sich nicht zu finden,
Von dessen Wiederkunft erfleht er Trost und Heil.
Das Zimmer, wie zu Doctor Faustus Tagen,
Noch unberührt seitdem er fern,
Erwartet seinen alten Herrn. 6665
Kaum wag' ich's mich herein zu wagen.
Was muß die Sternenstunde sein? —
Gemäuer scheint mir zu erbangen;
Thürpfosten bebten, Riegel sprangen,
Sonst kamt ihr selber nicht herein. 6670

Mephistopheles.

Wo hat der Mann sich hingethan?
Führt mich zu ihm, bringt ihn heran.

Famulus.

Ach! sein Verbot ist gar zu scharf,
Ich weiß nicht ob ich's wagen darf.
Monate lang, des großen Werkes willen, 6675
Lebt' er im allerstillsten Stillen.
Der zarteste gelehrter Männer
Er sieht aus wie ein Kohlenbrenner,
Geschwärzt vom Ohre bis zur Nasen,
Die Augen roth vom Feuerblasen, 6680
So lechzt er jedem Augenblick;
Geklirr der Zange gibt Musik.

Mephistopheles.

Sollt' er den Zutritt mir verneinen?
Ich bin der Mann das Glück ihm zu beschleunen.

Der Famulus geht ab, Mephistopheles setzt sich gravitätisch nieder.

6685 Kaum hab' ich Posto hier gefaßt
Regt sich dort hinten, mir bekannt, ein Gast.
Doch dießmal ist er von den Neusten,
Er wird sich gränzenlos erdreusten.

Baccalaureus den Gang herstürmend.

Thor und Thüre find' ich offen!
6690 Nun, da läßt sich endlich hoffen,
Daß nicht, wie bisher, im Moder
Der Lebendige wie ein Todter
Sich verkümmere, sich verderbe,
Und am Leben selber sterbe.

6695 Diese Mauern, diese Wände
Neigen, senken sich zum Ende
Und wenn wir nicht bald entweichen
Wird uns Fall und Sturz erreichen.
Bin verwegen, wie nicht einer,
6700 Aber weiter bringt mich keiner.

Doch was soll ich heut erfahren!
War's nicht hier, vor so viel Jahren,
Wo ich, ängstlich und beklommen,
War als guter Fuchs gekommen?
6705 Wo ich diesen Bärtigen traute,
Mich an ihrem Schnack erbaute.

Aus den alten Bücherkrusten
Logen sie mir was sie wußten,

Was sie wußten, selbst nicht glaubten,
Sich und mir das Leben raubten. 6710
Wie? — Dort hinten in der Zelle,
Sitzt noch Einer dunkel-helle!

Nahend seh' ich's mit Erstaunen,
Sitzt er noch im Pelz, dem braunen;
Wahrlich wie ich ihn verließ, 6715
Noch gehüllt im rauhen Vließ!
Damals schien er zwar gewandt,
Als ich ihn noch nicht verstand.
Heute wird es nichts verfangen,
Frisch an ihn herangegangen! 6720

Wenn, alter Herr, nicht Lethe's trübe Fluthen
Das schiefgesenkte kahle Haupt durchschwommen,
Seht anerkennend hier den Schüler kommen,
Entwachsen akademischen Ruthen.
Ich find' euch noch wie ich euch sah; 6725
Ein Anderer bin ich wieder da.

Mephistopheles.

Mich freut daß ich euch hergeläutet.
Ich schätzt' euch damals nicht gering;
Die Raupe schon, die Chrysalide deutet
Den künftigen bunten Schmetterling. 6730
Am Lockenkopf und Spitzenkragen
Empfandet ihr ein kindliches Behagen. —
Ihr trugt wohl niemals einen Zopf? —
Heut schau' ich euch im Schwedenkopf.
Ganz resolut und wacker seht ihr aus, 6735
Kommt nur nicht absolut nach Haus.

Baccalaureus

Mein alter Herr! Wir sind am alten Orte,
Bedenkt jedoch erneuter Zeiten Lauf
Und sparet doppelsinnige Worte;
6740 Wir passen nun ganz anders auf.
Ihr hänseltet den guten treuen Jungen,
Das ist euch ohne Kunst gelungen,
Was heut zu Tage niemand wagt.

Mephistopheles.

Wenn man der Jugend reine Wahrheit sagt
6745 Die gelben Schnäbeln keineswegs behagt,
Sie aber hinterdrein nach Jahren
Das alles derb an eigner Haut erfahren,
Dann dünkeln sie es käm' aus eignem Schopf;
Da heißt es denn: der Meister war ein Tropf.

Baccalaureus.

6750 Ein Schelm vielleicht! — denn welcher Lehrer spricht
Die Wahrheit uns direct in's Angesicht?
Ein jeder weiß zu mehren wie zu mindern,
Bald ernst, bald heiter klug zu frommen Kindern.

Mephistopheles.

Zum Lernen gibt es freilich eine Zeit,
6755 Zum Lehren seid ihr, merk' ich, selbst bereit.
Seit manchen Monden, einigen Sonnen
Erfahrungsfülle habt ihr wohl gewonnen.

Baccalaureus.

Erfahrungswesen! Schaum und Duft!
Und mit dem Geist nicht ebenbürtig.
6760 Gesteht! was man von je gewußt
Es ist durchaus nicht wissenswürdig . . .

Mephistopheles nach einer Pause.

Mich deucht es längst. Ich war ein Thor,
Nun komm' ich mir recht schaal und albern vor.

Baccalaureus.

Das freut mich sehr! Da hör' ich doch Verstand;
Der erste Greis, den ich vernünftig fand! 6765

Mephistopheles.

Ich suchte nach verborgen=goldnem Schatze,
Und schauerliche Kohlen trug ich fort.

Baccalaureus.

Gesteht nur, euer Schädel, eure Glatze
Ist nicht mehr werth als jene hohlen dort?

Mephistopheles gemüthlich.

Du weißt wohl nicht, mein Freund, wie grob du bist? 6770

Baccalaureus.

Im Deutschen lügt man, wenn man höflich ist.

Mephistopheles der mit seinem Rollstuhle immer näher in's Proscenium rückt, zum Parterre.

Hier oben wird mir Licht und Luft benommen,
Ich finde wohl bei euch ein Unterkommen?

Baccalaureus.

Anmaßlich find' ich daß zur schlecht'sten Frist
Man etwas sein will, wo man nichts mehr ist. 6775
Des Menschen Leben lebt im Blut, und wo
Bewegt das Blut sich wie im Jüngling so?

Das ist lebendig Blut in frischer Kraft,
Das neues Leben sich aus Leben schafft.
6780 Da regt sich alles, da wird was gethan,
Das Schwache fällt, das Tüchtige tritt heran.
Indessen wir die halbe Welt gewonnen
Was habt ihr denn gethan? genickt, gesonnen,
Geträumt, erwogen, Plan und immer Plan.
6785 Gewiß! das Alter ist ein kaltes Fieber
Im Frost von grillenhafter Noth.
Hat einer dreißig Jahr vorüber,
So ist er schon so gut wie todt.
Am besten wär's euch zeitig todtzuschlagen.

Mephistopheles.

6790 Der Teufel hat hier weiter nichts zu sagen.

Baccalaureus.

Wenn ich nicht will, so darf kein Teufel sein.

Mephistopheles abseits.

Der Teufel stellt dir nächstens doch ein Bein.

Baccalaureus.

Dieß ist der Jugend edelster Beruf!
Die Welt sie war nicht eh' ich sie erschuf;
6795 Die Sonne führt'ich aus dem Meer herauf;
Mit mir begann der Mond des Wechsels Lauf;
Da schmückte sich der Tag auf meinen Wegen,
Die Erde grünte, blühte mir entgegen.
Auf meinen Wink, in jener ersten Nacht,
6800 Entfaltete sich aller Sterne Pracht.
Wer, außer mir, entband euch aller Schranken
Philisterhaft einklemmender Gedanken?

Ich aber frei, wie mir's im Geiste spricht,
Verfolge froh mein innerliches Licht,
Und wandle rasch, im eigensten Entzücken, 6805
Das Helle vor mir, Finsterniß im Rücken.

Ab.

Mephistopheles.

Original, fahr' hin in deiner Pracht! —
Wie würde dich die Einsicht kränken:
Wer kann was Dummes, wer was Kluges denken
Das nicht die Vorwelt schon gedacht? — 6810
Doch sind wir auch mit diesem nicht gefährdet,
In wenig Jahren wird es anders sein:
Wenn sich der Most auch ganz absurd gebärdet,
Es gibt zuletzt doch noch e' Wein.

Zu dem jüngern Parterre das nicht applaudirt.

Ihr bleibt bei meinem Worte kalt, 6815
Euch guten Kindern lass' ich's gehen;
Bedenkt: der Teufel der ist alt,
So werdet alt, ihn zu verstehen!

Laboratorium

im Sinne des Mittelalters, weitläufige unbehülfliche Apparate, zu phantastischen Zwecken.

Wagner am Herde.

Die Glocke tönt, die fürchterliche,
6820 Durchschauert die berußten Mauern.
Nicht länger kann das Ungewisse
Der ernstesten Erwartung dauern.
Schon hellen sich die Finsternisse;
Schon in der innerstern Phiole
6825 Erglüht es wie lebendige Kohle,
Ja wie der herrlichste Carfunkel,
Verstrahlend Blitze durch das Dunkel;
Ein helles weißes Licht erscheint!
O daß ich's dießmal nicht verliere! —
6830 Ach Gott! was rasselt an der Thüre?

Mephistopheles eintretend.

Willkommen! es ist gut gemeint.

Wagner ängstlich.

Willkommen! zu dem Stern der Stunde.

Leise.

Doch haltet Wort und Athem fest im Munde,
Ein herrlich Werk ist gleich zu Stand gebracht.

Mephistopheles leiser.

Was gibt es denn?

Wagner leiser.

Es wird ein Mensch gemacht. 6835

Mephistopheles.

Ein Mensch? Und welch verliebtes Paar
Habt ihr in's Rauchloch eingeschlossen?

Wagner.

Behüte Gott! wie sonst das Zeugen Mode war
Erklären wir für eitel Possen.
Der zarte Punct aus dem das Leben sprang, 6840
Die holde Kraft die aus dem Innern drang
Und nahm und gab, bestimmt sich selbst zu zeichnen,
Erst Nächstes, dann sich Fremdes anzueignen,
Die ist von ihrer Würde nun entsetzt;
Wenn sich das Thier noch weiter dran ergetzt, 6845
So muß der Mensch mit seinen großen Gaben
Doch künftig höhern, höhern Ursprung haben.

Zum Herd gewendet.

Es leuchtet! seht! — Nun läßt sich wirklich hoffen,
Daß, wenn wir aus viel hundert Stoffen
Durch Mischung, denn auf Mischung kommt es an, 6850
Den Menschenstoff gemächlich componiren,
In einen Kolben verlutiren
Und ihn gehörig cohobiren,
So ist das Werk im Stillen abgethan.

Zum Herd gewendet.

Es wird! die Masse regt sich klarer, 6855
Die Überzeugung wahrer, wahrer:

Was man an der Natur Geheimnißvolles pries,
Das wagen wir verständig zu probiren,
Und was sie sonst organisiren ließ,
6860 Das lassen wir krystallisiren.

Mephistopheles.

Wer lange lebt hat viel erfahren,
Nichts Neues kann für ihn auf dieser Welt geschehn,
Ich habe schon, in meinen Wanderjahren,
Krystallisirtes Menschenvolk gesehn.

Wagner bisher immer aufmerksam auf die Phiole.

6865 Es steigt, es blitzt, es häuft sich an,
Im Augenblick ist es gethan.
Ein großer Vorsatz scheint im Anfang toll;
Doch wollen wir des Zufalls künftig lachen,
Und so ein Hirn, das trefflich denken soll,
6870 Wird künftig auch ein Denker machen.

Entzückt die Phiole betrachtend.

Das Glas erklingt von lieblicher Gewalt,
Es trübt, es klärt sich; also muß es werden!
Ich seh' in zierlicher Gestalt
Ein artig Männlein sich gebärden.
6875 Was wollen wir, was will die Welt nun mehr?
Denn das Geheimniß liegt am Tage.
Gebt diesem Laute nur Gehör,
Er wird zu Stimme, wird zur Sprache.

Homunculus in der Phiole zu Wagner.

Nun Väterchen! wie steht's? es war kein Scherz.
6880 Komm, drücke mich recht zärtlich an dein Herz,
Doch nicht zu fest, damit das Glas nicht springe.
Das ist die Eigenschaft der Dinge:

Natürlichem genügt das Weltall kaum,
Was künstlich ist, verlangt geschloss'nen Raum.

Zu Mephistopheles.

Du aber Schalk, Herr Vetter, bist du hier? 6885
Im rechten Augenblick, ich danke dir.
Ein gut Geschick führt dich zu uns herein,
Dieweil ich bin, muß ich auch thätig sein.
Ich möchte mich sogleich zur Arbeit schürzen.
Du bist gewandt, die Wege mir zu kürzen. 6890

Wagner.

Nur noch ein Wort! bisher mußt' ich mich schämen,
Denn alt und jung bestürmt mich mit Problemen.
Zum Beispiel nur: noch niemand konnt' es fassen
Wie Seel' und Leib so schön zusammenpassen,
So fest sich halten als um nie zu scheiden, 6895
Und doch den Tag sich immerfort verleiden.
Sodann —

Mephistopheles.

Halt' ein! ich wollte lieber fragen:
Warum sich Mann und Frau so schlecht vertragen?
Du kommst, mein Freund, hierüber nie in's Reine.
Hier gibt's zu thun, das eben will der Kleine. 6900

Homunculus.

Was gibt's zu thun?

Mephistopheles auf eine Seitenthüre deutend.

Hier zeige deine Gabe!

Wagner immer in die Phiole schauend.

Fürwahr, du bist ein allerliebster Knabe!

Die Seitenthür öffnet sich, man sieht Faust auf dem Lager hingestreckt.

Homunculus erstaunt.

Bedeutend! —

Die Phiole entschlüpft aus Wagners Händen, schwebt über Faust und beleuchtet ihn.

Schön umgeben! — Klar Gewässer
Im dichten Haine, Fraun die sich entkleiden;
6905 Die allerliebsten! — Das wird immer besser.
Doch eine läßt sich glänzend unterscheiden,
Aus höchstem Helden=, wohl aus Götterstamme.
Sie setzt den Fuß in das durchsichtig Helle;
Des edlen Körpers holde Lebensflamme
6910 Kühlt sich im schmiegsamen Krystall der Welle.
Doch welch Getöse rasch bewegter Flügel,
Welch Sausen, Plätschern wühlt im glatten Spiegel?
Die Mädchen fliehn verschüchtert; doch allein
Die Königin sie blickt gelassen drein
6915 Und sieht, mit stolzem weiblichem Vergnügen,
Der Schwäne Fürsten ihrem Knie sich schmiegen,
Zudringlich=zahm. Er scheint sich zu gewöhnen. —
Auf einmal aber steigt ein Dunst empor
Und deckt mit dichtgewebtem Flor
6920 Die lieblichste von allen Scenen.

Mephistopheles.

Was du nicht alles zu erzählen hast!
So klein du bist, so groß bist du Phantast.
Ich sehe nichts —

Homunculus.

Das glaub' ich. Du aus Norden,
Im Nebelalter jung geworden,
6925 Im Wust von Ritterthum und Pfäfferei,

Wo wäre da dein Auge frei!
Im Düstern bist du nur zu Hause.

Umherschauend.

Verbräunt Gestein, bemodert, widrig,
Spitzbögig, schnörkelhaftest, niedrig! —
Erwacht uns dieser, gibt es neue Noth, 6930
Er bleibt gleich auf der Stelle todt.
Waldquellen, Schwäne, nackte Schönen,
Das war sein ahnungsvoller Traum;
Wie wollt' er sich hierher gewöhnen!
Ich, der bequemste, duld' es kaum. 6935
Nun fort mit ihm.

Mephistopheles.

Der Ausweg soll mich freuen.

Homunculus.

Befiehl den Krieger in die Schlacht,
Das Mädchen führe du zum Reihen,
So ist gleich alles abgemacht.
Jetzt eben, wie ich schnell bedacht, 6940
Ist classische Walpurgisnacht;
Das Beste was begegnen könnte
Bringt ihn zu seinem Elemente.

Mephistopheles.

Dergleichen hab' ich nie vernommen.

Homunculus.

Wie wollt' es auch zu euren Ohren kommen? 6945
Romantische Gespenster kennt ihr nur allein,
Ein echt Gespenst auch classisch hat's zu sein.

Mephistopheles.

Wohin denn aber soll die Fahrt sich regen?
Mich widern schon antikische Collegen.

Homunculus.

6950 Nordwestlich, Satan, ist dein Lustrevier;
Südöstlich dießmal aber segeln wir —
An großer Fläche fließt Peneios frei,
Umbuscht, umbaumt, in still= und feuchten Buchten,
Die Ebne dehnt sich zu der Berge Schluchten,
6955 Und oben liegt Pharsalus alt und neu.

Mephistopheles.

O weh! hinweg! und laßt mir jene Streite
Von Tyrannei und Sklaverei bei Seite.
Mich langeweilt's, denn kaum ist's abgethan,
So fangen sie von vorne wieder an;
6960 Und keiner merkt: er ist doch nur geneckt
Vom Asmodeus der dahinter steckt.
Sie streiten sich, so heißt's, um Freiheitsrechte,
Genau besehn sind's Knechte gegen Knechte.

Homunculus.

Den Menschen laß ihr widerspenstig Wesen,
6965 Ein jeder muß sich wehren wie er kann,
Vom Knaben auf, so wird's zuletzt ein Mann.
Hier fragt sich's nur wie dieser kann genesen?
Hast du ein Mittel so erprob' es hier,
Vermagst du's nicht so überlaß es mir.

Mephistopheles.

6970 Manch Brockenstückchen wäre durchzuproben,
Doch Heidenriegel find' ich vorgeschoben.

Das Griechenvolk es taugte nie recht viel!
Doch blendet's euch mit freiem Sinnen-Spiel,
Verlockt des Menschen Brust zu heitern Sünden,
Die unsern wird man immer düster finden. 6975
Und nun was soll's?

Homunculus.

Du bist ja sonst nicht blöde;
Und wenn ich von thessalischen Hexen rede,
So denk' ich hab' ich was gesagt.

Mephistopheles lüstern.

Thessalische Hexen! Wohl! das sind Personen
Nach denen hab' ich lang gefragt. 6980
Mit ihnen Nacht für Nacht zu wohnen
Ich glaube nicht daß es behagt;
Doch zum Besuch! Versuch!

Homunculus.

Den Mantel her,
Und um den Ritter umgeschlagen!
Der Lappen wird euch, wie bisher, 6985
Den einen mit dem andern tragen,
Ich leuchte vor.

Wagner ängstlich.

Und ich?

Homunculus.

Eh nun
Du bleibst zu Hause Wichtigstes zu thun.
Entfalte du die alten Pergamente,
Nach Vorschrift sammle Lebens-Elemente 6990
Und füge sie mit Vorsicht eins an's andre.

Das W a s bedenke, mehr bedenke W i e?
Indessen ich ein Stückchen Welt durchwandre
Entdeck' ich wohl das Tüpfchen auf das J.
6995 Dann ist der große Zweck erreicht,
Solch einen Lohn verdient ein solches Streben:
Gold, Ehre, Ruhm, gesundes langes Leben,
Und Wissenschaft und Tugend — auch vielleicht.
Leb' wohl!

W a g n e r betrübt.

Leb' wohl! Das drückt das Herz mir nieder.
7000 Ich fürchte schon ich seh' dich niemals wieder.

M e p h i s t o p h e l e s.

Nun zum Peneios frisch hinab,
Herr Vetter ist nicht zu verachten.

Ad Spectatores.

Am Ende hängen wir doch ab
Von Creaturen die wir machten.

Classische Walpurgisnacht.

Pharsalische Felder.

Finsterniß.

Erichtho.

Zum Schauderfeste dieser Nacht, wie öfter schon, 7005
Tret' ich einher, Erichtho, ich die düstere;
Nicht so abscheulich wie die leidigen Dichter mich
Im Übermaß verlästern. . . Endigen sie doch nie
In Lob und Tadel. . . Überbleicht erscheint mir schon
Von grauer Zelten Woge weit das Thal dahin, 7010
Als Nachgesicht der sorg= und grauenvollsten Nacht.
Wie oft schon wiederholt' sich's! Wird sich immerfort
In's Ewige wiederholen. . . Keiner gönnt das Reich
Dem andern, dem gönnt's keiner der's mit Kraft erwarb
Und kräftig herrscht. Denn jeder, der sein innres Selbst 7015
Nicht zu regieren weiß, regierte gar zu gern
Des Nachbars Willen, eignem stolzem Sinn gemäß. . .
Hier aber ward ein großes Beispiel durchgekämpft:
Wie sich Gewalt Gewaltigerem entgegenstellt,
Der Freiheit holder tausendblumiger Kranz zerreißt, 7020
Der starre Lorbeer sich um's Haupt des Herrschers biegt.
Hier träumte Magnus früher Größe Blüthentag,

Dem schwanken Zünglein lauschend wachte Cäsar dort!
Das wird sich messen. Weiß die Welt doch wem's gelang.

7025 Wachfeuer glühen, rothe Flammen spendende,
Der Boden haucht vergoss'nen Blutes Widerschein,
Und angelockt von seltnem Wunderglanz der Nacht
Versammelt sich hellenischer Sage Legion.
Um alle Feuer schwankt unsicher, oder sitzt
7030 Behaglich, alter Tage fabelhaft Gebild...
Der Mond, zwar unvollkommen, aber leuchtend hell,
Erhebt sich, milden Glanz verbreitend überall;
Der Zelten Trug verschwindet, Feuer brennen blau.

Doch, über mir! welch unerwartet Meteor?
7035 Es leuchtet und beleuchtet körperlichen Ball.
Ich wittre Leben. Da geziemen will mir's nicht
Lebendigem zu nahen, dem ich schädlich bin;
Das bringt mir bösen Ruf und frommt mir nicht.
Schon sinkt es nieder. Weich' ich aus mit Wohlbedacht!

Entfernt sich.

Die Luftfahrer oben.

Homunculus.

7040 Schwebe noch einmal die Runde
Über Flamm- und Schaudergrauen;
Ist es doch in Thal und Grunde
Gar gespenstisch anzuschauen.

Mephistopheles.

Seh' ich, wie durch's alte Fenster
7045 In des Nordens Wust und Graus,
Ganz abscheuliche Gespenster;
Bin ich hier wie dort zu Haus.

Homunculus.

Sieh! da schreitet eine Lange
Weiten Schrittes vor uns hin.

Mephistopheles.

Ist es doch als wär' ihr bange; 7050
Sah uns durch die Lüfte ziehn.

Homunculus.

Laß sie schreiten! setz' ihn nieder
Deinen Ritter, und sogleich
Kehret ihm das Leben wieder,
Denn er sucht's im Fabelreich. 7055

Faust den Boden berührend.

Wo ist sie? —

Homunculus.

Wüßten's nicht zu sagen,
Doch hier wahrscheinlich zu erfragen.
In Eile magst du, eh' es tagt,
Von Flamm' zu Flamme spürend gehen:
Wer zu den Müttern sich gewagt 7060
Hat weiter nichts zu überstehen.

Mephistopheles.

Auch ich bin hier an meinem Theil;
Doch wüßt' ich Besseres nicht zu unserm Heil
Als: jeder möge durch die Feuer
Versuchen sich sein eigen Abentheuer. 7065
Dann, um uns wieder zu vereinen,
Laß deine Leuchte, Kleiner, tönend scheinen.

Homunculus.

So soll es blitzen, soll es klingen.

Das Glas dröhnt und leuchtet gewaltig.

Nun frisch zu neuen Wunderdingen!

Ab.

Faust allein.

7070 Wo ist sie! — Frage jetzt nicht weiter nach...
Wär's nicht die Scholle die sie trug,
Die Welle nicht die ihr entgegen schlug,
So ist's die Luft die ihre Sprache sprach.
Hier! durch ein Wunder, hier in Griechenland!
7075 Ich fühlte gleich den Boden wo ich stand;
Wie mich, den Schläfer, frisch ein Geist durchglühte,
So steh' ich, ein Antäus an Gemüthe.
Und find' ich hier das Seltsamste beisammen,
Durchforsch' ich ernst dieß Labyrinth der Flammen.

Entfernt sich.

Mephistopheles umherspürend.

7080 Und wie ich diese Feuerchen durchschweife,
So find' ich mich doch ganz und gar entfremdet,
Fast alles nackt, nur hie und da behemdet:
Die Sphinxe schamlos, unverschämt die Greife,
Und was nicht alles, lockig und beflügelt,
7085 Von vorn und hinten sich im Auge spiegelt...
Zwar sind auch wir von Herzen unanständig,
Doch das Antike find' ich zu lebendig;
Das müßte man mit neustem Sinn bemeistern
Und mannichfaltig modisch überkleistern....
7090 Ein widrig Volk! doch darf mich's nicht verdrießen
Als neuer Gast anständig sie zu grüßen....
Glückzu! den schönen Fraun, den klugen Greisen.

Greif schnarrend.

Nicht Greisen! Greifen! — Niemand hört es gern
Daß man ihn Greis nennt. Jedem Worte klingt
Der Ursprung nach wo es sich her bedingt: 7095
Grau, grämlich, griesgram, greulich, Gräber, grimmig,
Etymologisch gleicherweise stimmig,
Verstimmen uns.

Mephistopheles.

Und doch, nicht abzuschweifen,
Gefällt das Grei im Ehrentitel Greifen.

Greif wie oben und immer so fort.

Natürlich! die Verwandtschaft ist erprobt, 7100
Zwar oft gescholten, mehr jedoch gelobt;
Man greife nun nach Mädchen, Kronen, Gold,
Dem Greifenden ist meist Fortuna hold.

Ameisen von der colossalen Art.

Ihr sprecht von Gold, wir hatten viel gesammelt,
In Fels- und Höhlen heimlich eingerammelt; 7105
Das Arimaspen-Volk hat's ausgespürt,
Sie lachen dort, wie weit sie's weggeführt.

Greife.

Wir wollen sie schon zum Geständniß bringen.

Arimaspen.

Nur nicht zur freien Jubelnacht.
Bis morgen ist's alles durchgebracht, 7110
Es wird uns diesmal wohl gelingen.

Mephistopheles hat sich zwischen die Sphinxe gesetzt.

Wie leicht und gern ich mich hierher gewöhne,
Denn ich verstehe Mann für Mann.

Sphinx.

Wir hauchen unsre Geistertöne
7115 Und ihr verkörpert sie alsdann.
Jetzt nenne dich bis wir dich weiter kennen.

Mephistopheles.

Mit vielen Namen glaubt man mich zu nennen —
Sind Briten hier? Sie reisen sonst so viel,
Schlachtfeldern nachzuspüren, Wasserfällen,
7120 Gestürzten Mauern, classisch dumpfen Stellen;
Das wäre hier für sie ein würdig Ziel.
Sie zeugten auch: Im alten Bühnen-Spiel
Sah man mich dort als old Iniquity.

Sphinx.

Wie kam man drauf?

Mephistopheles.

Ich weiß es selbst nicht wie.

Sphinx.

7125 Mag sein! Hast du von Sternen einige Kunde?
Was sagst du zu der gegenwärt'gen Stunde?

Mephistopheles aufschauend.

Stern schießt nach Stern, beschnittner Mond scheint helle
Und mir ist wohl an dieser trauten Stelle,
Ich wärme mich an deinem Löwenfelle.
7130 Hinauf sich zu versteigen wär' zum Schaden,
Gib Räthsel auf, gib allenfalls Charaden.

Sphinx.

Sprich nur dich selbst aus, wird schon Räthsel sein.
Versuch' einmal dich innigst aufzulösen:
„Dem frommen Manne nöthig wie dem bösen,
Dem ein Plastron, ascetisch zu rapiren, 7135
Cumpan dem andern, Tolles zu vollführen,
Und beides nur, um Zeus zu amüsiren."

Erster Greif schnarrend.

Den mag ich nicht!

Zweiter Greif stärker schnarrend.

Was will uns der?

Beide.

Der Garstige gehöret nicht hierher!

Mephistopheles brutal.

Du glaubst vielleicht des Gastes Nägel krauen 7140
Nicht auch so gut wie deine scharfen Klauen?
Versuch's einmal!

Sphinx milde.

Du magst nur immer bleiben,
Wird dich's doch selbst aus unsrer Mitte treiben;
In deinem Lande thust dir was zu Gute,
Doch, irr' ich nicht, hier ist dir schlecht zu Muthe. 7145

Mephistopheles.

Du bist recht appetitlich oben anzuschauen,
Doch unten hin, die Bestie macht mir Grauen.

Sphinx.

Du Falscher kommst zu deiner bittern Buße,
Denn unsre Tatzen sind gesund;
7150 Dir mit verschrumpftem Pferdefuße
Behagt es nicht in unserem Bund.

Sirenen präludiren oben.

Mephistopheles.

Wer sind die Vögel in den Ästen
Des Pappelstromes hingewiegt?

Sphinx.

Gewahrt euch nur! die Allerbesten
7155 Hat solch ein Sing-Sang schon besiegt.

Sirenen.

Ach was wollt ihr euch verwöhnen
In dem Häßlich-Wunderbaren!
Horcht, wir kommen hier zu Schaaren
Und in wohlgestimmten Tönen,
7160 So geziemet es Sirenen.

Sphinxe sie verspottend in derselben Melodie.

Nöthigt sie herabzusteigen!
Sie verbergen in den Zweigen
Ihre garstigen Habichtskrallen,
Euch verderblich anzufallen,
7165 Wenn ihr euer Ohr verleiht.

Sirenen.

Weg! das Hassen, weg! das Neiden;
Sammeln wir die klarsten Freuden,

Unter'm Himmel ausgestreut!
Auf dem Wasser, auf der Erde
Sei's die heiterste Gebärde 7170
Die man dem Willkommnen beut.

Mephistopheles.

Das sind die saubern Neuigkeiten
Wo aus der Kehle, von den Saiten
Ein Ton sich um den andern flicht.
Das Trallern ist bei mir verloren, 7175
Es krabbelt wohl mir um die Ohren
Allein zum Herzen dringt es nicht.

Sphinxe.

Sprich nicht vom Herzen! das ist eitel;
Ein lederner verschrumpfter Beutel
Das paßt dir eher zu Gesicht. 7180

Faust herantretend.

Wie wunderbar! das Anschaun thut mir G'nüge,
Im Widerwärtigen große, tüchtige Züge.
Ich ahne schon ein günstiges Geschick;
Wohin versetzt mich dieser ernste Blick?

Auf Sphinxe bezüglich.

Vor solchen hat einst Ödipus gestanden; 7185

Auf Sirenen bezüglich.

Vor solchen krümmte sich Ulyß in hänfnen Banden;

Auf Ameisen bezüglich.

Von solchen ward der höchste Schatz gespart;

Auf Greife bezüglich.

Von diesen treu und ohne Fehl bewahrt.
Vom frischen Geiste fühl' ich mich durchdrungen,
Gestalten groß, groß die Erinnerungen. 7190

Mephistopheles.

Sonst hättest du dergleichen weggeflucht,
Doch jetzo scheint es dir zu frommen;
Denn wo man die Geliebte sucht,
Sind Ungeheuer selbst willkommen.

Faust zu den Sphinxen.

7195 Ihr Frauenbilder müßt mir Rede stehn:
Hat eins der Euren Helena gesehn?

Sphinxe.

Wir reichen nicht hinauf zu ihren Tagen,
Die letztesten hat Hercules erschlagen.
Von Chiron könntest du's erfragen;
7200 Der sprengt herum in dieser Geisternacht,
Wenn er dir steht, so hast du's weit gebracht.

Sirenen.

Sollte dir's doch auch nicht fehlen!...
Wie Ulyß bei uns verweilte,
Schmähend nicht vorübereilte,
7205 Wußt' er vieles zu erzählen;
Würden alles dir vertrauen,
Wolltest du zu unsern Gauen
Dich an's grüne Meer verfügen.

Sphinx.

Laß dich, Edler, nicht betrügen.
7210 Statt daß Ulyß sich binden ließ,
Laß unsern guten Rath dich binden;
Kannst du den hohen Chiron finden,
Erfährst du was ich dir verhieß.

Faust entfernt sich.

Mephistopheles verdrießlich.

Was krächzt vorbei mit Flügelschlag?
So schnell daß man's nicht sehen mag, 7215
Und immer eins dem andern nach,
Den Jäger würden sie ermüden.

Sphinx.

Dem Sturm des Winterwinds vergleichbar,
Alcides Pfeilen kaum erreichbar;
Es sind die raschen Stymphaliden. 7220
Und wohlgemeint ihr Krächzegruß,
Mit Geierschnabel und Gänsefuß.
Sie möchten gern in unsern Kreisen
Als Stammverwandte sich erweisen.

Mephistopheles wie verschüchtert.

Noch andres Zeug zischt zwischen drein. 7225

Sphinx.

Vor diesen sei euch ja nicht bange,
Es sind die Köpfe der lernäischen Schlange,
Vom Rumpf getrennt, und glauben was zu sein.
Doch sagt, was soll nur aus euch werden?
Was für unruhige Gebärden? 7230
Wo wollt ihr hin? Begebt euch fort! ...
Ich sehe, jener Chorus dort
Macht euch zum Wendehals. Bezwingt euch nicht,
Geht hin! begrüßt manch reizendes Gesicht.
Die Lamien sind's, lustfeine Dirnen, 7235
Mit Lächelmund und frechen Stirnen,
Wie sie dem Satyrvolk behagen;
Ein Bocksfuß darf dort alles wagen.

Mephistopheles.

Ihr bleibt doch hier? daß ich euch wiederfinde.

Sphinxe.

7240 Ja! Mische dich zum luftigen Gesinde.
Wir, von Ägypten her, sind längst gewohnt
Daß unsereins in tausend Jahre thront.
Und respectirt nur unsre Lage,
So regeln wir die Mond= und Sonnentage.

7245 Sitzen vor den Pyramiden,
Zu der Völker Hochgericht;
Überschwemmung, Krieg und Frieden —
Und verziehen kein Gesicht.

Peneios

umgeben von Gewässern und **Nymphen.**

Peneios.

Rege dich du Schilfgeflüster!
Hauche leise Rohrgeschwister, 7250
Säuselt leichte Weidensträuche,
Lispelt Pappelzitterzweige
Unterbrochnen Träumen zu! . . .
Weckt mich doch ein grauslich Wittern,
Heimlich allbewegend Zittern 7255
Aus dem Wallestrom und Ruh.

Faust an den Fluß tretend.

Hör' ich recht, so muß ich glauben:
Hinter den verschränkten Lauben
Dieser Zweige, dieser Stauden
Tönt ein menschenähnlichs Lauten. 7260
Scheint die Welle doch ein Schwätzen,
Lüftlein wie — ein Scherzergetzen.

Nymphen zu Faust.

Am besten geschäh' dir,
Du legtest dich nieder,
Erholtest im Kühlen 7265
Ermüdete Glieder,

Genösseset der immer
Dich meidenden Ruh;
Wir säuseln, wir rieseln,
7270 Wir flüstern dir zu.

Faust.

Ich wache ja! O laßt sie walten
Die unvergleichlichen Gestalten
Wie sie dorthin mein Auge schickt.
So wunderbar bin ich durchdrungen!
7275 Sind's Träume? Sind's Erinnerungen?
Schon einmal warst du so beglückt.
Gewässer schleichen durch die Frische
Der dichten, sanft bewegten Büsche,
Nicht rauschen sie, sie rieseln kaum;
7280 Von allen Seiten hundert Quellen
Vereinen sich im reinlich hellen,
Zum Bade flach vertieften Raum.
Gesunde junge Frauenglieder
Vom feuchten Spiegel doppelt wieder
7285 Ergetztem Auge zugebracht!
Gesellig dann und fröhlich badend,
Erdreistet schwimmend, furchtsam watend;
Geschrei zuletzt und Wasserschlacht.
Begnügen sollt' ich mich an diesen,
7290 Mein Auge sollte hier genießen,
Doch immer weiter strebt mein Sinn.
Der Blick dringt scharf nach jener Hülle,
Das reiche Laub der grünen Fülle
Verbirgt die hohe Königin.

7295 Wundersam! auch Schwäne kommen
Aus den Buchten hergeschwommen,

Majestätisch rein bewegt.
Ruhig schwebend, zart gesellig,
Aber stolz und selbstgefällig
Wie sich Haupt und Schnabel regt.... 7300
Einer aber scheint vor allen
Brüstend kühn sich zu gefallen,
Segelnd rasch durch alle fort;
Sein Gefieder bläht sich schwellend,
Welle selbst, auf Wogen wellend, 7305
Dringt er zu dem heiligen Ort....
Die andern schwimmen hin und wieder
Mit ruhig glänzendem Gefieder,
Bald auch in regem prächtigen Streit
Die scheuen Mädchen abzulenken, 7310
Daß sie an ihren Dienst nicht denken,
Nur an die eigne Sicherheit.

Nymphen.

Leget, Schwestern, euer Ohr
An des Ufers grüne Stufe;
Hör' ich recht, so kommt mir's vor 7315
Als der Schall von Pferdes Hufe.
Wüßt' ich nur wer dieser Nacht
Schnelle Botschaft zugebracht.

Faust.

Ist mir doch als dröhnt' die Erde
Schallend unter eiligem Pferde. 7320
Dorthin mein Blick!
Ein günstiges Geschick,
Soll es mich schon erreichen?
O Wunder ohne Gleichen!

7325 Ein Reuter kommt herangetrabt,
Er scheint von Geist und Muth begabt,
Von blendend-weißem Pferd getragen....
Ich irre nicht, ich kenn' ihn schon,
Der Philyra berühmter Sohn! —
7330 Halt, Chiron! halt! Ich habe dir zu sagen....

Chiron.

Was gibt's? Was ist's?

Faust.

Bezähme deinen Schritt!

Chiron.

Ich raste nicht.

Faust.

So bitte! Nimm mich mit!

Chiron.

Sitz' auf! so kann ich nach Belieben fragen:
Wohin des Wegs? Du stehst am Ufer hier,
7335 Ich bin bereit dich durch den Fluß zu tragen.

Faust aufsitzend.

Wohin du willst. Für ewig dank' ich's dir....
Der große Mann, der edle Pädagog,
Der, sich zum Ruhm, ein Heldenvolk erzog,
Den schönen Kreis der edlen Argonauten
7340 Und alle die des Dichters Welt erbauten.

Chiron.

Das lassen wir an seinem Ort!
Selbst Pallas kommt als Mentor nicht zu Ehren;
Am Ende treiben sie's nach ihrer Weise fort
Als wenn sie nicht erzogen wären.

Faust.

Den Arzt, der jede Pflanze nennt, 7345
Die Wurzeln bis in's Tiefste kennt,
Dem Kranken Heil, dem Wunden Lindrung schafft,
Umarm' ich hier in Geist- und Körperkraft!

Chiron.

Ward neben mir ein Held verletzt,
Da wußt' ich Hülf' und Rath zu schaffen! 7350
Doch ließ ich meine Kunst zuletzt
Den Wurzelweibern und den Pfaffen.

Faust.

Du bist der wahre große Mann
Der Lobeswort nicht hören kann;
Er sucht bescheiden auszuweichen 7355
Und thut als gäb' es Seinesgleichen.

Chiron.

Du scheinest mir geschickt zu heucheln,
Dem Fürsten wie dem Volk zu schmeicheln.

Faust.

So wirst du mir denn doch gestehn:
Du hast die Größten deiner Zeit gesehn, 7360
Dem Edelsten in Thaten nachgestrebt,
Halbgöttlich ernst die Tage durchgelebt.
Doch unter den heroischen Gestalten
Wen hast du für den Tüchtigsten gehalten?

Chiron.

Im hehren Argonautenkreise 7365
War jeder brav nach seiner eignen Weise,

Und, nach der Kraft die ihn beseelte,
Konnt' er genügen, wo's den andern fehlte.
Die Dioskuren haben stets gesiegt
7370 Wo Jugendfüll' und Schönheit überwiegt.
Entschluß und schnelle That zu andrer Heil
Den Boreaden ward's zum schönen Theil.
Nachsinnend, kräftig, klug, im Rath bequem,
So herrschte Jason, Frauen angenehm.
7375 Dann Orpheus, zart und immer still bedächtig,
Schlug er die Leier allen übermächtig.
Scharfsichtig Lynceus, der, bei Tag und Nacht,
Das heil'ge Schiff durch Klipp' und Strand gebracht...
Gesellig nur läßt sich Gefahr erproben:
7380 Wenn einer wirkt, die andern alle loben.

Faust.

Von Hercules willst nichts erwähnen?

Chiron.

O weh! errege nicht mein Sehnen...
Ich hatte Phöbus nie gesehn,
Noch Ares, Hermes, wie sie heißen,
7385 Da sah ich mir vor Augen stehn
Was alle Menschen göttlich preisen.
So war er ein geborner König,
Als Jüngling herrlichst anzuschaun;
Dem ältern Bruder unterthänig
7390 Und auch den allerliebsten Fraun.
Den zweiten zeugt nicht Gäa wieder;
Nicht führt ihn Hebe himmelein;
Vergebens mühen sich die Lieder,
Vergebens quälen sie den Stein.

Faust.

So sehr auch Bildner auf ihn pochen, 7395
So herrlich kam er nie zur Schau.
Vom schönsten Mann hast du gesprochen,
Nun sprich auch von der schönsten Frau!

Chiron.

Was!.. Frauen-Schönheit will nichts heißen,
Ist gar zu oft ein starres Bild; 7400
Nur solch ein Wesen kann ich preisen
Das froh und lebenslustig quillt.
Die Schöne bleibt sich selber selig;
Die Anmuth macht unwiderstehlich,
Wie Helena, da ich sie trug. 7405

Faust.

Du trugst sie?

Chiron.

Ja, auf diesem Rücken.

Faust.

Bin ich nicht schon verwirrt genug,
Und solch ein Sitz muß mich beglücken!

Chiron.

Sie faßte so mich in das Haar
Wie du es thust.

Faust.

O ganz und gar 7410
Verlier' ich mich! Erzähle wie?
Sie ist mein einziges Begehren!
Woher? wohin? ach, trugst du sie?

Chiron.

Die Frage läßt sich leicht gewähren.
7415 Die Dioskuren hatten, jener Zeit,
Das Schwesterchen aus Räuberfaust befreit.
Doch diese, nicht gewohnt besiegt zu sein,
Ermannten sich und stürmten hinterdrein.
Da hielten der Geschwister eiligen Lauf
7420 Die Sümpfe bei Eleusis auf;
Die Brüder wateten, ich patschte, schwamm hinüber;
Da sprang sie ab und streichelte
Die feuchte Mähne, schmeichelte
Und dankte lieblich-klug und selbstbewußt.
7425 Wie war sie reizend! jung, des Alten Lust!

Faust.

Erst zehen Jahr! . . . .

Chiron.

Ich seh', die Philologen
Sie haben dich so wie sich selbst betrogen.
Ganz eigen ist's mit mythologischer Frau;
Der Dichter bringt sie, wie er's braucht, zur Schau:
7430 Nie wird sie mündig, wird nicht alt,
Stets appetitlicher Gestalt,
Wird jung entführt, im Alter noch umfreit;
G'nug, den Poeten bindet keine Zeit.

Faust.

So sei auch sie durch keine Zeit gebunden!
7435 Hat doch Achill auf Pherä sie gefunden,
Selbst außer aller Zeit. Welch seltnes Glück:
Errungen Liebe gegen das Geschick!

Und sollt' ich nicht, sehnsüchtigster Gewalt,
In's Leben ziehn die einzigste Gestalt?
Das ewige Wesen, Göttern ebenbürtig, 7440
So groß als zart, so hehr als liebenswürdig?
Du sahst sie einst, heut hab' ich sie gesehn,
So schön wie reizend, wie ersehnt so schön.
Nun ist mein Sinn, mein Wesen streng umfangen,
Ich lebe nicht, kann ich sie nicht erlangen. 7445

Chiron.

Mein fremder Mann! als Mensch bist du entzückt;
Doch unter Geistern scheinst du wohl verrückt.
Nun trifft sich's hier zu deinem Glücke;
Denn alle Jahr, nur wenig Augenblicke,
Pfleg' ich bei Manto vorzutreten, 7450
Der Tochter Äsculaps; im stillen Beten
Fleht sie zum Vater: daß, zu seiner Ehre,
Er endlich doch der Ärzte Sinn verkläre
Und vom verwegnen Todtschlag sie bekehre. . .
Die liebste mir aus der Sibyllengilde; 7455
Nicht fratzenhaft bewegt, wohlthätig milde;
Ihr glückt es wohl, bei einigem Verweilen,
Mit Wurzelkräften dich von Grund zu heilen.

Faust.

Geheilt will ich nicht sein, mein Sinn ist mächtig;
Da wär' ich ja wie andre niederträchtig. 7460

Chiron.

Versäume nicht das Heil der edlen Quelle!
Geschwind herab! Wir sind zur Stelle.

Faust.

Sag' an! Wohin hast du, in grauser Nacht,
Durch Kiesgewässer, mich an's Land gebracht?

Chiron.

7465 Hier trotzten Rom und Griechenland im Streite,
Peneios rechts, links den Olymp zur Seite,
Das größte Reich das sich im Sand verliert;
Der König flieht, der Bürger triumphirt.
Blick' auf! hier steht, bedeutend nah,
7470 Im Mondenschein der ewige Tempel da.

Manto inwendig träumend.

Von Pferdes Hufe
Erklingt die heilige Stufe,
Halbgötter treten heran.

Chiron.

Ganz recht!
7475 Nur die Augen aufgethan!

Manto erwachend.

Willkommen! ich seh' du bleibst nicht aus.

Chiron.

Steht dir doch auch dein Tempelhaus!

Manto.

Streifst du noch immer unermüdet?

Chiron.

Wohnst du doch immer still umfriedet,
7480 Indeß zu kreisen mich erfreut.

Manto.

Ich harre, mich umkreis't die Zeit.
Und dieser?

Chiron.

Die verrufene Nacht
Hat strudelnd ihn hierhergebracht.
Helenen, mit verrückten Sinnen,
Helenen will er sich gewinnen, 7485
Und weiß nicht wie und wo beginnen;
Asklepischer Cur vor andern werth.

Manto.

Den lieb' ich, der Unmögliches begehrt.

Chiron ist schon weit weg.

Manto.

Tritt ein, Verwegner, sollst dich freuen;
Der dunkle Gang führt zu Persephoneien. 7490
In des Olympus hohlem Fuß
Lauscht sie geheim verbotnem Gruß.
Hier hab' ich einst den Orpheus eingeschwärzt,
Benutz' es besser, frisch! beherzt!

Sie steigen hinab.

Am oberen Peneios

wie zuvor.

Sirenen.

7495 Stürzt euch in Peneios Fluth!
Plätschernd ziemt es da zu schwimmen,
Lied um Lieder anzustimmen,
Dem unseligen Volk zu Gut.
Ohne Wasser ist kein Heil!
7500 Führen wir mit hellem Heere
Eilig zum ägäischen Meere,
Würd' uns jede Lust zu Theil.

Erdbeben.

Sirenen.

Schäumend kehrt die Welle wieder,
Fließt nicht mehr im Bett darnieder;
7505 Grund erbebt, das Wasser staucht,
Kies und Ufer berstend raucht.
Flüchten wir! Kommt alle, kommt!
Niemand dem das Wunder frommt.

Fort! ihr edlen frohen Gäste
7510 Zu dem seeisch heitern Feste,
Blinkend, wo die Zitterwellen,
Ufernetzend, leise schwellen;

Da wo Luna doppelt leuchtet,
Uns mit heil'gem Thau befeuchtet.
Dort ein freibewegtes Leben, 7515
Hier ein ängstlich Erde-Beben;
Eile jeder Kluge fort!
Schauderhaft ist's um den Ort.

Seismos in der Tiefe brummend und polternd.

Einmal noch mit Kraft geschoben,
Mit den Schultern brav gehoben! 7520
So gelangen wir nach oben,
Wo uns alles weichen muß.

Sphinxe.

Welch ein widerwärtig Zittern,
Häßlich grausenhaftes Wittern!
Welch ein Schwanken, welches Beben, 7525
Schaukelnd Hin- und Widerstreben!
Welch unleidlicher Verdruß!
Doch wir ändern nicht die Stelle,
Bräche los die ganze Hölle.

Nun erhebt sich ein Gewölbe 7530
Wundersam. Es ist derselbe,
Jener Alte, längst Ergraute,
Der die Insel Delos baute,
Einer Kreißenden zu Lieb'
Aus der Wog' empor sie trieb. 7535
Er, mit Streben, Drängen, Drücken,
Arme straff, gekrümmt den Rücken,
Wie ein Atlas an Gebärde,
Hebt er Boden, Rasen, Erde,

7540 Kies und Gries und Sand und Letten,
Unsres Ufers stille Betten.
So zerreißt er eine Strecke
Quer des Thales ruhige Decke.
Angestrengtest, nimmer müde,
7545 Colossale Karyatide;
Trägt ein furchtbar Steingerüste,
Noch im Boden bis zur Büste;
Weiter aber soll's nicht kommen,
Sphinxe haben Platz genommen.

Seismos.

7550 Das hab' ich ganz allein vermittelt,
Man wird mir's endlich zugestehn;
Und hätt' ich nicht geschüttelt und gerüttelt,
Wie wäre diese Welt so schön? —
Wie ständen eure Berge droben
7555 In prächtig-reinem Ätherblau,
Hätt' ich sie nicht hervorgeschoben
Zu mahlerisch-entzückter Schau!
Als, angesichts der höchsten Ahnen,
Der Nacht, des Chaos, ich mich stark betrug
7560 Und, in Gesellschaft von Titanen,
Mit Pelion und Ossa als mit Ballen schlug.
Wir tollten fort in jugendlicher Hitze,
Bis überdrüssig, noch zuletzt,
Wir dem Parnaß, als eine Doppelmütze,
7565 Die beiden Berge frevelnd aufgesetzt ....
Apollen hält ein froh Verweilen
Dort nun mit seliger Musen Chor.
Selbst Jupitern und seinen Donnerkeilen
Hob ich den Sessel hoch empor.

Jetzt so, mit ungeheurem Streben, 7570
Drang aus dem Abgrund ich herauf
Und fordre laut, zu neuem Leben,
Mir fröhliche Bewohner auf.

Sphinxe.

Uralt müßte man gestehen
Sei das hier Emporgebürgte, 7575
Hätten wir nicht selbst gesehen
Wie sich's aus dem Boden würgte.
Bebuschter Wald verbreitet sich hinan,
Noch drängt sich Fels auf Fels bewegt heran;
Ein Sphinx wird sich daran nicht kehren: 7580
Wir lassen uns im heiligen Sitz nicht stören.

Greife.

Gold in Blättchen, Gold in Flittern
Durch die Ritzen seh' ich zittern.
Laßt euch solchen Schatz nicht rauben;
Imsen auf! es auszuklauben. 7585

Chor der Ameisen.

Wie ihn die Riesigen
Empor geschoben,
Ihr Zappelfüßigen
Geschwind nach oben!
Behendest aus und ein! 7590
In solchen Ritzen
Ist jedes Bröselein
Werth zu besitzen.
Das Allermindeste
Müßt ihr entdecken 7595
Auf das geschwindeste

In allen Ecken.
Allemsig müßt ihr sein,
Ihr Wimmelschaaren;
7600 Nur mit dem Gold herein!
Den Berg laßt fahren.

Greife.

Herein! Herein! Nur Gold zu Hauf,
Wir legen unsre Klauen drauf;
Sind Riegel von der besten Art,
7605 Der größte Schatz ist wohl verwahrt.

Pygmäen.

Haben wirklich Platz genommen,
Wissen nicht wie es geschah.
Fraget nicht woher wir kommen,
Denn wir sind nun einmal da!
7610 Zu des Lebens lustigem Sitze
Eignet sich ein jedes Land;
Zeigt sich eine Felsenritze,
Ist auch schon der Zwerg zur Hand.
Zwerg und Zwergin, rasch zum Fleiße,
7615 Musterhaft ein jedes Paar;
Weiß nicht, ob es gleicher Weise
Schon im Paradiese war.
Doch wir finden's hier zum besten,
Segnen dankbar unsern Stern;
7620 Denn, im Osten wie im Westen,
Zeugt die Mutter Erde gern.

Daktyle.

Hat sie in einer Nacht
Die Kleinen hervorgebracht;

Sie wird die Kleinsten erzeugen,
Finden auch Ihresgleichen. 7625

Pygmäen-Älteste.

Eilet bequemen
Sitz einzunehmen!
Eilig zum Werke;
Schnelle für Stärke!
Noch ist es Friede; 7630
Baut euch die Schmiede,
Harnisch und Waffen
Dem Heer zu schaffen.

Ihr Imsen alle,
Rührig im Schwalle, 7635
Schafft uns Metalle!
Und ihr Daktyle,
Kleinste, so viele,
Euch sei befohlen
Hölzer zu holen! 7640
Schichtet zusammen
Heimliche Flammen,
Schaffet uns Kohlen.

Generalissimus.

Mit Pfeil und Bogen
Frisch ausgezogen! 7645
An jenem Weiher
Schießt mir die Reiher,
Unzählig nistende,
Hochmüthig brüstende,
Auf einen Ruck! 7650

Alle wie Einen;
Daß wir erscheinen
Mit Helm und Schmuck.

Imsen und Daktyle.

Wer wird uns retten!
7655 Wir schaffen 's Eisen,
Sie schmieden Ketten.
Uns loszureißen
Ist noch nicht zeitig,
Drum seid geschmeidig.

Die Kraniche des Ibykus.

7660 Mordgeschrei und Sterbeklagen!
Ängstlich Flügelflatterschlagen!
Welch ein Ächzen, welch Gestöhn
Dringt herauf zu unsern Höhn!
Alle sind sie schon ertödtet,
7665 See von ihrem Blut geröthet;
Mißgestaltete Begierde
Raubt des Reihers edle Zierde.
Weht sie doch schon auf dem Helme
Dieser Fettbauch=Krummbein=Schelme.
7670 Ihr Genossen unsres Heeres,
Reihenwanderer des Meeres,
Euch berufen wir zur Rache
In so nahverwandter Sache;
Keiner spare Kraft und Blut,
7675 Ewige Feindschaft dieser Brut!

Zerstreuen sich krächzend in den Lüften.

Mephistopheles in der Ebne.

Die nordischen Hexen wußt' ich wohl zu meistern,
Mir wird's nicht just mit diesen fremden Geistern.
Der Blocksberg bleibt ein gar bequem Local,
Wo man auch sei, man findet sich zumal.
Frau Ilse wacht für uns auf ihrem Stein, 7680
Auf seiner Höh wird Heinrich munter sein,
Die Schnarcher schnauzen zwar das Elend an,
Doch alles ist für tausend Jahr gethan.
Wer weiß denn hier nur, wo er geht und steht,
Ob unter ihm sich nicht der Boden bläht?.. 7685
Ich wandle lustig durch ein glattes Thal
Und hinter mir erhebt sich auf einmal
Ein Berg, zwar kaum ein Berg zu nennen,
Von meinen Sphinxen mich jedoch zu trennen
Schon hoch genug — hier zuckt noch manches Feuer 7690
Das Thal hinab, und flammt um's Abentheuer...
Noch tanzt und schwebt mir lockend, weichend vor,
Spitzbübisch gaukelnd, der galante Chor.
Nur sachte drauf! Allzugewohnt an's Naschen
Wo es auch sei, man sucht was zu erhaschen. 7695

Lamien Mephistopheles nach sich ziehend.

Geschwind, geschwinder!
Und immer weiter!
Dann wieder zaudernd,
Geschwätzig plaudernd.
Es ist so heiter 7700
Den alten Sünder
Uns nach zu ziehen,
Zu schwerer Buße.
Mit starrem Fuße

7705 Kommt er geholpert,
Einher gestolpert;
Er schleppt das Bein,
Wie wir ihn fliehen,
Uns hinterdrein.

Mephistopheles stillstehend.

7710 Verflucht Geschick! Betrogne Mannsen!
Von Adam her verführte Hansen!
Alt wird man wohl, wer aber klug?
Warst du nicht schon vernarrt genug!

Man weiß, das Volk taugt aus dem Grunde nichts,
7715 Geschnürten Leibs, geschminkten Angesichts.
Nichts haben sie Gesundes zu erwidern,
Wo man sie anfaßt, morsch in allen Gliedern.
Man weiß, man sieht's, man kann es greifen,
Und dennoch tanzt man, wenn die Luder pfeifen!

Lamien innehaltend.

7720 Halt! er besinnt sich, zaudert, steht;
Entgegnet ihm daß er euch nicht entgeht!

Mephistopheles fortschreitend.

Nur zu! und laß dich in's Gewebe
Der Zweifelei nicht thörig ein;
Denn wenn es keine Hexen gäbe,
7725 Wer Teufel möchte Teufel sein!

Lamien anmuthigst.

Kreisen wir um diesen Helden;
Liebe wird in seinem Herzen
Sich gewiß für Eine melden.

Mephistopheles.

Zwar bei ungewissem Schimmer
Scheint ihr hübsche Frauenzimmer, 7730
Und so möcht' ich euch nicht schelten.

Empuse eindringend.

Auch nicht mich! als eine solche
Laßt mich ein in eure Folge.

Lamien.

Die ist in unserm Kreis zuviel,
Verdirbt doch immer unser Spiel. 7735

Empuse zu Mephistopheles.

Begrüßt von Mühmichen Empuse,
Der Trauten mit dem Eselsfuße;
Du hast nur einen Pferdefuß
Und doch, Herr Vetter, schönsten Gruß!

Mephistopheles.

Hier dacht' ich lauter Unbekannte 7740
Und finde leider Nahverwandte;
Es ist ein altes Buch zu blättern:
Vom Harz bis Hellas immer Vettern!

Empuse.

Entschieden weiß ich gleich zu handeln,
In vieles könnt' ich mich verwandeln; 7745
Doch euch zu Ehren hab' ich jetzt
Das Eselsköpfchen aufgesetzt.

Mephistopheles.

Ich merk' es hat bei diesen Leuten
Verwandtschaft Großes zu bedeuten;

7750 Doch mag sich was auch will eräugnen,
Den Eselskopf möcht' ich verläugnen.

Lamien.

Laß diese Garstige, sie verscheucht
Was irgend schön und lieblich deucht;
Was irgend schön und lieblich wär',
7755 Sie kommt heran, es ist nicht mehr!

Mephistopheles.

Auch diese Mühmchen, zart und schmächtig,
Sie sind mir allesammt verdächtig;
Und hinter solcher Wänglein Rosen
Fürcht' ich doch auch Metamorphosen.

Lamien.

7760 Versuch' es doch! sind unsrer viele.
Greif' zu! Und hast du Glück im Spiele,
Erhasche dir das beste Loos.
Was soll das lüsterne Geleier?
Du bist ein miserabler Freier,
7765 Stolzirst einher und thust so groß! —
Nun mischt er sich in unsre Schaaren;
Laßt nach und nach die Masken fahren
Und gebt ihm euer Wesen bloß.

Mephistopheles.

Die Schönste hab' ich mir erlesen....

Sie umfassend.

7770 O weh mir! welch ein dürrer Besen!

Eine andere ergreifend.

Und diese?.... Schmähliches Gesicht!

Lamien.

Verdienst du's besser? dünk' es nicht.

Mephistopheles.

Die Kleine möcht' ich mir verpfänden....
Lacerte schlüpft mir aus den Händen!
Und schlangenhaft der glatte Zopf. 7775
Dagegen fass' ich mir die Lange....
Da pack' ich eine Thyrsusstange!
Den Pinienapfel als den Kopf.
Wo will's hinaus?.... Noch eine Dicke,
An der ich mich vielleicht erquicke; 7780
Zum letztenmal gewagt! Es sei!
Recht quammig, quappig, das bezahlen
Mit hohem Preis Orientalen....
Doch ach! der Bovist platzt entzwei!

Lamien.

Fahrt auseinander, schwankt und schwebet 7785
Blitzartig, schwarzen Flugs umgebet
Den eingedrungnen Hexensohn!
Unsichre, schauderhafte Kreise!
Schweigsamen Fittigs, Fledermäuse!
Zu wohlfeil kommt er doch davon. 7790

Mephistopheles sich schüttlend.

Viel klüger, scheint es, bin ich nicht geworden;
Absurd ist's hier, absurd im Norden,
Gespenster hier wie dort vertrackt,
Volk und Poeten abgeschmackt.
Ist eben hier eine Mummenschanz, 7795
Wie überall ein Sinnentanz.

Ich griff nach holden Maskenzügen
Und faßte Wesen daß mich's schauerte . . . .
Ich möchte gerne mich betrügen,
7800 Wenn es nur länger dauerte.

Sich zwischen dem Gestein verirrend.

Wo bin ich denn? Wo will's hinaus?
Das war ein Pfad, nun ist's ein Graus.
Ich kam daher auf glatten Wegen,
Und jetzt steht mir Geröll entgegen.
7805 Vergebens klettr' ich auf und nieder,
Wo find' ich meine Sphinxe wieder?
So toll hätt' ich mir's nicht gedacht,
Ein solch Gebirg in Einer Nacht!
Das heiß' ich frischen Hexenritt,
7810 Die bringen ihren Blocksberg mit.

Oreas vom Naturfels.

Herauf hier! Mein Gebirg ist alt,
Steht in ursprünglicher Gestalt.
Verehre schroffe Felsensteige,
Des Pindus letztgedehnte Zweige.
7815 Schon stand ich unerschüttert so
Als über mich Pompejus floh.
Daneben, das Gebild des Wahns
Verschwindet schon bei'm Krähn des Hahns.
Dergleichen Mährchen seh' ich oft entstehn
7820 Und plötzlich wieder untergehn.

Mephistopheles.

Sei Ehre dir, ehrwürdiges Haupt!
Von hoher Eichenkraft umlaubt;

Der allerklarste Mondenschein
Dringt nicht zur Finsterniß herein. —
Doch neben am Gebüsche zieht 7825
Ein Licht das gar bescheiden glüht.
Wie sich das alles fügen muß!
Fürwahr! es ist Homunculus.
Woher des Wegs, du Kleingeselle?

Homunculus.

Ich schwebe so von Stell' zu Stelle 7830
Und möchte gern im besten Sinn entstehn,
Voll Ungeduld mein Glas entzwei zu schlagen;
Allein was ich bisher gesehn,
Hinein da möcht' ich mich nicht wagen.
Nur, um dir's im Vertraun zu sagen: 7835
Zwei Philosophen bin ich auf der Spur,
Ich horchte zu, es hieß: Natur! Natur!
Von diesen will ich mich nicht trennen,
Sie müssen doch das irdische Wesen kennen;
Und ich erfahre wohl am Ende 7840
Wohin ich mich am allerklügsten wende.

Mephistopheles.

Das thu' auf deine eigne Hand.
Denn, wo Gespenster Platz genommen,
Ist auch der Philosoph willkommen.
Damit man seiner Kunst und Gunst sich freue, 7845
Erschafft er gleich ein Dutzend neue.
Wenn du nicht irrst, kommst du nicht zu Verstand!
Willst du entstehn, entsteh auf eigne Hand!

Homunculus.

Ein guter Rath ist auch nicht zu verschmähn.

Mephistopheles.

7850 So fahre hin! Wir wollen's weiter sehn.

Trennen sich.

Anaxagoras zu Thales.

Dein starrer Sinn will sich nicht beugen,
Bedarf es Weitres dich zu überzeugen?

Thales.

Die Welle beugt sich jedem Winde gern,
Doch hält sie sich vom schroffen Felsen fern.

Anaxagoras.

7855 Durch Feuerdunst ist dieser Fels zu Handen.

Thales.

Im Feuchten ist Lebendiges erstanden.

Homunculus zwischen beiden.

Laßt mich an eurer Seite gehn,
Mir selbst gelüstet's zu entstehn!

Anaxagoras.

Hast du, o Thales, je, in Einer Nacht,
7860 Solch einen Berg aus Schlamm hervorgebracht?

Thales.

Nie war Natur und ihr lebendiges Fließen
Auf Tag und Nacht und Stunden angewiesen.
Sie bildet regelnd jegliche Gestalt,
Und selbst im Großen ist es nicht Gewalt.

Anaxagoras.

7865 Hier aber war's! Plutonisch grimmig Feuer,
Äolischer Dünste Knallkraft ungeheuer

Durchbrach des flachen Bodens alte Kruste
Daß neu ein Berg sogleich entstehen mußte.

Thales.

Was wird dadurch nun weiter fortgesetzt?
Er ist auch da, und das ist gut zuletzt. 7870
Mit solchem Streit verliert man Zeit und Weile
Und führt doch nur geduldig Volk am Seile.

Anaxagoras.

Schnell quillt der Berg von Myrmidonen,
Die Felsenspalten zu bewohnen,
Pygmäen, Imsen, Däumerlinge 7875
Und andre thätig kleine Dinge.

Zum Homunculus.

Nie hast du Großem nachgestrebt,
Einsiedlerisch-beschränkt gelebt;
Kannst du zur Herrschaft dich gewöhnen,
So lass' ich dich als König krönen. 7880

Homunculus.

Was sagt mein Thales?

Thales.

Will's nicht rathen;
Mit Kleinen thut man kleine Thaten,
Mit Großen wird der Kleine groß.
Sieh hin! die schwarze Kranich-Wolke!
Sie droht dem aufgeregten Volke 7885
Und würde so dem König drohn.
Mit scharfen Schnäbeln, krallen Beinen,
Sie stechen nieder auf die Kleinen;
Verhängniß wetterleuchtet schon.

7890 Ein Frevel tödtete die Reiher,
Umstellend ruhigen Friedensweiher.
Doch jener Mordgeschosse Regen
Schafft grausam-blut'gen Rache-Segen,
Erregt der Nahverwandten Wuth
7895 Nach der Pygmäen frevlem Blut.
Was nützt nun Schild und Helm und Speer?
Was hilft der Reiherstrahl den Zwergen?
Wie sich Daktyl und Imse bergen!
Schon wankt, es flieht, es stürzt das Heer.

Anaxagoras nach einer Pause feierlich.

7900 Konnt' ich bisher die Unterirdischen loben,
So wend' ich mich in diesem Fall nach oben....
Du! droben ewig unveraltete,
Dreinamig-Dreigestaltete,
Dich ruf' ich an bei meines Volkes Weh,
7905 Diana, Luna, Hekate!
Du Brust-erweiternde, im-Tiefsten-sinnige,
Du ruhig-scheinende, gewaltsam-innige,
Eröffne deiner Schatten grausen Schlund,
Die alte Macht sei ohne Zauber kund!

Pause.

7910 Bin ich zu schnell erhört!
Hat mein Flehn
Nach jenen Höhn
Die Ordnung der Natur gestört?

Und größer, immer größer nahet schon
7915 Der Göttin rundumschriebner Thron,
Dem Auge furchtbar, ungeheuer!
In's Düstre röthet sich sein Feuer..

Nicht näher! drohend-mächtige Runde,
Du richtest uns und Land und Meer zu Grunde!

So wär' es wahr, daß dich thessalische Frauen, 7920
In frevlend magischem Vertrauen,
Von deinem Pfad herabgesungen?
Verderblichstes dir abgerungen? . . .
Das lichte Schild hat sich umdunkelt,
Auf einmal reißt's und blitzt und funkelt! 7925
Welch ein Geprassel! Welch ein Zischen!
Ein Donnern, Windgethüm dazwischen! —
Demüthig zu des Thrones Stufen! —
Verzeiht! Ich hab' es hergerufen.

Wirft sich auf's Angesicht.

Thales.

Was dieser Mann nicht alles hört' und sah! 7930
Ich weiß nicht recht wie uns geschah;
Auch hab' ich's nicht mit ihm empfunden.
Gestehen wir, es sind verrückte Stunden,
Und Luna wiegt sich ganz bequem
An ihrem Platz so wie vordem. 7935

Homunculus.

Schaut hin nach der Pygmäen Sitz,
Der Berg war rund, jetzt ist er spitz.
Ich spürt' ein ungeheures Prallen,
Der Fels war aus dem Mond gefallen,
Gleich hat er, ohne nachzufragen, 7940
So Freund als Feind gequetscht, erschlagen.
Doch muß ich solche Künste loben,
Die schöpferisch, in einer Nacht,

Zugleich von unten und von oben,
7945 Dieß Berggebäu zu Stand gebracht.

Thales.

Sei ruhig! Es war nur gedacht.
Sie fahre hin die garstige Brut!
Daß du nicht König warst ist gut.
Nun fort zum heitern Meeresfeste,
7950 Dort hofft und ehrt man Wundergäste.

Entfernen sich.

Mephistopheles an der Gegenseite kletternd.

Da muß ich mich durch steile Felsentreppen,
Durch alter Eichen starre Wurzeln schleppen!
Auf meinem Harz der harzige Dunst
Hat was vom Pech und das hat meine Gunst;
7955 Zunächst der Schwefel. . . . . Hier, bei diesen Griechen
Ist von dergleichen kaum die Spur zu riechen;
Neugierig aber wär' ich, nachzuspüren
Womit sie Höllenqual und Flamme schüren.

Dryas.

In deinem Lande sei einheimisch klug,
7960 Im fremden bist du nicht gewandt genug.
Du solltest nicht den Sinn zur Heimath kehren,
Der heiligen Eichen Würde hier verehren.

Mephistopheles.

Man denkt an das was man verließ,
Was man gewohnt war bleibt ein Paradies.
7965 Doch sagt: was in der Höhle dort,
Bei schwachem Licht, sich dreifach hingekauert?

Dryas.

Die Phorkyaden! Wage dich zum Ort
Und sprich sie an, wenn dich nicht schauert.

Mephistopheles.

Warum denn nicht! — Ich sehe was, und staune.
So stolz ich bin, muß ich mir selbst gestehn: 7970
Dergleichen hab' ich nie gesehn,
Die sind ja schlimmer als Alraune. . . .
Wird man die urverworfnen Sünden
Im mindesten noch häßlich finden,
Wenn man dieß Dreigethüm erblickt? 7975
Wir litten sie nicht auf den Schwellen
Der grauenvollsten unsrer Höllen.
Hier wurzelt's in der Schönheit Land,
Das wird mit Ruhm antik genannt. . . .
Sie regen sich, sie scheinen mich zu spüren, 7980
Sie zwitschern pfeifend, Fledermaus-Vampyren.

Phorkyas.

Gebt mir das Auge, Schwestern, daß es frage,
Wer sich so nah an unsre Tempel wage.

Mephistopheles.

Verehrteste! Erlaubt mir euch zu nahen
Und euren Segen dreifach zu empfahen. 7985
Ich trete vor, zwar noch als Unbekannter,
Doch, irr' ich nicht, weitläufiger Verwandter.
Altwürdige Götter hab' ich schon erblickt,
Vor Ops und Rhea tieffstens mich gebückt.
Die Parzen selbst, des Chaos, eure Schwestern, 7990
Ich sah sie gestern — oder ehegestern;

Doch Euresgleichen hab' ich nie erblickt,
Ich schweige nun und fühle mich entzückt.

Phorkyaden.

Er scheint Verstand zu haben dieser Geist.

Mephistopheles.

7995 Nur wundert's mich daß euch kein Dichter preis't.
Und sagt! wie kam's, wie konnte das geschehn?
Im Bilde hab' ich nie euch Würdigste gesehn;
Versuch's der Meißel doch euch zu erreichen,
Nicht Juno, Pallas, Venus und dergleichen.

Phorkyaden.

8000 Versenkt in Einsamkeit und stillste Nacht
Hat unser Drei noch nie daran gedacht!

Mephistopheles.

Wie sollt' es auch? da ihr, der Welt entrückt,
Hier niemand seht und niemand euch erblickt.
Da müßtet ihr an solchen Orten wohnen
8005 Wo Pracht und Kunst auf gleichem Sitze thronen,
Wo jeden Tag, behend, im Doppelschritt,
Ein Marmorblock als Held in's Leben tritt.
Wo —

Phorkyaden.

Schweige still und gib uns kein Gelüsten!
Was hülf' es uns und wenn wir's besser wüßten?
8010 In Nacht geboren, Nächtlichem verwandt,
Beinah uns selbst, ganz allen unbekannt.

Mephistopheles.

In solchem Fall hat es nicht viel zu sagen,
Man kann sich selbst auch andern übertragen.

Euch Dreien g'nügt Ein Auge, g'nügt Ein Zahn,
Da ging' es wohl auch mythologisch an 8015
In zwei die Wesenheit der drei zu fassen,
Der dritten Bildniß mir zu überlassen,
Auf kurze Zeit.

Eine.

Wie dünkt's euch? ging' es an?

Die andern.

Versuchen wir's! — doch ohne Aug' und Zahn.

Mephistopheles.

Nun habt ihr g'rad das Beste weggenommen, 8020
Wie würde da das strengste Bild vollkommen!

Eine.

Drück' du ein Auge zu, 's ist leicht geschehn,
Laß alsofort den Einen Raffzahn sehn,
Und, im Profil, wirst du sogleich erreichen
Geschwisterlich vollkommen uns zu gleichen. 8025

Mephistopheles.

Viel Ehr'! Es sei!

Phorkyaden.

Es sei!

Mephistopheles als Phorkyas im Profil.

Da steh' ich schon,
Des Chaos vielgeliebter Sohn!

Phorkyaden.

Des Chaos Töchter sind wir unbestritten.

Mephistopheles.

Man schilt mich nun, o Schmach! Hermaphroditen.

Phorkyaden.

8030 Im neuen Drei der Schwestern welche Schöne!
Wir haben zwei der Augen, zwei der Zähne.

Mephistopheles.

Vor aller Augen muß ich mich verstecken,
Im Höllenpfuhl die Teufel zu erschrecken.

Ab.

Felsbuchten des ägäischen Meers.

Mond im Zenith verharrend.

Sirenen
auf den Klippen umher gelagert, flötend und singend.

Haben sonst bei nächtigem Grauen
Dich thessalische Zauberfrauen 8035
Frevelhaft herabgezogen,
Blicke ruhig von dem Bogen
Deiner Nacht auf Zitterwogen
Mildeblitzend Glanzgewimmel
Und erleuchte das Getümmel 8040
Das sich aus den Wogen hebt.
Dir zu jedem Dienst erbötig,
Schöne Luna, sei uns gnädig!

Nereiden und Tritonen als Meerwunder.

Tönet laut in schärfern Tönen,
Die das breite Meer durchdröhnen, 8045
Volk der Tiefe ruft fortan!
Vor des Sturmes grausen Schlünden
Wichen wir zu stillsten Gründen,
Holder Sang zieht uns heran.

8050 Seht! Wie wir im Hochentzücken
Uns mit goldenen Ketten schmücken,
Auch zu Kron- und Edelsteinen
Spang- und Gürtelschmuck vereinen.
Alles das ist eure Frucht.
8055 Schätze, scheiternd hier verschlungen,
Habt ihr uns herangesungen,
Ihr Dämonen unsrer Bucht.

Sirenen.

Wissen's wohl, in Meeresfrische
Glatt behagen sich die Fische,
8060 Schwanken Lebens ohne Leid;
Doch! Ihr festlich regen Schaaren,
Heute möchten wir erfahren
Daß ihr mehr als Fische seid.

Nereiden und Tritonen.

Ehe wir hieher gekommen
8065 Haben wir's zu Sinn genommen,
Schwestern, Brüder, jetzt geschwind!
Heut bedarf's der kleinsten Reise
Zum vollgültigsten Beweise
Daß wir mehr als Fische sind.

Entfernen sich.

Sirenen.

8070 Fort sind sie im Nu!
Nach Samothrace g'rade zu,
Verschwunden mit günstigem Wind.
Was denken sie zu vollführen
Im Reiche der hohen Kabiren?

Sind Götter! Wundersam eigen, 8075
Die sich immerfort selbst erzeugen
Und niemals wissen was sie sind.

Bleibe auf deinen Höhn,
Holde Luna, gnädig stehn;
Daß es nächtig verbleibe, 8080
Uns der Tag nicht vertreibe.

Thales am Ufer zu Homunculus.

Ich führte dich zum alten Nereus gern;
Zwar sind wir nicht von seiner Höhle fern,
Doch hat er einen harten Kopf,
Der widerwärtige Sauertopf. 8085
Das ganze menschliche Geschlecht
Macht's ihm, dem Griesgram, nimmer recht.
Doch ist die Zukunft ihm entdeckt,
Dafür hat jedermann Respect
Und ehret ihn auf seinem Posten; 8090
Auch hat er manchem wohlgethan.

Homunculus.

Probiren wir's und klopfen an!
Nicht gleich wird's Glas und Flamme kosten.

Nereus.

Sind's Menschenstimmen die mein Ohr vernimmt?
Wie es mir gleich im tiefsten Herzen grimmt! 8095
Gebilde, strebsam Götter zu erreichen,
Und doch verdammt sich immer selbst zu gleichen.
Seit alten Jahren konnt' ich göttlich ruhn,
Doch trieb mich's an den Besten wohlzuthun;

8100 Und schaut' ich dann zuletzt vollbrachte Thaten,
So war es ganz als hätt' ich nicht gerathen.

Thales.

Und doch, o Greis des Meers, vertraut man dir;
Du bist der Weise, treib' uns nicht von hier!
Schau' diese Flamme, menschenähnlich zwar,
8105 Sie deinem Rath ergibt sich ganz und gar.

Nereus.

Was Rath! Hat Rath bei Menschen je gegolten?
Ein kluges Wort erstarrt im harten Ohr.
So oft auch That sich grimmig selbst gescholten,
Bleibt doch das Volk selbstwillig wie zuvor.
8110 Wie hab' ich Paris väterlich gewarnt,
Eh' sein Gelüst ein fremdes Weib umgarnt.
Am griechischen Ufer stand er kühnlich da,
Ihm kündet' ich was ich im Geiste sah:
Die Lüfte qualmend, überströmend Roth,
8115 Gebälke glühend, unten Mord und Tod:
Troja's Gerichtstag, rhythmisch festgebannt,
Jahrtausenden so schrecklich als gekannt.
Des Alten Wort dem Frechen schien's ein Spiel,
Er folgte seiner Lust und Ilios fiel —
8120 Ein Riesenleichnam, starr nach langer Qual,
Des Pindus Adlern gar willkommnes Mahl.
Ulyssen auch! sagt' ich ihm nicht voraus
Der Circe Listen, des Cyklopen Graus?
Das Zaudern sein, der Seinen leichten Sinn,
8125 Und was nicht alles! Bracht' ihm das Gewinn?
Bis vielgeschaukelt ihn, doch spät genug,
Der Woge Gunst an gastlich Ufer trug.

Thales.

Dem weisen Mann gibt solch Betragen Qual,
Der gute doch versucht es noch einmal.
Ein Quentchen Danks wird, hoch ihn zu vergnügen, 8130
Die Centner Undanks völlig überwiegen.
Denn nicht Geringes haben wir zu flehn:
Der Knabe da wünscht weislich zu entstehn.

Nereus.

Verderbt mir nicht den seltensten Humor!
Ganz andres steht mir heute noch bevor: 8135
Die Töchter hab' ich alle herbeschieden,
Die Grazien des Meeres, die Doriden.
Nicht der Olymp, nicht euer Boden trägt
Ein schön Gebild das sich so zierlich regt.
Sie werfen sich, anmuthigster Gebärde, 8140
Vom Wasserdrachen auf Neptunus Pferde,
Dem Element auf's zarteste vereint,
Daß selbst der Schaum sie noch zu heben scheint.
Im Farbenspiel von Venus Muschelwagen
Kommt Galatee, die schönste, nun getragen, 8145
Die, seit sich Kypris von uns abgekehrt,
In Paphos wird als Göttin selbst verehrt.
Und so besitzt die Holde, lange schon,
Als Erbin, Tempelstadt und Wagenthron.

Hinweg! Es ziemt, in Vaterfreudenstunde, 8150
Nicht Haß dem Herzen, Scheltwort nicht dem Munde.
Hinweg zu Proteus! Fragt den Wundermann:
Wie man entstehn und sich verwandlen kann.

Entfernt sich gegen das Meer.

Thales.

Wir haben nichts durch diesen Schritt gewonnen,
8155 Trifft man auch Proteus, gleich ist er zerronnen;
Und steht er euch, so sagt er nur zuletzt
Was staunen macht und in Verwirrung setzt.
Du bist einmal bedürftig solchen Raths,
Versuchen wir's und wandlen unsres Pfads!

Entfernen sich.

Sirenen oben auf den Felsen.

8160 Was sehen wir von weiten
Das Wellenreich durchgleiten?
Als wie nach Windes Regel
Anzögen weiße Segel,
So hell sind sie zu schauen,
8165 Verklärte Meeresfrauen.
Laßt uns herunterklimmen,
Vernehmt ihr doch die Stimmen.

Nereiden und Tritonen.

Was wir auf Händen tragen
Soll allen euch behagen.
8170 Chelonens Riesen-Schilde
Entglänzt ein streng Gebilde:
Sind Götter die wir bringen;
Müßt hohe Lieder singen.

Sirenen.

Klein von Gestalt,
8175 Groß von Gewalt,
Der Scheiternden Retter,
Uralt verehrte Götter.

Nereiden und Tritonen.

Wir bringen die Kabiren,
Ein friedlich Fest zu führen;
Denn wo sie heilig walten, 8180
Neptun wird freundlich schalten.

Sirenen.

Wir stehen euch nach,
Wenn ein Schiff zerbrach,
Unwiderstehbar an Kraft
Schützt ihr die Mannschaft. 8185

Nereiden und Tritonen.

Drei haben wir mitgenommen,
Der vierte wollte nicht kommen,
Er sagte, er sei der rechte
Der für sie alle dächte.

Sirenen.

Ein Gott den andern Gott 8190
Macht wohl zu Spott.
Ehrt ihr alle Gnaden,
Fürchtet jeden Schaden.

Nereiden und Tritonen.

Sind eigentlich ihrer sieben.

Sirenen.

Wo sind die drei geblieben? 8195

Nereiden und Tritonen.

Wir wüßten's nicht zu sagen,
Sind in Olymp zu erfragen;

Dort west't auch wohl der achte,
An den noch niemand dachte.
8200 In Gnaden uns gewärtig,
Doch alle noch nicht fertig.

Diese unvergleichlichen
Wollen immer weiter,
Sehnsuchtsvolle Hungerleider
8205 Nach dem Unerreichlichen.

Sirenen.

Wir sind gewohnt,
Wo es auch thront,
In Sonn' und Mond
Hinzubeten, es lohnt.

Nereiden und Tritonen.

8210 Wie unser Ruhm zum höchsten prangt
Dieses Fest anzuführen!

Sirenen.

Die Helden des Alterthums
Ermangeln des Ruhms,
Wo und wie er auch prangt,
8215 Wenn sie das goldne Vließ erlangt,
Ihr die Kabiren.

Wiederholt als Allgesang.

Wenn sie das goldne Vließ erlangt,
Wir! ihr! die Kabiren.

Nereiden und Tritonen ziehen vorüber.

Homunculus.

Die Ungestalten seh' ich an
Als irden-schlechte Töpfe, 8220
Nun stoßen sich die Weisen dran
Und brechen harte Köpfe.

Thales.

Das ist es ja was man begehrt,
Der Rost macht erst die Münze werth.

Proteus unbemerkt.

So etwas freut mich alten Fabler! 8225
Je wunderlicher desto respectabler.

Thales.

Wo bist du, Proteus?

Proteus bauchrednerisch, bald nah, bald fern.

Hier! und hier!

Thales.

Den alten Scherz verzeih' ich dir;
Doch, einem Freund nicht eitle Worte!
Ich weiß, du sprichst vom falschen Orte. 8230

Proteus als aus der Ferne.

Leb' wohl!

Thales leise zu Homunculus.

Er ist ganz nah. Nun leuchte frisch,
Er ist neugierig wie ein Fisch;
Und wo er auch gestaltet stockt,
Durch Flammen wird er hergelockt.

Homunculus.

8235 Ergieß' ich gleich des Lichtes Menge,
Bescheiden doch, daß ich das Glas nicht sprenge.

Proteus in Gestalt einer Riesen-Schildkröte.

Was leuchtet so anmuthig schön?

Thales den Homunculus verhüllend.

Gut! Wenn du Lust hast, kannst du's näher sehn.
Die kleine Mühe laß dich nicht verdrießen
8240 Und zeige dich auf menschlich beiden Füßen.
Mit unsern Gunsten sei's, mit unserm Willen,
Wer schauen will was wir verhüllen.

Proteus edel gestaltet.

Weltweise Kniffe sind dir noch bewußt.

Thales.

Gestalt zu wechseln bleibt noch deine Lust.

Hat den Homunculus enthüllt.

Proteus erstaunt.

8245 Ein leuchtend Zwerglein! Niemals noch gesehn!

Thales.

Es fragt um Rath und möchte gern entstehn.
Er ist, wie ich von ihm vernommen,
Gar wundersam nur halb zur Welt gekommen.
Ihm fehlt es nicht an geistigen Eigenschaften,
8250 Doch gar zu sehr am greiflich Tüchtighaften.
Bis jetzt gibt ihm das Glas allein Gewicht,
Doch wär' er gern zunächst verkörperlicht.

Proteus.

Du bist ein wahrer Jungfern-Sohn,
Eh' du sein solltest bist du schon!

Thales leise.

Auch scheint es mir von andrer Seite kritisch, 8255
Er ist, mich dünkt, hermaphroditisch.

Proteus.

Da muß es desto eher glücken,
So wie er anlangt wird sich's schicken.
Doch gilt es hier nicht viel Besinnen,
Im weiten Meere mußt du anbeginnen! 8260
Da fängt man erst im Kleinen an
Und freut sich Kleinste zu verschlingen,
Man wächs't so nach und nach heran
Und bildet sich zu höherem Vollbringen.

Homunculus.

Hier weht gar eine weiche Luft, 8265
Es grunelt so und mir behagt der Duft!

Proteus.

Das glaub' ich, allerliebster Junge!
Und weiter hin wird's viel behäglicher,
Auf dieser schmalen Strandeszunge
Der Dunstkreis noch unsäglicher; 8270
Da vorne sehen wir den Zug,
Der eben herschwebt, nah genug.
Kommt mit dahin!

Thales.

Ich gehe mit.

Homunculus.

Dreifach merkwürd'ger Geisterschritt!

Telchinen von Rhodus

auf Hippokampen und Meerdrachen, Neptunens Dreizack handhabend.

Chor.

8275 Wir haben den Dreizack Neptunen geschmiedet
Womit er die regesten Wellen begütet.
Entfaltet der Donnrer die Wolken, die vollen,
Entgegnet Neptunus dem greulichen Rollen;
Und wie auch von oben es zackig erblitzt,
8280 Wird Woge nach Woge von unten gespritzt;
Und was auch dazwischen in Ängsten gerungen,
Wird, lange geschleudert, vom Tiefsten verschlungen,
Weßhalb er uns heute den Scepter gereicht,
Nun schweben wir festlich, beruhigt und leicht.

Sirenen.

8285 Euch, dem Helios Geweihten,
Heitern Tags Gebenedeiten,
Gruß zur Stunde, die bewegt
Luna's Hochverehrung regt!

Telchinen.

Allieblichste Göttin am Bogen da droben!
8290 Du hörst mit Entzücken den Bruder beloben.

Der seligen Rhodus verleihst du ein Ohr,
Dort steigt ihm ein ewiger Päan hervor.
Beginnt er den Tagslauf und ist es gethan,
Er blickt uns mit feurigem Strahlenblick an.
Die Berge, die Städte, die Ufer, die Welle 8295
Gefallen dem Gotte, sind lieblich und helle.
Kein Nebel umschwebt uns, und schleicht er sich ein,
Ein Strahl und ein Lüftchen, die Insel ist rein!
Da schaut sich der Hohe in hundert Gebilden,
Als Jüngling, als Riesen, den großen, den milden. 8300
Wir ersten wir waren's, die Göttergewalt
Aufstellten in würdiger Menschengestalt.

Proteus.

Laß du sie singen, laß sie prahlen!
Der Sonne heiligen Lebestrahlen
Sind todte Werke nur ein Spaß. 8305
Das bildet, schmelzend, unverdrossen;
Und haben sie's in Erz gegossen,
Dann denken sie, es wäre was.
Was ist's zuletzt mit diesen Stolzen?
Die Götterbilder standen groß, — 8310
Zerstörte sie ein Erdestoß;
Längst sind sie wieder eingeschmolzen.

Das Erdetreiben, wie's auch sei,
Ist immer doch nur Plackerei;
Dem Leben frommt die Welle besser; 8315
Dich trägt in's ewige Gewässer
Proteus-Delphin.

Er verwandelt sich.

Schon ist's gethan!

Da soll es dir zum schönsten glücken,
Ich nehme dich auf meinen Rücken,
8320 Vermähle dich dem Ocean.

Thales.

Gib nach dem löblichen Verlangen
Von vorn die Schöpfung anzufangen!
Zu raschem Wirken sei bereit!
Da regst du dich nach ewigen Normen,
8325 Durch tausend, abertausend Formen,
Und bis zum Menschen hast du Zeit.

Homunculus besteigt den Proteus-Delphin.

Proteus.

Komm geistig mit in feuchte Weite,
Da lebst du gleich in Läng' und Breite,
Beliebig regest du dich hier;
8330 Nur strebe nicht nach höheren Orden,
Denn bist du erst ein Mensch geworden,
Dann ist es völlig aus mit dir.

Thales.

Nachdem es kommt; 's ist auch wohl fein
Ein wackrer Mann zu seiner Zeit zu sein.

Proteus zu Thales.

8335 So einer wohl von deinem Schlag!
Das hält noch eine Weile nach;
Denn unter bleichen Geisterschaaren
Seh' ich dich schon seit vielen hundert Jahren.

S i r e n e n auf den Felsen.

Welch ein Ring von Wölkchen ründet
Um den Mond so reichen Kreis? 8340
Tauben sind es, liebentzündet,
Fittige wie Licht so weiß.
Paphos hat sie hergesendet,
Ihre brünstige Vogelschaar;
Unser Fest, es ist vollendet, 8345
Heitre Wonne voll und klar!

N e r e u s zu Thales tretend.

Nennte wohl ein nächtiger Wandrer
Diesen Mondhof Lufterscheinung;
Doch wir Geister sind ganz andrer
Und der einzig richtigen Meinung. 8350
Tauben sind es, die begleiten
Meiner Tochter Muschelfahrt,
Wunderflugs besondrer Art,
Angelernt vor alten Zeiten.

T h a l e s.

Auch ich halte das für's Beste 8355
Was dem wackern Mann gefällt,
Wenn im stillen, warmen Neste
Sich ein Heiliges lebend hält.

P s y l l e n und M a r s e n
auf Meerstieren, Meerkälbern und Widdern.

In Cyperns rauhen Höhle-Grüften,
Vom Meergott nicht verschüttet, 8360
Vom Seismos nicht zerrüttet,
Umweht von ewigen Lüften,

Und, wie in den ältesten Tagen,
In still-bewußtem Behagen
8365 Bewahren wir Cypriens Wagen
Und führen, bei'm Säuseln der Nächte,
Durch liebliches Wellengeflechte,
Unsichtbar dem neuen Geschlechte,
Die lieblichste Tochter heran.
8370 Wir leise Geschäftigen scheuen
Weder Adler noch geflügelten Leuen,
Weder Kreuz noch Mond,
Wie es oben wohnt und thront,
Sich wechselnd wegt und regt,
8375 Sich vertreibt und todtschlägt,
Saaten und Städte niederlegt.
Wir, so fortan,
Bringen die lieblichste Herrin heran.

Sirenen.

Leicht bewegt, in mäßiger Eile,
8380 Um den Wagen, Kreis um Kreis,
Bald verschlungen Zeil' an Zeile
Schlangenartig reihenweis,
Naht euch, rüstige Nereiden,
Derbe Fraun, gefällig wild,
8385 Bringet, zärtliche Doriden,
Galateen, der Mutter Bild:
Ernst, den Göttern gleich zu schauen,
Würdiger Unsterblichkeit,
Doch wie holde Menschenfrauen
8390 Lockender Anmuthigkeit.

Doriden.

im Chor an Nereus vorbeiziehend, sämmtlich auf Delphinen.

Leih' uns Luna Licht und Schatten,
Klarheit diesem Jugendflor;
Denn wir zeigen liebe Gatten
Unserm Vater bittend vor.

Zu Nereus.

Knaben sind's, die wir gerettet 8395
Aus der Brandung grimmem Zahn,
Sie, auf Schilf und Moos gebettet,
Aufgewärmt zum Licht heran,
Die es nun mit heißen Küssen
Treulich uns verdanken müssen; 8400
Schau' die Holden günstig an!

Nereus.

Hoch ist der Doppelgewinn zu schätzen:
Barmherzig sein, und sich zugleich ergetzen.

Doriden.

Lobst du, Vater, unser Walten,
Gönnst uns wohl erworbene Lust, 8405
Laß uns fest, unsterblich halten
Sie an ewiger Jugendbrust.

Nereus.

Mögt euch des schönen Fanges freuen,
Den Jüngling bildet euch als Mann;
Allein ich könnte nicht verleihen 8410
Was Zeus allein gewähren kann.
Die Welle, die euch wogt und schaukelt,
Läßt auch der Liebe nicht Bestand,

Und hat die Neigung ausgegaukelt,
8415 So setzt gemächlich sie an's Land.

Doriden.

Ihr, holde Knaben, seid uns werth,
Doch müssen wir traurig scheiden;
Wir haben ewige Treue begehrt,
Die Götter wollen's nicht leiden.

Die Jünglinge.

8420 Wenn ihr uns nur so ferner labt,
Uns wackre Schiffer-Knaben;
Wir haben's nie so gut gehabt
Und wollen's nicht besser haben.

Galatee auf dem Muschelwagen nähert sich

Nereus.

Du bist es, mein Liebchen!

Galatee.

O Vater! das Glück!
8425 Delphine, verweilet! mich fesselt der Blick.

Nereus.

Vorüber schon, sie ziehen vorüber
In kreisenden Schwunges Bewegung;
Was kümmert sie die innre herzliche Regung!
Ach! nähmen sie mich mit hinüber!
8430 Doch ein einziger Blick ergetzt,
Daß er das ganze Jahr ersetzt.

Thales.

Heil! Heil! auf's neue!
Wie ich mich blühend freue,
Vom Schönen, Wahren durchdrungen...
Alles ist aus dem Wasser entsprungen!! 8435
Alles wird durch das Wasser erhalten!
Ocean, gönn' uns dein ewiges Walten.
Wenn du nicht Wolken sendetest,
Nicht reiche Bäche spendetest,
Hin und her nicht Flüsse wendetest, 8440
Die Ströme nicht vollendetest,
Was wären Gebirge, was Ebnen und Welt?
Du bist's der das frischeste Leben erhält.

Echo. Chorus der sämmtlichen Kreise.

Du bist's dem das frischeste Leben entquellt.

Nereus.

Sie kehren schwankend fern zurück, 8445
Bringen nicht mehr Blick zu Blick;
In gedehnten Kettenkreisen
Sich festgemäß zu erweisen,
Windet sich die unzählige Schaar.
Aber Galatea's Muschelthron 8450
Seh' ich schon und aber schon.
Er glänzt wie ein Stern
Durch die Menge;
Geliebtes leuchtet durch's Gedränge,
Auch noch so fern 8455
Schimmert's hell und klar,
Immer nah und wahr.

Homunculus.

In dieser holden Feuchte
Was ich auch hier beleuchte
8460 Ist alles reizend schön.

Proteus.

In dieser Lebensfeuchte
Erglänzt erst deine Leuchte
Mit herrlichem Getön.

Nereus.

Welch neues Geheimniß in Mitte der Schaaren
8465 Will unseren Augen sich offengebahren?
Was flammt um die Muschel, um Galatee's Füße?
Bald lodert es mächtig, bald lieblich, bald süße,
Als wär' es von Pulsen der Liebe gerührt.

Thales.

Homunculus ist es, von Proteus verführt. . .
8470 Es sind die Symptome des herrischen Sehnens,
Mir ahnet das Ächzen beängsteten Dröhnens;
Er wird sich zerschellen am glänzenden Thron;
Jetzt flammt es, nun blitzt es, ergießet sich schon.

Sirenen.

Welch feuriges Wunder verklärt uns die Wellen,
8475 Die gegen einander sich funkelnd zerschellen?
So leuchtet's und schwanket und hellet hinan:
Die Körper sie glühen auf nächtlicher Bahn,
Und ringsum ist alles vom Feuer umronnen;
So herrsche denn Eros der alles begonnen!

Heil dem Meere! Heil den Wogen! 8480
Von dem heiligen Feuer umzogen;
Heil dem Wasser! Heil dem Feuer!
Heil dem seltnen Abentheuer!

All Alle!

Heil den mildgewogenen Lüften!
Heil geheimnißreichen Grüften! 8485
Hochgefeiert seid allhier,
Element' ihr alle vier!

Dritter Act.

Vor dem Palaste des Menelas zu Sparta.

Helena tritt auf und Chor gefangener Trojanerinnen. Panthalis Chorführerin.

Helena.

Bewundert viel und viel gescholten Helena
Vom Strande komm' ich wo wir erst gelandet sind,
8490 Noch immer trunken von des Gewoges regsamem
Geschaukel, das vom phrygischen Blachgefild uns her
Auf sträubig-hohem Rücken, durch Poseidons Gunst
Und Euros Kraft, in vaterländische Buchten trug.
Dort unten freuet nun der König Menelas
8495 Der Rückkehr sammt den tapfersten seiner Krieger sich.
Du aber heiße mich willkommen, hohes Haus,
Das Tyndareos, mein Vater, nah dem Hange sich
Von Pallas Hügel wiederkehrend aufgebaut
Und, als ich hier mit Klytämnestren schwesterlich,
8500 Mit Castor auch und Pollux fröhlich spielend wuchs,
Vor allen Häusern Sparta's herrlich ausgeschmückt.
Gegrüßet seid mir, der ehrnen Pforte Flügel ihr!
Durch euer gastlich ladendes Weiteröffnen einst
Geschah's daß mir, erwählt aus vielen, Menelas
8505 In Bräutigams-Gestalt entgegen leuchtete.

Eröffnet mir sie wieder, daß ich ein Eilgebot
Des Königs treu erfülle, wie der Gattin ziemt.
Laßt mich hinein! und alles bleibe hinter mir,
Was mich umstürmte bis hieher, verhängnißvoll.
Denn seit ich diese Schwelle sorgenlos verließ, 8510
Cytherens Tempel besuchend, heiliger Pflicht gemäß,
Mich aber dort ein Räuber griff, der phrygische,
Ist viel geschehen, was die Menschen weit und breit
So gern erzählen, aber der nicht gerne hört
Von dem die Sage wachsend sich zum Mährchen spann. 8515

Chor.

Verschmähe nicht, o herrliche Frau,
Des höchsten Gutes Ehrenbesitz!
Denn das größte Glück ist dir einzig beschert,
Der Schönheit Ruhm der vor allen sich hebt.
Dem Helden tönt sein Name voran, 8520
Drum schreitet er stolz,
Doch beugt sogleich hartnäckigster Mann
Vor der allbezwingenden Schöne den Sinn.

Helena.

Genug! mit meinem Gatten bin ich hergeschifft
Und nun von ihm zu seiner Stadt vorausgesandt; 8525
Doch welchen Sinn er hegen mag errath' ich nicht.
Komm' ich als Gattin? komm' ich eine Königin?
Komm' ich ein Opfer für des Fürsten bittern Schmerz
Und für der Griechen lang erduldetes Mißgeschick?
Erobert bin ich, ob gefangen weiß ich nicht! 8530
Denn Ruf und Schicksal bestimmten fürwahr die Unsterblichen
Zweideutig mir, der Schöngestalt bedenkliche
Begleiter, die an dieser Schwelle mir sogar

Mit düster drohender Gegenwart zur Seite stehn.
8535 Denn schon im hohlen Schiffe blickte mich der Gemahl
Nur selten an, auch sprach er kein erquicklich Wort.
Als wenn er Unheil sänne saß er gegen mir.
Nun aber, als des Eurotas tiefem Buchtgestad
Hinangefahren der vordern Schiffe Schnäbel kaum
8540 Das Land begrüßten, sprach er, wie vom Gott bewegt:
Hier steigen meine Krieger, nach der Ordnung, aus,
Ich mustre sie am Strand des Meeres hingereiht,
Du aber ziehe weiter, ziehe des heiligen
Eurotas fruchtbegabtem Ufer immer auf,
8545 Die Rosse lenkend auf der feuchten Wiese Schmuck,
Bis daß zur schönen Ebene du gelangen magst,
Wo Lakedämon, einst ein fruchtbar weites Feld,
Von ernsten Bergen nah umgeben, angebaut.
Betrete dann das hochgethürmte Fürstenhaus
8550 Und mustere mir die Mägde, die ich dort zurück
Gelassen, sammt der klugen alten Schaffnerin.
Die zeige dir der Schätze reiche Sammlung vor,
Wie sie dein Vater hinterließ und die ich selbst
In Krieg und Frieden, stets vermehrend, aufgehäuft.
8555 Du findest alles nach der Ordnung stehen: denn
Das ist des Fürsten Vorrecht, daß er alles treu
In seinem Hause, wiederkehrend, finde, noch
An seinem Platze jedes wie er's dort verließ.
Denn nichts zu ändern hat für sich der Knecht Gewalt.

Chor.

8560 Erquicke nun am herrlichen Schatz,
Dem stets vermehrten, Augen und Brust;
Denn der Kette Zier, der Krone Geschmuck
Da ruhn sie stolz und sie dünken sich was;

Doch tritt nur ein und fordre sie auf,
Sie rüsten sich schnell. 8565
Mich freuet zu sehn Schönheit in dem Kampf
Gegen Gold und Perlen und Edelgestein.

Helena.

Sodann erfolgte des Herren ferneres Herrscherwort:
Wenn du nun alles nach der Ordnung durchgesehn,
Dann nimm so manchen Dreifuß als du nöthig glaubst 8570
Und mancherlei Gefäße die der Opfrer sich
Zur Hand verlangt, vollziehend heiligen Festgebrauch.
Die Kessel, auch die Schalen, wie das flache Rund,
Das reinste Wasser aus der heiligen Quelle sei
In hohen Krügen, ferner auch das trockne Holz, 8575
Der Flammen schnell empfänglich, halte da bereit,
Ein wohlgeschliffnes Messer fehle nicht zuletzt;
Doch alles andre geb' ich deiner Sorge heim.
So sprach er, mich zum Scheiden drängend; aber nichts
Lebendigen Athems zeichnet mir der Ordnende 8580
Das er, die Olympier zu verehren, schlachten will.
Bedenklich ist es, doch ich sorge weiter nicht
Und alles bleibe hohen Göttern heimgestellt,
Die das vollenden, was in ihrem Sinn sie deucht,
Es möge gut von Menschen, oder möge bös 8585
Geachtet sein, die Sterblichen wir ertragen das.
Schon manchmal hob das schwere Beil der Opfernde
Zu des erdgebeugten Thieres Nacken weihend auf
Und konnt' es nicht vollbringen, denn ihn hinderte
Des nahen Feindes oder Gottes Zwischenkunft. 8590

Chor.

Was geschehen werde sinnst du nicht aus;
Königin, schreite dahin

Guten Muths.
Gutes und Böses kommt
8595 Unerwartet dem Menschen;
Auch verkündet glauben wir's nicht.
Brannte doch Troja, sahen wir doch
Tod vor Augen, schmählichen Tod;
Und sind wir nicht hier
8600 Dir gesellt, dienstbar freudig,
Schauen des Himmels blendende Sonne
Und das Schönste der Erde
Huldvoll, dich, uns Glücklichen.

Helena.

Sei's wie es sei! Was auch bevorsteht, mir geziemt
8605 Hinaufzusteigen ungesäumt in das Königshaus,
Das lang entbehrt und viel ersehnt und fast verscherzt
Mir abermals vor Augen steht, ich weiß nicht wie.
Die Füße tragen mich so muthig nicht empor
Die hohen Stufen die ich kindisch übersprang.

Ab.

Chor.

8610 Werfet, o Schwestern, ihr
Traurig gefangenen,
Alle Schmerzen in's Weite;
Theilet der Herrin Glück,
Theilet Helenens Glück,
8615 Welche zu Vaterhauses Herd,
Zwar mit spätzurückkehrendem,
Aber mit desto festerem
Fuße freudig herannaht.

Preiset die heiligen,
Glücklich herstellenden 8620
Und heimführenden Götter!
Schwebt der Entbundene
Doch wie auf Fittigen
Über das Rauhste, wenn umsonst
Der Gefangene sehnsuchtsvoll 8625
Über die Zinne des Kerkers hin
Armausbreitend sich abhärmt.

Aber sie ergriff ein Gott
Die Entfernte;
Und aus Ilios Schutt 8630
Trug er hierher sie zurück,
In das alte, das neugeschmückte
Vaterhaus,
Nach unsäglichen
Freuden und Qualen, 8635
Früher Jugendzeit
Angefrischt zu gedenken.

Panthalis als Chorführerin.

Verlasset nun des Gesanges freudumgebnen Pfad
Und wendet nach der Thüre Flügeln euren Blick.
Was seh' ich, Schwestern? Kehret nicht die Königin, 8640
Mit heftigen Schrittes Regung, wieder zu uns her?
Was ist es, große Königin, was konnte dir
In deines Hauses Hallen, statt der Deinen Gruß,
Erschütterndes begegnen? Du verbirgst es nicht;
Denn Widerwillen seh' ich an der Stirne dir, 8645
Ein edles Zürnen das mit Überraschung kämpft.

Helena welche die Thürflügel offen gelassen hat, bewegt.

Der Tochter Zeus geziemet nicht gemeine Furcht
Und flüchtig-leise Schreckenshand berührt sie nicht;
Doch das Entsetzen, das dem Schoos der alten Nacht
8650 Von Urbeginn entsteigend, vielgestaltet noch
Wie glühende Wolken, aus des Berges Feuerschlund,
Herauf sich wälzt, erschüttert auch des Helden Brust.
So haben heute grauenvoll die Stygischen
In's Haus den Eintritt mir bezeichnet, daß ich gern
8655 Von oft betretner, langersehnter Schwelle mich,
Entlass'nem Gaste gleich, entfernend scheiden mag.
Doch nein! gewichen bin ich her an's Licht, und sollt
Ihr weiter nicht mich treiben, Mächte, wer ihr seid.
Auf Weihe will ich sinnen, dann gereinigt mag
8660 Des Herdes Gluth die Frau begrüßen wie den Herrn.

Chorführerin.

Entdecke deinen Dienerinnen, edle Frau,
Die dir verehrend beistehn, was begegnet ist.

Helena.

Was ich gesehen sollt ihr selbst mit Augen sehn,
Wenn ihr Gebilde nicht die alte Nacht sogleich
8665 Zurück geschlungen in ihrer Tiefe Wunderschoos.
Doch daß ihr's wisset, sag' ich's euch mit Worten an:
Als ich des Königs-Hauses ernsten Binnenraum,
Der nächsten Pflicht gedenkend, feierlich betrat,
Erstaunt' ich ob der öden Gänge Schweigsamkeit.
8670 Nicht Schall der emsig Wandelnden begegnete
Dem Ohr, nicht raschgeschäftiges Eiligthun dem Blick,
Und keine Magd erschien mir, keine Schaffnerin,
Die jeden Fremden freundlich sonst begrüßenden.

Als aber ich dem Schoose des Herdes mich genaht,
Da sah ich, bei verglommner Asche lauem Rest, 8675
Am Boden sitzen welch verhülltes großes Weib,
Der Schlafenden nicht vergleichbar, wohl der Sinnenden.
Mit Herrscherworten ruf' ich sie zur Arbeit auf,
Die Schaffnerin mir vermuthend, die indeß vielleicht
Des Gatten Vorsicht hinterlassend angestellt; 8680
Doch eingefaltet sitzt die Unbewegliche;
Nur endlich rührt sie, auf mein Dräun, den rechten Arm,
Als wiese sie von Herd und Halle mich hinweg.
Ich wende zürnend mich ab von ihr und eile gleich
Den Stufen zu, worauf empor der Thalamos 8685
Geschmückt sich hebt und nah daran das Schatzgemach;
Allein das Wunder reißt sich schnell vom Boden auf,
Gebietrisch mir den Weg vertretend, zeigt es sich
In hagrer Größe, hohlen, blutig-trüben Blicks,
Seltsamer Bildung, wie sie Aug' und Geist verwirrt. 8690
Doch red' ich in die Lüfte; denn das Wort bemüht
Sich nur umsonst Gestalten schöpferisch aufzubaun.
Da seht sie selbst! sie wagt sogar sich an's Licht hervor!
Hier sind wir Meister, bis der Herr und König kommt.
Die grausen Nachtgeburten drängt der Schönheitsfreund, 8695
Phöbus, hinweg in Höhlen, oder bändigt sie.

Phorkyas

auf der Schwelle zwischen den Thürpfosten auftretend.

Chor.

Vieles erlebt' ich, obgleich die Locke
Jugendlich wallet mir um die Schläfe!
Schreckliches hab' ich vieles gesehen,
Kriegrischen Jammer, Ilios Nacht, 8700
Als es fiel.

Durch das umwölkte, staubende Tosen
Drängender Krieger hört' ich die Götter
Fürchterlich rufen, hört' ich der Zwietracht
8705 Eherne Stimme schallen durch's Feld,
Mauerwärts.

Ach! sie standen noch, Ilios
Mauern, aber die Flammengluth
Zog vom Nachbar zum Nachbar schon
8710 Sich verbreitend von hier und dort
Mit des eignen Sturmes Wehn
Über die nächtliche Stadt hin.

Flüchtend sah ich, durch Rauch und Gluth
Und der züngelnden Flamme Loh'n,
8715 Gräßlich zürnender Götter Nahn,
Schreitend Wundergestalten
Riesengroß durch düsteren
Feuerumleuchteten Qualm hin.

Sah ich's, oder bildete
8720 Mir der angstumschlungene Geist
Solches Verworrene? sagen kann
Nimmer ich's, doch daß ich dieß
Gräßliche hier mit Augen schau'
Solches gewiß ja weiß ich;
8725 Könnt' es mit Händen fassen gar,
Hielte von dem Gefährlichen
Nicht zurücke die Furcht mich.

Welche von Phorkys
Töchtern nur bist du?
8730 Denn ich vergleiche dich

Diesem Geschlechte.
Bist du vielleicht der graugebornen,
Eines Auges und Eines Zahns
Wechselsweis theilhaftigen
Graien eine gekommen? 8735

Wagest du Scheusal
Neben der Schönheit
Dich vor dem Kennerblick
Phöbus zu zeigen?
Tritt du dennoch hervor nur immer, 8740
Denn das Häßliche schaut Er nicht,
Wie sein heilig Auge noch
Nie erblickte den Schatten.

Doch uns Sterbliche nöthigt, ach,
Leider trauriges Mißgeschick 8745
Zu dem unsäglichen Augenschmerz,
Den das Verwerfliche, Ewig-unselige
Schönheitliebenden rege macht.

Ja so höre denn, wenn du frech
Uns entgegenest, höre Fluch, 8750
Höre jeglicher Schelte Drohn,
Aus dem verwünschenden Munde der Glücklichen
Die von Göttern gebildet sind.

Phorkyas.

Alt ist das Wort, doch bleibet hoch und wahr der Sinn,
Daß Scham und Schönheit nie zusammen, Hand in Hand, 8755
Den Weg verfolgen über der Erde grünen Pfad.
Tief eingewurzelt wohnt in beiden alter Haß,
Daß, wo sie immer irgend auch des Weges sich

Begegnen, jede der Gegnerin den Rücken kehrt.
8760 Dann eilet jede wieder heftiger, weiter fort,
Die Scham betrübt, die Schönheit aber frech gesinnt,
Bis sie zuletzt des Orcus hohle Nacht umfängt,
Wenn nicht das Alter sie vorher gebändigt hat.
Euch find' ich nun, ihr Frechen, aus der Fremde her
8765 Mit Übermuth ergossen, gleich der Kraniche
Laut-heiser klingendem Zug, der über unser Haupt,
In langer Wolke, krächzend sein Getön herab
Schickt, das den stillen Wandrer über sich hinauf
Zu blicken lockt; doch ziehn sie ihren Weg dahin,
8770 Er geht den seinen; also wird's mit uns geschehn.

Wer seid denn ihr? daß ihr des Königs Hochpalast
Mänadisch wild, Betrunknen gleich umtoben dürft?
Wer seid ihr denn, daß ihr des Hauses Schaffnerin
Entgegen heulet, wie dem Mond der Hunde Schaar?
8775 Wähnt ihr, verborgen sei mir welch Geschlecht ihr seid,
Du kriegerzeugte, schlachterzogne junge Brut?
Mannlustige du, so wie verführt verführende,
Entnervend beide, Kriegers auch und Bürgers Kraft.
Zu Hauf euch sehend scheint mir ein Cicaden-Schwarm
8780 Herabzustürzen, deckend grüne Feldersaat.
Verzehrerinnen fremden Fleißes! Naschende
Vernichterinnen aufgekeimten Wohlstands ihr,
Erobert', marktverkauft', vertauschte Waare du!

Helena.

Wer gegenwarts der Frau die Dienerinnen schilt,
8785 Der Gebietrin Hausrecht tastet er vermessen an;
Denn ihr gebührt allein das Lobenswürdige
Zu rühmen, wie zu strafen was verwerflich ist.

Auch bin des Dienstes ich wohl zufrieden, den sie mir
Geleistet als die hohe Kraft von Ilios
Umlagert stand und fiel und lag; nicht weniger 8790
Als wir der Irrfahrt kummervolle Wechselnoth
Ertrugen, wo sonst jeder sich der nächste bleibt.
Auch hier erwart' ich gleiches von der muntren Schaar;
Nicht was der Knecht sei, fragt der Herr, nur wie er dient.
Drum schweige du und grinse sie nicht länger an. 8795
Hast du das Haus des Königs wohl verwahrt bisher,
Anstatt der Hausfrau, solches dient zum Ruhme dir;
Doch jetzo kommt sie selber, tritt nun du zurück,
Damit nicht Strafe werde statt verdienten Lohns.

Phorkyas.

Den Hausgenossen drohen bleibt ein großes Recht, 8800
Das gottbeglückten Herrschers hohe Gattin sich
Durch langer Jahre weise Leitung wohl verdient.
Da du, nun Anerkannte! neu den alten Platz
Der Königin und Hausfrau wiederum betrittst,
So fasse längst erschlaffte Zügel, herrsche nun, 8805
Nimm in Besitz den Schatz und sämmtlich uns dazu.
Vor allem aber schütze mich die ältere
Vor dieser Schaar, die, neben deiner Schönheit Schwan,
Nur schlecht befittigt', schnatterhafte Gänse sind.

Chorführerin.

Wie häßlich neben Schönheit zeigt sich Häßlichkeit. 8810

Phorkyas.

Wie unverständig neben Klugheit Unverstand.

Von hier an erwidern die Choretiden, einzeln aus dem Chor heraustretend.

Choretide 1.

Von Vater Erebus melde, melde von Mutter Nacht.

Phorkyas.

So sprich von Scylla, leiblich dir Geschwisterkind.

Choretide 2.

An deinem Stammbaum steigt manch Ungeheur empor.

Phorkyas.

8815 Zum Orcus hin! da suche deine Sippschaft auf.

Choretide 3.

Die dorten wohnen sind dir alle viel zu jung.

Phorkyas.

Tiresias den Alten gehe buhlend an.

Choretide 4.

Orions Amme war dir Ur=Urenkelin.

Phorkyas.

Harpyen wähn' ich fütterten dich im Unflat auf.

Choretide 5.

8820 Mit was ernährst du so gepflegte Magerkeit?

Phorkyas.

Mit Blute nicht, wonach du allzulüstern bist.

Choretide 6.

Begierig du auf Leichen, ekle Leiche selbst!

Phorkyas.

Vampyren=Zähne glänzen dir im frechen Maul.

Chorführerin.

Das deine stopf' ich, wenn ich sage wer du seist.

Phorkyas.

So nenne dich zuerst, das Räthsel hebt sich auf. 8825

Helena.

Nicht zürnend, aber traurend schreit' ich zwischen euch,
Verbietend solchen Wechselstreites Ungestüm!
Denn Schädlicheres begegnet nichts dem Herrscherherrn
Als treuer Diener heimlich unterschworner Zwist.
Das Echo seiner Befehle kehrt alsdann nicht mehr 8830
In schnell vollbrachter That wohlstimmig ihm zurück,
Nein, eigenwillig brausend tos't es um ihn her,
Den selbstverirrten, in's Vergebne scheltenden.
Dieß nicht allein. Ihr habt in sittelosem Zorn
Unsel'ger Bilder Schreckgestalten hergebannt, 8835
Die mich umdrängen daß ich selbst zum Orcus mich
Gerissen fühle, vaterländ'scher Flur zum Trutz.
Ist's wohl Gedächtniß? war es Wahn, der mich ergreift?
War ich das alles? Bin ich's? Werd' ich's künftig sein,
Das Traum- und Schreckbild jener Städteverwüstenden? 8840
Die Mädchen schaudern, aber du die älteste
Du stehst gelassen, rede mir verständig Wort.

Phorkyas.

Wer langer Jahre mannichfaltigen Glücks gedenkt,
Ihm scheint zuletzt die höchste Göttergunst ein Traum.
Du aber hochbegünstigt, sonder Maß und Ziel, 8845
In Lebensreihe sahst nur Liebesbrünstige,
Entzündet rasch zum kühnsten Wagstück jeder Art.
Schon Theseus haschte früh dich, gierig aufgeregt,
Wie Herakles stark, ein herrlich schön geformter Mann.

Helena.

8850 Entführte mich, ein zehenjährig schlankes Reh,
Und mich umschloß Aphidnus Burg in Attika.

Phorkyas.

Durch Castor und durch Pollux aber bald befreit,
Umworben standst du ausgesuchter Helden-Schaar.

Helena.

Doch stille Gunst vor allen, wie ich gern gesteh',
8855 Gewann Patroclus, er des Peliden Ebenbild.

Phorkyas.

Doch Vaterwille traute dich an Menelas,
Den kühnen Seedurchstreicher, Hausbewahrer auch.

Helena.

Die Tochter gab er, gab des Reichs Bestellung ihm.
Aus ehlichem Beisein sproßte dann Hermione.

Phorkyas.

8860 Doch als er fern sich Creta's Erbe kühn erstritt,
Dir Einsamen da erschien ein allzuschöner Gast.

Helena.

Warum gedenkst du jener halben Witwenschaft?
Und welch Verderben gräßlich mir daraus erwuchs?

Phorkyas.

Auch jene Fahrt mir freigebornen Creterin
8865 Gefangenschaft erschuf sie, lange Sklaverei.

Helena.

Als Schaffnerin bestellt' er dich sogleich hieher,
Vertrauend vieles, Burg und kühn erworbnen Schatz.

Phorkyas.

Die du verließest, Ilios umthürmter Stadt
Und unerschöpften Liebesfreuden zugewandt.

Helena.

Gedenke nicht der Freuden! allzuherben Leids 8870
Unendlichkeit ergoß sich über Brust und Haupt.

Phorkyas.

Doch sagt man, du erschienst ein doppelhaft Gebild,
In Ilios gesehen und in Ägypten auch.

Helena.

Verwirre wüsten Sinnes Aberwitz nicht gar.
Selbst jetzo, welche denn ich sei, ich weiß es nicht. 8875

Phorkyas.

Dann sagen sie: aus hohlem Schattenreich herauf
Gesellte sich inbrünstig noch Achill zu dir!
Dich früher liebend gegen allen Geschicks Beschluß.

Helena.

Ich als Idol, ihm dem Idol verband ich mich.
Es war ein Traum, so sagen ja die Worte selbst. 8880
Ich schwinde hin und werde selbst mir ein Idol.

Sinkt dem Halbchor in die Arme.

Chor.

Schweige, schweige!
Mißblickende, mißredende du!
Aus so gräßlichen einzahnigen
Lippen was enthaucht wohl 8885
Solchem furchtbaren Greuelschlund.

Denn der Bösartige wohlthätig erscheinend,
Wolfesgrimm unter schafwolligem Vließ,
Mir ist er weit schrecklicher als des drei=
8890 köpfigen Hundes Rachen.
Ängstlich lauschend stehn wir da,
Wann? wie? wo nur bricht's hervor
Solcher Tücke
Tiefauflauerndes Ungethüm?

8895 Nun denn, statt freundlich mit Trost reich begabten,
Letheschenkenden, holdmildesten Worts
Regest du auf aller Vergangenheit
Böseстes mehr denn Gutes,
Und verdüsterst allzugleich
8900 Mit dem Glanz der Gegenwart
Auch der Zukunft
Mild aufschimmerndes Hoffnungslicht.

Schweige, schweige!
Daß der Königin Seele,
8905 Schon zu entfliehen bereit,
Sich noch halte, festhalte
Die Gestalt aller Gestalten
Welche die Sonne jemals beschien.

Helena hat sich erholt und steht wieder in der Mitte.

Phorkyas.

Tritt hervor aus flüchtigen Wolken, hohe Sonne dieses Tags,
8910 Die verschleiert schon entzückte, blendend nun im Glanze herrscht.

Wie die Welt sich dir entfaltet schaust du selbst mit holdem Blick.
Schelten sie mich auch für häßlich, kenn' ich doch das Schöne wohl.

Helena.

Tret' ich schwankend aus der Öde die im Schwindel mich umgab,
Pflegt' ich gern der Ruhe wieder, denn so müd' ist mein Gebein:
Doch es ziemet Königinnen, allen Menschen ziemt es wohl, 8915
Sich zu fassen, zu ermannen, was auch drohend überrascht.

Phorkyas.

Stehst du nun in deiner Großheit, deiner Schöne vor uns da,
Sagt dein Blick, daß du befiehlest, was befiehlst du? sprich es aus.

Helena.

Eures Haders frech Versäumniß auszugleichen seid bereit,
Eilt ein Opfer zu bestellen wie der König mir gebot. 8920

Phorkyas.

Alles ist bereit im Hause, Schale, Dreifuß, scharfes Beil,
Zum Besprengen, zum Beräuchern; das zu Opfernde zeig' an.

Helena.

Nicht bezeichnet' es der König.

Phorkyas.

Sprach's nicht aus? O Jammerwort!

Helena.

Welch ein Jammer überfällt dich?

Phorkyas.

Königin, du bist gemeint!

Helena.

8925 Ich?

Phorkyas.

Und diese.

Chor.

Weh und Jammer!

Phorkyas.

Fallen wirst du durch das Beil.

Helena.

Gräßlich! doch geahnt, ich Arme!

Phorkyas.

Unvermeidlich scheint es mir.

Chor.

Ach! Und uns? was wird begegnen?

Phorkyas.

Sie stirbt einen edlen Tod;
Doch am hohen Balken drinnen, der des Daches Giebel trägt,
Wie im Vogelfang die Drosseln, zappelt ihr der Reihe nach.

Helena und Chor stehen erstaunt und erschreckt, in bedeutender, wohl vorbereiteter Gruppe.

Phorkyas.

8930 Gespenster! — — — Gleich erstarrten Bildern steht ihr da,
Geschreckt vom Tag zu scheiden der euch nicht gehört.

Die Menschen, die Gespenster sämmtlich gleich wie ihr,
Entsagen auch nicht willig hehrem Sonnenschein;
Doch bittet oder rettet niemand sie vom Schluß;
Sie wissen's alle, wenigen doch gefällt es nur. 8935
Genug, ihr seid verloren! Also frisch an's Werk.

Klatscht in die Hände; darauf erscheinen an der Pforte vermummte Zwerggestalten, welche die ausgesprochenen Befehle alsobald mit Behendigkeit ausführen.

Herbei du düstres, kugelrundes Ungethüm,
Wälzt euch hieher, zu schaden gibt es hier nach Lust.
Dem Tragaltar, dem goldgehörnten, gebet Platz,
Das Beil, es liege blinkend über dem Silberrand, 8940
Die Wasserkrüge füllet, abzuwaschen gibt's
Des schwarzen Blutes greuelvolle Besudelung.
Den Teppich breitet köstlich hier am Staube hin,
Damit das Opfer niederkniee königlich
Und eingewickelt, zwar getrennten Haupts sogleich, 8945
Anständig würdig aber doch bestattet sei.

Chorführerin.

Die Königin stehet sinnend an der Seite hier,
Die Mädchen welken gleich gemähtem Wiesengras;
Mir aber deucht, der Ältesten, heiliger Pflicht gemäß
Mit dir das Wort zu wechseln, Ur-Urälteste. 8950
Du bist erfahren, weise, scheinst uns gut gesinnt,
Obschon verkennend hirnlos diese Schaar dich traf.
Drum sage, was du möglich noch von Rettung weißt.

Phorkyas.

Ist leicht gesagt: Von der Königin hängt allein es ab
Sich selbst zu erhalten, euch Zugaben auch mit ihr. 8955
Entschlossenheit ist nöthig und die behendeste.

Chor.

Ehrenwürdigste der Parzen, weiseste Sibylle du,
Halte gesperrt die goldene Schere, dann verkünd' uns Tag
und Heil;
Denn wir fühlen schon im Schweben, Schwanken, Bammeln
unergetzlich
8960 Unsere Gliederchen, die lieber erst im Tanze sich ergetzten,
Ruhten drauf an Liebchens Brust.

Helena.

Laß diese bangen! Schmerz empfind' ich, keine Furcht;
Doch kennst du Rettung, dankbar sei sie anerkannt.
Dem Klugen, Weitumsichtigen zeigt fürwahr sich oft
8965 Unmögliches noch als möglich. Sprich und sag' es an.

Chor.

Sprich und sage, sag' uns eilig: wie entrinnen wir den grausen,
Garstigen Schlingen? die bedrohlich, als die schlechtesten
Geschmeide,
Sich um unsre Hälse ziehen. Vorempfinden wir's, die Armen,
Zum Entathmen, zum Ersticken, wenn du, Rhea, aller Götter
8970 Hohe Mutter, dich nicht erbarmst.

Phorkyas.

Habt ihr Geduld des Vortrags langgedehnten Zug
Still anzuhören? Mancherlei Geschichten sind's.

Chor.

Geduld genug! Zuhörend leben wir indeß.

Phorkyas.

Dem der zu Hause verharrend edlen Schatz bewahrt
Und hoher Wohnung Mauern auszukitten weiß, 8975
Wie auch das Dach zu sichern vor des Regens Drang,
Dem wird es wohlgehn lange Lebenstage durch:
Wer aber seiner Schwelle heilige Richte leicht
Mit flüchtigen Sohlen überschreitet freventlich,
Der findet wiederkehrend wohl den alten Platz, 8980
Doch umgeändert alles, wo nicht gar zerstört.

Helena.

Wozu dergleichen wohlbekannte Sprüche hier?
Du willst erzählen, rege nicht an Verdrießliches.

Phorkyas.

Geschichtlich ist es, ist ein Vorwurf keineswegs.
Raubschiffend ruderte Menelas von Bucht zu Bucht, 8985
Gestad' und Inseln, alles streift' er feindlich an,
Mit Beute wiederkehrend, wie sie drinnen starrt.
Vor Ilios verbracht' er langer Jahre zehn,
Zur Heimfahrt aber weiß ich nicht wie viel es war.
Allein wie steht es hier am Platz um Tyndareos 8990
Erhabnes Haus? wie stehet es mit dem Reich umher?

Helena.

Ist dir denn so das Schelten gänzlich einverleibt,
Daß ohne Tadeln du keine Lippe regen kannst?

Phorkyas.

So viele Jahre stand verlassen das Thal-Gebirg,
Das hinter Sparta nordwärts in die Höhe steigt, 8995
Taygetos im Rücken, wo als muntrer Bach

Herab Eurotas rollt und dann durch unser Thal
An Rohren breit hinfließend eure Schwäne nährt.
Dort hinten still im Gebirgthal hat ein kühn Geschlecht
9000 Sich angesiedelt, dringend aus cimmerischer Nacht,
Und unersteiglich feste Burg sich aufgethürmt,
Von da sie Land und Leute placken wie's behagt.

Helena.

Das konnten sie vollführen? Ganz unmöglich scheint's.

Phorkyas.

Sie hatten Zeit, vielleicht an zwanzig Jahre sind's.

Helena.

9005 Ist Einer Herr? sind's Räuber viel, Verbündete?

Phorkyas.

Nicht Räuber sind es, Einer aber ist der Herr.
Ich schelt' ihn nicht und wenn er schon mich heimgesucht.
Wohl konnt' er alles nehmen, doch begnügt' er sich
Mit wenigen Freigeschenken, nannt' er's, nicht Tribut.

Helena.

9010 Wie sieht er aus?

Phorkyas.

Nicht übel! mir gefällt er schon.
Es ist ein munterer, kecker, wohlgebildeter,
Wie unter Griechen wenig' ein verständ'ger Mann.
Man schilt das Volk Barbaren, doch ich dächte nicht
Daß grausam einer wäre, wie vor Ilios
9015 Gar mancher Held sich menschenfresserisch erwies.
Ich acht' auf seine Großheit, ihm vertraut' ich mich.

Und seine Burg! die solltet ihr mit Augen sehn!
Das ist was anderes gegen plumpes Mauerwerk
Das eure Väter, mir nichts dir nichts, aufgewälzt,
Cyklopisch wie Cyklopen, rohen Stein sogleich 9020
Auf rohe Steine stürzend; dort hingegen, dort
Ist alles senk- und wagerecht und regelhaft.
Von außen schaut sie! himmelan sie strebt empor,
So starr, so wohl in Fugen, spiegelglatt wie Stahl.
Zu klettern hier — ja selbst der Gedanke gleitet ab. 9025
Und innen großer Höfe Raumgelasse, rings
Mit Baulichkeit umgeben, aller Art und Zweck'.
Da seht ihr Säulen, Säulchen, Bogen, Bögelchen,
Altane, Galerien, zu schauen aus und ein,
Und Wappen.

Chor.

Was sind Wappen?

Phorkyas.

Ajax führte ja 9030
Geschlungene Schlang' im Schilde, wie ihr selbst gesehn.
Die Sieben dort vor Theben trugen Bildnerein
Ein jeder auf seinem Schilde, reich bedeutungsvoll.
Da sah man Mond und Stern' am nächtigen Himmelsraum,
Auch Göttin, Held und Leiter, Schwerter, Fackeln auch, 9035
Und was Bedrängliches guten Städten grimmig droht.
Ein solch Gebilde führt auch unsre Heldenschaar
Von seinen Ur-Urahnen her in Farbenglanz.
Da seht ihr Löwen, Adler, Klau' und Schnabel auch,
Dann Büffelhörner, Flügel, Rosen, Pfauenschweif, 9040
Auch Streifen, gold und schwarz und silbern, blau und roth.

Dergleichen hängt in Sälen Reih an Reihe fort,
In Sälen, gränzenlosen, wie die Welt so weit;
Da könnt ihr tanzen!

Chor.

Sage, gibt's auch Tänzer da?

Phorkyas.

9045 Die besten! goldgelockte, frische Bubenschaar,
Die duften Jugend, Paris duftete einzig so,
Als er der Königin zu nahe kam.

Helena.

Du fällst
Ganz aus der Rolle, sage mir das letzte Wort!

Phorkyas.

Du sprichst das letzte, sagst mit Ernst vernehmlich ja!
9050 Sogleich umgeb' ich dich mit jener Burg.

Chor.

O sprich
Das kurze Wort! und rette dich und uns zugleich.

Helena.

Wie? sollt' ich fürchten, daß der König Menelas
So grausam sich verginge mich zu schädigen?

Phorkyas.

Hast du vergessen, wie er deinen Deiphobus,
9055 Des todtgekämpften Paris Bruder, unerhört
Verstümmelte, der starrsinnig Witwe dich erstritt

Und glücklich kebs'te; Nas' und Ohren schnitt er ab
Und stümmelte mehr so; Greuel war es anzuschaun.

Helena.

Das that er jenem, meinetwegen that er das.

Phorkyas.

Um jeneswillen wird er dir das Gleiche thun. 9060
Untheilbar ist die Schönheit; der sie ganz besaß
Zerstört sie lieber, fluchend jedem Theilbesitz.

Trompeten in der Ferne; der Chor fährt zusammen.

Wie scharf der Trompete Schmettern Ohr und Eingeweid'
Zerreißend anfaßt, also krallt sich Eifersucht
Im Busen fest des Mannes, der das nie vergißt 9065
Was einst er besaß und nun verlor, nicht mehr besitzt.

Chor.

Hörst du nicht die Hörner schallen? siehst der Waffen Blitze nicht?

Phorkyas.

Sei willkommen, Herr und König, gerne geb' ich Rechenschaft.

Chor.

Aber wir?

Phorkyas.

Ihr wißt es deutlich, seht vor Augen ihren Tod,
Merkt den eurigen da drinne; nein, zu helfen ist euch nicht. 9070

Pause.

Helena.

Ich sann mir aus das Nächste was ich wagen darf.
Ein Widerdämon bist du, das empfind' ich wohl

Und fürchte, Gutes wendest du zum Bösen um.
Vor allem aber folgen will ich dir zur Burg;
9075 Das andre weiß ich; was die Königin dabei
Im tiefen Busen geheimnißvoll verbergen mag,
Sei jedem unzugänglich. Alte! geh voran.

Chor.

O wie gern gehen wir hin,
Eilenden Fußes;
9080 Hinter uns Tod,
Vor uns abermals
Ragender Veste
Unzugängliche Mauer.
Schütze sie eben so gut,
9085 Eben wie Ilios Burg,
Die doch endlich nur
Niederträchtiger List erlag.

Nebel verbreiten sich, umhüllen den Hintergrund, auch die Nähe, nach Belieben.

Wie? aber wie?
Schwestern, schaut euch um!
9090 War es nicht heiterer Tag?
Nebel schwanken streifig empor
Aus Eurotas heil'ger Fluth;
Schon entschwand das liebliche
Schilfumkränzte Gestade dem Blick,
9095 Auch die frei, zierlich-stolz
Sanfthingleitenden Schwäne
In gesell'ger Schwimmlust
Seh' ich, ach, nicht mehr!

Doch, aber doch
Tönen hör' ich sie, 9100
Tönen fern heiseren Ton!
Tod verkündenden, sagen sie;
Ach daß uns er nur nicht auch,
Statt verheißener Rettung Heil,
Untergang verkünde zuletzt; 9105
Uns den schwangleichen, lang-
Schön weißhalsigen, und ach!
Unsrer Schwanerzeugten.
Weh uns, weh, weh!

Alles deckte sich schon 9110
Rings mit Nebel umher.
Sehen wir doch einander nicht!
Was geschieht? gehen wir?
Schweben wir nur
Trippelnden Schrittes am Boden hin? 9115
Siehst du nichts? schwebt nicht etwa gar
Hermes voran? Blinkt nicht der goldne Stab
Heischend, gebietend uns wieder zurück
Zu dem unerfreulichen, grautagenden,
Ungreifbarer Gebilde vollen, 9120
Überfüllten, ewig leeren Hades?

Ja, auf einmal wird es düster, ohne Glanz entschwebt der Nebel
Dunkelgräulich, mauerbräunlich. Mauern stellen sich dem Blicke,
Freiem Blicke starr entgegen. Ist's ein Hof? ist's tiefe Grube?
Schauerlich in jedem Falle! Schwestern, ach wir sind gefangen, 9125
So gefangen wie nur je.

Innerer Burghof, umgeben von reichen phantastischen Gebäuden des Mittelalters.

Chorführerin.

Vorschnell und thöricht, echt wahrhaftes Weibsgebild!
Vom Augenblick abhängig, Spiel der Witterung,
Des Glücks und Unglücks, keins von beiden wißt ihr je
9130 Zu bestehn mit Gleichmut. Eine widerspricht ja stets
Der andern heftig, überquer die andern ihr;
In Freud' und Schmerz nur heult und lacht ihr gleichen Tons.
Nun schweigt! und wartet horchend was die Herrscherin
Hochsinnig hier beschließen mag für sich und uns.

Helena.

9135 Wo bist du, Pythonissa? heiße wie du magst,
Aus diesen Gewölben tritt hervor der düstern Burg.
Gingst etwa du, dem wunderbaren Heldenherrn
Mich anzukündigen, Wohlempfang bereitend mir,
So habe Dank und führe schnell mich ein zu ihm;
9140 Beschluß der Irrfahrt wünsch' ich. Ruhe wünsch' ich nur.

Chorführerin.

Vergebens blickst du, Königin, allseits um dich her;
Verschwunden ist das leidige Bild, verblieb vielleicht
Im Nebel dort, aus dessen Busen wir hieher,
Ich weiß nicht wie, gekommen, schnell und sonder Schritt.
9145 Vielleicht auch irrt sie zweifelhaft im Labyrinth
Der wundersam aus vielen einsgewordnen Burg,

Den Herrn erfragend fürstlicher Hochbegrüßung halb.
Doch sieh, dort oben regt in Menge sich allbereits
In Galerien, am Fenster, in Portalen rasch
Sich hin und her bewegend viele Dienerschaft; 9150
Vornehm-willkommnen Gastempfang verkündet es.

Chor.

Aufgeht mir das Herz! o, seht nur dahin
Wie so sittig herab mit verweilendem Tritt
Jungholdeste Schaar anständig bewegt
Den geregelten Zug. Wie? auf wessen Befehl 9155
Nur erscheinen gereiht und gebildet so früh
Von Jünglingsknaben das herrliche Volk?
Was bewundr' ich zumeist! Ist es zierlicher Gang,
Etwa des Haupts Lockhaar um die blendende Stirn,
Etwa der Wänglein Paar, wie die Pfirsiche roth 9160
Und eben auch so weichwollig beflaumt?
Gern biss' ich hinein, doch ich schaudre davor,
Denn in ähnlichem Fall, da erfüllte der Mund
Sich, gräßlich zu sagen! mit Asche.
Aber die schönsten 9165
Sie kommen daher;
Was tragen sie nur?
Stufen zum Thron,
Teppich und Sitz,
Umhang und zelt- 9170
artigen Schmuck;
Über überwallt er,
Wolkenkränze bildend,
Unsrer Königin Haupt,
Denn schon bestieg sie 9175
Eingeladen herrlichen Pfühl.

Tretet heran,
Stufe für Stufe
Reihet euch ernst.
9180 Würdig, o würdig, dreifach würdig
Sei gesegnet ein solcher Empfang!

Alles vom Chor Ausgesprochene geschieht nach und nach.

Faust.

Nachdem Knaben und Knappen in langem Zug herabgestiegen, erscheint er oben an der Treppe in ritterlicher Hofkleidung des Mittelalters und kommt langsam würdig herunter.

Chorführerin ihn aufmerksam beschauend.

Wenn diesem nicht die Götter, wie sie öfter thun,
Für wenige Zeit nur wundernswürdige Gestalt,
Erhabnen Anstand, liebenswerthe Gegenwart
9185 Vorübergänglich liehen; wird ihm jedesmal
Was er beginnt gelingen, sei's in Männerschlacht,
So auch im kleinen Kriege mit den schönsten Fraun.
Er ist fürwahr gar vielen andern vorzuziehn,
Die ich doch auch als hochgeschätzt mit Augen sah.
9190 Mit langsam=ernstem, ehrfurchtsvoll gehaltnem Schritt
Seh' ich den Fürsten; wende dich, o Königin!

Faust herantretend, einen Gefesselten zur Seite.

Statt feierlichsten Grußes, wie sich ziemte,
Statt ehrfurchtsvollem Willkomm bring' ich dir
In Ketten hart geschlossen solchen Knecht,
9195 Der, Pflicht verfehlend, mir die Pflicht entwand.
Hier kniee nieder! dieser höchsten Frau

Bekenntniß abzulegen deiner Schuld.
Dieß ist, erhabne Herrscherin, der Mann
Mit seltnem Augenblitz vom hohen Thurm
Umherzuschaun bestellt, dort Himmelsraum 9200
Und Erdenbreite scharf zu überspähn,
Was etwa da und dort sich melden mag,
Vom Hügelkreis in's Thal zur festen Burg
Sich regen mag, der Heerden Woge sei's,
Ein Heereszug vielleicht; wir schützen jene, 9205
Begegnen diesem. Heute, welch Versäumniß!
Du kommst heran, er meldet's nicht, verfehlt
Ist ehrenvoller, schuldigster Empfang
So hohen Gastes. Freventlich verwirkt
Das Leben hat er, läge schon im Blut 9210
Verdienten Todes; doch nur du allein
Bestrafst, begnadigst, wie dir's wohl gefällt.

Helena.

So hohe Würde wie du sie vergönnst,
Als Richterin, als Herrscherin, und wär's
Versuchend nur, wie ich vermuthen darf; 9215
So üb' ich nun des Richters erste Pflicht,
Beschuldigte zu hören. Rede denn.

Thurmwärter Lynceus.

Laß mich knieen, laß mich schauen,
Laß mich sterben, laß mich leben,
Denn schon bin ich hingegeben 9220
Dieser gottgegebnen Frauen.

Harrend auf des Morgens Wonne,
Östlich spähend ihren Lauf,

Ging auf einmal mir die Sonne
9225 Wunderbar im Süden auf.

Zog den Blick nach jener Seite,
Statt der Schluchten, statt der Höhn,
Statt der Erd- und Himmelsweite,
Sie die Einzige zu spähn.

9230 Augenstrahl ist mir verliehen
Wie dem Luchs auf höchstem Baum,
Doch nun mußt' ich mich bemühen
Wie aus tiefem, düsterm Traum.

Wüßt' ich irgend mich zu finden?
9235 Zinne? Thurm? geschloss'nes Thor?
Nebel schwanken, Nebel schwinden,
Solche Göttin tritt hervor!

Aug' und Brust ihr zugewendet
Sog ich an den milden Glanz,
9240 Diese Schönheit wie sie blendet
Blendete mich Armen ganz.

Ich vergaß des Wächters Pflichten,
Völlig das beschworne Horn;
Drohe nur mich zu vernichten,
9245 Schönheit bändigt allen Zorn.

Helena.

Das Übel das ich brachte darf ich nicht
Bestrafen. Wehe mir! Welch streng Geschick
Verfolgt mich, überall der Männer Busen
So zu bethören, daß sie weder sich

Noch sonst ein Würdiges verschonten. Raubend jetzt, 9250
Verführend, fechtend, hin und her entrückend,
Halbgötter, Helden, Götter, ja Dämonen,
Sie führten mich im Irren her und hin.
Einfach die Welt verwirrt' ich, doppelt mehr,
Nun dreifach, vierfach bring' ich Noth auf Noth. 9255
Entferne diesen Guten, laß ihn frei;
Den Gottbethörten treffe keine Schmach.

Faust.

Erstaunt, o Königin, seh' ich zugleich
Die sicher Treffende, hier den Getroffnen;
Ich seh' den Bogen, der den Pfeil entsandt, 9260
Verwundet jenen. Pfeile folgen Pfeilen
Mich treffend. Allwärts ahn' ich überquer
Gefiedert schwirrend sie in Burg und Raum.
Was bin ich nun? Auf einmal machst du mir
Rebellisch die Getreusten, meine Mauern 9265
Unsicher. Also fürcht' ich schon, mein Heer
Gehorcht der siegend unbesiegten Frau.
Was bleibt mir übrig als mich selbst und alles,
Im Wahn das Meine, dir anheim zu geben?
Zu deinen Füßen laß mich, frei und treu, 9270
Dich Herrin anerkennen, die sogleich
Auftretend sich Besitz und Thron erwarb.

Lynceus

mit einer Kiste und Männer die ihm andere nachtragen.

Du siehst mich, Königin, zurück!
Der Reiche bettelt einen Blick,
Er sieht dich an und fühlt sogleich 9275
Sich bettelarm und fürstenreich.

Was war ich erst? was bin ich nun?
Was ist zu wollen? was zu thun?
Was hilft der Augen schärfster Blitz!
9280 Er prallt zurück an deinem Sitz.

Von Osten kamen wir heran
Und um den Westen war's gethan;
Ein lang- und breites Volksgewicht,
Der erste wußte vom letzten nicht.

9285 Der erste fiel, der zweite stand,
Des dritten Lanze war zur Hand;
Ein jeder hundertfach gestärkt,
Erschlagne Tausend unbemerkt.

Wir drängten fort, wir stürmten fort,
9290 Wir waren Herrn von Ort zu Ort;
Und wo ich herrisch heut befahl,
Ein andrer morgen raubt' und stahl.

Wir schauten, — eilig war die Schau;
Der griff die allerschönste Frau,
9295 Der griff den Stier von festem Tritt,
Die Pferde mußten alle mit.

Ich aber liebte zu erspähn
Das Seltenste was man gesehn,
Und was ein andrer auch besaß,
9300 Das war für mich gedörrtes Gras.

Den Schätzen war ich auf der Spur,
Den scharfen Blicken folgt' ich nur,
In alle Taschen blickt' ich ein,
Durchsichtig war mir jeder Schrein.

Und Haufen Goldes waren mein, 9305
Am herrlichsten der Edelstein:
Nun der Smaragd allein verdient
Daß er an deinem Herzen grünt.

Nun schwanke zwischen Ohr und Mund
Das Tropfenei aus Meeresgrund; 9310
Rubinen werden gar verscheucht,
Das Wangenroth sie niederbleicht.

Und so den allergrößten Schatz
Versetz' ich hier auf deinen Platz,
Zu deinen Füßen sei gebracht 9315
Die Ernte mancher blut'gen Schlacht.

So viele Kisten schlepp' ich her,
Der Eisenkisten hab' ich mehr;
Erlaube mich auf deiner Bahn
Und Schatzgewölbe füll' ich an. 9320

Denn du bestiegest kaum den Thron,
So neigen schon, so beugen schon
Verstand und Reichthum und Gewalt
Sich vor der einzigen Gestalt.

Das alles hielt ich fest und mein, 9325
Nun aber lose, wird es dein,
Ich glaubt' es würdig, hoch und baar,
Nun seh' ich, daß es nichtig war.

Verschwunden ist was ich besaß,
Ein abgemähtes, welkes Gras: 9330
O gib mit einem heitern Blick
Ihm seinen ganzen Werth zurück!

Faust.

Entferne schnell die kühn erworbne Last,
Zwar nicht getadelt, aber unbelohnt.
9335 Schon ist Ihr alles eigen was die Burg
Im Schoos verbirgt, Besondres Ihr zu bieten
Ist unnütz. Geh und häufe Schatz auf Schatz
Geordnet an. Der ungesehnen Pracht
Erhabnes Bild stell' auf! Laß die Gewölbe
9340 Wie frische Himmel blinken, Paradiese
Von lebelosem Leben richte zu.
Voreilend ihren Tritten laß beblümt
An Teppich Teppiche sich wälzen, ihrem Tritt
Begegne sanfter Boden, ihrem Blick,
9345 Nur Göttliche nicht blendend, höchster Glanz.

Lynceus.

Schwach ist was der Herr befiehlt,
Thut's der Diener, es ist gespielt:
Herrscht doch über Gut und Blut
Dieser Schönheit Übermuth.
9350 Schon das ganze Heer ist zahm,
Alle Schwerter stumpf und lahm,
Vor der herrlichen Gestalt
Selbst die Sonne matt und kalt,
Vor dem Reichthum des Gesichts
9355 Alles leer und alles nichts.

Ab.

Helena zu Faust.

Ich wünsche dich zu sprechen, doch herauf
An meine Seite komm! der leere Platz
Beruft den Herrn und sichert mir den meinen.

Faust.

Erst knieend laß die treue Widmung dir
Gefallen, hohe Frau; die Hand die mich 9360
An deine Seite hebt laß mich sie küssen.
Bestärke mich als Mitregenten deines
Gränzunbewußten Reichs, gewinne dir
Verehrer, Diener, Wächter all' in Einem.

Helena.

Vielfache Wunder seh' ich, hör' ich an, 9365
Erstaunen trifft mich, fragen möcht' ich viel.
Doch wünscht' ich Unterricht, warum die Rede
Des Manns mir seltsam klang, seltsam und freundlich.
Ein Ton scheint sich dem andern zu bequemen,
Und hat ein Wort zum Ohre sich gesellt, 9370
Ein andres kommt, dem ersten liebzukosen.

Faust.

Gefällt dir schon die Sprechart unsrer Völker,
O so gewiß entzückt auch der Gesang,
Befriedigt Ohr und Sinn im tiefsten Grunde.
Doch ist am sichersten wir üben's gleich, 9375
Die Wechselrede lockt es, ruft's hervor.

Helena.

So sage denn, wie sprech' ich auch so schön?

Faust.

Das ist gar leicht, es muß von Herzen gehn.
Und wenn die Brust von Sehnsucht überfließt,
Man sieht sich um und fragt —

Helena.

Wer mit genießt. 9380

Faust.

Nun schaut der Geist nicht vorwärts, nicht zurück,
Die Gegenwart allein —

Helena.

Ist unser Glück.

Faust.

Schatz ist sie, Hochgewinn, Besitz und Pfand;
Bestätigung wer gibt sie?

Helena.

Meine Hand.

Chor.

9385 Wer verdächt' es unsrer Fürstin,
Gönnet sie dem Herrn der Burg
Freundliches Erzeigen.
Denn gesteht, sämmtliche sind wir
Ja Gefangene, wie schon öfter,
9390 Seit dem schmählichen Untergang
Ilios und der ängstlich-
Labyrinthischen Kummerfahrt.

Fraun, gewöhnt an Männerliebe,
Wählerinnen sind sie nicht,
9395 Aber Kennerinnen.
Und wie goldlockigen Hirten,
Vielleicht schwarzborstigen Faunen,
Wie es bringt die Gelegenheit,
Über die schwellenden Glieder
9400 Vollertheilen sie gleiches Recht.

Nah und näher sitzen sie schon
An einander gelehnet,
Schulter an Schulter, Knie an Knie,
Hand in Hand wiegen sie sich
Über des Throns 9405
Aufgepolsterter Herrlichkeit.
Nicht versagt sich die Majestät
Heimlicher Freuden
Vor den Augen des Volkes
Übermüthiges Offenbarsein. 9410

Helena.

Ich fühle mich so fern und doch so nah
Und sage nur zu gern: da bin ich! da!

Faust.

Ich athme kaum, mir zittert, stockt das Wort,
Es ist ein Traum, verschwunden Tag und Ort.

Helena.

Ich scheine mir verlebt und doch so neu, 9415
In dich verwebt, dem Unbekannten treu.

Faust.

Durchgrüble nicht das einzigste Geschick,
Dasein ist Pflicht und wär's ein Augenblick.

Phorkyas heftig eintretend.

Buchstabirt in Liebes-Fibeln,
Tändelnd grübelt nur am Liebeln, 9420
Müßig liebelt fort im Grübeln,
Doch dazu ist keine Zeit.
Fühlt ihr nicht ein dumpfes Wettern?
Hört nur die Trompete schmettern,

9425 Das Verderben ist nicht weit.
Menelas mit Volkes-Wogen
Kommt auf euch herangezogen;
Rüstet euch zu herbem Streit!
Von der Sieger-Schaar umwimmelt,
9430 Wie Deiphobus verstümmelt
Büßest du das Fraun-Geleit.
Bammelt erst die leichte Waare,
Dieser gleich ist am Altare
Neugeschliffnes Beil bereit.

Faust.

9435 Verwegne Störung! widerwärtig dringt sie ein,
Auch nicht in Gefahren mag ich sinnlos Ungestüm.
Den schönsten Boten Unglücksbotschaft häßlicht ihn;
Du Häßlichste gar, nur schlimme Botschaft bringst du gern.
Doch dießmal soll dir's nicht gerathen, leeren Hauchs
9440 Erschüttere du die Lüfte. Hier ist nicht Gefahr,
Und selbst Gefahr erschiene nur als eitles Dräun.

Signale, Explosionen von den Thürmen, Trompeten und Zinken, kriegerische Musik, Durchmarsch gewaltiger Heereskraft.

Faust.

Nein, gleich sollst du versammelt schauen
Der Helden ungetrennten Kreis:
Nur der verdient die Gunst der Frauen,
9445 Der kräftigst sie zu schützen weiß.

Zu den Heerführern, die sich von den Colonnen absondern und herantreten.

Mit angehaltnem stillen Wüthen,
Das euch gewiß den Sieg verschafft,

Ihr Nordens jugendliche Blüthen,
Ihr Ostens blumenreiche Kraft.

In Stahl gehüllt, vom Strahl umwittert, 9450
Die Schaar die Reich um Reich zerbrach,
Sie treten auf, die Erde schüttert,
Sie schreiten fort, es donnert nach.

An Pylos traten wir zu Lande,
Der alte Nestor ist nicht mehr, 9455
Und alle kleinen Königsbande
Zersprengt das ungebundne Heer.

Drängt ungesäumt von diesen Mauern
Jetzt Menelas dem Meer zurück;
Dort irren mag er, rauben, lauern, 9460
Ihm war es Neigung und Geschick.

Herzoge soll ich euch begrüßen,
Gebietet Sparta's Königin,
Nun legt ihr Berg und Thal zu Füßen,
Und euer sei des Reichs Gewinn. 9465

Germane du! Corinthus Buchten
Vertheidige mit Wall und Schutz,
Achaia dann mit hundert Schluchten
Empfehl' ich, Gothe, deinem Trutz.

Nach Elis ziehn der Franken Heere, 9470
Messene sei der Sachsen Loos,
Normanne reinige die Meere
Und Argolis erschaff' er groß.

Dann wird ein jeder häuslich wohnen,
9475 Nach außen richten Kraft und Blitz;
Doch Sparta soll euch überthronen,
Der Königin verjährter Sitz.

All-Einzeln sieht sie euch genießen
Des Landes dem kein Wohl gebricht;
9480 Ihr sucht getrost zu ihren Füßen
Bestätigung und Recht und Licht.

Faust steigt herab, die Fürsten schließen einen Kreis um ihn, Befehl und Anordnung näher zu vernehmen.

Chor.

Wer die Schönste für sich begehrt,
Tüchtig vor allen Dingen
Seh' er nach Waffen weise sich um;
9485 Schmeichelnd wohl gewann er sich
Was auf Erden das Höchste;
Aber ruhig besitzt er's nicht:
Schleicher listig entschmeicheln sie ihm,
Räuber kühnlich entreißen sie ihm,
9490 Dieses zu hinderen sei er bedacht.

Unsern Fürsten lob' ich drum,
Schätz' ihn höher vor andern,
Wie er so tapfer klug sich verband
Daß die Starken gehorchend stehn
9495 Jedes Winkes gewärtig.
Seinen Befehl vollziehn sie treu,
Jeder sich selbst zu eignem Nutz
Wie dem Herrscher zu lohnendem Dank,
Beiden zu höchlichem Ruhmes-Gewinn.

Denn wer entreißet sie jetzt 9500
Dem gewalt'gen Besitzer?
Ihm gehört sie, ihm sei sie gegönnt,
Doppelt von uns gegönnt, die er
Sammt ihr zugleich innen mit sicherster Mauer,
Außen mit mächtigstem Heer umgab. 9505

Faust.

Die Gaben, diesen hier verliehen —
An jeglichen ein reiches Land —
Sind groß und herrlich, laß sie ziehen!
Wir halten in der Mitte Stand.

Und sie beschützen um die Wette, 9510
Ringsum von Wellen angehüpft,
Nichtinsel dich, mit leichter Hügelkette
Europens letztem Bergast angeknüpft.

Das Land, vor aller Länder Sonnen,
Sei ewig jedem Stamm beglückt, 9515
Nun meiner Königin gewonnen,
Das früh an ihr hinaufgeblickt.

Als, mit Eurotas Schilfgeflüster,
Sie leuchtend aus der Schale brach,
Der hohen Mutter, dem Geschwister 9520
Das Licht der Augen überstach.

Dieß Land, allein zu dir gekehret,
Entbietet seinen höchsten Flor;
Dem Erdkreis, der dir angehöret,
Dein Vaterland, o! zieh es vor. 9525

Und duldet auch auf seiner Berge Rücken
Das Zackenhaupt der Sonne kalten Pfeil,
Läßt nun der Fels sich angegrünt erblicken,
Die Ziege nimmt genäschig kargen Theil.

9530 Die Quelle springt, vereinigt stürzen Bäche,
Und schon sind Schluchten, Hänge, Matten grün.
Auf hundert Hügeln unterbrochner Fläche
Siehst Wollenheerden ausgebreitet ziehn.

Vertheilt, vorsichtig abgemessen schreitet
9535 Gehörntes Rind hinan zum jähen Rand,
Doch Obdach ist den sämmtlichen bereitet,
Zu hundert Höhlen wölbt sich Felsenwand.

Pan schützt sie dort und Lebensnymphen wohnen
In buschiger Klüfte feucht erfrischtem Raum,
9540 Und, sehnsuchtsvoll nach höhern Regionen,
Erhebt sich zweighaft Baum gedrängt an Baum.

Alt-Wälder sind's! Die Eiche starret mächtig
Und eigensinnig zackt sich Ast an Ast;
Der Ahorn mild, von süßem Safte trächtig,
9545 Steigt rein empor und spielt mit seiner Last.

Und mütterlich im stillen Schattenkreise
Quillt laue Milch bereit für Kind und Lamm;
Obst ist nicht weit, der Ebnen reife Speise,
Und Honig trieft vom ausgehöhlten Stamm.

9550 Hier ist das Wohlbehagen erblich,
Die Wange heitert wie der Mund,
Ein jeder ist an seinem Platz unsterblich:
Sie sind zufrieden und gesund.

Und so entwickelt sich am reinen Tage
Zu Vaterkraft das holde Kind. 9555
Wir staunen drob; noch immer bleibt die Frage:
Ob's Götter, ob es Menschen sind?

So war Apoll den Hirten zugestaltet
Daß ihm der schönsten einer glich;
Denn wo Natur im reinen Kreise waltet 9560
Ergreifen alle Welten sich.

Neben ihr sitzend.

So ist es mir, so ist es dir gelungen,
Vergangenheit sei hinter uns gethan;
O fühle dich vom höchsten Gott entsprungen,
Der ersten Welt gehörst du einzig an. 9565

Nicht feste Burg soll dich umschreiben!
Noch zirkt, in ewiger Jugendkraft
Für uns, zu wonnevollem Bleiben,
Arkadien in Sparta's Nachbarschaft.

Gelockt auf sel'gem Grund zu wohnen, 9570
Du flüchtetest in's heiterste Geschick!
Zur Laube wandeln sich die Thronen,
Arkadisch frei sei unser Glück!

Der Schauplatz verwandelt sich durchaus.

An eine Reihe von Felsenhöhlen lehnen sich geschloss'ne Lauben. Schattiger Hain bis an die rings umgebende Felsensteile hinan. Faust und Helena werden nicht gesehen. Der Chor liegt schlafend vertheilt umher.

Phorkyas.

Wie lange Zeit die Mädchen schlafen weiß ich nicht,
Ob sie sich träumen ließen was ich hell und klar 9575

Vor Augen sah, ist ebenfalls mir unbekannt.
Drum weck' ich sie. Erstaunen soll das junge Volk;
Ihr Bärtigen auch, die ihr da drunten sitzend harrt,
Glaubhafter Wunder Lösung endlich anzuschaun.
9580 Hervor! hervor! Und schüttelt eure Locken rasch;
Schlaf aus den Augen! Blinzt nicht so, und hört mich an!

Chor.

Rede nur, erzähl', erzähle was sich Wunderlichs begeben,
Hören möchten wir am liebsten was wir gar nicht glauben können,
Denn wir haben lange Weile diese Felsen anzusehn.

Phorkyas.

9585 Kaum die Augen ausgerieben, Kinder, langeweilt ihr schon?
So vernehmt: in diesen Höhlen, diesen Grotten, diesen Lauben
Schutz und Schirmung war verliehen, wie idyllischem Liebespaare,
Unserm Herrn und unsrer Frauen.

Chor.

Wie, da drinnen?

Phorkyas.

Abgesondert
Von der Welt, nur mich die Eine riefen sie zu stillem Dienste.
9590 Hochgeehrt stand ich zur Seite, doch, wie es Vertrauten ziemet,
Schaut' ich um nach etwas andrem. Wendete mich hier- und dorthin,
Suchte Wurzeln, Moos und Rinden, kundig aller Wirksamkeiten,
Und so blieben sie allein.

Chor.

Thust du doch als ob da drinnen ganze Welträume wären,
Wald und Wiese, Bäche, Seen; welche Mährchen spinnst
du ab! 9595

Phorkyas.

Allerdings, ihr Unerfahrnen! das sind unerforschte Tiefen:
Saal an Sälen, Hof an Höfen, diese spürt' ich sinnend aus.
Doch auf einmal ein Gelächter echo't in den Höhlen-Räumen;
Schau' ich hin, da springt ein Knabe von der Frauen Schoos zum
Manne,
Von dem Vater zu der Mutter; das Gekose, das Getändel, 9600
Thöriger Liebe Neckereien, Scherzgeschrei und Lustgejauchze
Wechselnd übertäuben mich.
Nackt ein Genius ohne Flügel, faunenartig ohne Thierheit,
Springt er auf den festen Boden, doch der Boden gegenwirkend
Schnellt ihn zu der luft'gen Höhe, und im zweiten, dritten
Sprunge 9605
Rührt er an das Hochgewölb.

Ängstlich ruft die Mutter: springe wiederholt und nach Belieben,
Aber hüte dich zu fliegen, freier Flug ist dir versagt.
Und so mahnt der treue Vater: in der Erde liegt die Schnellkraft,
Die dich aufwärts treibt, berühre mit der Zehe nur den
Boden, 9610
Wie der Erdensohn Antäus bist du alsobald gestärkt.
Und so hüpft er auf die Masse dieses Felsens, von der Kante
Zu dem andern und umher so wie ein Ball geschlagen springt.

Doch auf einmal in der Spalte rauher Schlucht ist er verschwunden,
Und nun scheint er uns verloren. Mutter jammert, Vater
tröstet, 9615

Achselzuckend steh' ich ängstlich. Doch nun wieder welch
Erscheinen!
Liegen Schätze dort verborgen? Blumenstreifige Gewande
Hat er würdig angethan.
Quasten schwanken von den Armen, Binden flattern um den
Busen,
9620 In der Hand die goldne Leier, völlig wie ein kleiner Phöbus
Tritt er wohlgemuth zur Kante, zu dem Überhang; wir
staunen.
Und die Eltern vor Entzücken werfen wechselnd sich an's
Herz.
Denn wie leuchtet's ihm zu Haupten? Was erglänzt ist
schwer zu sagen,
Ist es Goldschmuck, ist es Flamme übermächtiger Geisteskraft.
9625 Und so regt er sich gebärdend, sich als Knabe schon verkün-
dend
Künftigen Meister alles Schönen, dem die ewigen Melodien
Durch die Glieder sich bewegen; und so werdet ihr ihn
hören,
Und so werdet ihr ihn sehn zu einzigster Bewunderung.

Chor.

Nennst du ein Wunder dieß,
9630 Creta's Erzeugte?
Dichtend belehrendem Wort
Hast du gelauscht wohl nimmer?
Niemals noch gehört Joniens,
Nie vernommen auch Hellas
9635 Urväterlicher Sagen
Göttlich-heldenhaften Reichthum?

Alles was je geschieht
Heutigen Tages
Trauriger Nachklang ist's
Herrlicher Ahnherrn-Tage; 9640
Nicht vergleicht sich dein Erzählen
Dem was liebliche Lüge,
Glaubhaftiger als Wahrheit,
Von dem Sohne sang der Maja.

Diesen zierlich und kräftig doch 9645
Kaum geborenen Säugling
Faltet in reinster Windeln Flaum,
Strenget in köstlicher Wickeln Schmuck
Klatschender Wärterinnen Schaar
Unvernünftigen Wähnens. 9650
Kräftig und zierlich aber zieht
Schon der Schalk die geschmeidigen
Doch elastischen Glieder
Listig heraus, die purpurne
Ängstlich drückende Schale 9655
Lassend ruhig an seiner Statt;
Gleich dem fertigen Schmetterling,
Der aus starrem Puppenzwang
Flügel entfaltend behendig schlüpft,
Sonne-durchstrahlten Äther kühn 9660
Und muthwillig durchflatternd.

So auch er, der behendeste,
Daß er Dieben und Schälken,
Vortheilsuchenden allen auch
Ewig günstiger Dämon sei. 9665
Dieß bethätigt er alsobald
Durch gewandteste Künste.

Schnell des Meeres Beherrscher stiehlt
Er den Trident, ja dem Ares selbst
9670 Schlau das Schwert aus der Scheide;
Bogen und Pfeil dem Phöbus auch,
Wie dem Hephästos die Zange;
Selber Zeus, des Vaters, Blitz
Nähm' er, schreckt' ihn das Feuer nicht;
9675 Doch dem Eros siegt er ob
In beinstellendem Ringerspiel;
Raubt auch Cyprien, wie sie ihm kos't,
Noch vom Busen den Gürtel.

Ein reizendes, reinmelodisches Saitenspiel erklingt aus der Höhle. Alle merken auf und scheinen bald innig gerührt. Von hier an bis zur bemerkten Pause durchaus mit vollstimmiger Musik.

Phorkyas.

Höret allerliebste Klänge,
9680 Macht euch schnell von Fabeln frei,
Eurer Götter alt Gemenge
Laßt es hin, es ist vorbei.

Niemand will euch mehr verstehen,
Fordern wir doch höhern Zoll:
9685 Denn es muß von Herzen gehen,
Was auf Herzen wirken soll.

Sie zieht sich nach den Felsen zurück.

Chor.

Bist du, fürchterliches Wesen,
Diesem Schmeichelton geneigt,
Fühlen wir, als frisch genesen,
9690 Uns zur Thränenlust erweicht.

Laß der Sonne Glanz verschwinden,
Wenn es in der Seele tagt,
Wir im eignen Herzen finden
Was die ganze Welt versagt.

Helena, Faust, Euphorion in dem oben beschriebenen Costüm.

Euphorion.

Hört ihr Kindeslieder singen, 9695
Gleich ist's euer eigner Scherz;
Seht ihr mich im Tacte springen,
Hüpft euch elterlich das Herz.

Helena.

Liebe, menschlich zu beglücken
Nähert sie ein edles Zwei, 9700
Doch zu göttlichem Entzücken
Bildet sie ein köstlich Drei.

Faust.

Alles ist sodann gefunden:
Ich bin dein und du bist mein;
Und so stehen wir verbunden, 9705
Dürft' es doch nicht anders sein!

Chor.

Wohlgefallen vieler Jahre
In des Knaben mildem Schein
Sammelt sich auf diesem Paare.
O! wie rührt mich der Verein. 9710

Euphorion.

Nun laßt mich hüpfen,
Nun laßt mich springen,
Zu allen Lüften
Hinauf zu dringen
9715 Ist mir Begierde,
Sie faßt mich schon.

Faust.

Nur mäßig! mäßig!
Nicht in's Verwegne,
Daß Sturz und Unfall
9720 Dir nicht begegne,
Zu Grund uns richte
Der theure Sohn.

Euphorion.

Ich will nicht länger
Am Boden stocken;
9725 Laßt meine Hände,
Laßt meine Locken,
Laßt meine Kleider,
Sie sind ja mein.

Helena.

O denk'! o denke
9730 Wem du gehörest!
Wie es uns kränke,
Wie du zerstörest
Das schön errungene
Mein, Dein und Sein.

Chor.

Bald löst', ich fürchte, 9735
Sich der Verein!

Helena und Faust.

Bändige! bändige!
Eltern zu Liebe
Überlebendige,
Heftige Triebe! 9740
Ländlich im Stillen
Ziere den Plan.

Euphorion.

Nur euch zu Willen
Halt' ich mich an.

Durch den Chor sich schlingend und ihn zum Tanze fortziehend.

Leichter umschweb' ich hie 9745
Muntres Geschlecht.
Ist nun die Melodie,
Ist die Bewegung recht?

Helena.

Ja, das ist wohlgethan,
Führe die Schönen an 9750
Künstlichem Reihn.

Faust.

Wäre das doch vorbei!
Mich kann die Gaukelei
Gar nicht erfreun.

Euphorion und Chor tanzend und singend bewegen sich in verschlungenem Reihen.

Chor.

9755 Wenn du der Arme Paar
Lieblich bewegest,
Im Glanz dein lockig Haar
Schüttelnd erregest,
Wenn dir der Fuß so leicht
9760 Über die Erde schleicht,
Dort und da wieder hin
Glieder um Glied sich ziehn,
Hast du dein Ziel erreicht,
Liebliches Kind;
9765 All' unsre Herzen sind
All' dir geneigt.

Pause.

Euphorion.

Ihr seid so viele
Leichtfüßige Rehe,
Zu neuem Spiele
9770 Frisch aus der Nähe,
Ich bin der Jäger,
Ihr seid das Wild.

Chor.

Willst du uns fangen,
Sei nicht behende,
9775 Denn wir verlangen
Doch nur am Ende

Dich zu umarmen,
Du schönes Bild!

Euphorion.

Nur durch die Haine!
Zu Stock und Steine! 9780
Das leicht Errungene
Das widert mir,
Nur das Erzwungene
Ergetzt mich schier.

Helena und Faust.

Welch ein Muthwill'! welch ein Rasen! 9785
Keine Mäßigung ist zu hoffen.
Klingt es doch wie Hörnerblasen
Über Thal und Wälder dröhnend;
Welch ein Unfug! welch Geschrei!

Chor einzeln schnell eintretend.

Uns ist er vorbei gelaufen, 9790
Mit Verachtung uns verhöhnend
Schleppt er von dem ganzen Haufen
Nun die Wildeste herbei.

Euphorion ein junges Mädchen hereintragend.

Schlepp' ich her die derbe Kleine
Zu erzwungenem Genusse. 9795
Mir zur Wonne, mir zur Lust
Drück' ich widerspenstige Brust,

Küss' ich widerwärtigen Mund,
Thue Kraft und Willen kund.

Mädchen.

9800 Laß mich los! In dieser Hülle
Ist auch Geistes Muth und Kraft,
Deinem gleich ist unser Wille
Nicht so leicht hinweggerafft.
Glaubst du wohl mich im Gedränge?
9805 Deinem Arm vertraust du viel!
Halte fest, und ich versenge
Dich den Thoren mir zum Spiel.
Sie flammt auf und lodert in die Höhe.
Folge mir in leichte Lüfte,
Folge mir in starre Grüfte,
9810 Hasche das verschwundne Ziel.

Euphorion die letzten Flammen abschüttelnd.

Felsengedränge hier
Zwischen dem Waldgebüsch,
Was soll die Enge mir,
Bin ich doch jung und frisch.
9815 Winde sie sausen ja,
Wellen sie brausen da,
Hör' ich doch beides fern,
Nah wär' ich gern.
Er springt immer höher felsauf.

Helena, Faust und Chor.

Wolltest du den Gemsen gleichen?
9820 Vor dem Falle muß uns graun.

Euphorion.

Immer höher muß ich steigen,
Immer weiter muß ich schaun.
Weiß ich nun wo ich bin!
Mitten der Insel drin,
Mitten in Pelops Land, 9825
Erde- wie seeverwandt.

Chor.

Magst nicht in Berg und Wald
Friedlich verweilen?
Suchen wir alsobald
Reben in Zeilen, 9830
Reben am Hügelrand;
Feigen und Apfelgold.
Ach in dem holden Land
Bleibe du hold!

Euphorion.

Träumt ihr den Friedenstag? 9835
Träume wer träumen mag.
Krieg! ist das Losungswort.
Sieg! und so klingt es fort.

Chor.

Wer im Frieden
Wünschet sich Krieg zurück 9840
Der ist geschieden
Vom Hoffnungsglück.

Euphorion.

Welche dieß Land gebar
Aus Gefahr in Gefahr,

9845 Frei, unbegränzten Muths,
Verschwendrisch eignen Bluts;
Dem nicht zu dämpfenden
Heiligen Sinn,
Alle den Kämpfenden
9850 Bring' es Gewinn!

Chor.

Seht hinauf wie hoch gestiegen!
Und er scheint uns doch nicht klein,
Wie im Harnisch, wie zum Siegen,
Wie von Erz und Stahl der Schein.

Euphorion.

9855 Keine Wälle, keine Mauern,
Jeder nur sich selbst bewußt;
Feste Burg um auszudauern
Ist des Mannes ehrne Brust.
Wollt ihr unerobert wohnen,
9860 Leicht bewaffnet rasch in's Feld;
Frauen werden Amazonen
Und ein jedes Kind ein Held.

Chor.

Heilige Poesie,
Himmelan steige sie,
9865 Glänze, der schönste Stern,
Fern und so weiter fern,
Und sie erreicht uns doch
Immer, man hört sie noch,
Vernimmt sie gern.

Euphorion.

Nein, nicht ein Kind bin ich erschienen, 9870
In Waffen kommt der Jüngling an;
Gesellt zu Starken, Freien, Kühnen,
Hat er im Geiste schon gethan.
Nun fort!
Nun dort 9875
Eröffnet sich zum Ruhm die Bahn.

Helena und Faust.

Kaum in's Leben eingerufen,
Heitrem Tag gegeben kaum,
Sehnest du von Schwindelstufen
Dich zu schmerzenvollem Raum. 9880
Sind denn wir
Gar nichts dir?
Ist der holde Bund ein Traum?

Euphorion.

Und hört ihr donnern auf dem Meere?
Dort widerdonnern Thal um Thal, 9885
In Staub und Wellen Heer dem Heere,
In Drang um Drang zu Schmerz und Qual.
Und der Tod
Ist Gebot,
Das versteht sich nun einmal. 9890

Helena, Faust und Chor.

Welch Entsetzen! welches Grauen!
Ist der Tod denn dir Gebot?

Euphorion.

Sollt' ich aus der Ferne schauen?
Nein! ich theile Sorg' und Noth.

Die Vorigen.

9895 Übermuth und Gefahr,
Tödtliches Loos!

Euphorion.

Doch! — und ein Flügelpaar
Faltet sich los!
Dorthin! Ich muß! ich muß!
9900 Gönnt mir den Flug!

Er wirft sich in die Lüfte, die Gewande tragen ihn einen Augenblick, sein Haupt strahlt, ein Lichtschweif zieht nach.

Chor.

Ikarus! Ikarus!
Jammer genug.

Ein schöner Jüngling stürzt zu der Eltern Füßen, man glaubt in dem Todten eine bekannte Gestalt zu erblicken; doch das Körperliche verschwindet sogleich, die Aureole steigt wie ein Komet zum Himmel auf, Kleid, Mantel und Lyra bleiben liegen.

Helena und Faust.

Der Freude folgt sogleich
Grimmige Pein.

Euphorions Stimme aus der Tiefe.

9905 Laß mich im düstern Reich,
Mutter, mich nicht allein!

Pause.

Chor. Trauergesang.

Nicht allein! — wo du auch weilest,
Denn wir glauben dich zu kennen,
Ach! wenn du dem Tag enteilest,
Wird kein Herz von dir sich trennen. 9910
Wüßten wir doch kaum zu klagen,
Neidend singen wir dein Loos:
Dir in klar- und trüben Tagen
Lied und Muth war schön und groß.

Ach! zum Erdenglück geboren, 9915
Hoher Ahnen, großer Kraft,
Leider! früh dir selbst verloren,
Jugendblüthe weggerafft.
Scharfer Blick die Welt zu schauen,
Mitsinn jedem Herzensdrang, 9920
Liebesgluth der besten Frauen
Und ein eigenster Gesang.

Doch du ranntest unaufhaltsam
Frei in's willenlose Netz,
So entzweitest du gewaltsam 9925
Dich mit Sitte, mit Gesetz;
Doch zuletzt das höchste Sinnen
Gab dem reinen Muth Gewicht,
Wolltest Herrliches gewinnen,
Aber es gelang dir nicht. 9930

Wem gelingt es? — Trübe Frage,
Der das Schicksal sich vermummt,
Wenn am unglückseligsten Tage
Blutend alles Volk verstummt.

9935 Doch erfrischet neue Lieder,
Steht nicht länger tief gebeugt:
Denn der Boden zeugt sie wieder,
Wie von je er sie gezeugt.

Völlige Pause. Die Musik hört auf.

Helena zu Faust.

Ein altes Wort bewährt sich leider auch an mir:
9940 Daß Glück und Schönheit dauerhaft sich nicht vereint.
Zerrissen ist des Lebens wie der Liebe Band,
Bejammernd beide, sag' ich schmerzlich Lebewohl!
Und werfe mich noch einmal in die Arme dir.
Persephoneia, nimm den Knaben auf und mich.

Sie umarmt Faust, das Körperliche verschwindet, Kleid und Schleier bleiben ihm in den Armen.

Phorkyas zu Faust.

9945 Halte fest was dir von allem übrig blieb.
Das Kleid laß es nicht los. Da zupfen schon
Dämonen an den Zipfeln, möchten gern
Zur Unterwelt es reißen. Halte fest!
Die Göttin ist's nicht mehr die du verlorst,
9950 Doch göttlich ist's. Bediene dich der hohen,
Unschätzbarn Gunst und hebe dich empor,
Es trägt dich über alles Gemeine rasch
Am Äther hin, so lange du dauern kannst.
Wir sehn uns wieder, weit, gar weit von hier.

Helenens Gewande lösen sich in Wolken auf, umgeben Faust, heben ihn in die Höhe und ziehen mit ihm vorüber.

Phorkyas nimmt Euphorions Kleid, Mantel und Lyra von der Erde, tritt in's Proscenium, hebt die Exuvien in die Höhe und spricht:

Noch immer glücklich aufgefunden! 9955
Die Flamme freilich ist verschwunden,
Doch ist mir um die Welt nicht leid.
Hier bleibt genug, Poeten einzuweihen,
Zu stiften Gild- und Handwerksneid;
Und kann ich die Talente nicht verleihen, 9960
Verborg' ich wenigstens das Kleid.

Sie setzt sich im Proscenium an eine Säule nieder.

Panthalis.

Nun eilig, Mädchen! Sind wir doch den Zauber los,
Der alt-thessalischen Vettel wüsten Geisteszwang;
So des Geklimpers viel-verworrner Töne Rausch,
Das Ohr verwirrend, schlimmer noch den innern Sinn. 9965
Hinab zum Hades! Eilte doch die Königin
Mit ernstem Gang hinunter. Ihrer Sohle sei
Unmittelbar getreuer Mägde Schritt gefügt.
Wir finden sie am Throne der Unerforschlichen.

Chor.

Königinnen freilich überall sind sie gern; 9970
Auch im Hades stehen sie oben an,
Stolz zu ihres Gleichen gesellt,
Mit Persephonen innigst vertraut;
Aber wir im Hintergrunde
Tiefer Asphodelos-Wiesen, 9975
Langgestreckten Pappeln,
Unfruchtbaren Weiden zugesellt,
Welchen Zeitvertreib haben wir?

Fledermaus-gleich zu piepsen
9980 Geflüster, unerfreulich, gespenstig.

Panthalis.

Wer keinen Namen sich erwarb, noch Edles will,
Gehört den Elementen an, so fahret hin!
Mit meiner Königin zu sein verlangt mich heiß;
Nicht nur Verdienst, auch Treue wahrt uns die Person.

Ab.

Alle.

9985 Zurückgegeben sind wir dem Tageslicht,
Zwar Personen nicht mehr,
Das fühlen, das wissen wir,
Aber zum Hades kehren wir nimmer.
Ewig lebendige Natur
9990 Macht auf uns Geister,
Wir auf sie vollgültigen Anspruch.

Ein Theil des Chors.

Wir in dieser tausend Äste Flüsterzittern, Säuselschweben,
Reizen tändlend, locken leise, wurzelauf des Lebens Quellen
Nach den Zweigen; bald mit Blättern, bald mit Blüthen überschwänglich
9995 Zieren wir die Flatterhaare frei zu luftigem Gedeihn.
Fällt die Frucht, sogleich versammeln lebenslustig Volk und Heerden
Sich zum Greifen, sich zum Naschen, eilig kommend, emsig drängend;
Und, wie vor den ersten Göttern, bückt sich alles um uns her.

Ein andrer Theil.

Wir, an dieser Felsenwände weithinleuchtend glattem Spiegel
Schmiegen wir, in sanften Wellen uns bewegend, schmei-
cheln an; 10000
Horchen, lauschen jedem Laute, Vogelsängen, Röhrigflöten,
Sei es Pans furchtbarer Stimme, Antwort ist sogleich
bereit;
Säuselt's, säuseln wir erwidernd, donnert's, rollen unsre
Donner
In erschütterndem Verdoppeln, dreifach, zehnfach hinten nach.

Ein dritter Theil.

Schwestern! Wir, bewegtern Sinnes, eilen mit den Bächen
weiter; 10005
Denn es reizen jener Ferne reichgeschmückte Hügelzüge,
Immer abwärts, immer tiefer, wässern wir, mäandrisch
wallend,
Jetzt die Wiese, dann die Matten, gleich den Garten um
das Haus.
Dort bezeichnen's der Cypressen schlanke Wipfel, über
Landschaft,
Uferzug und Wellenspiegel nach dem Äther steigende. 10010

Ein vierter Theil.

Wallt ihr andern wo's beliebet, wir umzingeln, wir um-
rauschen
Den durchaus bepflanzten Hügel, wo am Stab die Rebe
grünt;
Dort zu aller Tage Stunden läßt die Leidenschaft des
Winzers
Uns des liebevollsten Fleißes zweifelhaft Gelingen sehn.

10015 Bald mit Hacke, bald mit Spaten, bald mit Häufeln,
Schneiden, Binden,
Betet er zu allen Göttern, förderſamſt zum Sonnengott.
Bacchus kümmert ſich, der Weichling, wenig um den treu=
en Diener,
Ruht in Lauben, lehnt in Höhlen, faſelnd mit dem jüng=
ſten Faun.
Was zu ſeiner Träumereien halbem Rauſch er je bedurfte,
10020 Immer bleibt es ihm in Schläuchen, ihm in Krügen und
Gefäßen
Rechts und links der kühlen Grüfte ewige Zeiten aufbe=
wahrt.
Haben aber alle Götter, hat nun Helios vor allen,
Lüftend, feuchtend, wärmend, gluthend Beeren=Füllhorn
aufgehäuft,
Wo der ſtille Winzer wirkte, dort auf einmal wird's le=
bendig,
10025 Und es rauſcht in jedem Laube, raſchelt um von Stock zu
Stock.
Körbe knarren, Eimer klappern, Tragebutten ächzen hin,
Alles nach der großen Kufe zu der Keltrer kräft'gem Tanz;
Und ſo wird die heilige Fülle reingeborner ſaftiger Beeren
Frech zertreten, ſchäumend, ſprühend miſcht ſich's widerlich
zerquetſcht.
10030 Und nun gellt in's Ohr der Cymbeln mit der Becken Erz=
getöne,
Denn es hat ſich Dionyſos aus Myſterien enthüllt;
Kommt hervor mit Ziegenfüßlern, ſchwenkend Ziegenfüß=
lerinnen,
Und dazwiſchen ſchreit unbändig grell Silenus öhrig Thier.
Nichts geſchont! Geſpaltne Klauen treten alle Sitte nieder,
10035 Alle Sinne wirbeln taumlich, gräßlich übertäubt das Ohr.

Nach der Schale tappen Trunkne, überfüllt sind Kopf und Wänste,
Sorglich ist noch ein- und andrer, doch vermehrt er die Tumulte,
Denn um neuen Most zu bergen, leert man rasch den alten Schlauch!

Der Vorhang fällt.

Phorkyas

im Proscenium richtet sich riesenhaft auf, tritt aber von den Kothurnen herunter, lehnt Maske und Schleier zurück und zeigt sich als Mephistopheles, um, in sofern es nöthig wäre, im Epilog das Stück zu commentiren.

Vierter Act.

Hochgebirg,

starre, zackige Felsen-Gipfel. Eine Wolke zieht herbei, lehnt sich an, senkt sich auf eine vorstehende Platte herab. Sie theilt sich.

Faust tritt hervor.

Der Einsamkeiten tiefste schauend unter meinem Fuß,
10040 Betret' ich wohlbedächtig dieser Gipfel Saum,
Entlassend meiner Wolke Tragewerk, die mich sanft
An klaren Tagen über Land und Meer geführt.
Sie lös't sich langsam, nicht zerstiebend, von mir ab.
Nach Osten strebt die Masse mit geballtem Zug,
10045 Ihr strebt das Auge staunend in Bewundrung nach.
Sie theilt sich wandelnd, wogenhaft, veränderlich.
Doch will sich's modeln.—Ja! das Auge trügt mich nicht!—
Auf sonnbeglänzten Pfühlen herrlich hingestreckt,
Zwar riesenhaft, ein göttergleiches Fraungebild,
10050 Ich seh's! Junonen ähnlich, Leda'n, Helenen,
Wie majestätisch lieblich mir's im Auge schwankt.
Ach! schon verrückt sich's! Formlos breit und aufgethürmt,
Ruht es in Osten, fernen Eisgebirgen gleich,
Und spiegelt blendend flücht'ger Tage großen Sinn.

10055 Doch mir umschwebt ein zarter lichter Nebelstreif
Noch Brust und Stirn, erheiternd, kühl und schmeichelhaft.

Nun steigt es leicht und zaudernd hoch und höher auf,
Fügt sich zusammen. — Täuscht mich ein entzückend Bild,
Als jugenderstes, längstentbehrtes höchstes Gut?
Des tiefsten Herzens frühste Schätze quellen auf, 10060
Aurorens Liebe, leichten Schwung bezeichnet's mir,
Den schnellempfundnen, ersten, kaum verstandnen Blick,
Der, festgehalten, überglänzte jeden Schatz.
Wie Seelenschönheit steigert sich die holde Form,
Löst sich nicht auf, erhebt sich in den Äther hin 10065
Und zieht das Beste meines Innern mit sich fort.

Ein Sieben-Meilenstiefel tappt auf. Ein anderer folgt alsbald. Mephistopheles steigt ab. Die Stiefel schreiten eilig weiter.

Mephistopheles.

Das heiß' ich endlich vorgeschritten!
Nun aber sag', was fällt dir ein?
Steigst ab in solcher Greuel Mitten,
Im gräßlich gähnenden Gestein? 10070
Ich kenn' es wohl, doch nicht an dieser Stelle,
Denn eigentlich war das der Grund der Hölle.

Faust.

Es fehlt dir nie an närrischen Legenden,
Fängst wieder an dergleichen auszuspenden.

Mephistopheles ernsthaft.

Als Gott der Herr — ich weiß auch wohl warum — 10075
Uns, aus der Luft, in tiefste Tiefen bannte,
Da, wo centralisch glühend, um und um,
Ein ewig Feuer flammend sich durchbrannte,

Wir fanden uns bei allzugroßer Hellung
10080 In sehr gedrängter, unbequemer Stellung.
Die Teufel fingen sämmtlich an zu husten,
Von oben und von unten aus zu pusten;
Die Hölle schwoll von Schwefel-Stank und Säure,
Das gab ein Gas! Das ging in's Ungeheure,
10085 So daß gar bald der Länder flache Kruste,
So dick sie war, zerkrachend bersten mußte.
Nun haben wir's an einem andern Zipfel,
Was ehmals Grund war ist nun Gipfel.
Sie gründen auch hierauf die rechten Lehren
10090 Das Unterste in's Oberste zu kehren.
Denn wir entrannen knechtisch-heißer Gruft
In's Übermaß der Herrschaft freier Luft.
Ein offenbar Geheimniß wohl verwahrt
Und wird nur spät den Völkern offenbart.

(Ephes. 6. 12.)

Faust.

10095 Gebirgesmasse bleibt mir edel-stumm,
Ich frage nicht woher und nicht warum?
Als die Natur sich in sich selbst gegründet,
Da hat sie rein den Erdball abgeründet,
Der Gipfel sich, der Schluchten sich erfreut
10100 Und Fels an Fels und Berg an Berg gereiht;
Die Hügel dann bequem hinabgebildet,
Mit sanftem Zug sie in das Thal gemildet.
Da grünt's und wächst's, und um sich zu erfreuen
Bedarf sie nicht der tollen Strudeleien.

Mephistopheles.

10105 Das sprecht ihr so! Das scheint euch sonnenklar,
Doch weiß es anders der zugegen war.

Ich war dabei, als noch da drunten, siedend,
Der Abgrund schwoll und strömend Flammen trug;
Als Molochs Hammer, Fels an Felsen schmiedend,
Gebirges-Trümmer in die Ferne schlug. 10110
Noch starrt das Land von fremden Centnermassen;
Wer gibt Erklärung solcher Schleudermacht?
Der Philosoph er weiß es nicht zu fassen,
Da liegt der Fels, man muß ihn liegen lassen,
Zu Schanden haben wir uns schon gedacht. — 10115
Das treu-gemeine Volk allein begreift
Und läßt sich im Begriff nicht stören;
Ihm ist die Weisheit längst gereift:
Ein Wunder ist's, der Satan kommt zu Ehren.
Mein Wandrer hinkt, an seiner Glaubenskrücke, 10120
Zum Teufelsstein, zur Teufelsbrücke.

Faust.

Es ist doch auch bemerkenswerth zu achten,
Zu sehn wie Teufel die Natur betrachten.

Mephistopheles.

Was geht mich's an! Natur sei wie sie sei!
's ist Ehrenpunct! — Der Teufel war dabei. 10125
Wir sind die Leute Großes zu erreichen;
Tumult, Gewalt und Unsinn! sieh das Zeichen! —
Doch, daß ich endlich ganz verständlich spreche,
Gefiel dir nichts an unsrer Oberfläche?
Du übersahst, in ungemess'nen Weiten, 10130
Die Reiche der Welt und ihre Herrlichkeiten;
(Matth. 4.)
Doch, ungenügsam wie du bist,
Empfandest du wohl kein Gelüst?

Faust.

Und doch! ein Großes zog mich an.
10135 Errathe!

Mephistopheles.

Das ist bald gethan.
Ich suchte mir so eine Hauptstadt aus,
Im Kerne Bürger-Nahrungs-Graus,
Krummenge Gäßchen, spitze Giebeln,
Beschränkten Markt, Kohl, Rüben, Zwiebeln;
10140 Fleischbänke wo die Schmeißen hausen
Die fetten Braten anzuschmausen;
Da findest du zu jeder Zeit
Gewiß Gestank und Thätigkeit.
Dann weite Plätze, breite Straßen,
10145 Vornehmen Schein sich anzumaßen;
Und endlich, wo kein Thor beschränkt,
Vorstädte gränzenlos verlängt.
Da freut' ich mich an Rollekutschen,
Am lärmigen Hin- und Widerrutschen,
10150 Am ewigen Hin- und Widerlaufen
Zerstreuter Ameis-Wimmelhaufen.
Und wenn ich führe, wenn ich ritte,
Erschien' ich immer ihre Mitte,
Von Hunderttausenden verehrt.

Faust.

10155 Das kann mich nicht zufrieden stellen!
Man freut sich daß das Volk sich mehrt,
Nach seiner Art behäglich nährt,
Sogar sich bildet, sich belehrt,
Und man erzieht sich nur Rebellen.

Mephistopheles.

Dann baut' ich, grandios, mir selbst bewußt, 10160
Am lustigen Ort ein Schloß zur Lust.
Wald, Hügel, Flächen, Wiesen, Feld
Zum Garten prächtig umbestellt.
Vor grünen Wänden Sammet-Matten,
Schnurwege, kunstgerechte Schatten, 10165
Cascadensturz, durch Fels zu Fels gepaart,
Und Wasserstrahlen aller Art;
Ehrwürdig steigt es dort, doch an den Seiten
Da zischt's und pißt's in tausend Kleinigkeiten.
Dann aber ließ' ich allerschönsten Frauen 10170
Vertraut-bequeme Häuslein bauen;
Verbrächte da gränzenlose Zeit
In allerliebst-geselliger Einsamkeit.
Ich sage Fraun; denn ein für allemal
Denk' ich die Schönen im Plural. 10175

Faust.

Schlecht und modern! Sardanapal!

Mephistopheles.

Erräth man wohl wornach du strebtest?
Es war gewiß erhaben kühn.
Der du dem Mond um so viel näher schwebtest,
Dich zog wohl deine Sucht dahin? 10180

Faust.

Mit nichten! dieser Erdenkreis
Gewährt noch Raum zu großen Thaten.
Erstaunenswürdiges soll gerathen,
Ich fühle Kraft zu kühnem Fleiß.

Mephistopheles.

10185 Und also willst du Ruhm verdienen?
Man merkt's du kommst von Heroinen.

Faust.

Herrschaft gewinn' ich, Eigenthum!
Die That ist alles, nichts der Ruhm.

Mephistopheles.

Doch werden sich Poeten finden,
10190 Der Nachwelt deinen Glanz zu künden,
Durch Thorheit Thorheit zu entzünden.

Faust.

Von allem ist dir nichts gewährt.
Was weißt du was der Mensch begehrt?
Dein widrig Wesen, bitter, scharf,
10195 Was weiß es was der Mensch bedarf?

Mephistopheles.

Geschehe denn nach deinem Willen!
Vertraue mir den Umfang deiner Grillen.

Faust.

Mein Auge war auf's hohe Meer gezogen,
Es schwoll empor, sich in sich selbst zu thürmen.
10200 Dann ließ es nach und schüttete die Wogen,
Des flachen Ufers Breite zu bestürmen.
Und das verdroß mich; wie der Übermuth
Den freien Geist, der alle Rechte schätzt,
Durch leidenschaftlich aufgeregtes Blut
10205 In's Mißbehagen des Gefühls versetzt.
Ich hielt's für Zufall, schärfte meinen Blick,
Die Woge stand und rollte dann zurück,

Entfernte sich vom stolz erreichten Ziel;
Die Stunde kommt, sie wiederholt das Spiel.

Mephistopheles ad Spectatores.

Da ist für mich nichts Neues zu erfahren, 10210
Das kenn' ich schon seit hunderttausend Jahren.

Faust leidenschaftlich fortfahrend.

Sie schleicht heran, an abertausend Enden
Unfruchtbar selbst Unfruchtbarkeit zu spenden;
Nun schwillt's und wächs't und rollt und überzieht
Der wüsten Strecke widerlich Gebiet. 10215
Da herrschet Well' auf Welle kraftbegeistet,
Zieht sich zurück und es ist nichts geleistet,
Was zur Verzweiflung mich beängstigen könnte!
Zwecklose Kraft unbändiger Elemente!
Da wagt mein Geist sich selbst zu überfliegen; 10220
Hier möcht' ich kämpfen, dieß möcht' ich besiegen.

Und es ist möglich! — fluthend wie sie sei,
An jedem Hügel schmiegt sie sich vorbei;
Sie mag sich noch so übermüthig regen,
Geringe Höhe ragt ihr stolz entgegen, 10225
Geringe Tiefe zieht sie mächtig an.
Da faßt' ich schnell im Geiste Plan auf Plan:
Erlange dir das köstliche Genießen
Das herrische Meer vom Ufer auszuschließen,
Der feuchten Breite Gränzen zu verengen 10230
Und, weit hinein, sie in sich selbst zu drängen.
Von Schritt zu Schritt wußt' ich mir's zu erörtern;
Das ist mein Wunsch, den wage zu befördern!

Trommeln und kriegerische Musik im Rücken der Zuschauer, aus der Ferne, von der rechten Seite her.

Mephistopheles.

Wie leicht ist das! Hörst du die Trommeln fern?

Faust.

10235 Schon wieder Krieg! der Kluge hört's nicht gern.

Mephistopheles.

Krieg oder Frieden. Klug ist das Bemühen
Zu seinem Vortheil etwas auszuziehen.
Man paßt, man merkt auf jedes günstige Nu.
Gelegenheit ist da, nun, Fauste, greife zu!

Faust.

10240 Mit solchem Räthselkram verschone mich!
Und kurz und gut, was soll's? Erkläre dich.

Mephistopheles.

Auf meinem Zuge blieb mir nicht verborgen,
Der gute Kaiser schwebt in großen Sorgen;
Du kennst ihn ja. Als wir ihn unterhielten,
10245 Ihm falschen Reichthum in die Hände spielten,
Da war die ganze Welt ihm feil.
Denn jung ward ihm der Thron zu Theil,
Und ihm beliebt' es falsch zu schließen:
Es könne wohl zusammengehn,
10250 Und sei recht wünschenswerth und schön,
Regieren und zugleich genießen.

Faust.

Ein großer Irrthum. Wer befehlen soll,
Muß im Befehlen Seligkeit empfinden.
Ihm ist die Brust von hohem Willen voll,
10255 Doch was er will, es darf's kein Mensch ergründen.

Was er den Treusten in das Ohr geraunt,
Es ist gethan und alle Welt erstaunt.
So wird er stets der Allerhöchste sein,
Der Würdigste —, Genießen macht gemein.

Mephistopheles.

So ist er nicht! Er selbst genoß und wie? 10260
Indeß zerfiel das Reich in Anarchie,
Wo groß und klein sich kreuz und quer befehdeten,
Und Brüder sich vertrieben, tödteten,
Burg gegen Burg, Stadt gegen Stadt,
Zunft gegen Adel — Fehde hat, 10265
Der Bischof mit Capitel und Gemeinde;
Was sich nur ansah waren Feinde.
In Kirchen Mord und Todtschlag, vor den Thoren
Ist jeder Kauf- und Wandersmann verloren.
Und allen wuchs die Kühnheit nicht gering; 10270
Denn leben hieß sich wehren — Nun, das ging.

Faust.

Es ging, es hinkte, fiel, stand wieder auf;
Dann überschlug sich's, rollte plump zu Hauf.

Mephistopheles.

Und solchen Zustand durfte niemand schelten,
Ein jeder konnte, jeder wollte gelten. 10275
Der Kleinste selbst er galt für voll.
Doch war's zuletzt den Besten allzutoll.
Die Tüchtigen sie standen auf mit Kraft
Und sagten: Herr ist der uns Ruhe schafft.
Der Kaiser kann's nicht, will's nicht — laßt uns wählen, 10280
Den neuen Kaiser neu das Reich beseelen,

Indem er jeden sicher stellt,
In einer frisch geschaffnen Welt
Fried' und Gerechtigkeit vermählen.

Faust.

10285 Das klingt sehr pfäffisch.

Mephistopheles.

Pfaffen waren's auch,
Sie sicherten den wohlgenährten Bauch.
Sie waren mehr als andere betheiligt.
Der Aufruhr schwoll, der Aufruhr ward geheiligt;
Und unser Kaiser, den wir froh gemacht,
10290 Zieht sich hieher, vielleicht zur letzten Schlacht.

Faust.

Er jammert mich, er war so gut und offen.

Mephistopheles.

Komm, sehn wir zu, der Lebende soll hoffen.
Befrein wir ihn aus diesem engen Thale!
Einmal gerettet ist's für tausendmale.
10295 Wer weiß wie noch die Würfel fallen?
Und hat er Glück, so hat er auch Vasallen.

Sie steigen über das Mittelgebirg herüber und beschauen die Anordnung des Heeres im Thal. Trommeln und Kriegsmusik schallt von unten auf.

Mephistopheles.

Die Stellung, seh' ich, gut ist sie genommen;
Wir treten zu, dann ist der Sieg vollkommen.

Faust.

Was kann da zu erwarten sein?
10300 Trug! Zauberblendwerk! Hohler Schein.

Mephistopheles.

Kriegslist um Schlachten zu gewinnen!
Befestige dich bei großen Sinnen,
Indem du deinen Zweck bedenkst.
Erhalten wir dem Kaiser Thron und Lande,
So kniest du nieder und empfängst 10305
Die Lehn von gränzenlosem Strande.

Faust.

Schon manches hast du durchgemacht,
Nun, so gewinn' auch eine Schlacht.

Mephistopheles.

Nein, du gewinnst sie! Diesesmal
Bist du der Obergeneral. 10310

Faust.

Das wäre mir die rechte Höhe
Da zu befehlen wo ich nichts verstehe!

Mephistopheles.

Laß du den Generalstab sorgen
Und der Feldmarschall ist geborgen.
Kriegsunrath hab' ich längst verspürt, 10315
Den Kriegsrath gleich voraus formirt
Aus Urgebirgs Urmenschenkraft;
Wohl dem der sie zusammenrafft.

Faust.

Was seh' ich dort was Waffen trägt?
Hast du das Bergvolk aufgeregt? 10320

Mephistopheles.

Nein! aber, gleich Herrn Peter Squenz,
Vom ganzen Praß die Quintessenz.

Die drei Gewaltigen treten auf.
(Sam. II. 23. 8.)

Mephistopheles.

Da kommen meine Bursche ja!
Du siehst, von sehr verschiednen Jahren,
10325 Verschiednem Kleid und Rüstung sind sie da,
Du wirst nicht schlecht mit ihnen fahren.
Ad Spectatores.
Es liebt sich jetzt ein jedes Kind
Den Harnisch und den Ritterkragen;
Und, allegorisch wie die Lumpe sind,
10330 Sie werden nur um desto mehr behagen.

Raufebold jung, leicht bewaffnet, bunt gekleidet.

Wenn einer mir in's Auge sieht,
Werd' ich ihm mit der Faust gleich in die Fresse fahren,
Und eine Memme, wenn sie flieht,
Fass' ich bei ihren letzten Haaren.

Habebald männlich, wohl bewaffnet, reich gekleidet.

10335 So leere Händel das sind Possen,
Damit verdirbt man seinen Tag;
Im Nehmen sei nur unverdrossen,
Nach allem andern frag' hernach.

Haltefest bejahrt, stark bewaffnet, ohne Gewand.

Damit ist auch nicht viel gewonnen,
10340 Bald ist ein großes Gut zerronnen,

Es rauscht im Lebensstrom hinab.
Zwar nehmen ist recht gut, doch besser ist's behalten;
Laß du den grauen Kerl nur walten
Und niemand nimmt dir etwas ab.

Sie steigen allzusammen tiefer.

Auf dem Vorgebirg.

Trommeln und kriegerische Musik von unten. Des Kaisers Zelt wird aufgeschlagen.

Kaiser. Obergeneral. Trabanten.

Obergeneral.

10345 Noch immer scheint der Vorsatz wohl erwogen,
Daß wir, in dieß gelegene Thal,
Das ganze Heer gedrängt zurückgezogen;
Ich hoffe fest uns glückt die Wahl.

Kaiser.

Wie es nun geht, es muß sich zeigen;
10350 Doch mich verdrießt die halbe Flucht, das Weichen.

Obergeneral.

Schau hier, mein Fürst, auf unsre rechte Flanke.
Solch ein Terrain wünscht sich der Kriegsgedanke;
Nicht steil die Hügel, doch nicht allzu gänglich,
Den Unsern vortheilhaft, dem Feind verfänglich.
10355 Wir, halb versteckt, auf wellenförmigem Plan;
Die Reiterei sie wagt sich nicht heran.

Kaiser.

Mir bleibt nichts übrig als zu loben;
Hier kann sich Arm und Brust erproben.

Obergeneral.

Hier, auf der Mittelwiese flachen Räumlichkeiten,
Siehst du den Phalanx, wohlgemuth zu streiten. 10360
Die Piken blinken flimmernd in der Luft,
Im Sonnenglanz, durch Morgennebelduft.
Wie dunkel wogt das mächtige Quadrat!
Zu Tausenden glüht's hier auf große That.
Du kannst daran der Masse Kraft erkennen, 10365
Ich trau' ihr zu der Feinde Kraft zu trennen.

Kaiser.

Den schönen Blick hab' ich zum erstenmal.
Ein solches Heer gilt für die Doppelzahl.

Obergeneral.

Von unsrer Linken hab' ich nichts zu melden,
Den starren Fels besetzen wackere Helden. 10370
Das Steingeklipp, das jetzt von Waffen blitzt,
Den wichtigen Paß der engen Klause schützt.
Ich ahne schon hier scheitern Feindeskräfte
Unvorgesehn im blutigen Geschäfte.

Kaiser.

Dort ziehn sie her die falschen Anverwandten, 10375
Wie sie mich Oheim, Vetter, Bruder nannten,
Sich immer mehr und wieder mehr erlaubten,
Dem Scepter Kraft, dem Thron Verehrung raubten,
Dann, unter sich entzweit, das Reich verheerten
Und nun gesammt sich gegen mich empörten. 10380

Die Menge schwankt im ungewissen Geist,
Dann strömt sie nach wohin der Strom sie reißt.

Obergeneral.

Ein treuer Mann, auf Kundschaft ausgeschickt,
Kommt eilig felsenab; sei's ihm geglückt!

Erster Kundschafter.

10385 Glücklich ist sie uns gelungen,
Listig, muthig unsre Kunst,
Daß wir hin und her gedrungen;
Doch wir bringen wenig Gunst,
Viele schwören reine Huldigung
10390 Dir, wie manche treue Schaar;
Doch Unthätigkeits-Entschuldigung:
Innere Gährung, Volksgefahr.

Kaiser.

Sich selbst erhalten bleibt der Selbstsucht Lehre,
Nicht Dankbarkeit und Neigung, Pflicht und Ehre.
10395 Bedenkt ihr nicht, wenn eure Rechnung voll,
Daß Nachbars Hausbrand Euch verzehren soll?

Obergeneral.

Der zweite kommt, nur langsam steigt er nieder,
Dem müden Manne zittern alle Glieder.

Zweiter Kundschafter.

Erst gewahrten wir vergnüglich
10400 Wilden Wesens irren Lauf;
Unerwartet, unverzüglich
Trat ein neuer Kaiser auf.

Und auf vorgeschriebnen Bahnen
Zieht die Menge durch die Flur;
Den entrollten Lügenfahnen 10405
Folgen alle. — Schafsnatur.

Kaiser.

Ein Gegenkaiser kommt mir zum Gewinn,
Nun fühl' ich erst daß Ich der Kaiser bin.
Nur als Soldat legt' ich den Harnisch an,
Zu höherm Zweck ist er nun umgethan. 10410
Bei jedem Fest, wenn's noch so glänzend war,
Nichts ward vermißt, mir fehlte die Gefahr.
Wie ihr auch seid, zum Ringspiel riethet ihr,
Mir schlug das Herz, ich athmete Turnier.
Und hättet ihr mir nicht vom Kriegen abgerathen, 10415
Jetzt glänzt' ich schon in lichten Heldenthaten.
Selbstständig fühlt' ich meine Brust besiegelt,
Als ich mich dort im Feuerreich bespiegelt,
Das Element drang gräßlich auf mich los,
Es war nur Schein, allein der Schein war groß. 10420
Von Sieg und Ruhm hab' ich verwirrt geträumt,
Ich bringe nach was frevelhaft versäumt.

Die Herolde werden abgefertigt zu Herausforderung des Gegenkaisers.

Faust geharnischt, mit halbgeschloss'nem Helme. Die drei Gewaltigen gerüstet und gekleidet wie oben.

Faust.

Wir treten auf und hoffen, ungescholten;
Auch ohne Noth hat Vorsicht wohl gegolten.

10425 Du weißt das Bergvolk denkt und simulirt,
Ist in Natur- und Felsenschrift studirt.
Die Geister, längst dem flachen Land entzogen,
Sind mehr als sonst dem Felsgebirg gewogen.
Sie wirken still durch labyrinthische Klüfte,
10430 Im edlen Gas metallisch reicher Düfte;
In stetem Sondern, Prüfen und Verbinden,
Ihr einziger Trieb ist Neues zu erfinden.
Mit leisem Finger geistiger Gewalten
Erbauen sie durchsichtige Gestalten;
10435 Dann im Krystall und seiner ewigen Schweigniß
Erblicken sie der Oberwelt Ereigniß.

Kaiser.

Vernommen hab' ich's und ich glaube dir;
Doch, wackrer Mann, sag' an: was soll das hier?

Faust.

Der Nekromant von Norcia, der Sabiner,
10440 Ist dein getreuer, ehrenhafter Diener.
Welch greulich Schicksal droht' ihm ungeheuer,
Das Reisig prasselte, schon züngelte das Feuer;
Die trocknen Scheite, rings umher verschränkt,
Mit Pech und Schwefelruthen untermengt;
10445 Nicht Mensch, noch Gott, noch Teufel konnte retten,
Die Majestät zersprengte glühende Ketten.
Dort war's in Rom. Er bleibt dir hoch verpflichtet,
Auf deinen Gang in Sorge stets gerichtet.
Von jener Stund' an ganz vergaß er sich,
10450 Er fragt den Stern, die Tiefe nur für Dich.
Er trug uns auf, als eiligstes Geschäfte,
Bei dir zu stehn. Groß sind des Berges Kräfte;

Da wirkt Natur so übermächtig frei,
Der Pfaffen Stumpfsinn schilt es Zauberei.

Kaiser.

Am Freudentag wenn wir die Gäste grüßen, 10455
Die heiter kommen, heiter zu genießen,
Da freut uns jeder wie er schiebt und drängt,
Und, Mann für Mann, der Säle Raum verengt.
Doch höchst willkommen muß der Biedre sein,
Tritt er als Beistand kräftig zu uns ein, 10460
Zur Morgenstunde, die bedenklich waltet,
Weil über ihr des Schicksals Wage schaltet.
Doch lenket hier, im hohen Augenblick,
Die starke Hand vom willigen Schwert zurück,
Ehrt den Moment, wo manche Tausend schreiten, 10465
Für oder wider mich zu streiten.
Selbst ist der Mann! Wer Thron und Kron' begehrt,
Persönlich sei er solcher Ehren werth.
Sei das Gespenst, das gegen uns erstanden
Sich Kaiser nennt und Herr von unsern Landen, 10470
Des Heeres Herzog, Lehnsherr unsrer Großen,
Mit eigner Faust in's Todtenreich gestoßen!

Faust.

Wie es auch sei das Große zu vollenden,
Du thust nicht wohl dein Haupt so zu verpfänden.
Ist nicht der Helm mit Kamm und Busch geschmückt? 10475
Er schützt das Haupt das unsern Muth entzückt.
Was, ohne Haupt, was förderten die Glieder?
Denn schläfert jenes, alle sinken nieder,
Wird es verletzt, gleich alle sind verwundet,
Erstehen frisch, wenn jenes rasch gesundet. 10480

Schnell weiß der Arm sein starkes Recht zu nützen,
Er hebt den Schild den Schädel zu beschützen,
Das Schwert gewahret seiner Pflicht sogleich,
Lenkt kräftig ab und wiederholt den Streich;
10485 Der tüchtige Fuß nimmt Theil an ihrem Glück,
Setzt dem Erschlagnen frisch sich in's Genick.

Kaiser.

Das ist mein Zorn, so möcht' ich ihn behandeln,
Das stolze Haupt in Schemeltritt verwandeln!

Herolde kommen zurück.

Wenig Ehre, wenig Geltung
10490 Haben wir daselbst genossen,
Unsrer kräftig edlen Meldung
Lachten sie als schaler Possen:
„Euer Kaiser ist verschollen,
Echo dort im engen Thal;
10495 Wenn wir sein gedenken sollen,
Mährchen sagt: — Es war einmal.“

Faust.

Dem Wunsch gemäß der Besten ist's geschehn,
Die, fest und treu, an deiner Seite stehn.
Dort naht der Feind, die Deinen harren brünstig,
10500 Befiehl den Angriff, der Moment ist günstig.

Kaiser.

Auf das Commando leist' ich hier Verzicht.

Zum Oberfeldherrn.

In deinen Händen, Fürst, sei deine Pflicht.

Obergeneral.

So trete denn der rechte Flügel an!
Des Feindes Linke, eben jetzt im Steigen,

Soll, eh' sie noch den letzten Schritt gethan, 10505
Der Jugendkraft geprüfter Treue weichen.

Faust.

Erlaube denn daß dieser muntre Held
Sich ungesäumt in deine Reihen stellt,
Sich deinen Reihen innigst einverleibt
Und, so gesellt, sein kräftig Wesen treibt. 10510

Er deutet zur Rechten.

Raufebold tritt vor.

Wer das Gesicht mir zeigt der kehrt's nicht ab
Als mit zerschlagnen Unter- und Oberbacken;
Wer mir den Rücken kehrt, gleich liegt ihm schlapp
Hals, Kopf und Schopf hinschlotternd graß im Nacken.
Und schlagen deine Männer dann 10515
Mit Schwert und Kolben wie ich wüthe,
So stürzt der Feind, Mann über Mann,
Ersäuft im eigenen Geblüte.

Ab.

Obergeneral.

Der Phalanx unsrer Mitte folge sacht,
Dem Feind begegn' er, klug mit aller Macht, 10520
Ein wenig rechts, dort hat bereits, erbittert,
Der Unsern Streitkraft ihren Plan erschüttert.

Faust auf den Mittelsten deutend.

So folge denn auch dieser deinem Wort.
Er ist behend, reißt alles mit sich fort.

Habebald tritt hervor.

Dem Heldenmuth der Kaiserschaaren 10525
Soll sich der Durst nach Beute paaren;

Und allen sei das Ziel gestellt:
Des Gegenkaisers reiches Zelt.
Er prahlt nicht lang auf seinem Sitze,
10530 Ich ordne mich dem Phalanx an die Spitze.

Eilebeute Marketenderin, sich an ihn anschmiegend.

Bin ich auch ihm nicht angeweibt,
Er mir der liebste Buhle bleibt.
Für uns ist solch ein Herbst gereift!
Die Frau ist grimmig wenn sie greift,
10535 Ist ohne Schonung wenn sie raubt;
Im Sieg voran! und alles ist erlaubt.

Beide ab.

Obergeneral.

Auf unsre Linke, wie vorauszusehn,
Stürzt ihre Rechte, kräftig. Widerstehn
Wird Mann für Mann dem wüthenden Beginnen
10540 Den engen Paß des Felswegs zu gewinnen.

Faust winkt nach der Linken.

So bitte, Herr, auch diesen zu bemerken,
Es schadet nichts, wenn Starke sich verstärken.

Haltefest tritt vor.

Dem linken Flügel keine Sorgen!
Da wo ich bin ist der Besitz geborgen;
10545 In ihm bewähret sich der Alte,
Kein Strahlblitz spaltet was ich halte.

Ab.

Mephistopheles von oben herunter kommend.

Nun schauet wie im Hintergrunde
Aus jedem zackigen Felsenschlunde

Bewaffnete hervor sich drängen,
Die schmalen Pfade zu verengen, 10550
Mit Helm und Harnisch, Schwertern, Schilden
In unserm Rücken eine Mauer bilden,
Den Wink erwartend zuzuschlagen.

Leise zu den Wissenden.

Woher das kommt müßt ihr nicht fragen.
Ich habe freilich nicht gesäumt, 10555
Die Waffensäle ringsum ausgeräumt;
Da standen sie zu Fuß, zu Pferde
Als wären sie noch Herrn der Erde;
Sonst waren's Ritter, König, Kaiser,
Jetzt sind es nichts als leere Schneckenhäuser; 10560
Gar manch Gespenst hat sich darein geputzt,
Das Mittelalter lebhaft aufgestutzt.
Welch Teufelchen auch drinne steckt,
Für dießmal macht es doch Effect.

Laut.

Hört wie sie sich voraus erbosen, 10565
Blechklappernd aneinander stoßen!
Auch flattern Fahnenfetzen bei Standarten,
Die frischer Lüftchen ungeduldig harrten.
Bedenkt, hier ist ein altes Volk bereit
Und mischte gern sich auch zum neuen Streit. 10570

Furchtbarer Posaunenschall von oben, im feindlichen Heere merkliche Schwankung.

Faust.

Der Horizont hat sich verdunkelt,
Nur hie und da bedeutend funkelt
Ein rother ahnungsvoller Schein;
Schon blutig blinken die Gewehre,

10575 Der Fels, der Wald, die Atmosphäre,
Der ganze Himmel mischt sich ein.

Mephistopheles.

Die rechte Flanke hält sich kräftig;
Doch seh' ich, ragend unter diesen,
Hans Raufbold, den behenden Riesen,
10580 Auf seine Weise rasch geschäftig.

Kaiser.

Erst sah ich Einen Arm erhoben,
Jetzt seh' ich schon ein Dutzend toben,
Naturgemäß geschieht es nicht.

Faust.

Vernahmst du nichts von Nebelstreifen
10585 Die auf Siciliens Küsten schweifen?
Dort, schwankend klar, im Tageslicht,
Erhoben zu den Mittellüften,
Gespiegelt in besondern Düften,
Erscheint ein seltsames Gesicht:
10590 Da schwanken Städte hin und wider,
Da steigen Gärten auf und nieder,
Wie Bild um Bild den Äther bricht.

Kaiser.

Doch wie bedenklich! Alle Spitzen
Der hohen Speere seh' ich blitzen;
10595 Auf unsrer Phalanx blanken Lanzen
Seh' ich behende Flämmchen tanzen.
Das scheint mir gar zu geisterhaft.

Faust.

Verzeih, o Herr, das sind die Spuren
Verschollner geistiger Naturen,

Ein Widerschein der Dioskuren, 10600
Bei denen alle Schiffer schwuren;
Sie sammeln hier die letzte Kraft.

Kaiser.

Doch sage: wem sind wir verpflichtet
Daß die Natur, auf uns gerichtet,
Das Seltenste zusammenrafft? 10605

Mephistopheles.

Wem als dem Meister, jenem hohen,
Der dein Geschick im Busen trägt?
Durch deiner Feinde starkes Drohen
Ist er im Tiefsten aufgeregt.
Sein Dank will dich gerettet sehen, 10610
Und sollt' er selbst daran vergehen.

Kaiser.

Sie jubelten mich pomphaft umzuführen,
Ich war nun was, das wollt' ich auch probiren
Und fand's gelegen, ohne viel zu denken,
Dem weißen Barte kühle Luft zu schenken. 10615
Dem Klerus hab' ich eine Lust verdorben
Und ihre Gunst mir freilich nicht erworben.
Nun sollt' ich, seit so manchen Jahren,
Die Wirkung frohen Thuns erfahren?

Faust.

Freiherzige Wohlthat wuchert reich; 10620
Laß deinen Blick sich aufwärts wenden!
Mich deucht Er will ein Zeichen senden,
Gib Acht, es deutet sich sogleich.

Kaiser.

Ein Adler schwebt im Himmelhohen,
10625 Ein Greif ihm nach mit wildem Drohen.

Faust.

Gib Acht: gar günstig scheint es mir.
Greif ist ein fabelhaftes Thier;
Wie kann er sich so weit vergessen
Mit echtem Adler sich zu messen?

Kaiser.

10630 Nunmehr, in weitgedehnten Kreisen,
Umziehn sie sich; — in gleichem Nu,
Sie fahren auf einander zu
Sich Brust und Hälse zu zerreißen.

Faust.

Nun merke wie der leidige Greif,
10635 Zerzerrt, zerzaus't, nur Schaden findet
Und mit gesenktem Löwenschweif,
Zum Gipfelwald gestürzt, verschwindet.

Kaiser.

Sei's wie gedeutet, so gethan!
Ich nehm' es mit Verwundrung an.

Mephistopheles gegen die Rechte.

10640 Dringend wiederholten Streichen
Müssen unsre Feinde weichen,
Und, mit ungewissem Fechten,
Drängen sie nach ihrer Rechten
Und verwirren so im Streite
10645 Ihrer Hauptmacht linke Seite.

Unsers Phalanx feste Spitze
Zieht sich rechts und gleich dem Blitze
Fährt sie in die schwache Stelle. —
Nun, wie sturmerregte Welle
Sprühend, wüthen gleiche Mächte 10650
Wild in doppeltem Gefechte;
Herrlichers ist nichts ersonnen,
Uns ist diese Schlacht gewonnen!

Kaiser an der linken Seite zu Faust.

Schau! Mir scheint es dort bedenklich,
Unser Posten steht verfänglich. 10655
Keine Steine seh' ich fliegen,
Niedre Felsen sind erstiegen,
Obre stehen schon verlassen.
Jetzt! — Der Feind, zu ganzen Massen
Immer näher angedrungen, 10660
Hat vielleicht den Paß errungen,
Schlußerfolg unheiligen Strebens!
Eure Künste sind vergebens.

Pause.

Mephistopheles.

Da kommen meine beiden Raben,
Was mögen die für Botschaft haben? 10665
Ich fürchte gar es geht uns schlecht.

Kaiser.

Was sollen diese leidigen Vögel?
Sie richten ihre schwarzen Segel
Hierher vom heißen Felsgefecht.

Mephistopheles zu den Raben.

10670 Setzt euch ganz nah zu meinen Ohren.
Wen ihr beschützt ist nicht verloren,
Denn euer Rath ist folgerecht.

Faust zum Kaiser.

Von Tauben hast du ja vernommen,
Die aus den fernsten Landen kommen,
10675 Zu ihres Nestes Brut und Kost.
Hier ist's mit wichtigen Unterschieden:
Die Taubenpost bedient den Frieden,
Der Krieg befiehlt die Rabenpost.

Mephistopheles.

Es meldet sich ein schwer Verhängniß,
10680 Seht hin! gewahret die Bedrängniß
Um unsrer Helden Felsenrand.
Die nächsten Höhen sind erstiegen,
Und würden sie den Paß besiegen,
Wir hätten einen schweren Stand.

Kaiser.

10685 So bin ich endlich doch betrogen!
Ihr habt mich in das Netz gezogen,
Mir graut seitdem es mich umstrickt.

Mephistopheles.

Nur Muth! Noch ist es nicht mißglückt.
Geduld und Pfiff zum letzten Knoten;
10690 Gewöhnlich geht's am Ende scharf.
Ich habe meine sichern Boten,
Befehlt daß ich befehlen darf.

Obergeneral der indessen herangekommen.

Mit diesen hast du dich vereinigt,
Mich hat's die ganze Zeit gepeinigt,
Das Gaukeln schafft kein festes Glück. 10695
Ich weiß nichts an der Schlacht zu wenden,
Begannen sie's, sie mögen's enden,
Ich gebe meinen Stab zurück.

Kaiser.

Behalt' ihn bis zu bessern Stunden,
Die uns vielleicht das Glück verleiht. 10700
Mir schaudert vor dem garstigen Kunden
Und seiner Rabentraulichkeit.

Zu Mephistopheles.

Den Stab kann ich dir nicht verleihen,
Du scheinst mir nicht der rechte Mann,
Befiehl und such' uns zu befreien; 10705
Geschehe, was geschehen kann.

Ab in's Zelt mit dem Obergeneral.

Mephistopheles.

Mag ihn der stumpfe Stab beschützen!
Uns andern könnt' er wenig nützen,
Es war so was vom Kreuz daran.

Faust.

Was ist zu thun?

Mephistopheles.

Es ist gethan! — 10710
Nun, schwarze Vettern, rasch im Dienen,
Zum großen Bergsee! grüßt mir die Undinen

Und bittet sie um ihrer Fluthen Schein.
Durch Weiberkünste, schwer zu kennen,
10715 Verstehen sie vom Sein den Schein zu trennen,
Und jeder schwört das sei das Sein.

Pause.

Faust.

Den Wasserfräulein müssen unsre Raben
Recht aus dem Grund geschmeichelt haben,
Dort fängt es schon zu rieseln an.
10720 An mancher trocknen, kahlen Felsenstelle
Entwickelt sich die volle, rasche Quelle,
Um jener Sieg ist es gethan.

Mephistopheles.

Das ist ein wunderbarer Gruß,
Die kühnsten Klettrer sind confus.

Faust.

10725 Schon rauscht Ein Bach zu Bächen mächtig nieder,
Aus Schluchten kehren sie gedoppelt wieder,
Ein Strom nun wirft den Bogenstrahl,
Auf einmal legt er sich in flache Felsenbreite
Und rauscht und schäumt, nach der und jener Seite,
10730 Und stufenweise wirft er sich in's Thal.
Was hilft ein tapfres, heldenmäßiges Stemmen?
Die mächtige Woge strömt sie wegzuschwemmen.
Mir schaudert selbst vor solchem wilden Schwall.

Mephistopheles.

Ich sehe nichts von diesen Wasserlügen,
10735 Nur Menschen-Augen lassen sich betrügen

Und mich ergetzt der wunderliche Fall.
Sie stürzen fort zu ganzen hellen Haufen,
Die Narren wähnen zu ersaufen,
Indem sie frei auf festem Lande schnaufen
Und lächerlich mit Schwimmgebärden laufen. 10740
Nun ist Verwirrung überall.

Die Raben sind wieder gekommen

Ich werd' euch bei dem hohen Meister loben;
Wollt ihr euch nun als Meister selbst erproben,
So eilet zu der glühnden Schmiede,
Wo das Gezwerg-Volk, nimmer müde, 10745
Metall und Stein zu Funken schlägt.
Verlangt, weitläufig sie beschwatzend,
Ein Feuer, leuchtend, blinkend, platzend,
Wie man's im hohen Sinne hegt.
Zwar Wetterleuchten in der weiten Ferne, 10750
Blickschnelles Fallen allerhöchster Sterne
Mag jede Sommernacht geschehn;
Doch Wetterleuchten in verworrnen Büschen
Und Sterne die am feuchten Boden zischen,
Das hat man nicht so leicht gesehn. 10755
So müßt ihr, ohn' euch viel zu quälen,
Zuvörderst bitten, dann befehlen.

Raben ab. Es geschieht wie vorgeschrieben.

Mephistopheles.

Den Feinden dichte Finsternisse!
Und Tritt und Schritt in's Ungewisse!
Irrfunken-Blick an allen Enden, 10760
Ein Leuchten plötzlich zu verblenden.
Das alles wäre wunderschön,
Nun aber braucht's noch Schreckgetön.

Faust.

Die hohlen Waffen aus der Säle Grüften
10765 Empfinden sich erstarkt in freien Lüften;
Da droben klappert's, rasselt's lange schon,
Ein wunderbarer, falscher Ton.

Mephistopheles.

Ganz recht! sie sind nicht mehr zu zügeln,
Schon schallt's von ritterlichen Prügeln,
10770 Wie in der holden alten Zeit.
Armschienen, wie der Beine Schienen,
Als Guelfen und als Ghibellinen,
Erneuen rasch den ewigen Streit.
Fest, im ererbten Sinne wöhnlich,
10775 Erweisen sie sich unversöhnlich,
Schon klingt das Tosen weit und breit.
Zuletzt, bei allen Teufelsfesten,
Wirkt der Parteihaß doch zum besten,
Bis in den allerletzten Graus;
10780 Schallt wider-widerwärtig panisch,
Mitunter grell und scharf-satanisch,
Erschreckend in das Thal hinaus.

Kriegstumult im Orchester, zuletzt übergehend in militärisch heitre Weisen.

Des Gegenkaisers Zelt.

Thron, reiche Umgebung.

Habebald. Eilebeute.

Eilebeute.

So sind wir doch die ersten hier!

Habebald.

Kein Rabe fliegt so schnell als wir.

Eilebeute.

O! welch ein Schatz liegt hier zu Hauf! 10785
Wo fang' ich an? Wo hör' ich auf?

Habebald.

Steht doch der ganze Raum so voll!
Weiß nicht wozu ich greifen soll.

Eilebeute.

Der Teppich wär' mir eben recht,
Mein Lager ist oft gar zu schlecht. 10790

Habebald.

Hier hängt von Stahl ein Morgenstern,
Dergleichen hätt' ich lange gern.

Eilebeute.

Den rothen Mantel goldgesäumt,
So etwas hatt' ich mir geträumt.

Habebald die Waffe nehmend.

10795 Damit ist es gar bald gethan,
Man schlägt ihn todt und geht voran.
Du hast soviel schon aufgepackt
Und doch nichts Rechtes eingesackt.
Den Plunder laß an seinem Ort,
10800 Nehm' eines dieser Kistchen fort!
Dieß ist des Heers beschiedner Sold,
In seinem Bauche lauter Gold.

Eilebeute.

Das hat ein mörderisch Gewicht,
Ich heb' es nicht, ich trag' es nicht.

Habebald.

10805 Geschwinde duck' dich! Mußt dich bücken!
Ich hucke dir's auf den starken Rücken.

Eilebeute.

O weh! O weh, nun ist's vorbei!
Die Last bricht mir das Kreuz entzwei.

Das Kistchen stürzt und springt auf.

Habebald.

Da liegt das rothe Gold zu Hauf,
10810 Geschwinde zu und raff' es auf.

Eilebeute kauert nieder.

Geschwinde nur zum Schoos hinein!
Noch immer wird's zur G'nüge sein.

Habebald.

Und so genug! und eile doch!

Sie steht auf.

O weh, die Schürze hat ein Loch!
Wohin du gehst und wo du stehst 10815
Verschwenderisch die Schätze säst.

Trabanten unsres Kaisers.

Was schafft ihr hier am heiligen Platz?
Was kramt ihr in dem Kaiserschatz?

Habebald.

Wir trugen unsre Glieder feil
Und holen unser Beutetheil. 10820
In Feindes-Zelten ist's der Brauch
Und wir, Soldaten sind wir auch.

Trabanten.

Das passet nicht in unsern Kreis
Zugleich Soldat und Diebsgeschmeiß,
Und wer sich unserm Kaiser naht 10825
Der sei ein redlicher Soldat.

Habebald.

Die Redlichkeit die kennt man schon,
Sie heißet: Contribution.
Ihr alle seid auf gleichem Fuß:
Gib her! das ist der Handwerksgruß. 10830

Zu Eilebeute.

Mach' fort und schleppe was du hast,
Hier sind wir nicht willkommner Gast.

Ab.

Erster Trabant.

Sag', warum gabst du nicht sogleich
Dem frechen Kerl einen Backenstreich?

Zweiter.

10835 Ich weiß nicht, mir verging die Kraft,
Sie waren so gespensterhaft.

Dritter.

Mir ward es vor den Augen schlecht,
Da flimmert' es, ich sah nicht recht.

Vierter.

Wie ich es nicht zu sagen weiß:
10840 Es war den ganzen Tag so heiß,
So bänglich, so beklommen schwül,
Der eine stand, der andre fiel,
Man tappte hin und schlug zugleich,
Der Gegner fiel vor jedem Streich,
10845 Vor Augen schwebt' es wie ein Flor,
Dann summt's und saust's und zischt' im Ohr.
Das ging so fort, nun sind wir da
Und wissen selbst nicht wie's geschah.

Kaiser mit vier Fürsten treten auf.

Die Trabanten entfernen sich.

Kaiser.

Es sei nun wie ihm sei! uns ist die Schlacht gewonnen,
10850 Des Feinds zerstreute Flucht im flachen Feld zerronnen.
Hier steht der leere Thron, verrätherischer Schatz,
Von Teppichen umhüllt, verengt umher den Platz.

Wir, ehrenvoll geschützt von eigenen Trabanten,
Erwarten Kaiserlich der Völker Abgesandten;
Von allen Seiten her kommt frohe Botschaft an: 10855
Beruhigt sei das Reich, uns freudig zugethan.
Hat sich in unsern Kampf auch Gaukelei geflochten,
Am Ende haben wir uns nur allein gefochten.
Zufälle kommen ja dem Streitenden zu Gut,
Vom Himmel fällt ein Stein, dem Feinde regnet's Blut, 10860
Aus Felsenhöhlen tönt's von mächtigen Wunderklängen,
Die unsre Brust erhöhn, des Feindes Brust verengen.
Der Überwundne fiel, zu stets erneutem Spott,
Der Sieger, wie er prangt, preis't den gewognen Gott.
Und alles stimmt mit ein, er braucht nicht zu befehlen, 10865
Herr Gott, dich loben wir! aus Millionen Kehlen.
Jedoch zum höchsten Preis wend' ich den frommen Blick,
Das selten sonst geschah, zur eignen Brust zurück.
Ein junger, muntrer Fürst mag seinen Tag vergeuden,
Die Jahre lehren ihn des Augenblicks Bedeuten. 10870
Deßhalb denn ungesäumt verbind' ich mich sogleich
Mit euch vier Würdigen, für Haus und Hof und Reich.

Zum ersten.

Dein war, o Fürst! des Heers geordnet kluge Schichtung,
Sodann, im Hauptmoment, heroisch kühne Richtung;
Im Frieden wirke nun wie es die Zeit begehrt, 10875
Erzmarschall nenn' ich dich, verleihe dir das Schwert.

Erzmarschall.

Dein treues Heer, bis jetzt im Inneren beschäftigt,
Wenn's an der Gränze dich und deinen Thron bekräftigt,
Dann sei es uns vergönnt, bei Festesdrang im Saal
Geräumiger Väterburg, zu rüsten dir das Mahl. 10880

Blank trag' ich's dir dann vor, blank halt' ich dir's zur Seite,
Der höchsten Majestät zu ewigem Geleite.

Der **Kaiser** zum zweiten.

Der sich, als tapfrer Mann, auch zart gefällig zeigt,
Du! sei Erzkämmerer, der Auftrag ist nicht leicht.
10885 Du bist der Oberste von allem Hausgesinde,
Bei deren innerm Streit ich schlechte Diener finde;
Dein Beispiel sei fortan in Ehren aufgestellt,
Wie man dem Herrn, dem Hof und allen wohlgefällt.

Erzkämmerer.

Des Herren großen Sinn zu fördern bringt zu Gnaden,
10890 Den Besten hülfreich sein, den Schlechten selbst nicht schaden,
Dann klar sein ohne List, und ruhig ohne Trug!
Wenn du mich, Herr, durchschaust, geschieht mir schon genug.
Darf sich die Phantasie auf jenes Fest erstrecken?
Wenn du zur Tafel gehst, reich' ich das goldne Becken,
10895 Die Ringe halt' ich dir, damit zur Wonnezeit
Sich deine Hand erfrischt, wie mich dein Blick erfreut.

Kaiser.

Zwar fühl' ich mich zu ernst auf Festlichkeit zu sinnen,
Doch sei's! Es fördert auch frohmüthiges Beginnen.

Zum dritten.

Dich wähl' ich zum Erztruchseß! Also sei fortan
10900 Dir Jagd, Geflügel-Hof und Vorwerk unterthan;
Der Lieblingsspeisen Wahl laß mir zu allen Zeiten
Wie sie der Monat bringt und sorgsam zubereiten.

Erztruchseß.

Streng Fasten sei für mich die angenehmste Pflicht,
Bis, vor dich hingestellt, dich freut ein Wohlgericht.

Der Küche Dienerschaft soll sich mit mir vereinigen, 10905
Das Ferne beizuziehn, die Jahrszeit zu beschleunigen.
Dich reizt nicht Fern und Früh womit die Tafel prangt,
Einfach und kräftig ist's wornach dein Sinn verlangt.

Kaiser zum vierten.

Weil unausweichlich hier sich's nur von Festen handelt,
So sei mir, junger Held, zum Schenken umgewandelt. 10910
Erzschenke, sorge nun daß unsre Kellerei
Auf's reichlichste versorgt mit gutem Weine sei.
Du selbst sei mäßig, laß nicht über Heiterkeiten,
Durch der Gelegenheit Verlocken, dich verleiten.

Erzschenk.

Mein Fürst, die Jugend selbst, wenn man ihr nur vertraut, 10915
Steht, eh' man sich's versieht, zu Männern auferbaut.
Auch ich versetze mich zu jenem großen Feste;
Ein Kaiserlich Büffet schmück' ich auf's allerbeste,
Mit Prachtgefäßen, gülden, silbern allzumal,
Doch wähl' ich dir voraus den lieblichsten Pokal: 10920
Ein blank venedisch Glas, worin Behagen lauschet,
Des Weins Geschmack sich stärkt und nimmermehr berauschet.
Auf solchen Wunderschatz vertraut man oft zu sehr;
Doch deine Mäßigkeit, du Höchster, schützt noch mehr.

Kaiser.

Was ich euch zugedacht in dieser ernsten Stunde, 10925
Vernahmt ihr mit Vertraun aus zuverläßigem Munde.
Des Kaisers Wort ist groß und sichert jede Gift,
Doch zur Bekräftigung bedarf's der edlen Schrift,
Bedarf's der Signatur. Die förmlich zu bereiten,
Seh' ich den rechten Mann zu rechter Stunde schreiten. 10930

Der Erzbischof=Erzcanzler tritt auf.

Kaiser.

Wenn ein Gewölbe sich dem Schlußstein anvertraut,
Dann ist's mit Sicherheit für ewige Zeit erbaut.
Du siehst vier Fürsten da! Wir haben erst erörtert,
Was den Bestand zunächst von Haus und Hof befördert.
10935 Nun aber, was das Reich in seinem Ganzen hegt,
Sei, mit Gewicht und Kraft, der Fünfzahl auferlegt.
An Ländern sollen sie vor allen andern glänzen,
Deßhalb erweitr' ich gleich jetzt des Besitzthums Gränzen,
Vom Erbtheil jener die sich von uns abgewandt.
10940 Euch Treuen sprech' ich zu so manches schöne Land,
Zugleich das hohe Recht euch, nach Gelegenheiten,
Durch Anfall, Kauf und Tausch in's Weitre zu verbreiten;
Dann sei bestimmt vergönnt zu üben ungestört
Was von Gerechtsamen euch Landesherrn gehört.
10945 Als Richter werdet ihr die Endurtheile fällen,
Berufung gelte nicht von euern höchsten Stellen.
Dann Steuer, Zins und Beth', Lehn und Geleit und Zoll,
Berg=, Salz= und Münzregal euch angehören soll.
Denn meine Dankbarkeit vollgültig zu erproben,
10950 Hab' ich euch ganz zunächst der Majestät erhoben.

Erzbischof.

Im Namen aller sei dir tiefster Dank gebracht,
Du machst uns stark und fest und stärkest deine Macht.

Kaiser.

Euch fünfen will ich noch erhöhtere Würde geben.
Noch leb' ich meinem Reich und habe Lust zu leben;
10955 Doch hoher Ahnen Kette zieht bedächtigen Blick
Aus rascher Strebsamkeit in's Drohende zurück.

Auch werd' ich, seiner Zeit, mich von den Theuren trennen,
Dann sei es eure Pflicht den Folger zu ernennen.
Gekrönt erhebt ihn hoch auf heiligem Altar,
Und friedlich ende dann was jetzt so stürmisch war. 10960

Erzcanzler.

Mit Stolz in tiefster Brust, mit Demuth an Gebärde,
Stehn Fürsten dir gebeugt, die ersten auf der Erde.
So lang das treue Blut die vollen Adern regt,
Sind wir der Körper den dein Wille leicht bewegt.

Kaiser.

Und also sei, zum Schluß, was wir bisher bethätigt, 10965
Für alle Folgezeit durch Schrift und Zug bestätigt.
Zwar habt ihr den Besitz als Herren völlig frei,
Mit dem Beding jedoch, daß er untheilbar sei.
Und wie ihr auch vermehrt was ihr von uns empfangen,
Es soll's der ält'ste Sohn in gleichem Maß erlangen. 10970

Erzcanzler.

Dem Pergament alsbald vertrau' ich wohlgemuth,
Zum Glück dem Reich und uns, das wichtigste Statut;
Reinschrift und Sieglung soll die Canzelei beschäftigen,
Mit heiliger Signatur wirst du's, der Herr, bekräftigen.

Kaiser.

Und so entlass' ich euch, damit den großen Tag, 10975
Gesammelt, jedermann sich überlegen mag.

Die weltlichen Fürsten entfernen sich.

Der geistliche bleibt und spricht pathetisch.

Der Canzler ging hinweg, der Bischof ist geblieben,
Vom ernsten Warnegeist zu deinem Ohr getrieben!
Sein väterliches Herz von Sorge bangt's um dich.

Kaiser.

10980 Was hast du Bängliches zur frohen Stunde? sprich!

Erzbischof.

Mit welchem bittern Schmerz find' ich, in dieser Stunde,
Dein hochgeheiligt Haupt mit Satanas im Bunde.
Zwar, wie es scheinen will, gesichert auf dem Thron,
Doch leider! Gott dem Herrn, dem Vater Papst zum Hohn.
10985 Wenn dieser es erfährt, schnell wird er sträflich richten,
Mit heiligem Strahl dein Reich, das sündige, zu vernichten.
Denn noch vergaß er nicht wie du, zur höchsten Zeit,
An deinem Krönungstag den Zauberer befreit.
Von deinem Diadem, der Christenheit zum Schaden,
10990 Traf das verfluchte Haupt der erste Strahl der Gnaden.
Doch schlag' an deine Brust und gib, vom frevlen Glück,
Ein mäßig Schärflein gleich dem Heiligthum zurück;
Den breiten Hügelraum, da wo dein Zelt gestanden,
Wo böse Geister sich zu deinem Schutz verbanden,
10995 Dem Lügenfürsten du ein horchsam Ohr geliehn,
Den stifte, fromm belehrt, zu heiligem Bemühn;
Mit Berg und dichtem Wald, so weit sie sich erstrecken,
Mit Höhen die sich grün zu fetter Weide decken,
Fischreichen, klaren Seen, dann Bächlein ohne Zahl,
11000 Wie sie sich, eilig schlängelnd, stürzen ab zu Thal;
Das breite Thal dann selbst, mit Wiesen, Gauen, Gründen;
Die Reue spricht sich aus, und du wirst Gnade finden.

Kaiser.

Durch meinen schweren Fehl bin ich so tief erschreckt,
Die Gränze sei von dir nach eignem Maß gesteckt.

Erzbischof.

11005 Erst! der entweihte Raum, wo man sich so versündigt,
Sei alsobald zum Dienst des Höchsten angekündigt.

Behende steigt im Geist Gemäuer stark empor,
Der Morgensonne Blick erleuchtet schon das Chor,
Zum Kreuz erweitert sich das wachsende Gebäude,
Das Schiff erlängt, erhöht sich zu der Gläubigen Freude, 11010
Sie strömen brünstig schon durch's würdige Portal,
Der erste Glockenruf erscholl durch Berg und Thal,
Von hohen Thürmen tönt's, wie sie zum Himmel streben,
Der Büßer kommt heran, zu neugeschaffnem Leben.
Dem hohen Weihetag, er trete bald herein! 11015
Wird deine Gegenwart die höchste Zierde sein.

Kaiser.

Mag ein so großes Werk den frommen Sinn verkündigen,
Zu preisen Gott den Herrn, so wie mich zu entsündigen.
Genug! Ich fühle schon wie sich mein Sinn erhöht.

Erzbischof.

Als Canzler förd' ich nun Schluß und Formalität. 11020

Kaiser.

Ein förmlich Document, der Kirche das zu eignen,
Du legst es vor, ich will's mit Freuden unterzeichnen.

Erzbischof

hat sich beurlaubt, kehrt aber bei'm Ausgang um.

Dann widmest du zugleich dem Werke, wie's entsteht,
Gesammte Landsgefälle: Zehnten, Zinsen, Beth',
Für ewig. Viel bedarf's zu würdiger Unterhaltung, 11025
Und schwere Kosten macht die sorgliche Verwaltung.
Zum schnellen Aufbau selbst auf solchem wüsten Platz
Reichst du uns einiges Gold, aus deinem Beuteschatz.
Daneben braucht man auch, ich kann es nicht verschweigen,
Entferntes Holz und Kalk und Schiefer und dergleichen. 11030

Die Fuhren thut das Volk, vom Predigtstuhl belehrt,
Die Kirche segnet den der ihr zu Diensten fährt.

Ab.

Kaiser.

Die Sünd' ist groß und schwer womit ich mich beladen,
Das leidige Zaubervolk bringt mich in harten Schaden.

Erzbischof

abermals zurückkehrend mit tiefster Verbeugung.

11035 Verzeih, o Herr! Es ward dem sehr verrufnen Mann
Des Reiches Strand verliehn; doch diesen trifft der Bann,
Verleihst du reuig nicht der hohen Kirchenstelle
Auch dort den Zehnten, Zins und Gaben und Gefälle.

Kaiser verdrießlich.

Das Land ist noch nicht da, im Meere liegt es breit.

Erzbischof.

11040 Wer's Recht hat und Geduld für den kommt auch die Zeit.
Für uns mög' Euer Wort in seinen Kräften bleiben!

Ab.

Kaiser allein.

So könnt' ich wohl zunächst das ganze Reich verschreiben.

Fünfter Act.

Offene Gegend.

Wandrer.

Ja! sie sind's die dunkeln Linden,
Dort, in ihres Alters Kraft.
Und ich soll sie wieder finden, 11045
Nach so langer Wanderschaft!
Ist es doch die alte Stelle,
Jene Hütte, die mich barg,
Als die sturmerregte Welle
Mich an jene Dünen warf! 11050
Meine Wirthe möcht' ich segnen,
Hülfsbereit, ein wackres Paar,
Das, um heut mir zu begegnen,
Alt schon jener Tage war.
Ach! das waren fromme Leute! 11055
Poch' ich? ruf' ich? — Seid gegrüßt!
Wenn, gastfreundlich, auch noch heute
Ihr des Wohlthuns Glück genießt.

Baucis. Mütterchen, sehr alt.

Lieber Kömmling! Leise! Leise!
Ruhe! laß den Gatten ruhn! 11060
Langer Schlaf verleiht dem Greise
Kurzen Wachens rasches Thun.

Wandrer.

Sage, Mutter, bist du's eben,
Meinen Dank noch zu empfahn,
11065 Was du für des Jünglings Leben
Mit dem Gatten einst gethan?
Bist du Baucis, die, geschäftig,
Halberstorbnen Mund erquickt?

Der Gatte tritt auf.

Du Philemon, der, so kräftig,
11070 Meinen Schatz der Fluth entrückt?
Eure Flammen raschen Feuers,
Eures Glöckchens Silberlaut,
Jenes grausen Abentheuers
Lösung war euch anvertraut.

11075 Und nun laßt hervor mich treten,
Schaun das gränzenlose Meer;
Laßt mich knieen, laßt mich beten,
Mich bedrängt die Brust so sehr.

Er schreitet vorwärts auf der Düne.

Philemon zu Baucis.

Eile nur den Tisch zu decken,
11080 Wo's im Gärtchen munter blüht.
Laß ihn rennen, ihn erschrecken,
Denn er glaubt nicht was er sieht.

Neben dem Wandrer stehend.

Das euch grimmig mißgehandelt,
Wog' auf Woge, schäumend wild,
11085 Seht als Garten ihr behandelt,
Seht ein paradiesisch Bild.

Älter, war ich nicht zu Handen,
Hülfreich nicht wie sonst bereit,
Und, wie meine Kräfte schwanden,
War auch schon die Woge weit. 11090
Kluger Herren kühne Knechte
Gruben Gräben, dämmten ein,
Schmälerten des Meeres Rechte,
Herrn an seiner Statt zu sein.
Schaue grünend Wies' an Wiese, 11095
Anger, Garten, Dorf und Wald. —
Komm nun aber und genieße,
Denn die Sonne scheidet bald. —
Dort im Fernsten ziehen Segel!
Suchen nächtlich sichern Port. 11100
Kennen doch ihr Nest die Vögel,
Denn jetzt ist der Hafen dort.
So erblickst du in der Weite
Erst des Meeres blauen Saum,
Rechts und links, in aller Breite, 11105
Dichtgedrängt bewohnten Raum.

Am Tische zu drei, im Gärtchen.

Baucis.

Bleibst du stumm? und keinen Bissen
Bringst du zum verlechzten Mund?

Philemon.

Möcht' er doch vom Wunder wissen,
Sprichst so gerne, thu's ihm kund. 11110

Baucis.

Wohl! ein Wunder ist's gewesen!
Läßt mich heut noch nicht in Ruh;

Denn es ging das ganze Wesen
Nicht mit rechten Dingen zu.

Philemon.

11115 Kann der Kaiser sich versünd'gen
Der das Ufer ihm verliehn?
Thät's ein Herold nicht verkünd'gen
Schmetternd im Vorüberziehn?
Nicht entfernt von unsern Dünen
11120 Ward der erste Fuß gefaßt,
Zelte, Hütten! — Doch im Grünen
Richtet bald sich ein Palast.

Baucis.

Tags umsonst die Knechte lärmten,
Hack' und Schaufel, Schlag um Schlag;
11125 Wo die Flämmchen nächtig schwärmten
Stand ein Damm den andern Tag.
Menschenopfer mußten bluten,
Nachts erscholl des Jammers Qual,
Meerab flossen Feuergluthen,
11130 Morgens war es ein Canal.
Gottlos ist er, ihn gelüstet
Unsre Hütte, unser Hain;
Wie er sich als Nachbar brüstet
Soll man unterthänig sein.

Philemon.

11135 Hat er uns doch angeboten
Schönes Gut im neuen Land!

Baucis.

Traue nicht dem Wasserboden,
Halt' auf deiner Höhe Stand!

Philemon.

Laßt uns zur Capelle treten!
Letzten Sonnenblick zu schaun. 11140
Laßt uns läuten, knieen, beten!
Und dem alten Gott vertraun.

Palast.

Weiter Ziergarten, großer gradgeführter Canal.

Faust im höchsten Alter wandelnd, nachdenkend.

Lynceus der Thürmer durch's Sprachrohr.

Die Sonne sinkt, die letzten Schiffe
Sie ziehen munter hafenein.
11145 Ein großer Kahn ist im Begriffe
Auf dem Canale hier zu sein.
Die bunten Wimpel wehen fröhlich,
Die starren Masten stehn bereit,
In dir preis't sich der Bootsmann selig,
11150 Dich grüßt das Glück zur höchsten Zeit.

Das Glöckchen läutet auf der Düne.

Faust auffahrend.

Verdammtes Läuten! Allzuschändlich
Verwundet's, wie ein tückischer Schuß;
Vor Augen ist mein Reich unendlich,
Im Rücken neckt mich der Verdruß,
11155 Erinnert mich durch neidische Laute:
Mein Hochbesitz er ist nicht rein,
Der Lindenraum, die braune Baute,
Das morsche Kirchlein ist nicht mein.

Und wünscht' ich dort mich zu erholen,
Vor fremdem Schatten schaudert mir, 11160
Ist Dorn den Augen, Dorn den Sohlen,
O! wär' ich weit hinweg von hier!

Thürmer wie oben.

Wie segelt froh der bunte Kahn
Mit frischem Abendwind heran!
Wie thürmt sich sein behender Lauf 11165
In Kisten, Kasten, Säcken auf!

Prächtiger Kahn, reich und bunt beladen mit Erzeugnissen fremder Weltgegenden.

Mephistopheles. Die drei gewaltigen Gesellen.

Chorus.

Da landen wir,
Da sind wir schon.
Glückan! dem Herren,
Dem Patron. 11170

Sie steigen aus, die Güter werden an's Land geschafft.

Mephistopheles.

So haben wir uns wohl erprobt,
Vergnügt wenn der Patron es lobt.
Nur mit zwei Schiffen ging es fort,
Mit zwanzig sind wir nun im Port.
Was große Dinge wir gethan, 11175
Das sieht man unsrer Ladung an.
Das freie Meer befreit den Geist,
Wer weiß da was Besinnen heißt!

Da fördert nur ein rascher Griff,
11180 Man fängt den Fisch, man fängt ein Schiff,
Und ist man erst der Herr zu drei,
Dann hakelt man das vierte bei;
Da geht es denn dem fünften schlecht,
Man hat Gewalt, so hat man Recht.
11185 Man fragt um's Was? und nicht um's Wie?
Ich müßte keine Schifffahrt kennen:
Krieg, Handel und Piraterie,
Dreieinig sind sie, nicht zu trennen.

Die drei gewaltigen Gesellen.

Nicht Dank und Gruß!
11190 Nicht Gruß und Dank!
Als brächten wir
Dem Herrn Gestank.
Er macht ein
Widerlich Gesicht;
11195 Das Königsgut
Gefällt ihm nicht.

Mephistopheles.

Erwartet weiter
Keinen Lohn,
Nahmt ihr doch
11200 Euren Theil davon.

Die Gesellen.

Das ist nur für
Die Langeweil,
Wir alle fordern
Gleichen Theil.

Mephistopheles.

Erst ordnet oben 11205
Saal an Saal
Die Kostbarkeiten
Allzumal.
Und tritt er zu
Der reichen Schau, 11210
Berechnet er alles
Mehr genau,
Er sich gewiß
Nicht lumpen läßt
Und gibt der Flotte 11215
Fest nach Fest.
Die bunten Vögel kommen morgen,
Für die werd' ich zum besten sorgen.

Die Ladung wird weggeschafft.

Mephistopheles zu Faust.

Mit ernster Stirn, mit düstrem Blick
Vernimmst du dein erhaben Glück. 11220
Die hohe Weisheit wird gekrönt,
Das Ufer ist dem Meer versöhnt;
Vom Ufer nimmt, zu rascher Bahn,
Das Meer die Schiffe willig an;
So sprich daß hier, hier vom Palast 11225
Dein Arm die ganze Welt umfaßt.
Von dieser Stelle ging es aus,
Hier stand das erste Breterhaus;
Ein Gräbchen ward hinabgeritzt
Wo jetzt das Ruder emsig spritzt. 11230

Dein hoher Sinn, der Deinen Fleiß
Erwarb des Meers, der Erde Preis.
Von hier aus —

Faust.

Das verfluchte hier!
Das eben, leidig lastet's mir.
11235 Dir Vielgewandtem muß ich's sagen,
Mir gibt's im Herzen Stich um Stich,
Mir ist's unmöglich zu ertragen!
Und wie ich's sage schäm' ich mich.
Die Alten droben sollten weichen,
11240 Die Linden wünscht' ich mir zum Sitz,
Die wenig Bäume, nicht mein eigen,
Verderben mir den Welt-Besitz.
Dort wollt' ich, weit umher zu schauen,
Von Ast zu Ast Gerüste bauen,
11245 Dem Blick eröffnen weite Bahn,
Zu sehn was alles ich gethan,
Zu überschaun mit einem Blick
Des Menschengeistes Meisterstück,
Bethätigend, mit klugem Sinn,
11250 Der Völker breiten Wohngewinn.

So sind am härt'sten wir gequält
Im Reichthum fühlend was uns fehlt.
Des Glöckchens Klang, der Linden Duft
Umfängt mich wie in Kirch' und Gruft.
11255 Des allgewaltigen Willens Kür
Bricht sich an diesem Sande hier.
Wie schaff' ich mir es vom Gemüthe!
Das Glöcklein läutet und ich wüthe.

Mephistopheles.

Natürlich! daß ein Hauptverdruß
Das Leben dir vergällen muß. 11260
Wer läugnet's! Jedem edlen Ohr
Kommt das Geklingel widrig vor.
Und das verfluchte Bim-Baum-Bimmel,
Umnebelnd heitern Abendhimmel,
Mischt sich in jegliches Begebniß, 11265
Vom ersten Bad bis zum Begräbniß,
Als wäre, zwischen Bim und Baum,
Das Leben ein verschollner Traum.

Faust.

Das Widerstehn, der Eigensinn
Verkümmern herrlichsten Gewinn, 11270
Daß man, zu tiefer, grimmiger Pein,
Ermüden muß gerecht zu sein.

Mephistopheles.

Was willst du dich denn hier geniren,
Mußt du nicht längst colonisiren?

Faust.

So geht und schafft sie mir zur Seite! — 11275
Das schöne Gütchen kennst du ja,
Das ich den Alten ausersah.

Mephistopheles.

Man trägt sie fort und setzt sie nieder,
Eh' man sich umsieht stehn sie wieder;
Nach überstandener Gewalt 11280
Versöhnt ein schöner Aufenthalt.

Er pfeift gellend.

Die Drei treten auf.

Mephistopheles.

Kommt! Wie der Herr gebieten läßt,
Und morgen gibt's ein Flottenfest.

Die Drei.

Der alte Herr empfing uns schlecht,
11285 Ein flottes Fest ist uns zu Recht.

Ab.

Mephistopheles ad Spectatores.

Auch hier geschieht was längst geschah,
Denn Naboths Weinberg war schon da.

(Regum I. 21.)

Tiefe Nacht.

Lynceus der Thürmer
auf der Schloßwarte, singend.

Zum Sehen geboren,
Zum Schauen bestellt,
Dem Thurme geschworen 11290
Gefällt mir die Welt.
Ich blick' in die Ferne,
Ich seh' in der Näh
Den Mond und die Sterne
Den Wald und das Reh. 11295
So seh' ich in allen
Die ewige Zier,
Und wie mir's gefallen
Gefall' ich auch mir.
Ihr glücklichen Augen 11300
Was je ihr gesehn,
Es sei wie es wolle,
Es war doch so schön!

Pause.

Nicht allein mich zu ergetzen
Bin ich hier so hoch gestellt; 11305
Welch ein greuliches Entsetzen
Droht mir aus der finstern Welt!

Funkenblicke seh' ich sprühen
Durch der Linden Doppelnacht,
11310 Immer stärker wühlt ein Glühen
Von der Zugluft angefacht.
Ach! die innre Hütte lodert,
Die bemoos't und feucht gestanden,
Schnelle Hülfe wird gefodert,
11315 Keine Rettung ist vorhanden.
Ach! die guten alten Leute,
Sonst so sorglich um das Feuer,
Werden sie dem Qualm zur Beute!
Welch ein schrecklich Abentheuer!
11320 Flamme flammet, roth in Gluthen
Steht das schwarze Moosgestelle;
Retteten sich nur die Guten
Aus der wildentbrannten Hölle!
Züngelnd lichte Blitze steigen
11325 Zwischen Blättern, zwischen Zweigen;
Äste dürr, die flackernd brennen,
Glühen schnell und stürzen ein.
Sollt ihr Augen dieß erkennen!
Muß ich so weitsichtig sein!
11330 Das Capellchen bricht zusammen
Von der Äste Sturz und Last.
Schlängelnd sind, mit spitzen Flammen,
Schon die Gipfel angefaßt.
Bis zur Wurzel glühn die hohlen
11335 Stämme, purpurroth im Glühn. —

Lange Pause, Gesang.

Was sich sonst dem Blick empfohlen,
Mit Jahrhunderten ist hin.

Faust auf dem Balcon, gegen die Dünen.

Von oben welch ein singend Wimmern?
Das Wort ist hier, der Ton zu spat;
Mein Thürmer jammert; mich, im Innern, 11340
Verdrießt die ungeduld'ge That.
Doch sei der Lindenwuchs vernichtet
Zu halbverkohlter Stämme Graun,
Ein Luginsland ist bald errichtet,
Um in's Unendliche zu schaun. 11345
Da seh' ich auch die neue Wohnung,
Die jenes alte Paar umschließt,
Das, im Gefühl großmüthiger Schonung,
Der späten Tage froh genießt.

Mephistopheles und die Dreie unten.

Da kommen wir mit vollem Trab, 11350
Verzeiht! es ging nicht gütlich ab.
Wir klopften an, wir pochten an,
Und immer ward nicht aufgethan:
Wir rüttelten, wir pochten fort,
Da lag die morsche Thüre dort; 11355
Wir riefen laut und drohten schwer,
Allein wir fanden kein Gehör.
Und wie's in solchem Fall geschicht,
Sie hörten nicht, sie wollten nicht;
Wir aber haben nicht gesäumt, 11360
Behende dir sie weggeräumt.
Das Paar hat sich nicht viel gequält,
Vor Schrecken fielen sie entseelt.
Ein Fremder, der sich dort versteckt
Und fechten wollte, ward gestreckt. 11365

In wilden Kampfes kurzer Zeit,
Von Kohlen, rings umher gestreut,
Entflammte Stroh. Nun lodert's frei,
Als Scheiterhaufen dieser drei.

Faust.

11370 Wart ihr für meine Worte taub!
Tausch wollt' ich, wollte keinen Raub.
Dem unbesonnenen wilden Streich
Ihm fluch' ich, theilt es unter euch!

Chorus.

Das alte Wort, das Wort erschallt:
11375 Gehorche willig der Gewalt!
Und bist du kühn und hältst du Stich,
So wage Haus und Hof und — Dich.

Ab.

Faust auf dem Balcon.

Die Sterne bergen Blick und Schein,
Das Feuer sinkt und lodert klein;
11380 Ein Schauerwindchen fächelt's an,
Bringt Rauch und Dunst zu mir heran.
Geboten schnell, zu schnell gethan! —
Was schwebet schattenhaft heran?

Mitternacht.

Vier graue Weiber treten auf.

Erste.

Ich heiße der Mangel.

Zweite.

Ich heiße die Schuld.

Dritte.

Ich heiße die Sorge.

Vierte.

Ich heiße die Noth. 11385

Zu drei.

Die Thür ist verschlossen, wir können nicht ein,
Drinn wohnet ein Reicher, wir mögen nicht 'nein.

Mangel.

Da werd' ich zum Schatten.

Schuld.

Da werd' ich zu nicht.

Noth.

Man wendet von mir das verwöhnte Gesicht.

Sorge.

11390 Ihr Schwestern, ihr könnt nicht und dürft nicht hinein.
Die Sorge sie schleicht sich durch's Schlüsselloch ein.

Sorge verschwindet.

Mangel.

Ihr, graue Geschwister, entfernt euch von hier.

Schuld.

Ganz nah an der Seite verbind' ich mich dir.

Noth.

Ganz nah an der Ferse begleitet die Noth.

Zu drei.

11395 Es ziehen die Wolken, es schwinden die Sterne!
Dahinten, dahinten! von ferne, von ferne,
Da kommt er der Bruder, da kommt er der — — — Tod.

Ab.

Faust im Palast.

Vier sah ich kommen, drei nur gehn,
Den Sinn der Rede konnt' ich nicht verstehn.
11400 Es klang so nach als hieß es — Noth,
Ein düstres Reimwort folgte — Tod.
Es tönte hohl, gespensterhaft gedämpft.
Noch hab' ich mich in's Freie nicht gekämpft.
Könnt' ich Magie von meinem Pfad entfernen,
11405 Die Zaubersprüche ganz und gar verlernen;
Stünd' ich, Natur! vor dir ein Mann allein,
Da wär's der Mühe werth ein Mensch zu sein.

Das war ich sonst, eh' ich's im Düstern suchte,
Mit Frevelwort mich und die Welt verfluchte.
Nun ist die Luft von solchem Spuk so voll 11410
Daß niemand weiß wie er ihn meiden soll.
Wenn auch Ein Tag uns klar vernünftig lacht,
In Traumgespinnst verwickelt uns die Nacht;
Wir kehren froh von junger Flur zurück,
Ein Vogel krächzt; was krächzt er? Mißgeschick. 11415
Von Aberglauben früh und spat umgarnt:
Es eignet sich, es zeigt sich an, es warnt.
Und so verschüchtert stehen wir allein.
Die Pforte knarrt und niemand kommt herein.

Erschüttert.

Ist jemand hier?

Sorge.

Die Frage fordert ja! 11420

Faust.

Und du, wer bist denn du?

Sorge.

Bin einmal da.

Faust.

Entferne dich!

Sorge.

Ich bin am rechten Ort.

Faust erst ergrimmt, dann besänftigt für sich.

Nimm dich in Acht und sprich kein Zauberwort.

Sorge.

Würde mich kein Ohr vernehmen,
Müßt' es doch im Herzen dröhnen; 11425

In verwandelter Gestalt
Üb' ich grimmige Gewalt.
Auf den Pfaden, auf der Welle,
Ewig ängstlicher Geselle,
11430 Stets gefunden, nie gesucht,
So geschmeichelt wie verflucht.
Hast du die Sorge nie gekannt?

Faust.

Ich bin nur durch die Welt gerannt.
Ein jed Gelüst ergriff ich bei den Haaren,
11435 Was nicht genügte ließ ich fahren,
Was mir entwischte ließ ich ziehn.
Ich habe nur begehrt und nur vollbracht,
Und abermals gewünscht und so mit Macht
Mein Leben durchgestürmt; erst groß und mächtig;
11440 Nun aber geht es weise, geht bedächtig.
Der Erdenkreis ist mir genug bekannt,
Nach drüben ist die Aussicht uns verrannt;
Thor! wer dorthin die Augen blinzelnd richtet,
Sich über Wolken Seinesgleichen dichtet;
11445 Er stehe fest und sehe hier sich um;
Dem Tüchtigen ist diese Welt nicht stumm;
Was braucht er in die Ewigkeit zu schweifen;
Was er erkennt läßt sich ergreifen;
Er wandle so den Erdentag entlang;
11450 Wenn Geister spuken, geh' er seinen Gang,
Im Weiterschreiten find' er Qual und Glück,
Er! unbefriedigt jeden Augenblick.

Sorge.

Wen ich einmal mir besitze
Dem ist alle Welt nichts nütze,

Ewiges Düstre steigt herunter, 11455
Sonne geht nicht auf noch unter,
Bei vollkommnen äußern Sinnen
Wohnen Finsternisse drinnen,
Und er weiß von allen Schätzen
Sich nicht in Besitz zu setzen. 11460
Glück und Unglück wird zur Grille,
Er verhungert in der Fülle,
Sei es Wonne, sei es Plage
Schiebt er's zu dem andern Tage,
Ist der Zukunft nur gewärtig 11465
Und so wird er niemals fertig.

Faust.

Hör' auf! so kommst du mir nicht bei!
Ich mag nicht solchen Unsinn hören.
Fahr' hin! die schlechte Litanei
Sie könnte selbst den klügsten Mann bethören. 11470

Sorge.

Soll er gehen, soll er kommen,
Der Entschluß ist ihm genommen;
Auf gebahnten Weges Mitte
Wankt er tastend halbe Schritte.
Er verliert sich immer tiefer, 11475
Siehet alle Dinge schiefer,
Sich und andre lästig drückend,
Athem holend und erstickend;
Nicht erstickt und ohne Leben,
Nicht verzweiflend, nicht ergeben. 11480
So ein unaufhaltsam Rollen,
Schmerzlich Lassen, widrig Sollen,

Bald Befreien, bald Erdrücken,
Halber Schlaf und schlecht Erquicken
11485 Heftet ihn an seine Stelle
Und bereitet ihn zur Hölle.

Faust.

Unselige Gespenster! so behandelt ihr
Das menschliche Geschlecht zu tausendmalen;
Gleichgültige Tage selbst verwandelt ihr
11490 In garstigen Wirrwarr netzumstrickter Qualen.
Dämonen, weiß ich, wird man schwerlich los,
Das geistig-strenge Band ist nicht zu trennen;
Doch deine Macht, o Sorge, schleichend groß,
Ich werde sie nicht anerkennen.

Sorge.

11495 Erfahre sie, wie ich geschwind
Mich mit Verwünschung von dir wende!
Die Menschen sind im ganzen Leben blind,
Nun Fauste! werde du's am Ende.

Sie haucht ihn an. Ab.

Faust erblindet.

Die Nacht scheint tiefer tief hereinzudringen,
11500 Allein im Innern leuchtet helles Licht,
Was ich gedacht ich eil' es zu vollbringen;
Des Herren Wort es gibt allein Gewicht.
Vom Lager auf, ihr Knechte! Mann für Mann!
Laßt glücklich schauen was ich kühn ersann.
11505 Ergreift das Werkzeug, Schaufel rührt und Spaten!
Das Abgesteckte muß sogleich gerathen.

Auf strenges Ordnen, raschen Fleiß
Erfolgt der allerschönste Preis;
Daß sich das größte Werk vollende
Genügt Ein Geist für tausend Hände. 11510

Großer Vorhof des Palasts.

Fackeln.

Mephistopheles als Aufseher, voran.

Herbei, herbei! Herein, herein!
Ihr schlotternden Lemuren,
Aus Bändern, Sehnen und Gebein
Geflickte Halbnaturen.

Lemuren im Chor.

11515 Wir treten dir sogleich zur Hand,
Und, wie wir halb vernommen,
Es gilt wohl gar ein weites Land
Das sollen wir bekommen.

Gespitzte Pfähle die sind da,
11520 Die Kette lang zum Messen;
Warum an uns der Ruf geschah
Das haben wir vergessen.

Mephistopheles.

Hier gilt kein künstlerisch Bemühn;
Verfahret nur nach eignen Maßen;
11525 Der Längste lege längelang sich hin,
Ihr andern lüftet rings umher den Rasen;

Wie man's für unsre Väter that,
Vertieft ein längliches Quadrat!
Aus dem Palast in's enge Haus,
So dumm läuft es am Ende doch hinaus. 11530

Lemuren mit neckischen Gebärden grabend.

Wie jung ich war und lebt' und liebt',
Mich deucht das war wohl süße,
Wo's fröhlich klang und lustig ging
Da rührten sich meine Füße.

Nun hat das tückische Alter mich 11535
Mit seiner Krücke getroffen;
Ich stolpert' über Grabes Thür,
Warum stand sie just offen!

Faust aus dem Palaste tretend tastet an den Thürpfosten.

Wie das Geklirr der Spaten mich ergetzt!
Es ist die Menge, die mir fröhnet, 11540
Die Erde mit sich selbst versöhnet,
Den Wellen ihre Gränze setzt,
Das Meer mit strengem Band umzieht.

Mephistopheles bei Seite.

Du bist doch nur für uns bemüht
Mit deinen Dämmen, deinen Buhnen; 11545
Denn du bereitest schon Neptunen,
Dem Wasserteufel, großen Schmaus.
In jeder Art seid ihr verloren; —
Die Elemente sind mit uns verschworen,
Und auf Vernichtung läuft's hinaus. 11550

Faust.

Aufseher!

Mephistopheles.

Hier!

Faust.

Wie es auch möglich sei
Arbeiter schaffe Meng' auf Menge,
Ermuntere durch Genuß und Strenge,
Bezahle, locke, presse bei!
11555 Mit jedem Tage will ich Nachricht haben
Wie sich verlängt der unternommene Graben.

Mephistopheles halblaut.

Man spricht, wie man mir Nachricht gab,
Von keinem Graben, doch vom Grab.

Faust.

Ein Sumpf zieht am Gebirge hin,
11560 Verpestet alles schon Errungene;
Den faulen Pfuhl auch abzuziehn,
Das Letzte wär' das Höchsterrungene.
Eröffn' ich Räume vielen Millionen,
Nicht sicher zwar, doch thätig-frei zu wohnen.
11565 Grün das Gefilde, fruchtbar; Mensch und Heerde
Sogleich behaglich auf der neusten Erde,
Gleich angesiedelt an des Hügels Kraft,
Den aufgewälzt kühn-emsige Völkerschaft.
Im Innern hier ein paradiesisch Land,
11570 Da rase draußen Fluth bis auf zum Rand,
Und wie sie nascht gewaltsam einzuschießen,
Gemeindrang eilt die Lücke zu verschließen.
Ja! diesem Sinne bin ich ganz ergeben,
Das ist der Weisheit letzter Schluß:
11575 Nur der verdient sich Freiheit wie das Leben,

Der täglich sie erobern muß.
Und so verbringt, umrungen von Gefahr,
Hier Kindheit, Mann und Greis sein tüchtig Jahr.
Solch ein Gewimmel möcht' ich sehn,
Auf freiem Grund mit freiem Volke stehn. 11580
Zum Augenblicke dürft' ich sagen:
Verweile doch, du bist so schön!
Es kann die Spur von meinen Erdetagen
Nicht in Äonen untergehn. —
Im Vorgefühl von solchem hohen Glück 11585
Genieß' ich jetzt den höchsten Augenblick.

Faust sinkt zurück, die Lemuren fassen ihn auf und legen ihn auf den Boden.

Mephistopheles.

Ihn sättigt keine Lust, ihm g'nügt kein Glück,
So buhlt er fort nach wechselnden Gestalten;
Den letzten, schlechten, leeren Augenblick
Der Arme wünscht ihn fest zu halten. 11590
Der mir so kräftig widerstand,
Die Zeit wird Herr, der Greis hier liegt im Sand.
Die Uhr steht still —

Chor.

Steht still! Sie schweigt wie Mitternacht.
Der Zeiger fällt.

Mephistopheles.

Er fällt, es ist vollbracht.

Chor.

Es ist vorbei.

Mephistopheles.

Vorbei! ein dummes Wort. 11595
Warum vorbei?

Part of the Pisan Fresco "Il Trionfo della Morte."

Vorbei und reines Nicht, vollkommnes Einerlei!
Was soll uns denn das ew'ge Schaffen!
Geschaffenes zu nichts hinwegzuraffen!
11600 Da ist's vorbei! Was ist daran zu lesen?
Es ist so gut als wär' es nicht gewesen,
Und treibt sich doch im Kreis als wenn es wäre.
Ich liebte mir dafür das Ewig-Leere.

Grablegung.

Lemur. Solo.

Wer hat das Haus so schlecht gebaut,
11605 Mit Schaufeln und mit Spaten?

Lemuren. Chor.

Dir, dumpfer Gast im hänfnen Gewand,
Ist's viel zu gut gerathen.

Lemur. Solo.

Wer hat den Saal so schlecht versorgt?
Wo blieben Tisch und Stühle?

Lemuren. Chor.

11610 Es war auf kurze Zeit geborgt;
Der Gläubiger sind so viele.

Mephistopheles.

Der Körper liegt und will der Geist entfliehn,
Ich zeig' ihm rasch den blutgeschriebnen Titel; —
Doch leider hat man jetzt so viele Mittel
11615 Dem Teufel Seelen zu entziehn.
Auf altem Wege stößt man an,
Auf neuem sind wir nicht empfohlen;

Sonst hätt' ich es allein gethan,
Jetzt muß ich Helfershelfer holen.

Uns geht's in allen Dingen schlecht! 11620
Herkömmliche Gewohnheit, altes Recht,
Man kann auf gar nichts mehr vertrauen.
Sonst mit dem letzten Athem fuhr sie aus,
Ich paßt' ihr auf und, wie die schnellste Maus,
Schnapps! hielt ich sie in fest verschloss'nen Klauen. 11625
Nun zaudert sie und will den düstern Ort,
Des schlechten Leichnams ekles Haus nicht lassen;
Die Elemente die sich hassen,
Die treiben sie am Ende schmählich fort.
Und wenn ich Tag' und Stunden mich zerplage, 11630
Wann? wie? und wo? das ist die leidige Frage;
Der alte Tod verlor die rasche Kraft,
Das Ob? sogar ist lange zweifelhaft;
Oft sah ich lüstern auf die starren Glieder;
Es war nur Schein, das rührte, das regte sich wieder. 11635

Phantastisch-flügelmännische Beschwörungs-Gebärden.

Nur frisch heran! verdoppelt euren Schritt,
Ihr Herrn vom g'raden, Herrn vom krummen Horne,
Von altem Teufelsschrot und Korne,
Bringt ihr zugleich den Höllenrachen mit.
Zwar hat die Hölle Rachen viele! viele! 11640
Nach Standsgebühr und Würden schlingt sie ein;
Doch wird man auch bei diesem letzten Spiele
In's künftige nicht so bedenklich sein.

Der greuliche Höllenrachen thut sich links auf.

Eckzähne klaffen; dem Gewölb des Schlundes
Entquillt der Feuerstrom in Wuth, 11645
Und in dem Siedequalm des Hintergrundes

Part of the Pisan Fresco "L'Inferno."

Seh' ich die Flammenstadt in ewiger Gluth.
Die rothe Brandung schlägt hervor bis an die Zähne,
Verdammte, Rettung hoffend, schwimmen an;
11650 Doch colossal zerknirscht sie die Hyäne
Und sie erneuen ängstlich heiße Bahn.
In Winkeln bleibt noch vieles zu entdecken,
So viel Erschrecklichstes im engsten Raum!
Ihr thut sehr wohl die Sünder zu erschrecken,
11655 Sie halten's doch für Lug und Trug und Traum.

Zu den Dickteufeln vom kurzen, g'raden Horne.

Nun wanstige Schuften mit den Feuerbacken!
Ihr glüht so recht vom Höllenschwefel feist;
Klotzartige, kurze, nie bewegte Nacken!
Hier unten lauert ob's wie Phosphor gleißt:
11660 Das ist das Seelchen, Psyche mit den Flügeln,
Die rupft ihr aus, so ist's ein garstiger Wurm;
Mit meinem Stempel will ich sie besiegeln,
Dann fort mit ihr im Feuer-Wirbel-Sturm.

Paßt auf die niedern Regionen,
11665 Ihr Schläuche, das ist eure Pflicht;
Ob's ihr beliebte da zu wohnen,
So accurat weiß man das nicht.
Im Nabel ist sie gern zu Haus,
Nehmt es in Acht, sie wischt euch dort heraus.

Zu den Dürrteufeln vom langen, krummen Horne.

11670 Ihr Firlefanze, flügelmännische Riesen,
Greift in die Luft, versucht euch ohne Rast;
Die Arme strack, die Klauen scharf gewiesen,
Daß ihr die flatternde, die flüchtige faßt.
Es ist ihr sicher schlecht im alten Haus
11675 Und das Genie es will gleich obenaus.

Glorie von oben, rechts.

Himmlische Heerschaar.

Folget Gesandte
Himmelsverwandte,
Gemächlichen Flugs:
Sündern vergeben,
Staub zu beleben; 11680
Allen Naturen
Freundliche Spuren
Wirket im Schweben
Des weilenden Zugs.

Mephistopheles.

Mißtöne hör' ich, garstiges Geklimper, 11685
Von oben kommt's mit unwillkommnem Tag;
Es ist das bübisch-mädchenhafte Gestümper,
Wie frömmelnder Geschmack sich's lieben mag.
Ihr wißt wie wir, in tiefverruchten Stunden,
Vernichtung sannen menschlichem Geschlecht; 11690
Das Schändlichste was wir erfunden
Ist ihrer Andacht eben recht.

Sie kommen gleisnerisch die Laffen!
So haben sie uns manchen weggeschnappt,
Bekriegen uns mit unsern eignen Waffen; 11695
Es sind auch Teufel, doch verkappt.
Hier zu verlieren wär' euch ew'ge Schande;
An's Grab heran und haltet fest am Rande!

Chor der Engel Rosen streuend.

Rosen, ihr blendenden,
Balsam versendenden! 11700

Flatternde, schwebende,
Heimlich belebende,
Zweiglein beflügelte,
Knospen entsiegelte,
11705 Eilet zu blühn.

Frühling entsprieße,
Purpur und Grün;
Tragt Paradiese
Dem Ruhenden hin.

Mephistopheles zu den Satanen.

11710 Was duckt und zuckt ihr? ist das Höllenbrauch?
So haltet Stand und laßt sie streuen.
An seinen Platz ein jeder Gauch!
Sie denken wohl mit solchen Blümeleien
Die heißen Teufel einzuschneien;
11715 Das schmilzt und schrumpft vor eurem Hauch.
Nun pustet, Püstriche! — Genug, genug!
Vor eurem Broden bleicht der ganze Flug. —
Nicht so gewaltsam! schließet Maul und Nasen!
Fürwahr ihr habt zu stark geblasen.
11720 Daß ihr doch nie die rechten Maße kennt.
Das schrumpft nicht nur, es bräunt sich, dorrt, es brennt!
Schon schwebt's heran mit giftig klaren Flammen,
Stemmt euch dagegen, drängt euch fest zusammen!
Die Kraft erlischt, dahin ist aller Muth!
11725 Die Teufel wittern fremde Schmeichelgluth.

Engel. Chor.

Blüthen die seligen,
Flammen die fröhlichen,

Liebe verbreiten sie,
Wonne bereiten sie,
Herz wie es mag. 11730
Worte die wahren,
Äther im Klaren.
Ewigen Schaaren
Überall Tag.

Mephistopheles.

O Fluch! o Schande solchen Tröpfen! 11735
Satane stehen auf den Köpfen,
Die Plumpen schlagen Rad auf Rad
Und stürzen ärschlings in die Hölle.
Gesegn' euch das verdiente heiße Bad!
Ich aber bleib' auf meiner Stelle. — 11740

Sich mit den schwebenden Rosen herumschlagend.

Irrlichter, fort! du! leuchte noch so stark,
Du bleibst gehascht ein ekler Gallert-Quark.
Was flatterst du? Willst du dich packen! —
Es klemmt wie Pech und Schwefel mir im Nacken.

Engel. Chor.

Was euch nicht angehört 11745
Müsset ihr meiden,
Was euch das Innre stört
Dürft ihr nicht leiden.
Dringt es gewaltig ein,
Müssen wir tüchtig sein. 11750
Liebe nur Liebende
Führet herein.

Mephistopheles.

Mir brennt der Kopf, das Herz, die Leber brennt,
Ein überteuflisch Element!
11755 Weit spitziger als Höllenfeuer.—
Drum jammert ihr so ungeheuer,
Unglückliche Verliebte! die, verschmäht,
Verdrehten Halses nach der Liebsten späht.

Auch mir! Was zieht den Kopf auf jene Seite?
11760 Bin ich mit ihr doch in geschwornem Streite!
Der Anblick war mir sonst so feindlich scharf.
Hat mich ein Fremdes durch und durch gedrungen?
Ich mag sie gerne sehn die allerliebsten Jungen;
Was hält mich ab daß ich nicht fluchen darf? —
11765 Und wenn ich mich bethören lasse,
Wer heißt denn künftighin der Thor?
Die Wetterbuben die ich hasse
Sie kommen mir doch gar zu lieblich vor! —

Ihr schönen Kinder, laßt mich wissen:
11770 Seid ihr nicht auch von Lucifers Geschlecht?
Ihr seid so hübsch, fürwahr ich möcht' euch küssen,
Mir ist's als kämt ihr eben recht.
Es ist mir so behaglich, so natürlich
Als hätt' ich euch schon tausendmal gesehn,
11775 So heimlich-kätzchenhaft begierlich;
Mit jedem Blick auf's neue schöner schön.
O nähert euch, o gönnt mir Einen Blick!

Engel.

Wir kommen schon, warum weichst du zurück?
Wir nähern uns und wenn du kannst so bleib'.

Die Engel nehmen, umherziehend, den ganzen Raum ein.

Mephistopheles der in's Proscenium gedrängt wird.

Ihr scheltet uns verdammte Geister 11780
Und seid die wahren Hexenmeister;
Denn ihr verführet Mann und Weib. —
Welch ein verfluchtes Abentheuer!
Ist dieß das Liebeselement?
Der ganze Körper steht in Feuer, 11785
Ich fühle kaum daß es im Nacken brennt. —
Ihr schwanket hin und her, so senkt euch nieder,
Ein bißchen weltlicher bewegt die holden Glieder;
Fürwahr der Ernst steht euch recht schön.
Doch möcht' ich euch nur einmal lächeln sehn; 11790
Das wäre mir ein ewiges Entzücken.
Ich meine so, wie wenn Verliebte blicken,
Ein kleiner Zug am Mund so ist's gethan.
Dich, langer Bursche, dich mag ich am liebsten leiden,
Die Pfaffenmiene will dich gar nicht kleiden, 11795
So sieh mich doch ein wenig lüstern an!
Auch könntet ihr anständig-nackter gehen,
Das lange Faltenhemd ist übersittlich —
Sie wenden sich — Von hinten anzusehen! —
Die Racker sind doch gar zu appetitlich. 11800

Chor der Engel.

Wendet zur Klarheit
Euch, liebende Flammen!
Die sich verdammen
Heile die Wahrheit;
Daß sie vom Bösen 11805
Froh sich erlösen,
Um in dem Allverein
Selig zu sein.

Mephistopheles sich fassend.

Wie wird mir! — Hiobsartig, Beul' an Beule
11810 Der ganze Kerl, dem's vor sich selber graut,
Und triumphirt zugleich, wenn er sich ganz durchschaut,
Wenn er auf sich und seinen Stamm vertraut;
Gerettet sind die edlen Teufelstheile,
Der Liebespuk er wirft sich auf die Haut;
11815 Schon ausgebrannt sind die verruchten Flammen,
Und, wie es sich gehört, fluch' ich euch allzusammen!

Chor der Engel.

Heilige Gluthen!
Wen sie umschweben
Fühlt sich im Leben
11820 Selig mit Guten.
Alle vereinigt
Hebt euch und preis't,
Luft ist gereinigt,
Athme der Geist!

Sie erheben sich, Faustens Unsterbliches entführend.

Mephistopheles sich umsehend.

11825 Doch wie? — wo sind sie hingezogen?
Unmündiges Volk, du hast mich überrascht,
Sind mit der Beute himmelwärts entflogen;
Drum haben sie an dieser Gruft genascht!
Mir ist ein großer, einziger Schatz entwendet,
11830 Die hohe Seele die sich mir verpfändet
Die haben sie mir pfiffig weggepascht.

Bei wem soll ich mich nun beklagen?
Wer schafft mir mein erworbenes Recht?

Du bist getäuscht in deinen alten Tagen,
Du hast's verdient, es geht dir grimmig schlecht. 11835
Ich habe schimpflich mißgehandelt,
Ein großer Aufwand, schmählich! ist verthan,
Gemein Gelüst, absurde Liebschaft wandelt
Den ausgepichten Teufel an.
Und hat mit diesem kindisch-tollen Ding 11840
Der Klugerfahrne sich beschäftigt,
So ist fürwahr die Thorheit nicht gering
Die seiner sich am Schluß bemächtigt.

St. Jerome in the Wilderness.

Bergschluchten,

Wald, Fels, Einöde.

Heilige Anachoreten gebirgauf vertheilt, gelagert zwischen Klüften.

Chor und Echo.

Waldung, sie schwankt heran,
11845 Felsen, sie lasten dran,
Wurzeln, sie klammern an,
Stamm dicht an Stamm hinan.
Woge nach Woge spritzt,
Höhle die tiefste schützt.
11850 Löwen, sie schleichen stumm-
Freundlich um uns herum,
Ehren geweihten Ort,
Heiligen Liebeshort.

Pater ecstaticus auf- und abschwebend.

Ewiger Wonnebrand,
11855 Glühendes Liebeband,
Siedender Schmerz der Brust,
Schäumende Gottes-Lust.
Pfeile, durchdringet mich,
Lanzen, bezwinget mich,

Keulen, zerschmettert mich, 11860
Blitze, durchwettert mich;
Daß ja das Nichtige
Alles verflüchtige,
Glänze der Dauerstern,
Ewiger Liebe Kern. 11865

Pater profundus. Tiefe Region.

Wie Felsenabgrund mir zu Füßen
Auf tiefem Abgrund lastend ruht,
Wie tausend Bäche strahlend fließen
Zum grausen Sturz des Schaums der Fluth,
Wie strack, mit eignem kräftigen Triebe, 11870
Der Stamm sich in die Lüfte trägt,
So ist es die allmächtige Liebe
Die alles bildet, alles hegt.

Ist um mich her ein wildes Brausen,
Als wogte Wald und Felsengrund, 11875
Und doch stürzt, liebevoll im Sausen,
Die Wasserfülle sich zum Schlund,
Berufen gleich das Thal zu wässern;
Der Blitz, der flammend niederschlug,
Die Atmosphäre zu verbessern 11880
Die Gift und Dunst im Busen trug;

Sind Liebesboten, sie verkünden
Was ewig schaffend uns umwallt.
Mein Innres mög' es auch entzünden
Wo sich der Geist, verworren, kalt, 11885
Verquält in stumpfer Sinne Schranken,
Scharfangeschloss'nem Kettenschmerz.

O Gott! beschwichtige die Gedanken,
Erleuchte mein bedürftig Herz.

Pater Seraphicus. Mittlere Region.

11890 Welch ein Morgenwölkchen schwebet
Durch der Tannen schwankend Haar;
Ahn' ich was im Innern lebet?
Es ist junge Geisterschaar.

Chor seliger Knaben.

Sag' uns, Vater, wo wir wallen,
11895 Sag' uns, Guter, wer wir sind?
Glücklich sind wir, allen, allen,
Ist das Dasein so gelind.

Pater Seraphicus.

Knaben! Mitternachts Geborne,
Halb erschlossen Geist und Sinn,
11900 Für die Eltern gleich Verlorne,
Für die Engel zum Gewinn.
Daß ein Liebender zugegen
Fühlt ihr wohl, so naht euch nur;
Doch von schroffen Erdewegen,
11905 Glückliche! habt ihr keine Spur.
Steigt herab in meiner Augen
Welt- und erdgemäß Organ,
Könnt sie als die euern brauchen,
Schaut euch diese Gegend an.

Er nimmt sie in sich.

11910 Das sind Bäume, das sind Felsen,
Wasserstrom, der abestürzt
Und mit ungeheurem Wälzen
Sich den steilen Weg verkürzt.

Selige Knaben von innen.

Das ist mächtig anzuschauen,
Doch zu düster ist der Ort, 11915
Schüttelt uns mit Schreck und Grauen,
Edler, Guter, laß uns fort.

Pater Seraphicus.

Steigt hinan zu höherm Kreise,
Wachset immer unvermerkt,
Wie, nach ewig reiner Weise, 11920
Gottes Gegenwart verstärkt.
Denn das ist der Geister Nahrung
Die im freisten Äther waltet,
Ewigen Liebens Offenbarung
Die zur Seligkeit entfaltet. 11925

Chor seliger Knaben um die höchsten Gipfel kreisend.

Hände verschlinget
Freudig zum Ringverein,
Regt euch und singet
Heil'ge Gefühle drein;
Göttlich belehret 11930
Dürft ihr vertrauen,
Den ihr verehret
Werdet ihr schauen.

Engel schwebend in der höheren Atmosphäre, Faustens Unsterbliches tragend.

Gerettet ist das edle Glied
Der Geisterwelt vom Bösen, 11935
„Wer immer strebend sich bemüht
Den können wir erlösen."

Und hat an ihm die Liebe gar
Von oben Theil genommen,
11940 Begegnet ihm die selige Schaar
Mit herzlichem Willkommen.

Die jüngeren Engel.

Jene Rosen aus den Händen
Liebend-heiliger Büßerinnen,
Halfen uns den Sieg gewinnen,
11945 Uns das hohe Werk vollenden,
Diesen Seelenschatz erbeuten.
Böse wichen als wir streuten,
Teufel flohen als wir trafen.
Statt gewohnter Höllenstrafen
11950 Fühlten Liebesqual die Geister;
Selbst der alte Satans-Meister
War von spitzer Pein durchdrungen.
Jauchzet auf! es ist gelungen.

Die vollendeteren Engel.

Uns bleibt ein Erdenrest
11955 Zu tragen peinlich,
Und wär' er von Asbest
Er ist nicht reinlich.
Wenn starke Geisteskraft
Die Elemente
11960 An sich herangerafft,
Kein Engel trennte
Geeinte Zwienatur
Der innigen Beiden,
Die ewige Liebe nur
11965 Vermag's zu scheiden.

Die jüngeren Engel.

Nebelnd um Felsenhöh
Spür' ich so eben,
Regend sich in der Näh,
Ein Geister-Leben.
Die Wölkchen werden klar, 11970
Ich seh' bewegte Schaar
Seliger Knaben,
Los von der Erde Druck,
Im Kreis gesellt,
Die sich erlaben 11975
Am neuen Lenz und Schmuck
Der obern Welt.
Sei er zum Anbeginn,
Steigendem Vollgewinn
Diesen gesellt! 11980

Die seligen Knaben.

Freudig empfangen wir
Diesen im Puppenstand;
Also erlangen wir
Englisches Unterpfand.
Löset die Flocken los 11985
Die ihn umgeben,
Schon ist er schön und groß
Von heiligem Leben.

Doctor Marianus. In der höchsten, reinlichsten Zelle.

Hier ist die Aussicht frei,
Der Geist erhoben. 11990
Dort ziehen Fraun vorbei,
Schwebend nach oben.

Die Herrliche, mitteninn,
Im Sternenkranze,
11995 Die Himmelskönigin,
Ich seh's am Glanze.

Entzückt.

Höchste Herrscherin der Welt!
Lasse mich, im blauen
Ausgespannten Himmelszelt,
12000 Dein Geheimniß schauen.
Billige was des Mannes Brust
Ernst und zart beweget
Und mit heiliger Liebeslust
Dir entgegen träget.

12005 Unbezwinglich unser Muth
Wenn du hehr gebietest,
Plötzlich mildert sich die Gluth
Wie du uns befriedest.
Jungfrau, rein im schönsten Sinn,
12010 Mutter, Ehren würdig,
Uns erwählte Königin,
Göttern ebenbürtig.

Um sie verschlingen
Sich leichte Wölkchen,
12015 Sind Büßerinnen,
Ein zartes Völkchen,
Um Ihre Kniee
Den Äther schlürfend,
Gnade bedürfend.

Dir, der Unberührbaren, 12020
Ist es nicht benommen
Daß die leicht Verführbaren
Traulich zu dir kommen.

In die Schwachheit hingerafft
Sind sie schwer zu retten; 12025
Wer zerreißt aus eigner Kraft
Der Gelüste Ketten?
Wie entgleitet schnell der Fuß
Schiefem, glattem Boden?
Wen bethört nicht Blick und Gruß, 12030
Schmeichelhafter Odem?

Mater gloriosa schwebt einher.

Chor der Büßerinnen.

Du schwebst zu Höhen
Der ewigen Reiche,
Vernimm das Flehen,
Du Ohnegleiche, 12035
Du Gnadenreiche!

Magna peccatrix (St. Lucae VII. 36).

Bei der Liebe die den Füßen
Deines gottverklärten Sohnes
Thränen ließ zum Balsam fließen,
Trotz des Pharisäer-Hohnes; 12040
Beim Gefäße das so reichlich
Tropfte Wohlgeruch hernieder,
Bei den Locken die so weichlich
Trockneten die heil'gen Glieder —

Mulier Samaritana (St. Joh. IV).

Bei dem Bronn zu dem schon weiland 12045
Abram ließ die Heerde führen,
Bei dem Eimer der dem Heiland
Kühl die Lippe durft' berühren;
Bei der reinen, reichen Quelle
Die nun dorther sich ergießet, 12050
Überflüssig, ewig helle,
Rings durch alle Welten fließet —

Maria Aegyptiaca (Acta Sanctorum).

Bei dem hochgeweihten Orte
Wo den Herrn man niederließ,
Bei dem Arm der von der Pforte 12055
Warnend mich zurücke stieß;
Bei der vierzigjährigen Buße
Der ich treu in Wüsten blieb,
Bei dem seligen Scheidegruße
Den im Sand ich niederschrieb — 12060

Zu drei.

Die du großen Sünderinnen
Deine Nähe nicht verweigerst
Und ein büßendes Gewinnen
In die Ewigkeiten steigerst,
Gönn' auch dieser guten Seele, 12065
Die sich einmal nur vergessen,
Die nicht ahnte daß sie fehle,
Dein Verzeihen angemessen!

Una Poenitentium sonst Gretchen genannt.

Sich anschmiegend.

Neige, neige,
Du Ohnegleiche, 12070
Du Strahlenreiche,
Dein Antlitz gnädig meinem Glück.
Der früh Geliebte,
Nicht mehr Getrübte
Er kommt zurück. 12075

Selige Knaben in Kreisbewegung sich nähernd.

Er überwächs't uns schon
An mächtigen Gliedern;
Wird treuer Pflege Lohn
Reichlich erwiedern.
Wir wurden früh entfernt 12080
Von Lebechören,
Doch dieser hat gelernt,
Er wird uns lehren.

Die eine Büßerin sonst Gretchen genannt.

Vom edlen Geisterchor umgeben,
Wird sich der Neue kaum gewahr, 12085
Er ahnet kaum das frische Leben,
So gleicht er schon der heiligen Schaar.
Sieh! wie er jedem Erdenbande
Der alten Hülle sich entrafft,
Und aus ätherischem Gewande 12090
Hervortritt erste Jugendkraft.
Vergönne mir ihn zu belehren,
Noch blendet ihn der neue Tag.

Mater gloriosa

Komm! hebe dich zu höhern Sphären,
12095 Wenn er dich ahnet, folgt er nach.

Doctor Marianus auf dem Angesicht anbetend.

Blicket auf zum Retterblick,
Alle reuig Zarten,
Euch zu seligem Geschick
Dankend umzuarten.
12100 Werde jeder bess're Sinn
Dir zum Dienst erbötig;
Jungfrau, Mutter, Königin,
Göttin, bleibe gnädig!

Chorus mysticus.

Alles Vergängliche
12105 Ist nur ein Gleichniß;
Das Unzulängliche
Hier wird's Ereigniß;
Das Unbeschreibliche
Hier ist's gethan;
12110 Das Ewig-Weibliche
Zieht uns hinan.

Finis.

NOTES.

Anmuthige Gegend.

Cf. Intr. p. xxx and p. xlvi. — The situation is Swiss. Under date of May 6, 1827, Eckermann represents Goethe as speaking at some length of his visit to Switzerland, in the year 1797, and of the impression produced upon him by the grand scenery of the Lucerne region. Eckermann suggested that the monologue of Faust in *terza rima* might be a reminiscence of the visit. Goethe at once confirmed the guess, adding that 'without the fresh impressions of that wonderful scenery he would not have been able to imagine the contents of the *Terzinen* at all.' So the lines were written while the impressions were 'fresh.' Feb. 21, 1798, Goethe wrote to Schiller that he had on hand a poetic project that had led him to experiment with the *terza rima*, but he did not like the meter because it had no 'rest.' On the strength of these two notices it seems safe to conclude that the monologue was written in the winter of 1798, though it may have been retouched and amplified at a later date. That the preceding fairy-choruses were written at the same time is unlikely. They belong probably to the year 1827.

In the dramatic economy of *Faust* this scene must be thought of as following shortly after the death of Gretchen, such being the clear implication of ll. 4623–5. But since the experiences of this one night symbolize a healing process which in real life requires a long time, the Faust who appears at court may properly be thought of as older by several years than the lover of Gretchen.

4612+. **schwebend bewegt,** 'hovering unsteadily' in the air above Faust. — **Ariel;** the familiar 'airy spirit' of Shakespeare, introduced here as the leader of a band of nocturnal fairies whose office is to assuage human pain.

4613. **Frühlings-Regen;** not that the time is spring, for it is midsummer (l. 4657). The meaning is that the good fairies are especially active in the season of the flowers and foliage which furnish them a home in the day-time. And the flowers are conceived in fairy lore as 'descending lightly' from above in a 'vernal shower.'

4616. **blinkt,** with dat., 'beams upon,' more literally, 'gleams for.' A free use of the dat. where normal usage would prefer a prepositional construction is very common in the Second Part. Cf. ll. 4721, 4909, 5272, 5330, 6681, and other cases collected by Strehlke Wb., *sub voce* Dativ.

4617. **Kleiner ... Geistergröße,** 'little fairies with the large-mindedness of spirits.' According to Grimm Wb., Geistergröße is a pregnant compound = Geistesgröße von Geistern. The 'magnanimity' of the fairies consists in their lofty indifference to the moral standards of men. Just as Nature sends her rain upon the just and upon the unjust, so they perform their kindly offices for every one who is unhappy, without regard to his character. W. von Biedermann, *Goethe-Forschungen*, II, 106, regards the elves as minions of Mephistopheles, sent to prevent Faust from becoming a penitent and thus escaping from the devil's power. But cf. Intr. p. xxx. — **Elfen,** instead of the proper German form Elben, is an English importation of the 18th century.

4621–33. These lines are spoken, while the preceding ones are sung. Musical passages, which are very numerous, are marked everywhere by the indention of the lines.

4626. **Pausen,** 'watches'; in allusion to the four Roman *vigiliae* of three hours each.

4629. **Lethe's Fluth;** the night-dew, by which the fairies are to render Faust oblivious of his past pain, is regarded, by a poetic figure, as coming from Lethe, the river of forgetfulness. But according to the Greek myth it was a draught of Lethe, and not a bath in its waters, that produced oblivion.

4630. **krampferstarrten,** 'cramp-stiffened.' Faust is thought of as a tired traveller.

4633. **Gebt ... zurück,** 'restore him,' in the pregnant sense of 'give him back restored,' — namely, in the morning.

4633+. **Einzeln ... gesammelt;** that is, the following songs are to be treated as solos, duets, and choruses, the voices alternating and combining *ad libitum*.

4634–65. These chants accompany the four watches of the night and carry out the commands of Ariel (ll. 4628 ff.). The first is an evening-song, describing the hush of nightfall and the coming-on of sleep, the second depicts the time of deepest slumber, the third the first break of dawn, and the fourth the sunrise. On the authority of the composer Eberwein Schröer prints the musical superscriptions *sérénade, notturno, mattutino,* and *réveille.* But these do not proceed from Goethe.

4634–5. Wenn ... Plan, 'when the zephyrs fill with coolness round about the green-girt field'; **sich füllen** = durchdrungen werden, 'become permeated.'—**Lau** is a factitive predicate,—the air 'fills cool,' i.e., becomes cool. The adjective applies to that which has been hot, but is so no longer. As used here of the summer-evening air, therefore, it comes nearer to Eng. 'cool' than to 'warm.'—**Plan** here of an Alpine meadow surrounded with trees.

4636. Süße Düfte. The fragrance of the flowers becomes more noticeable in the still, moist, evening air; hence the twilight is said to 'send down' the odors.

4638–41. The verbs are probably 3. sing., with Dämmerung as subject, though Schröer and others take them as 2. plu. The fairies have had their *orders* from Ariel, and do not need to order one another. The language is descriptive, as in the following songs, save where Faust is addressed.

4641. des Tages Pforte; the eyelids—without any mythological allusion, such as Strehlke sees, to the Homeric cloud-gates (*Iliad,* 5, 749) which are kept by the Horæ.

4643. heilig, 'solemnly'; but the word is more deeply expressive than feierlich. It is used, as in Stolberg's Süße, heilige Natur, to suggest the divine order in nature. The procession of the stars attunes the mind to 'holy' thoughts. So too the light is 'holy' for the fairies (l. 4633).

4647. klarer Nacht = in der klaren Nacht; an adverbial gen. of place, not of time.

4648. Tiefsten Ruhens, 'of deepest resting.' The verbal has a durative force which makes the phrase more expressive than tiefster Ruhe would be.

4651. Hingeschwunden ... Glück. The bath in the dews of Lethe (l. 4629) has now done its work.

4653. neuem Tagesblick. Attention may be called once for all to the frequent omission of the article as one of the stylistic peculiarities of the Second Part. A selection from the multitude of cases is given by Strehlke Wb., *sub voce* Auslassung.

4654. Thäler . . . schwellen, 'vales grow green and hills are swelling'; i.e., the green valleys and swelling hills of the landscape (to be thought of probably as far below) are beginning to emerge in the morning twilight.

4655. Buschen sich, 'cover themselves with bushy verdure'; a rather un-German substitute for bebüschen sich.

4656. schwanken, 'unsteady,' 'rippling,' 'billowy,' as in l. 6009, rather than = schwankend dünn, as Schröer thinks.

4657. Wogt . . . . zu, 'sways toward the harvest-time.' The morning breeze ruffles the sea of growing grain.

4658. Wunsch um Wünsche, 'wish upon wish,' i.e., the acme of thy wishes. Goethe is fond of using the plu. instead of the sing. in the second member of such formulæ. Cf. Thräne folgt den Thränen, l. 29; von Sturz zu Sturzen, l. 4718; Schaum an Schäume, l. 4720; Kreis um Kreise, l. 5527; Lied um Lieder, l. 7497, etc.

4659. Glanze; not yet the sun itself, but the premonitory glow in the east.

4663. zaudernd schweift, 'loiters irresolutely.' — **Wenn** in the sense of indem, 'while' (as in l. 6093).

4666. dem . . . Horen, 'the onset of the Hours.' The imagery seems to have been suggested primarily by Guido's well-known picture of the Sun-god in his chariot preceded by Aurora and attended by the dancing Hours. — The MS. at Weimar (H) and the first print (C) both read:

> Horchet! horcht! dem Sturm der Horen
> Tönend wird u.s.w.,

which makes it necessary to construe dem Sturm as a kind of ablative dat. with wird geboren (dem Sturm = von dem Sturm). We have followed the punctuation of the Weimar editor, though the arbitrary change is not quite in harmony with the general principles adopted for the Weimar edition.

4667. Tönend; cf. l. 243. Goethe blends the philosophic (Pythagorean) idea of spheral music with the myth of Helios and his chariot. See n. to l. 4674.

4669. **knarren rasselnd,** 'creak and clatter,' as they are thrown open to admit the chariot.

4672. **Es . . . posaunet,** 'there's blare of trumpets, peal of trombones.' The rhythmic clatter of the wheels and clanging of the gates produce *the effect* of a loud burst of orchestral music. There are no instruments in Guido's painting, though, as Taylor ingeniously remarks, 'the picture suggests noise and the sound of trumpets.' The loud-creaking gates may be a reminiscence of *Iliad*, 5, 749, where we read that 'the gates of heaven, which the Hours kept, opened of their own accord with a loud noise' (to admit the chariot of Hera).

4674. **Unerhörtes . . . nicht,** 'the unheard-of is not to be listened to.' A difficult line which has been variously explained. On the whole it seems best to take hört in the durative sense of anhören or zuhören. The sense will then be: Solch unerhörte Musik läßt sich nicht anhören. That is, the nocturnal fairies can, and safely may, hear the 'storm' of the sunrise from afar, so long as the sun is below the horizon. But if they wait to listen until the glare of the sun itself strikes them, the music becomes intolerable, — they are made deaf by it.

4676. **Tiefer, tiefer;** to be taken with schlüpfet: 'Creep into the flower-cups — farther, farther.'

4679–4727. The meter is the difficult *terza rima*, or triple rime, of Dante (cf. the introductory note above). The rimes are all feminine, interlaced according to the scheme *ababcbcdcdedef* etc. Loeper justly reckons these verses among 'the most beautiful that have ever been written in the German language.'

4684. **du regst und rührst,** 'thou dost arouse'; a common alliterative formula.

4688. **Thal aus, Thal ein,** 'vale in, vale out,' i.e., over all the vales. Adverbial acc. of the way, as in bergauf, bergunter.

4699. **grüngesenkten,** 'green-girt,' lit. 'sunk in green,' grün- being taken substantively, as in ll. 1071, 4635. The tree-girt meadows up the mountain-side give the effect of depressions in the general mass of green. The compound, while grammatically odd, is poetically accurate and picturesque. It is not merely a substitute for grünen, gesenkten.

4701. **stufenweis . . . gelungen,** 'step by step downward the work is done,' — the work of lighting up the landscape completely.

4702. **Sie;** the sun.

4703. **vom Augenschmerz durchdrungen,** 'with eyes pained by the piercing glare.'

4704–14. Faust rehearses his present experience with the Alpine sunrise as typical of a common experience in life, namely, that the complete realization of a cherished wish does not yield the pure gratification we have expected, but overwhelms us, so that we hardly know whether it is pleasure or pain that we feel. In a letter of 1826, perhaps in reminiscence of this passage, Goethe likens himself to a 'traveller walking toward the east at dawn, gazing with joy at the increasing light, eagerly awaiting the appearance of the great fire-ball, and then, when it appears, turning away his eyes, unable to endure the wished-for splendor.'

4705. **sich . . . zugerungen (hat),** 'has won its way to intimacy with.' Traulich is to be taken factitively. Light is thrown upon its meaning by the use of vertraut in the following passage from *Wilhelm Meister*, which also illustrates the thought in other respects: Der Mensch scheint mit nichts vertrauter zu sein als mit seinen Hoffnungen und Wünschen, . . . und doch wenn sie ihm nun begegnen, . . . erkennt er sie nicht und weicht vor ihnen zurück. — **Dem höchsten Wunsch** is to be understood in a general way of *any* supreme desire. — On the asyndeton between ll. 4705 and 4706 cf. l. 1180.

4709. **Des . . . entzünden,** 'we wished to light the torch of life,' i.e., we hoped for a moderate gratification of a familiar and calculable kind —hoped for fire enough to light our torch, and our prayer is answered with a 'sea of flame.'

4711. **die . . . . umwinden.** The antecedent of die is the Flammen of Flammen-Übermaß, the thought being: Is it love or hate, does it bode good or ill — this sea of glowing flames that envelops us? But for the exigency of the meter we should have: Ist's Lieb'? Ist's Haß? was glühend uns umwindet, u. s. w.

4712. **wechselnd ungeheuer,** 'changing stupendously.'

4714. **Zu bergen . . . . Schleier,** 'to hide ourselves in her most grateful veil.' The act of turning away from the glare of the sun to look at the green earth is conceived as a veiling of the face. Jugendlich of the matutinal freshness of Nature; cf. Richter's use of the word in *Titan:* Hinaus in den freudigen Tag, in den jugendlichen Garten. Loeper paraphrases it with morgendlich. The use of the absolute superlative without modifier (in jugendlichstem Schleier = in ihrem äußerst wohlthuenden Schleier) is somewhat forced, though abundant parallel examples can be found in Goethe's later writings.

4718. **Sturzen.** The plu. without umlaut is unusual, but occurs also in other writers, e.g., in Kant.

4719. **abertausend.** The prefix aber= denotes repetition, as in abermals, 'yet again.' Hence tausend und abertausend, 'a thousand and yet another thousand,' i.e., 'myriads.'

4720. **sausend**; here used transitively in the sense of 'sending with a roar.' The cataract 'leaps from plunge to plunge, breaking in a myriad streams and *roaring* masses of foam high into the air.' But Schröer thinks this inadmissible, and would connect Schaum an Schäume with wälzt.

4721. **diesem Sturm erspriessend** = aus diesem Sturm hervorgehend. The MS. has entspriessend, which makes the ablative dat. more natural.

4725–7. Faust sees in the ever-changing rainbow, which is the 'colored reflection' of ever-varying conditions, a symbol of human life. The essence of the analogy is that life takes its character from its surroundings. The white light of ideal purpose (Bestreben) manifests itself only as it breaks upon and is reflected back in visible colors by the facts of life. In an 'Essay toward a Theory of the Weather,' published in 1825, Goethe writes: 'The true, identical with the divine, is never cognized by us directly; we see it only in the reflection (Abglanz), the example, the symbol, in particular and in related phenomena.' Taylor quotes a kindred thought from Shelley's *Adonais:*

> Life, like a dome of many-colored glass,
> Stains the white radiance of Eternity.

Kaiserliche Pfalz.

Saal des Thrones.

Cf. Intr. p. xxxi and p. xlvii. — The prose sketch of 1816 locates this scene at Augsburg in the time of the Diet held there by Emperor Maximilian I, who reigned from 1493 to 1519. This is in harmony with the later forms of the legend, beginning with Widman, though the original Faust-book makes the magician appear instead at the court of Maximilian's grandson, Karl V. Maximilian is known in history as 'the last of the knights,' and his character has furnished some traits for Goethe's Emperor. Thus he was fond of æsthetic pleasures and of imperial glamour, impatient of reformers, and always in straits for money. It may be remarked, too, that the general situation depicted by Goethe, — that is, the incohesiveness of the Empire, with its internal anarchy and *Faustrecht*, its rotten administration, and its impotent insistence upon antiquated forms, — corresponds with the conditions which actually existed at this time, the time of the breaking-up of feudalism. But aside from these generalities our poet does not trouble himself about the 'facts' of a particular life or a particular epoch. His picture is broadly but not pedantically historical. What he aimed at in his portrait of the Emperor is indicated in a conversation with Eckermann, to which we have already referred (Intr. p. xxxii).

The original conception of this scene, or what appears to have been such, was communicated in some way to Johannes Falk, who has left an account of it in his book, *Goethe aus näherem persönlichem Umgange dargestellt.* Falk's account locates the scene at Frankfurt, on the occasion of a coronation festival, and gives details altogether different from those of the final version. A remnant of this early conception is preserved, probably, in the curious bit of dialogue published in the Weimar *Goethe* as Paralipomenon No. 65. But as neither of these documents, however interesting in themselves, has any discernible relation to the text of the completed poem, it is unnecessary to discuss them. Cf. Strehlke, *Paralipomena*, pp. 49, 59.

4728. **Getreuen, Lieben.** Lieber Getreuer was the usual form of ceremonious address from a monarch to his 'faithful,' oath-bound minister. The Emperor begins a formal speech of welcome, but breaks off because he misses his fool. He resumes in l. 4761.

4733. **Stürzt' .... zusammen,** 'collapsed,' 'dropped down'—paralyzed by Mephistopheles, who wanted the office for himself.

4743-50. The answer is, in each case, the court-fool,—with varying reference to the court-fool in general, the old fool, and the new fool.

4754. **Da löse du,** 'try your hand there at solving.' Read: Da l ö s e du, with stress on the verb. Da is used somewhat indefinitely for bei den Räthseln dieser Herrn, i.e., in the approaching council of state. The thought is: I have riddles enough, propounded by my ministers; what I need is a solver.

4755. **weit in's Weite,** 'on a far, far journey.' The Emperor wrongly thinks him dead.

4756+. **Gemurmel der Menge.** Here and elsewhere the Gemurmel is not to be understood as a chorus, and still less as an imitation of the Greek chorus, Taylor's note being quite erroneous. It consists rather of individual grumblings, each half-line being spoken by a different person. This is indicated by the dashes. The court-people do not like their Emperor's partiality for fools and astrologers.—On the other hand, as the grumblings are made to rime and are of the nature of comment on the proceedings, they are properly indented in the manner of musical passages. After all they are nearer to chorus than to dialogue.

4759. **Der hat verthan,** 'it's up with him,' 'he's done for'; from verthun in the sense of 'to finish one's doing.'

4766. **entschlagen;** inf. with wollten below.

4767. **Schönbärte,** 'masks'; originally 'bearded mask,' the Schön being a perversion of M.H.G. *scheme*, 'mask', which early dropped out of use in this sense, and so ceased to be understood.—**Mummenschänzlich,** 'masquerade-fashion'; an adv. found only here. Translate: When we would escape from cares, don the masquerading guise, etc.

4771. **Geschehen ist's,** 'the thing 's been done,' i.e., a meeting of the council has been called; **so sei's gethan,** 'so let the business be despatched.'

4771+. **Canzler.** The imperial Chancellor, called also Arch-chancellor (Erzkanzler), was the Archbishop of Mainz. Hence the variety of his titles in *Faust*. See Act 4, l. 10930+.

4774. **sie** refers to Tugend, but at the same time anticipates Gerechtigkeit; — **gültig,** 'validly,' 'effectively.'

4781. **Übel . . . überbrütet,** 'evil o'erhatches itself in evils,' i. e., hatches out an excessive progeny of evils.

4783. **schwerer Traum,** 'nightmare.'

4784. **Mißgestalt;** here used in about the sense of 'disorder.' 'Disorder rules amid disorders, and lawlessness holds sway under forms of law.'

4786. **Irrthums;** here = Verirrung, 'aberration,' 'perversity.'

4796. **Mitschuldigste,** 'most guilty accomplices.'

4800. **vernichtigen;** supply will sich. Vernichtigen, from nichtig, means 'to make futile' (not the same as vernichten, 'annihilate'). 'Thus all the world is going to pieces and the right (was sich gebührt) is becoming an empty form.' This seems better than to take was sich gebührt as object.

4801–2. **der Sinn . . . der führt;** the law-abiding spirit.

4804. **Neigt sich,** 'becomes accessible.'

4807. **dichtern,** 'thicker' — but thicker than what? One can not, with Schröer, ignore the comparative. The sense seems to be: I have painted a black picture, yet not so black as the facts warrant. I have veiled it somewhat, but I should like to draw a still thicker veil over it.

4811. **Geht . . . zu Raub** = wird zur Beute, 'becomes a spoil,' 'goes to ruin.'

4811+. **Heermeister,** 'master of the army,' conceived by Goethe like a modern minister of war. No such dignity was known to the politics of the Empire, though it was known to certain knightly orders.

4817. **auszudauern;** often transitive, as here, in the sense of 'to hold out against,' 'withstand.'

4827. **Man läßt . . . hausen,** 'their violence is allowed to rage on'; wüthend being an adv. and hausen an inf. = übel wirtschaften, wüsten. So the MS. and the first print; but the edition of 1833 has: Man läßt ihr Toben, wüthend Hausen, i.e., läßt es bleiben.

4828. **verthan,** 'done for,' 'lost.' Cf. l. 4759.

4829. **draußen**, 'outside' the limits of the Empire. The complaint is that foreign princes, though friendly, do not bother themselves over the internal affairs of the Empire.

4831. **pochen auf jemand** = 'to rely upon'; pochen auf etwas (l. 4795), 'to brag of.'

4833. **Wie . . . aus**, 'like piped water, fail to appear.' The capricious uncertainty of piped water is proverbial in German. See Grimm Wb. under Röhrwasser; also *Dichtung u. Wahrheit*, bk. 4, paragraphs 7 and 8.

4836. **ein Neuer**, 'a new man,' *novus homo*. Upstarts that decline to continue the tribute paid by their predecessors have displaced the old feudal nobility.

4841. **wie sie heißen**, 'whatever their name' = wie sie auch heißen. The context means that selfishness is stronger than party spirit.

4845–6. 'Before the middle of the 15th century,' says Bryce, *Holy Roman Empire*, p. 306, 'the names of Guelf and Ghibelline had ceased to have any sense or meaning.' Goethe uses the old, far-famed party-names to typify all parties whatever. If the warring factions are quiet for the moment, it is not out of respect for imperial authority, but only to get breath for new quarrels.

4851+. **Marschalk**, 'steward'; older form of Marschall, which occurs in Act 4, l. 10876+. The functionary thus denoted is usually called Hofmarschall. The imperial Marschall was the Elector of Saxony, but the care of the Emperor's kitchen devolved upon another potentate — the Truchseß (cf. n. to l. 10876).

4856. After thut supply in thought zwar — correlative with jedoch in l. 4861.

4859. **Deputate**, 'allowances-in-kind'; i.e., meat, wood, fruits, etc., 'deputed' to be paid by tenants, instead of money, as part of the rent due.

4863. **Berg' und Jahresläufte**, 'vineyards and vintages'; Berg' = Weinberge. Lauft was formerly more common than Lauf.

4864. **Gesäufte**, 'toping'; a variation of Gesäufe and Gesaufe, which seems to have lingered in Goethe's mind from his reading of Hans von Schweinichen.

4866. **sein Lager verzapfen**, 'tap its supply.' The council of a medieval city usually had a wine-cellar (Rathskeller) in the town-hall.

4867. **Humpen, Napfen,** 'bowls and basins' (instead of decent wine-glasses). The usual plu. of Napf is Näpfe.

4871. **Anticipationen,** 'advances,' 'loans,' — against future income.

4875. **vorgegessen Brot,** 'bread already eaten' is proverbial for bread got with borrowed money.

4877. **Den Glanz . . . schauen,** 'to behold the splendor round about!' The exclamatory infinitive requires nothing to be supplied.

4896. **Natur- und Geisteskraft** = natürliche Geisteskraft, 'native ability.'

4897. **Natur und Geist.** The Chancellor, a high prelate of the church, scents heresy and wickedness in this proposed reliance upon 'nature' and 'mind' (instead of authority and faith).

4903. **Uns nicht so**; sc. kommt man nicht. 'None of that for us!' — Landen is probably an ablative dat., possibly a dat. of interest.

4904. **Geschlechter**; here = Stände, 'estates,' the reference being to the 'saints,' i.e., the clergy, and the 'knights,' i.e., the nobility. Nur is used as if the following Sie were a relative. 'Only two estates have arisen which worthily support the throne.'

4909. **Pöbelsinn,** 'seditious bent,' 'unruliness'; the dat. = gegen den Pöbelsinn.

4911. **Die . . . Hexenmeister,** 'I mean the heretics, the sorcerers'; i.e., these are the 'muddled minds' to which I refer.

4913. **du**; namely, Mephistopheles.

4915. **Ihr . . . Herzen.** Both the reference of the pronoun and the meaning of the verb are moot-questions. Ihr can hardly refer to Mephistopheles, as Strehlke thinks, nor, as many others think, to the Emperor alone, he being regularly addressed with Du. It seems rather to refer in a general way to the whole council, the sense being: 'You (gentlemen) are taking up with a depraved heart.' Sich hegen an is much like sich anschließen an, but more expressive; it suggests the idea of 'cherishing,' 'taking to one's heart' (cf. hegen in l. 4901).

4916. A more logical form for the idea would be: Der Narr ist ihnen nah verwandt.

4924. **du**; the Chancellor, whose outburst against the heretics strikes the Emperor like an inopportune Lenten sermon.

4931. **Schreckensläuften,** 'times of terror'; in allusion to the great

Germanic migrations, the Hunnish invasions, etc. So Cornelius, in Marlowe's *Faustus*, promises that spirits shall fetch

> the wealth that our forefathers hid
> Within the massy entrails of the earth.

4940. **des . . . Recht**, the Emperor's right from of old; in allusion to old laws which provided that treasure found buried in the earth below the reach of a plowshare belonged wholly or in part to the imperial fiscus; *al schatz der tiefer denn ein pflug ge, gehoret zu der kuniglichen Gewalt*, says the *Sachsenspiegel* I, 35.

4942. **Es . . . Dingen.** The meaning is that it is wicked — not to be accomplished without the devil's aid. Cf. n. to l. 2894.

4949. **In Kreis um Kreise**, 'in circle after circle' (cf. n. to l. 4658), i.e., in all the circles of the sky. A horoscope was usually drawn in the form of a circle or ellipse with inner concentric curves and radii. The segments cut off by these radii were known as 'houses.'

4953. **mattgesungen . . . Gedicht**, 'played-out old lie'; Gedicht, as often, = Erdichtung; mattgesungen, 'sung until it has become stale.' The crowd rightly suspect a collusion between the new fool and the old visionary.

4955–70. In the jargon of the astrologers the heavenly bodies corresponded to metals as follows: the sun, gold; the moon, silver; Venus, copper; Mars, iron; Jupiter, tin; Saturn, lead; Mercury, quicksilver. The lingo here blends this symbolism with mythological allusions and statements of simple physical fact. It has no point except to lead up to a hearty recommendation of Mephistopheles (l. 4969).

4957. **angethan**, 'bewitched.'

4958. **So . . . spat**, 'in youth and in age.' For spat = spät cf. l. 3112.

4959. **launet grillenhaft**, 'is subject to whimsical caprices.' The moon is changeable.

4960. **dräut**, 'threatens'; in allusion to the dread god of war, and also, probably, to the red Mars in the sky, which was regarded as ominous.

4965. **fein**, 'modestly,' 'in her maiden modesty.' The logic of the following lines is, that there is now a conjunction of Sol and Luna, — gold and silver, — which means unbounded wealth. Only it needs a wise man (Mephistopheles) to get it up.

4973. **Gedroschner** = abgedroschner, 'threshed-out,' 'stale.'

4974. **Kalenderei,** 'calender-making,' 'astrology'; **Chymisterei,** 'alchemy.' The crowd suspect the familiar old swindle of gold-making.

4976. **er,** the promised wonder-worker; **Gauch** here = 'rogue,' 'swindler.'

4979–80. **der eine . . . Hund,** 'one babbles of alrauns, another of the black dog.' Mephistopheles rallies the crowd for cherishing vulgar superstitions and being at the same time skeptical with regard to *his* great 'find.' The alraun is the wonder-working mandrake (the 'shrieking mandrake' of *Romeo and Juliet*, IV, 3), which grows in human form under a gallows (whence called Galgenmännlein). If pulled up violently it gives forth a scream which is fatal to him who hears it. To obtain the alraun one must stop his ears with wax, dig around the root, fasten it to a hungry black dog, tempt the dog with food and at the same time blow a blast upon a large horn in order to drown the deadly sound. When the root is thus pulled up the dog will fall dead, but the alraun, on being washed with red wine, wrapped in a red cloth, and laid away in a box, becomes a valuable possession (*Hausgeist*) which enables its owner to do all sorts of wonderful things. For a full account of this curious superstition see E. O. Lippmann, *Über einen naturwissenschaftlichen Aberglauben*, Halle, 1894. Our illustration is borrowed from Lippmann, who reproduces it from a picture in the Nürnberg museum.

4981 ff. The meaning is: Why pretend to despise my occult science when you are all subject to those mysterious sensations (such as a tickling of the foot or a sudden stumbling) by which the presence of subterraneous treasure is indicated. The allusion is to the occult art of 'metal-feeling,' in which Goethe took a poetic interest. In *Meisters Wanderjahre* he introduces a man who 'felt the strong effect of subterraneous streams, deposits of metal,' etc., and whose 'sensations changed with every change of the soil.'

4988. **Schmiegt . . . herauf,** 'comes creeping up.'

4992. **Da . . . Spielmann,** 'there lies the fiddler.' Da liegt ein Spielmann begraben is a proverb used when people stumble or have an irresistible desire to go on dancing after the music has stopped (cf. *Des Knaben Wunderhorn*, 328). The buried fiddler furnishes the music, i.e., he is a good friend, the spot is lucky. *Per contra* one says, Da liegt ein Schuster begraben, of the place where one gets bad cards (the cobbler does the dealing). Goethe uses the proverb of the fiddler in the

ALRAUN AND BLACK DOG.

general sense of 'That's the lucky spot,' and then makes the meaning definite by adding: 'There lies the treasure.'

5000. **Erprobe . . . Lügenschäume,** 'put to the test your froth of lies.' The Emperor is at once credulous and skeptical.

5006. The line is a facetious 'aside,' as shown by the dash, the doch of the next line resuming from l. 4992.

5011. **Leimenwand,** 'clay wall.' The usual form is Lehmwand or Leimwand. The plowman turns up a vessel of clay pottery which he thinks to scrape for saltpeter (which was once esteemed as a medicine), but finds full of gold. The 'clay wall' is the surface of the Goldtopf; cf. *Zeits. f. d. Ph.*, 24, 509. Strehlke however takes Leimenwand in the sense of 'clay stratum in the soil,' while Düntzer and others make it mean a mud-plastered wall of masonry. Old walls were formerly a source of supply for saltpeter.

5012. **golden-goldne Rolle;** emphatic reduplication, as in Eng. 'the wide, wide world.' For Rolle in the sense of 'gold coin' cf. l. 5718.

5013. **kümmerlicher,** 'miserable.' Logically the adj. goes with Bauer, but the transference to Hand (the part for the whole) is natural enough in poetry and heightens the effect of the picture.

5016. **Schatzbewußte,** 'treasure-expert'; one who is 'conscious,' through his subjective sensations, of the presence of treasure near him.

5018. **altverwahrten,** 'preserved from of old.' Goethe has elsewhere das altverborgene Gold. Thus the MS., but the first print has allverwahrten, i.e., 'fully preserved.'

5023. **Naß;** wine.

5026. **Der Weinstein schuf;** in allusion to the popular belief, said by Taylor to be 'general' in Germany, that the tartar deposited on the sides of a buried wine-cask may form a vessel solid enough to hold the wine after the staves have rotted away.

5029. **Nacht und Graus;** hendiadys for nächtlichem Graus, 'darksome horror.'

5030. **unverdrossen,** 'undismayed' by the horror.

5031. **Am Tag . . . Possen,** 'to recognize things in the daylight is child's play.'

5036. Popular proverbs expressive of the idea that darkness obliterates distinctions of color.

5040. **macht dich groß,** 'will make you great,' i.e., will redound to your honor, make you the subject of a saga, as in the case of Cincinnatus and others. The devil can not mean that the toil would be good for his Majesty's character.

5041. **goldner Kälber;** in allusion to the 'golden calf' of Exodus. 'A herd of golden calves' is, however, simply an extravagant metaphor for boundless wealth.

5045. Farb= und Glanzgestein, 'colored brilliant.'

5050. Zerstreutes Wesen = Zerstreutheit, 'distraction.' The scatter-brained mood of the carnival is not favorable to our proposed undertaking (that of digging for the treasure). Mephistopheles has a scheme that is better than digging, and so, to gain time, he has the Astrologer declare that the digging must be done in Lent.

5051. in Fassung uns versühnen, 'do penance in a calm frame of mind.' Versühnen is the earlier form of **versöhnen.**

5052. Das . . . verdienen, 'deserve the lower (i.e. riches) by means of the higher (i.e. religious exercises).' Schröer quotes appositely a passage from *Dichtung und Wahrheit*, in which Goethe speaks of Lavater and Basedow as men who were capable of 'using spiritual means for earthly ends,' and thus 'sacrificing the upper to the lower.'

5053–6. All four lines express the thought: Whoso wishes a blessing, let him look to himself and patiently adapt means to ends.

(Kaiserliche Pfalz.)

Weitläufiger Saal.

Cf. Intr. p. xxxii and p. xlvii. As is there remarked, the Masquerade should be taken for just what it purports to be, and not for an 'allegory of society' or anything of that sort. There are some allegorical figures, as is common enough in masquerades; but these are simply features of the spectacle. The thing aimed at is not philosophy, but picturesque effect. It is all a picture to be *seen*, an exuberant play of poetic fancy luxuriating in the joyous *Farbenpracht* of the south. Nominally we have a German imitation of the Italian carnival, but a close imitation is not attempted. The figures introduced were suggested partly by Goethe's recollections of the Roman carnival (see his well-known description, *Werke*, H. 16, 297), partly by his well-trained instinct for the picturesque in court-spectacles (cf. his various *Maskenzüge*), and partly by his reading. Among his literary sources the most important was Grazzini's *Canti Carnascialeschi*, a compilation giving the text of songs and poems used in connection with various Florentine festivals of the

16th century. The records of the court library at Weimar show that Goethe had Grazzini's work from Aug. 11 to Oct. 9, 1827. It furnished him with various hints for the Masquerade. — For the details of Greek mythology, here and elsewhere, his main resource was Hederich's *Lexicon Mythologicum*, a quaint, lumbering, pedantic, but withal very serviceable work, which is still to be found in the poet's little study at Weimar, among his few books of reference.

5064+. **Herold.** The 'Herald' is here a sort of master of ceremonies. His office is to announce what is coming and give needed explanations.

5066. **Von;** used loosely in the sense of 'abounding in,' 'characterized by.' The thought is: Do not expect a Shrovetide spectacle of the familiar German kind, with its grotesque and gruesome features.—The Dance of Death, Fr. *danse macabre*, is familiar in symbolic art as a skeleton leading a bevy of frolicking maidens.

5067. **heitres,** 'cheerful'; like 'sunny' Italy. Cf. heitres Reich below in l. 5071.

5072. **an heiligen Sohlen,** 'at the feet of the pope.' The emperors were regularly crowned in Rome (where they had to kiss the pope's slipper), down to the time of Maximilian. — Goethe first wrote Der Kaiser an den and then changed it to the more colloquial Der Kaiser, er.

5075. **Kappe,** 'fool's cap,' emblem of All Fools' Day. It was not really an importation from Italy.

5079. **ähnlet,** 'makes like'; for the more usual ähnelt. Cf. Wimmlens, l. 6014; verwandlen, l. 8153; wandlen, l. 8159; traurend, l. 8826; tändlend, l. 9993, etc. In general Goethe's spelling of the contract forms of verbs in -eln and -ern accords with present usage, but he was not perfectly consistent. The capricious exceptions noted above might as well have been normalized by the Weimar editor.

5084. **unverdrossen,** 'undismayed,' by the novelty of the scene or any feeling that the foolishness is undignified. The Herald wants them to feel at home in this little world of fools, remembering that the big world is of the same ilk.

5087. **einzig;** adj. with Thor. The MS. has einziger.

5087+. **Gärtnerinnen.** Girls with flower-baskets on their heads are familiar figures in the Italian carnival. As Florence is the city of flowers, *these* girls are made to come from Florence, and as they have wandered so far from home (according to the fiction), their flowers are artificial.

5096. **es**; the wearing of artificial flowers.

5100–1. **Allerlei . . . gethan**; a somewhat forced locution = allerlei gefärbte Schnitzel wurden symmetrisch arrangirt.

5109. **Häupten**; an archaic plu. still preserved in the phrase zu Häupten.

5116. **Feilschet**, 'bargain,' 'chaffer.' The company are invited to go through the pantomime of buying flowers, but are warned that there is to be no actual sale (the artistic arrangement is not to be disturbed). The girls then take up one flower after another and, under the pretence of inviting a purchaser, describe its character in language which purports to come from the flower itself.

5137. **Theophrast**; the favorite pupil of Aristotle, called the father of botany. Goethe first wrote: Würde selbst kein Humboldt sagen, — which would have been a too flagrant anachronism.

5140. **mich . . . eignen** = gehören, 'belong to.'

5143+. **Ausforderung** stands for Rosenknospen, die Phantasieblumen herausfordernd; i.e., the lines following are a 'challenge' of the modest rosebuds to the gaudy artificial flowers. Ll. 5144–9 are sung by one of the girls while she is rummaging in her basket after a hidden cluster of rosebuds; ll. 5150–7 after she has suddenly produced them from their hiding-place.

5157+. **Theorben.** The gardeners have *theorbi*, lute-like instruments with a lower register than the mandolins of the flower-girls.

5160. **wollen . . . verführen.** The thought is: Our fruits, unlike these flowers you see about your heads (addressed to the people under the arbors), do not try to seduce the eye; *they* appeal to the taste.

5162. **bräunliche Gesichter**; by metonymy for the sun-browned gardeners themselves.

5170–3. Addressed to the flower-girls.

5177+. **Guitarren**, 'guitars'; probably a mere oversight for Mandolinen (l. 5087+). But the two instruments are much alike.

5194. **dritter Mann**; the name of a social game, called also Dreimannhoch and Plumpsack. For a description see Grimm Wb. under Drittermann.

5198+. **Holzhauer,** 'Wood-cutters,' such as Goethe had probably seen in the Italian carnival. It is not likely that he had in mind the *ὑλοφόροι* or 'wood-carriers' of Attic comedy. — The preceding stage-directions, like some others further on, give the content of a scene or part of a scene, which Goethe probably meant at one time to elaborate in verse. One can see no very good reason why they were allowed to stand on the final revision — perhaps as a suggestion for pantomime.

5199. **Blöße,** 'clearing.' The Wood-cutters use a technical term of their craft.

5206. **Bringt . . . Reine,** 'straighten this out.' The sense is: Construe these rough manners to our credit.

5214+. **Pulcinelle.** 'Pulcinello,' literally 'chick,' is the name given to an Italian clown belonging originally to the low comedy of Naples. Goethe describes the type (*Werke*, H. 24, 203) as 'calm, composed, to a degree indifferent, almost loaferish, and yet humorous.' Here they are introduced, by way of contrast to the hard-working Wood-cutters, as lazy street-loafers, 'lubberly almost to silliness.'

5226. **Einher zu laufen;** dependent on müßig. 'We are always at leisure to run along' etc.

5229. **Auf,** 'at,' i.e., 'in answer to'. The loafers collect in response to the cat-calls of their kind.

5236+. **Parasiten.** The 'fawning esurient' parasite was a stock figure of ancient comedy, both Greek and Roman. Grazzini, Parte I, p. 450, has a *Canto de' Buffoni e Parassiti.*

5237. **Ihr . . . Träger;** to the Wood-cutters.

5247 ff. The meaning is: Of what use would all our antics be, even though fire should fall miraculously from heaven, if there were no wood and coal for the cooks to burn?

5252. **Kohlentrachten,** 'loads of coal.' Tracht = was man trägt.

5255. **prudelt,** 'sizzles.' Prudeln is the same as brodeln or brudeln.

5262+. **Trunkner.** Among the masks seen at the Roman carnival Goethe mentions drunken German bakers.

5268. **Tinke, Tinke;** onomatopœia for the clinking of glasses.

5269. **du;** addressed in genuine carnival fashion to some one back in the crowd.

5270. **so ist's gethan** = so ist's recht, 'that's the thing.'

5272. **Rümpfte . . . Rock,** 'turned up her nose at this gaudy coat.' The simple dat. with rümpfen is bold and unidiomatic. It is worth noting that the MS. has diesen corrected in the poet's own hand to diesem.

5274. **Maskenstock;** the stick on which masks are hung or an effigy built up. Say 'scarecrow.'

5290+. **Chor.** The Drunken Man must be thought of as accompanied by a number of bibulous friends who keep erect a little longer than their leader.

5293. **Bank und Span,** 'bench and board.' Span is obscure, but seems to mean a thin board, lath, shingle, — anything that a drunken man might think available for a temporary support.

5294+. Cf. n. to l. 5198+. The Herald introduces a bevy of poets competing for popular favor; and so very anxious are they to say what everybody likes, that one of them, of a cynical turn, thinks it would be the joy of his life to say what nobody would like. The satire was to turn, if the passage had been fully elaborated, upon the eulogistic toothlessness of the Minerva press. In his essay upon *Epochs of German Literature* Goethe refers to his own epoch as the 'encomiastic era.'

5298+. The 'nocturnal and sepulchral poets' are those that exploit the gruesome and the horrible. Under date of March 14, 1830, Eckermann makes Goethe say, in speaking of recent French poetry: 'In place of the beautiful Greek mythology, devils, witches, and vampyres are coming into fashion; while the noble heroes of the olden time must give way to criminals and galley-slaves. That sort of thing is piquant. It produces an effect.' Cf. also Goethe's review of Mérimée's *La Guzla* (1827), in which he speaks (*Werke*, H. 29, 704) of the Frenchman's predilection for nocturnal horrors and 'the most hideous vampyrism.'

5300+. **Hegemone.** The names and number of the Graces are variously given by the ancients, but Goethe probably got his lore from Hederich, in whom he read: 'Some reckon two of them, namely Auxo and Hegemone, . . . others, and in fact the most, three, namely, Aglaia, Thalia, and Euphrosyne. . . . They were the goddesses of amenity (Annehmlichkeit), benefits, and gratitude. . . . There are three of them, because one bestows the favor, the second accepts it, and the third returns or requites it. . . . Without them nothing was gracious and pleasing (anmuthig und gefällig).' There was thus good enough authority for putting Hegemone in place of Thalia, whose name is better known as that of the Muse of Comedy.

5304+. **Die Parzen,** 'the Fates.' According to the common tradition, Klotho holds the distaff, Lachesis spins, and Atropos cuts the thread. But since the dread goddesses in their proper character would hardly comport with a heitres Fest (l. 5067), Goethe changes their rôles, making Atropos do the spinning and Lachesis wind the thread upon her reel. The awful shears are in charge of Klotho, but are hidden away in a box — no one has anything to fear from them. So Lachesis winds off the thread until the Weaver takes the skein. — Grazzini has a *Trionfo delle tre Parche*, introducing

> Queste tre Parche, in cui la Puerizia,
> La Gioventù, la Senettù riluce.

5322. **an . . . Luft;** dat., not acc., the sense being: She (Atropos) lets worthless persons live long, and cuts off prematurely lives that are full of promise.

5339. **überschweifen,** 'slip off' from the reel.

5343. **zählen, messen.** The verbs are used intransitively in the pregnant sense of 'Hours count off hours, years measure off years.'

5344. **Strang** = Strähne, 'skein.' Lachesis means to say that under the new arrangement the end of mortal life is not left to the caprice of her incompetent sisters, but to the all-wise Weaver, who at his pleasure takes the skein of the individual life and weaves it into the great fabric of history.

5352. **Tauben;** in allusion to Matt. x, 16: 'Be ye therefore wise as serpents and harmless as doves.'

5356+. **Die Furien.** The Furies, whom the Greeks conceived as horrible old hags with snaky hair, and whose office was to avenge blood-guiltiness, are introduced into the heitres Fest as handsome young women whose business it is to excite jealousy in lovers, provoke feuds between married people, and avenge marital infidelity. Grazzini, Parte I, p. 254, has a *Trionfo delle Furie;* but Goethe borrows nothing specific from the Italian.

5357. **Was . . . euch,** 'what good does it do you,' viz., to have been warned by the Herald as to our character?

5360. **krauen,** 'scratch gently,' 'tickle.'

5376. **erwarmen**; used *metri gratia* for erwärmen, the 'warming of the frost' being the symbol of a crazy, chimerical purpose. Will am Frost erwarmen would suit the connection better.

5378. **Asmodi**; Asmodæus, Asmodi, or Ashmedai, the 'evil spirit' of Tobit iii, 8, regarded in later tradition as an *Eheteufel*, or fomenter of discord between husband and wife.

5386. **Gischt und Galle** = Gift und Galle, which is a common alliterative phrase.

5388. **beging'**; subjunctive. 'There is no debating *how* he did it — he simply pays the penalty.'

5393 ff. The Herald announces an allegorical group consisting, as we presently learn, of an elephant with Prudence seated on his neck as driver, and Victory mounted on his back as radiant 'goddess of all activities.' On either side walk Hope and Fear in fetters. That is, Prudence guides the living colossus of politics and takes no counsel of panicky Fear or seductive Hope, — these goddesses being held in subjection. — In a conversation with Eckermann, reported under date of Dec. 20, 1829, Goethe discussed the possibility of representing this scene, and said among other things: 'It would not be the first elephant on the stage. There is one in Paris that plays a regular rôle. He belongs to a party, and takes the crown from one king and puts it on another, which must indeed be very fine.' This is a sufficient hint. The conceit is a bit of spectacular extravagance which should not be pressed for political doctrine beyond the obvious import of the text. — Kuno Francke surmises, but on rather doubtful evidence, that Goethe may have got the hint for his allegorical elephant from a picture by Mantegna (see *Harvard Studies in Philology and Literature*, 1892, p. 125 ff.).

5412. **Verdacht,** 'suspicion,' namely, that they have all turned traitor to Fear.

5421. **drüben** = draußen in der Welt. Escape to the outside world would be of no use, since all men are enemies of Fear (in carnival time).

5423–40. During carnival time the ladies are more or less on their guard against the illusions of Hope (they live in the present), but when it is over they will be easy victims again.

5440+. Klugheit, 'Prudence.' Grazzini, Parte I, p. 35, has an allegorical *Trionfo della Prudenza* which introduces Hope and Fear (Speranza and Paura) as 'two great enemies of our life' (due gran nimiche di nostra vita).

5450. Göttin; supply seht ihr.

5452. hinzuwenden; to be construed with behenden. 'With broad wings quick to turn' etc.

5456+. Zoilo-Thersites. Zoilus was a Greek grammarian of the third century B.C., who distinguished himself as a carping critic of Homer, and thus acquired the nickname of Homeromastix, or Scourge of Homer. Goethe compounds his name with that of the well-known Homeric Thersites who gets beaten by Odysseus for abusing his betters (*Iliad*, 2, 202 ff.), to make the name of a grumbling marplot. The figure, that of a hideous two-headed dwarf, must be understood as a magical creation of Mephistopheles, whose contribution to the Masquerade here begins to cross the pre-arranged program (cf. Intr. p. xlviii). As the dwarf approaches deriding the majestic Lady Victory, the Herald, whose duty it is to keep aloof disturbing elements (l. 5498), strikes him with his staff, and is himself as much surprised as any one when the monster changes into a crawling adder and a fluttering bat, which cause consternation in the crowd.

5486. umflicht; here in the general sense of 'encircles,' 'circles about.'

5494 ff. The Herald describes what he sees, confessing that he does not understand it. What he sees — again a work of Mephistopheles — is a magic chariot drawn through the air over the heads of the people (l. 5514) by four dragons. The charioteer is Poetry (who alone could manage this kind of vehicle) and the occupants are Faust in the mask of Plutus, the Greek god of wealth, and Mephistopheles as Avarice. In the chariot is a box of treasure.

5520+. Knabe Wagenlenker. Dec. 20, 1829, Goethe assured Eckermann that the Boy Charioteer is Euphorion. 'How can that be,' queried Eckermann very naturally, 'when Euphorion is not born until

Act 3?' 'Euphorion,' Goethe answered, 'is not a human, but an allegorical being, a personification of Poesy, which is not bound to time, place, or person.' The MS. shows **Euphorion** crossed out and **Knabe Wagenlenker** written in place of it. The poet probably felt that however 'philosophical' his whim might be, it was needlessly confusing and destructive of poetic illusion.

5542. **Wort.** The 'riddle's cheery word' is the answer to the riddle.

5549. **zu Wohl und Weh,** 'for weal or woe,' 'for better or worse'; i.e., 'on a pinch.'

5558–9. The thought is: His delight in giving is greater than his delight in having and enjoying.

5565. At the end of the line supply something like **lassen sich einigermaßen beschreiben.**

5568. A herald would naturally know the insignia of a king.

5575. **sein eigenst Gut,** i.e., his most intimate self. One is reminded of Goethe's saying concerning his own *Tasso*, that it was 'bone of his bone and flesh of his flesh.'

5582 ff. The Charioteer snaps his fingers and precious jewels appear to fall on every hand. The crowd rush for them and are victimized by Mephisto's hocus-pocus. We get a hint that the gems of poesy are not for the rabble.

5588. **Flämmchen;** symbolical of 'words that burn'—if they fall in the right place (cf. l. 5635 ff.).

5595. **griffe;** not subj., but archaic indic. Cf. Thomas's *German Grammar*, § 327, 3.

5603. **frevle;** here = 'worthless,' 'insignificant' (in contrast with **solider**). Grimm Wb. suggests that the word may have been used with a thought of Fr. *frivole.*

5612. **Windesbraut;** cf. n. to l. 3936.

5629. The line is an adaptation of Matt. iii, 17.

5642. **Gekauzt da hintendrauf,** 'squatting up there behind.' Mephistopheles, as Lean Man, or Living Skeleton, guards the box of treasure in the mask of Avarice, or Stinginess, thus making a picturesque contrast to Wealth-Faust and Prodigality-Poesy. In the work of Grazzini, Parte I, p. 38, we find a *Trionfo in Dispregio dell' Oro, dell' Avarizia, e del Guadagno.*

5648 ff. Since abstract qualities are usually personified as feminine, the Lean Person has to account for his sex. The point of the banter is that in the good old times he was a woman — Avaritia — and the ally of the women in their domestic economies; but now that they have all become reckless spendthrifts he has changed his sex and become, as der Geiz, the ally of their husbands.

5653. **Das . . . sein,** 'that actually had to count as a vice,' — i. e., with the *men*. They called my economy stinginess, and classed me with the vices.

5660. **erspulen,** 'earn with the Spule,' i.e. with the Webspule, or weaver's spool; 'earn by weaving.'

5666. **Mit . . . geizen,** 'let the dragon play the miser with dragons'; i.e., they are the proper company for his Cadaverousness. In a letter of 1780, Goethe playfully applies the name Drache to his friend Merck, who was also a gaunt man.

5671. **Marterholz,** 'wooden cross'; in sarcastic allusion to the Lean Person's appearance.

5678. **bewegt,** 'excitedly'; adv. with entfalten.

5681. **Umschuppte** = beschuppte, 'scaly.'

5685-6. **haben . . . herangetragen.** The dragons (without hands, hence the marvel) take the box, with Mephistopheles sitting on it, out of the chariot and bring it to (heran) where Faust is standing.

5691. **schäckig,** 'motley.'

5696. **zur Einsamkeit.** Cf. the words of the Poet in the Prelude, ll. 59 ff.

5706. **verrathen.** Poetry is self-revelation, i.e., self-betrayal. Cf. the lines in the *West-Östlicher Divan*, IX, 19:

> Erst sich im Geheimniß wiegen,
> Dann verplaudern früh und spat!
> Dichter ist umsonst verschwiegen,
> Dichten selbst ist schon Verrath.

5712. **goldnem Blute;** figurative for the red-golden liquid which rises in the pots and threatens to dissolve the jewels.

5717. **schmelzen sich,** 'are melting,' i.e., 'are on the point of melting,' — whence the need of seizing them quickly.

5718. **Gemünzte Rollen,** 'minted rolls,' i.e., coins.

5719. **Dukaten . . . geprägt** = Goldstücke wie geprägte Dukaten, 'pieces like genuine ducats.' But Schröer says **wie geprägt = wie neu geprägt.**

5730. **Gold und Werth**; i.e., werthvolles (wirkliches) Gold.

5735–6. The meaning is: What 's the use of truth for such as you, ever the ready victims of stupid illusion?—**An allen Zipfeln packen,** 'to lay hold of by every tag,' i.e., to lay hold of with all one's might.

5753. **all' und all',** 'all together,' 'every one of us.' Cf. All Alle in l. 8483+.

5761–2. Plutus as magician draws an invisible line to keep back the crowd — as a 'pledge' for the maintenance of the order established. **Unterpfand,** dat. rather than appositive to Band.

5791. **wiederwärtig**; here = 'disgusted,' 'shocked.'

5792. **übelfertig,** 'ready for mischief.' He molds the plastic gold into a phallus.

5797. **er ahnet nicht.** Plutus-Faust pretends that his confederate does not know of what is coming, i.e., of the Emperor's approach in the mask of Pan.

5798. **Narrentheidung**; one of the many variant forms of Narrentheiding, 'fool's conduct,' 'nonsense.'

5800. The meaning is: In a moment the entire space within the magic circle will be filled with the cohorts of Pan; thus the immodest antics will be brought to an end by a simple 'need' of space to perform in, which 'need' is more potent than any 'law' imposed by the magic wand for which the Herald has asked.

5801–6. The lines must be taken as a general marching-chorus of the Fauns, Satyrs, Gnomes, etc., who are to speak for themselves in separate groups further on. This being so, we should expect them to say:

> W i r feiern u n s e r n großen Pan,
> W i r wissen doch u.s.w.

Instead of this the 'Wild Army' describes itself in the third person, as if the lines were spoken by the Herald for the information of the crowd. A like incongruity occurs in ll. 5816 ff., 5819 ff., 5829 ff., and 5864 ff.

5801. **zumal** = zusammen auf einmal.

5805. **was keiner weiß**; viz., that Pan is the Emperor.

5810. **schuldig,** 'as in duty bound.'

5814. The Wild Army knew nothing of the magic line, and rushed in without knowing that they were getting into a place where strange things might happen.

5815. **Du;** the masqueraders, whose gay dress and 'tinsel show' are contrasted unfavorably by the Wild Army with their own uncouth roughness.

5831. **sollen . . . sein,** 'they ought to be slender and sinewy'; i.e., they need to be, in view of his mode of life. Goethe represents the (Roman) faun as fond of human society, especially of dancing with women; the kindred (Greek) satyr on the other hand as a shy, chamois-like haunter of the mountains.

5841. **Paar und Paar.** While the Fauns are fond of dancing and would like partners (ll. 5826–8), the constraint of keeping time is not for the little Gnomes, whose nature it is to be bustling about their work in helter-skelter fashion, each one for himself, like ants.

5845. **Leuchtameisen,** 'shining ants'; an invention of Goethe, formed after the analogy of Leuchtkäfer. The Gnomes with their little miners' lamps look like phosphorescent ants — if there were such a thing. — **Wimmelhaft** = wimmelnd, 'thronging.'

5846. **wuselt** = wimmelt; South German dialect.

5848. **Gütchen,** 'good-fellows.' The word 'gnome,' in German as in English, is not a folk-word. The 'gnomes,' i.e., the little moss-coated miners who live underground, are popularly known as Gütchen, Gutgesellen, gute Holden, and Erdmännlein.

5849. **Felsschirurgen,** 'rock-surgeons'; because they 'cup,' i.e., tap, the veins of the mountains.

5859. **allgemeinen Mord,** 'general murder,' i.e., 'war.'

5860. **drei Gebot';** against theft and adultery (l. 5857), and murder (l. 5859).

5862–3. The Gnomes, like the fairies of ll. 4619–20, are indifferent to human standards of morality. They do their work in a spirit of good will toward man, but are not responsible for the bad use he makes of the gold and iron they furnish him.

5864. **Die wilden Männer.** The 'Wild Man,' or 'Woodsman' (Waldmann), is a well-known figure of German folk-lore (see Grimm D.M. I,

402). He is conceived as a gigantic faun. — The harsh elision ſ' for ſie is found also in Goethe's lyric poems.

5870. **Schurz;** in apposition with Band. The 'stocky girdle' consists of leafy branches which are bound about their loins, forming the 'coarsest of aprons.'

5871. **Leibwache.** The gigantic 'Wild Men' make a better body-guard for Pan than the pope has in his tall Swiss guards.

5873. **das All der Welt.** Goethe follows a well-known false etymology which is given thus by Hederich, *sub voce* Pan: Dieſen (Namen) hat er von πᾶν, weil er ein Bild der geſammten Natur iſt.

5880–2. **Auch . . . doch.** The logical connection is: Pan wishes us to be happy, and has thus far kept awake himself even under the blue-arched roof (of the palace, decorated to represent a rustic scene at noon); still, the conditions are such as invite him to his mid-day nap, and when he goes to sleep the merriment must end. — According to the Greek myth, all nature was quiescent while Pan slept at noon.

5890 ff. Panics were supposed to be caused by Pan.

5897+. **Deputation der Gnomen.** The Gnomes have discovered a glowing vein of precious metal (proceeding from Mephisto's magic chest), to which, as experts, they invite his Majesty's attention.

5909. **Was . . . war;** viz., riches in abundance.

5910. **zu vollenden;** viz., by signing the paper presented at this point. Cf. n. to l. 6068.

5914. **im . . . Sinne,** 'serenely.' The magician gives a polite warning that something terrible is coming, but no one is to be frightened. It is only a harmless illusion — a Flammengaukelſpiel (l. 5987).

5917. **ſich eräugnen,** 'be manifested'; earlier form of ſich ereignen.

5929. **ſolchem Weſen;** the fiery manifestations.

5932 ff. The youthful, smooth-faced Emperor, who enjoys the sport, is suddenly unmasked by magic. He puts his hand to his face in surprise at the sudden loss of his Pan's beard, but the blazing beard flies back to its place and seems to set him on fire. — Commentators think that Goethe's imagination may have been influenced in this scene by a story told in J. L. Gottfried's *Chronika* concerning a disastrous carnival-frolic that took place at the court of the French king Charles VI. The king and several gentlemen had dressed themselves up as 'wild men' or satyrs, the shaggy coat of the satyr being produced by means of pitch and tow. In the course of the proceedings the king's dress was accidentally set on fire by a torch in the hands of the Duc d'Orléans. The attendants rushed to his assistance, but were themselves set on fire, and four of them burned to death, though the king was saved. — It is worth noting that the Faust-book of 1587 makes Doctor Faustus divert the Turkish Emperor at table with 'great streams of fire such that everyone ran up to extinguish them' (Cap. xxvi).

5934. **Ungeschick** = Mißgeschick or Unglück.

5956. **Brüll-Gesang** = brüllender Gesang, 'boisterous song.'

5959. **bezirken,** 'confine within limits'; = umschränken.

5962. **Wald**; with reference to the rustic decorations. Cf. n. to l. 5880.

5964. **holzverschränkten Deckenband,** 'wooden framework of the ceiling.' The temporary structure which 'binds' together the ceiling and supports the decorations is made of 'joggled' timbers.

5970 ff. The sham fire is now put out by a sham shower of mist, througn which the flames soon appear like harmless 'heat lightning.'

5977. **schwangre Streifen**; the 'streaks' of mist, which look as if they were 'pregnant' with moisture.

5979. An unrimed line, which was no doubt intended to make two lines, but was written and printed as one through inadvertence.

(Kaiserliche Pfalz.)

Lustgarten.

From the preceding scene the Emperor is aware that two magicians have arrived at his court, but he does not know their names nor the relation existing between them. He must suppose, presumably, that Faust's is the master-hand, since the legerdemain of the fire and mist must have appeared to him as Faust's work. Instead of being offended at the trick played upon him, the Emperor is eager for more, and in order to have the wonder-workers always at hand, appoints them custodians of his subterraneous treasure. — The humbug of irredeemable paper money was brought to Goethe's attention by the depreciation of French assignats during the Revolution. Cf. the conversation with Soret, reported by Eckermann under date of Feb. 15, 1830, in which the story is told of Grimm's paying three hundred thousand francs for a pair of cuffs.

5990. **Pluto**; here, as often, a name for the devil.

5991. **Nacht und Kohlen**; hendiadys for kohlenschwarzer Nacht (aus = bestehend aus).

5992. **Schlund**; ablative dat. (aufwirbelten = entwirbelten aufwärts).

5995. **Zum . . . Dome** refers factitively to the dome of flame, not to the dome of the palace.

5998. **Völker**, 'nations.' By a magic illusion the Emperor saw himself as Plutonic majesty, receiving the homage of subject nations in a palace of fire. Since it *was* an illusion we need not wonder that his description does not tally with that of the Herald in ll. 5920 ff. Cf. ll. 10417 ff. — Loeper understands by Völker the different classes present, as courtiers, invited guests, and gazing people.

6013–14. The very walls (of circumambient water) 'enjoy life'; i.e., they are 'alive' with thronging denizens of the sea, that dart to and fro with arrowy swiftness. — **Wimmlens**; cf. n. to l. 5079.

6022. **Nereiden**; Nereid nymphs, daughters of Nereus, the old man of the sea. One of the Nereids, Thetis, was the wife of Peleus, by whom she became the mother of Achilles.

6025. **Die spätern**, 'the more tardy.' The older and wiser nymphs approach more warily.

6027. **Den Sitz**; sc. hast du. Mephisto's gorgeous program does not end with promising the Kaiser an immortal wife, but proposes to make him one of the Olympian gods — a literal *divus imperator*.

6032. **Tausend Einer Nacht**, 'Thousand and One Nights,' commonly called in Eng. 'Arabian Nights'; here = 'the land of wonders.' The usual title is Tausend u n d Eine Nacht. On the sing. Nacht see Thomas's *German Grammar*, § 297, *a*.

6033. **Scheherazade**; the queen who tells the wonderful stories of the *Arabian Nights*.

6035. **Tageswelt**, 'world of fact,' 'every-day reality.'

6039. **Als**; used somewhat loosely, as if solch had preceded Verkündung. 'I never expected to make (such an) announcement of supreme good fortune as this,' etc.

6047. **Lanzknecht,** 'mercenary.' The form is a perversion of Landsknecht. — **Fühlt sich frisches Blut,** 'feels fresh blood within him' (sich dat., Blut acc., as in ob er sich eignen Wert fühlt in *Hermann u. Dorothea*). But Grimm Wb. regards sich as acc., Blut as nom.

6061. **damit**; here = daß. 'Provision has been made that' etc.

6068. **sprach . . . heran** = kam heran und sprach. The incident here recalled is not found in the Masquerade, but would come in most naturally at l. 5897+, or perhaps at l. 5906. Monarchs often make use of a holiday to grant amnesties and other special favors; so here the easy-going Emperor was quite satisfied on being told that the paper presented for his signature was 'for the people's good.' That the Chancellor-Archbishop, with all his pious horror of magic and magicians, should be given the rôle here assigned him seems a little unnatural.

6072. **Tausendkünstler,** 'wonder-workers'; i. e., the printers, with their wonderful new art.

6081. **überzählig,** 'redundant' in letters; the only letters necessary henceforth being those of the imperial signature.

6082. **Zeichen**; with allusion to Constantine's *In hoc signo vinces.*

6087. **Mit Blitzeswink** = blitzschnell. Wink is often used as a symbol of great quickness.

6088. **Die . . . auf,** 'the money-changers' shops stand wide open.' So great is the crowd coming and going that the doors are never shut. For **Wechsler-Bänke,** since the word refers to the 'shops' and not specifically to the 'benches' or 'counters,' modern usage would prefer Wechselbanken. — **Sperrig** = sperrweit, angelweit, i. e., 'wide open.'

6093. **Wenn** = indem, 'while,' as in l. 4663; **neu in Kleidern** = in neuen Kleidern.

6100. **Schedel,** 'piece of paper,' 'bill'; from Lat. *schedula.*

6108. **Gürtel . . . Lenden,** 'the girdle of his loins,' i. e., his money-belt. He lightens it by exchanging his copper money for paper.

6111. **erstarrt,** 'stagnant,' as not circulating.

6117. **würdig** = a restrictive relative clause; 'minds such as are worthy to take a deep view,' i.e., to be let into the deep secrets of nature.

6121. The meaning is: No more dickering and trading with coins of various mintage and doubtful weight and fineness.

6125. **Pokal**; cf. l. 5021.

6126. **amortisirt,** 'extinguished' as tokens of indebtedness, i.e., 'redeemed' in metal.

6139–40. **Wo . . . zusammenstellt,** i. e., here on the surface of the earth. The Emperor appoints the two magicians as keepers of his underground treasure, and bespeaks harmony between them and the regular Schatzmeister.

6141. **kein fernster** = nicht der entfernteste, 'not the remotest,' 'not the slightest.'

6155. **Gnaden,** 'tokens of grace.'

6156. **wieder**; cf. ll. 4733, 4755.

6163. The Fool means that he has often before risen from the dead (dead drunkenness), but never as now to find himself boundlessly rich.

6170. **gestrengen Herrn,** 'worshipful sir'; the common title of landed proprietors and high functionaries. Cf. Schiller's *Tell*, l. 1860.

6172. **Witz.** The fool's 'wit' consists in his decision to invest his money in real estate; but the First Banneret is equally wise. Of course the reader divines that the sudden salvation wrought by the devil's paper money is not destined to last. The sequel comes in Act 4.

(Kaiserliche Pfalz.)

Finstere Gallerie.

Cf. Intr. p. xxxiii and p. xlix. — In the preceding scene Faust goes out first and is soon followed by the Emperor, who asks to see Helena and Paris. Faust promises, and being himself unable to do the thing desired, goes in search of his confederate, who avoids him as if he knew of the hard task coming. At last they meet, and Faust draws him away into a dark corridor to explain the situation.

For the grandiose myth of the Mothers (we must regard it as an invented myth and not as an allegory) Goethe got the initial hint, as he himself tells us, from Plutarch (cf. Eckermann, under Jan. 10, 1830). In his *Life of Marcellus* Plutarch tells of goddesses worshipped at Engyium in Sicily under the name of 'the Mothers,' and relates a story of Nikias, an influential citizen of the place, who saved himself from his enemies by feigning madness and crying out that the Mothers were pursuing him. This furnished the awe-inspiring name, but nothing further. Another suggestion was got, however, from the same writer's treatise *On the Cessation of Oracles*, where we read that the universe consists of one hundred and eighty-three worlds arranged in the form of a triangle. The inclosed space is called the Field of Truth; and here 'lie motionless the causes, forms, and primordial images of all things that have ever existed or are destined ever to exist. They are surrounded by Eternity, from which Time flows out as an effluence upon the worlds.' This gave the hint for a *locus* (so to speak) outside of time and space; a realm where eternal beings await existence and return after existing. That any real myths, as, for example, of awful Fates or Norns living in some mysterious far-away ἄδυτον, may have influenced the conception is possible, as Loeper suggests, but there are no clear traces of such influence.

The whole scene is a delightful *jeu d'esprit*, if only one does not try to find too much 'meaning' in the details. Above all, Mephisto's humorous pretence of embarrassment must not be taken too seriously, *for he has the key.* He might call up the apparitions directly, as he does in the legend; but he has to do with an idealist, and knowing his man, and knowing that his man knows him (l. 6258), he invents a line of hocus-pocus suited to the problem. On hearing the scene read, Eckermann, always intent on philosophic culture, was disposed to ask questions; but Goethe's only reply was to assume a mysterious look, open wide his eyes and repeat the line:

Die Mütter! Mütter! 's klingt so wunderlich!

This is a sufficient hint as to how the scene should be taken.

6177–8. The sense is: Don't talk as if *I* cared for your silly tricks; you wore *that* tone out long ago. Cf. ll. 1675 ff. and 1765.

6180. um . . . stehen, 'to prevent my getting speech of you.' The meaning is: *You* may think this dodging great sport, but it is no sport for me, since the Steward and Chamberlain are after me.

6181. **zu thun,** 'to be doing things.'

6193. **es . . . sogleich,** 'that it is readily manageable.'

6194. **steilern,** 'steeper' than in any of our previous undertakings.

6196. **machst . . . Schulden,** 'you will incur new debts,' i. e., burden yourself with responsibility to powers that as yet you know nothing of. The language is perhaps purposely vague.

6199. **Hexen-Fexen,** 'witch-monstrosities,' i.e., 'revolting witches'; but the meaning is a little uncertain. Fex, written also Fächs and Fecks, means properly a person afflicted with cretinism, and is used dialectically, according to Schröer, of persons or things that are ridiculous because of some excessive deformity. This seems to suit best the intended contrast with Helena. But the word also means 'clown,' and Grimm Wb., followed by Strehlke, gives Hexen-Fex as = Hexenhafter-Possenreißer, i.e., 'witch-like clown.' — **Gespenst-Gespinnsten,** 'spook-phantoms'; cf. Hirngespinst and Traumgespinst. One might say 'spectre-spectacles.'

6200. **Kielkröpfigen Zwergen,** 'impish dwarfs.' A Kielkropf is the changeling child of devil and witch. In the *Anthropodemus Plutonicus* of Prätorius, a book used by Goethe for the devil-lore of *Faust*, we read, p. 378: Es sind aber Kiel-Kröpfe solche Kinder, die der Teufel selbst in die Hexen Leibe formieret und sie solche läßt gebehren, in welche er sich selbst setzet und anstatt der Seelen durch sie redet, ihren Leib beweget u.s.w.

6206. **neuen Lohn.** No 'new reward' has really been asked for. The logic is: You are bound to serve me through life on the chance of a great reward hereafter; but whenever I ask a particular favor you grumble and make difficulties, as if you expected special pay for each service.

6208. **Wie . . . umschaut,** 'while one is looking around him,' i.e., in an instant.

6220. **schürfen,** 'dig down'; a miner's word.

6223–4. **an's . . . Erbittende,** 'to the Unbesought, the Unbeseechable.' The realm of the Mothers (i.e., of 'ideals') is inaccessible to flesh and blood, and entreaty avails nothing.

6229. **das . . . Hexenküche,** 'that savors of the Witch's Kitchen';

i.e., you are again resorting to humbug and the help of mysterious old women for what you might just as well do yourself. Cf. ll. 2366 ff.

6231–8. A very perplexing passage, since the experiences alluded to are not only not provided for in the preceding text, but are inconsistent with it. The lines tell plainly of a Faust who as university teacher excites hostility by his radical views (like Paracelsus, cf. Intr. to Part I, p. xxxi), is driven from his chair in consequence, and becomes a hermit in the woods. Here he is visited by the devil, with whom, in his disgust, he leagues himself for the sake of companionship. The 'repulsive pranks' of l. 6235 suggest annoying demonstrations by students. All this being totally out of tune with the plot as we have it, there is no resource but to suppose with Scherer (G.-J., VI, 249) that the matter of the lines is a reminiscence of an early plan that was dropped. Curiously enough in the MS. ll. 6228–38 are written on a separate slip of paper and *pasted over* ll. 6228–30. This is thought by the Weimar editor to disprove Scherer's hypothesis. But does it? The question of age touches only the substance, not the form. What the MS. shows is that ll. 6231–8 were an afterthought. As the scene was first written Faust's speech consisted of three lines only. Then, feeling the need of an explicit answer to the question **Hast du Begriff von Öd' und Einsamkeit?** the poet recalled (from memory or from some written reminder) the old Paracelsus-motive which had once occupied his thoughts, versified it, and interpolated the new verses. In any case it is clear that the details of his youthful plot, as he had finally determined it after much travail, were no longer vividly present to his mind. He may have thought, and probably fancied his readers would think, of the scene 'Forest and Cavern.' But in that scene Faust's retreat to the woods is in no way connected with his teaching or with 'repulsive pranks.' Moreover he has *already* given himself up to the devil; and finally, instead of taking up with the devil's society as better than none, he hates it and would prefer to be left alone.

6236. **Wilderniß** = Wildniß. The form is unusual, but occurs in Gryphius.

6237. **versäumt** = verlassen, — as often in Luther.

6244. **Gestillter,** 'hushed' after a storm.

6251. **umgekehrt,** 'reversely.' The mystagogue usually seeks to *at-*

tract the neophyte by telling of wonders to be seen and heard; you seek to *overawe* him by telling of a horrific void where nothing is to be seen or heard.

6253. **jene Katze,** 'that cat' in the well-known fable of the monkey and the chestnuts.

6256. Faust is not yet enamored of Helena in particular, but he *is* an idealist, and has heard enough to show him that he is to visit the realm of 'ideals.' These are 'everything' to him, though they are 'nothing' to the sensualist Mephistopheles.

6258. **daß du . . . kennst**; i.e., that you understand the point of view from which the devil speaks of this realm as an absolute void.

6259. **Schlüssel.** The magic key must be taken naively, like the magic wand, ring, or purse, met with in fairy tales. We are not to inquire with philosophic mind what it means or how it comes to be in possession of a devil who knows nothing of the realm that it is to unlock.

6267. **beschränkt,** i.e., so beschränkt, 'so narrow-minded.'

6269. **weiter**; here = künftighin, 'henceforth.'

6270. **gewohnt**; here with gen., as often in early modern German.

6271. **Erstarren,** 'torpidity,' 'nonchalance.'

6272. **Schaudern,** 'the thrill of awe.'

6273–4. The pronouns refer to der Mensch, implied in Menschheit. — **Vertheure,** 'make dear,' 'make scarce,' hence 'tend to stifle.' The thought is, that *man* has a capacity for awe in presence of the stupendous, though the world — i.e. life — may tend to make the sentiment 'rare.'

6279. **Wie . . . Getreibe,** 'the restless throng moves sinuously like films of cloud'; i.e., your way will lie through something that will look like floating patches of cloud — the Urbilder, or archetypal forms, that exist in the realm of the Mothers as unsubstantial wraiths. Strehlke gives Getreibe as = bewegtes Treiben, 'hurly-burly'; it denotes a multitude in motion.

6283. **Dreifuß.** Just as the sacred tripod at Delphi was the emblem of Apollo's power and the instrument of his revelations, so the Mothers have a tripod in their holy of holies as the emblem and instrument of *their* power.

6291. Gefahr. The danger — of a paralytic shock — is a part of the hocus-pocus and intended to prepare the way for the final explosion. Cf. n. introductory to the scene Rittersaal.

(Kaiserliche Pfalz.)

Hell erleuchtete Säle.

An episodical scene, in which Mephistopheles, in the rôle of court-doctor, prescribes magic remedies for freckles, chilblains, recreant love, etc.

6324. eure Pantherkätzchen, 'your (favorite) spotted kittens.'

6325. cohobirt, 'cohobate,' i.e., redistil; a term used by the early chemists.

6327. wenn er abnimmt, 'when it wanes' (the moon, implied in Mondlicht).

6329. umschranzen, 'fawn around,' in the manner of Hofschranzen, i. e., 'sycophants.'

6336. zu . . . . Gleiches. Goethe's humor makes the devil a homœopathist.

6357. von einem Scheiterhaufen = von einer Art Scheiterhaufen, viz., the witch-burnings. As these were really at their height in the time of Doctor Faust, the passage involves an anachronism.

6359. für voll halten, 'take seriously.' The lady thinks him too young.

(Kaiserliche Pfalz.)

Rittersaal.

Cf. Intr. p. xxxiii. — In the original Faust-book, of 1587, Faust is made to visit the court of Karl V. The emperor wishes to see the spirits of Alexander the Great and his wife, and Faust promises to comply on condition that his Majesty shall not speak or ask questions. When Alexander appears the emperor starts to rise and receive him, but is at once checked by Faust. So, too, when Helena is produced for the students (cf. Intr. p. xi), Faust first cautions them 'not to speak or rise from the table or presume to receive her' (sie zu empfahen anmassen). In these instances the passivity enjoined by the magician is duly observed and nothing startling happens; not so, however, in an earlier version of the story which Goethe may have read in Hans Sachs. In a poem of Hans Sachs, dated Oct. 12, 1564, and entitled Wunderbarlich gesicht Keiser Maximiliani löblicher gedechtnus von einem nigromanten, we read how a certain 'necromancer,' whose name is not given, called up spirits for the diversion of Emperor Maximilian. The list is headed by the 'beautiful Helena of Lacedemonia, . . . who was carried away by Paris,' etc. Finally the emperor wishes to see his own wife, Mary of Burgundy; but when she appears, as natural as life, his love overcomes him, and, contrary to the magician's warning, he attempts to embrace her, whereat the spirit instantly vanishes, 'amid noise and smoke and loud tumult,' such that the emperor is greatly frightened. In view of Goethe's early interest in Hans Sachs, it is easy to believe with Schröer that he remembered this story and got from it the germ of his own ghost-scene, viz., the idea of producing Helena at court (Paris was then a natural concomitant) and of letting the scene end 'tumultuously' because of a rash attempt to touch the apparition. That the magician himself should be the one to suffer from this rash attempt may have been suggested by Anthony (Antoine) Hamilton's story *L'Enchanteur Faustus*. Hamilton makes Faust appear at the court of Queen Elizabeth of England, and there evoke the shades of various renowned beauties, beginning with Helena. When at last Fair Rosamond is made to appear, the queen, who has received the usual warning, is so delighted that she rushes forward with open arms to embrace her. Whereupon a 'loud clap of thunder shook the palace, a thick black smoke filled the gallery, bright flashes darted here and there,' etc., and when the darkness disappeared Faust was seen 'lying on his back (les quatre fers en l'air) foaming like a wild-boar, his cap at one side, his wand at the other, and his magic alcoran between his legs.' The collected works of Hamilton (1646–1720) were first published in 1749, and afterwards often reprinted. Düntzer's supposition that Goethe may have read the French tale of Faustus is thus entirely reasonable.

6378. **verkümmert,** 'interferes with.'

6380. **verworrene;** here = 'mysterious,' 'uncanny.'

6384. **der großen Zeit;** probably of the medieval empire, possibly of classical antiquity.

6395–6. The end-wall parts vertically in the middle, and the two halves fold back against the side.

6398. **Proscenium;** here simply the front part of the stage. The Astrologer needs to be near the prompter, who occupies a 'hole' (Souffleurloch) in the middle of the fore part of the stage, his head being concealed from the audience by a hood-like screen. This arrangement is still common in the German theatres.

6400. 'Promptings' are the devil's specialty, his 'art of speech' runs in that direction; perhaps with allusion to the original 'prompting' of Mother Eve. Ll. 6399–400 are a facetious 'aside.'

6412. **Schmal=Pfeiler . . . strebend** seems to mean simply schmale Strebepfeiler, i.e., 'narrow buttresses.' The Architect speaks as a friend of the Gothic style.

6417. **weit heran,** 'hither from afar.' Fancy is to come from her distant home and be the goddess of the hour in place of the fettered Reason.

6434. 'The canopy of day and the vault of night' is simply a figurative expression for the earthly life, with its alternating day and night. At their own good pleasure the Mothers send forth their 'ideal' children for a temporary embodiment on earth, and this is the *natural* course of things alluded to in l. 6435. The unembodied wraiths can reach earth, however, only by the aid of magic (l. 6436).

6442. **verschränkt,** 'intervolved,' 'interwrought.' The longish volume of vapor parts into two globular masses which for a moment cleave together, so that each is a part of the other. In this state they are **verschränkt.** They then part completely and form a pair, one to become Paris, the other Helena.

6445. **ein Weißnichtwie,** 'a know-not-how,' i. e., 'a marvel' — of aerial tones; patterned after Fr. *un je ne sais quoi.*

6447. **Triglyphe.** The triglyph is the vertically channeled tablet of the Doric frieze. So our temple is a *Doric* temple.

6469. **er . . . vor,** 'he's only playing a part,' — he intends no impropriety.

6477. **Ambrosia.** The old lady gives a would-be wise explanation of the 'ambrosial' fragrance that exhales from the sleeping Paris as a 'perfume of youth' (cf. l. 9046). In *Iliad* 14, 170, Hera makes herself fragrant with ambrosia. Cf. also *Odyssey* 4, 445. Goethe may have read in Hederich that Paris was a 'great lover of costly unguents and cosmetics.' Riemer quotes from Balzac: 'Il exhalait comme un parfum de jeunesse qui vous rafraîchissait.'

6483. **Feuerzungen**; in allusion to the 'tongues like as of fire' of Acts ii, 3. Supply the apodosis: I could not describe it.

6495. **voreinst**; cf. ll. 2429 ff.

6497. **Schaumbild,** 'frothy counterfeit.' Grimm Wb. gives the unique word as = trügerisches Schattenbild ohne Wert, sich schnell verflüchtigend.

6500+. **Kasten**; the Souffleurloch of l. 6398+.

6502–3. The Greek ideal of womanly beauty, as seen in the antique statues, is apt to strike the uninstructed modern as having the head too small and the feet too large.

6509. **Endymion und Luna.** The pose described was evidently suggested by Sebastian Conca's picture of Diana and Endymion, an engraving of which, by Le Sueur, is to be found in Goethe's collection, and is here reproduced.

6519. The lady speaks ironically, meaning: A handsome youth with whom to wanton is nothing wonderful to *her*, but something quite familiar to her experience.

6529. **Verguldung** = Vergoldung.

6530. **Vom zehnten Jahr**; cf. n. to l. 7426.

6538. The allusion is to *Iliad* 3, 158, where the old men of Troy liken Helen to the immortal goddesses.

6549. **was Raub**; cf. was Rath in l. 8106. Such exclamations are due to the analogy of others, like was Teufel, was Henker, in which the noun was originally gen. They have the effect of an indignant repetition of the noun.

6555. **Das Doppelreich,** 'the double realm,' is the realm of the real and the ideal, or perhaps the new world created by their interaction. The language is at best somewhat obscure.

6560. **Fauste**; cf. n. to l. 1525.

6563. **Nu! im Nu!** 'now then! in a trice!' The Astrologer

prompted by Mephistopheles, who has foreseen the end from the beginning, prepares the spectators for the *grande finale*.

Hochgewölbtes Zimmer.

Cf. Intr. p. xxxv and p. l. The fiction presupposes a lapse of years (time enough for the 'boy' of Part I to have become a 'youth') since Faust deserted his study. Wagner has remained at his post and piously kept the place unchanged, always hoping for the great man's return. Meanwhile he has himself become a bright light of science and has a famulus of his own named Nicodemus. Imagine the study at the end of a long, dark passage with ups and downs (cf. Treppe, l. 6621), in an old, rickety building where professors teach and experiment as well as 'live.' At the summons of the bell which sets the old rookery a-quaking, Nicodemus comes staggering along the passage until he sees a tall stranger through the door of the study which is usually kept locked.

The Baccalaureus episode, which re-introduces the timid freshman of Part I in the rôle of conceited young graduate (Baccalaureus = Bachelor of Arts), is lacking in verisimilitude of details. The youth comes 'storming,' without any obvious errand, into a rickety building which he at first takes to be deserted and fears may tumble about his head. He does not at once recognize the place, though he must be supposed to have been very familiar with it at no distant date. Presently he descries a former acquaintance in Faust's old coat, and, forgetting his fears, advances boldly to guy the old fellow who had once guyed him. But *then* he supposed that he was talking with Professor Faust. Does he suppose so now? Has he not heard of Faust's disappearance? The fiction does not answer these questions clearly, and the matter becomes still less thinkable when we hear, l. 6727, that the youth is 'rung in,' for why should *he* heed Mephisto's bell? — All this means that Goethe here abandons completely the ground of academic realism to paint a symbolical picture of youthful extravagance. This is further indicated by the lyrical character given to ll. 6689–6720, which thus become a sort of triumphal march of young egotism. There is reason to think that these musical verses are of much later origin than the ensuing dialogue; for according to information obtained by Düntzer from the younger Fichte, Frau von Kalb once claimed to have heard, as early as 1796, an unpublished scene of *Faust*, in which Mephistopheles has to do with an extravagant young idealist. In particular she recalled an expression about killing people over thirty years of age (cf. l. 6787). This, according to the younger Fichte, was currently taken as a hit at his father, the famous philosopher, who does say something like that — very remotely like it — in one of his published writings. (The passage is quoted in Taylor's notes.) If this testimony can be relied upon we must suppose that not long after the beginning of Fichte's great vogue at Jena, in 1790, Goethe wrote or sketched a Faust-scene in which the bashful 'Schüler' should re-appear after a lapse of years in the character of an absolute idealist of the Fichtean school, profoundly contemptuous of the old, jubilantly confident of the new and of his own greatness. This may have been the germ of a fragmentary scene written down by Goethe in some form or other, read occasionally to his friends with oral explanation of the connection, and then worked over, in the light of later observations, into what we now have. That the scene in its final form is not to be taken *primarily* as a parody of philosophic idealism is made clear by Goethe's own words. "We spoke of the figure of Baccalaureus," writes Eckermann under date of Dec. 6, 1829. "'Does he not represent,' said I, 'a certain class of idealistic philosophers?' 'No,' said Goethe, 'he personifies the presumption which is especially characteristic of youth, and of which we had such notable examples after our war of liberation. Moreover everyone believes in his youth that the world is really beginning with him, and that everything exists only for his sake. There actually was a man once in the Orient who gathered his people about him every morning and would not let them go to their work until he had commanded the sun to rise.'" Cf. l. 6795.

6582. **Pelz**; the 'long coat' of l. 1850+.

6587. **Rauchwarme,** i.e., rauhwarme, 'rough warm.' In early German rauch is more common than rauh as stem-form.

6588. **Mich . . . erbrüsten,** 'swagger,' 'show off' — in the rôle of infallible professor. Sich erbrüsten properly = sich in die Brust werfen.

6590. 's = the professorial air of inerrancy.

6591+. **Farfarellen,** 'moths.' Goethe seems to have confounded It. *farfalla*, *farfaletta*, 'butterfly,' with *farfarello*, 'kobold.' In the much earlier *Claudine* he uses the same form as here, in the sense of Grillen (Farfarellen sind dir in den Leib gefahren).

6593. **Patron,** 'liege-lord.' Cf. ll. 1516–17.

6600–3. The sense is: You are a sly rogue. Even we, who are great hiders, reveal ourselves in our true colors sooner than you.

6615. **muß . . . geben,** there must always be 'maggots,' i.e., you will always have society; with a play on the two meanings of Grillen.

6617. **Principal,** 'boss'; applied usually to the head of a business concern.

6624. **Springt das Estrich,** 'the pavement cracks'; not the plastered ceiling, though that also cracks.

6635. **Oremus,** 'let us pray'; a kind of verbal sign-of-the-cross which the Famulus, already frightened by the other diabolical portents, resorts to as a charm against evil spirits when the stranger calls him by name. Cf. l. 1582.

6637. **es;** used loosely for the *status* of Nicodemus as bemoostes Haupt, or academic 'old boy.'

6642. **ein Beschlagner,** 'a clever one.'

6651. **Das Untre so** (= wie) **das Obre,** 'the lower and the higher' realm of knowledge; the material and the spiritual.

6650. **wie Sanct Peter**; allusion to Matt. xvi, 19.

6655. **Der . . . erfand,** 'who has found out things,' 'made original discoveries.' Erfinden, now = 'invent,' was once common in the sense of entdecken, 'discover.' Zum Entdecken gehört Glück, zum Erfinden Geist, says Grimm Wb.

6666. The tautology is a little harsh, but not much more so than the Eng. 'I scarcely dare to venture in.'

6667. **Sternenstunde.** Nicodemus is interested in the astrologic aspect of the recent earthquake.

6670 **kamt** = wäret gekommen. Cf. Thomas's *German Grammar*, § 359, 2.

6681. **lechzt . . . Augenblick,** 'pants for every moment,' i.e., looks eagerly forward to, and hence grudges, every moment; the dat. = **jedem Augenblick** entgegen.

6682. gibt Musik. The very rattling of his tongs is music to his ears, so absorbed is he.

6684. beschleunen = beschleunigen, 'hasten,' 'expedite.'

6685. Posto, 'post,' 'position.'

6686. dort hinten, 'off yonder,' at the end of the passage; not 'back,' for in l. 6711 Mephistopheles is dort hinten to Baccalaureus.

6688. erdreusten; *metri gratia*, as often, for erdreisten.

6705. Bärtigen, 'long-beards,' i.e., professors. Cf. l. 2055.

6707. Bücherkrusten, 'board-bound volumes,' 'ponderous tomes'; -kruste with reference to their thick, heavy binding.

6708. was sie wußten; object-clause with logen, rather than, as Schröer thinks, = so viel sie konnten. The sense is: They 'stuffed' me with false knowledge which they knew to be false.

6712. dunkel-helle = im Dunkelhellen, 'in the dim light.'

6721. Fluthen; object of durchschwommen (hat). Cf. n. to l. 4629.

6727. hergeläutet, 'rung in'; cf. introductory note above. Imagine, *faute de mieux*, that Baccalaureus was passing by, heard the shrill peal of the bell, and noticing the strange signs that followed, entered to see what was going on. Not until he is in the dark corridor does he recognize familiar ground.

6733. Ihr . . . Zopf, 'you never wore,' i.e., 'you are too young to have worn, a queue;' an anachronism, since the time thought of is the end of the 18th century. The 'queue' began to disappear before the Revolution, but held its own sporadically into the new century. As Swedes took the lead in rejecting it, the short hair of the new *régime* came to be known as a 'Swedish cut.'

6736. absolut. An 'absolutist' in the matter of hair would be a person without any at all; in philosophy, one who believes in the possibility of knowledge 'absolutely' independent of experience.

6745. gelben Schnäbeln = Gelbschnäbeln, 'callow goslings.'

6758. Erfahrungswesen, 'experience-business.' The young man is death on empiricism.

6767. schauerliche, 'despicable.' There is a Latin adage, *carbonem pro thesauro invenire*, 'to find coal (i.e., something common and worthless) instead of treasure.'

6790. That is, the devil, as Genius of Destruction (cf. ll. 1341 ff.), couldn't wish for anything better.

6791. Commentators see here an allusion to Fichte's doctrine that the phenomenal world exists only as it is created, i.e., 'thought,' by the Absolute Ego. But this is perhaps going needlessly far for an explanation. Mephistopheles had promised the boy (l. 2048) that he should become 'as God,' and now the youth proceeds to identify himself with the Creator.

6814. **e' Wein** = einen Wein; Frankfurt dialect.

Laboratorium.

Cf. Intr. pp. xxxv–xxxviii and pp. l–lii. — The notion of *homunculi* is a product of the learned superstition of the humanistic period. Paracelsus discusses them at some length in two of his treatises, the *De Generatione Rerum* and the *De Imaginibus*. He explains that they have the shape of a man, but are very small, transparent, and 'without body.' He also tells how to make them: The materials must be 'putrefied' until the homunculus becomes alive and begins to move. Thus they get their life 'by art' (*we* should say by knowledge), and therefore 'art is innate in them.' They are good for various purposes, as 'for the health of men,' for the 'favor of men,' to bring men from distant lands, and to protect men from danger. We see, then, that homunculi, like the alrauns, belong to the general order of helpful familiar spirits, their specific character being found in the fact that they are produced by chemistry and serve men of learning. Like other familiar spirits, they are characterized by wonderful knowingness — the great mind in the little body.

Closely connected with this conception is that of the bottle-imp, the bottle being the cage or prison in which the puissant magician confines his familiar. The so-called 'Cartesian devil' gets its name from this bit of superstition. Loeper (II, xxxiv) gives a number of quotations which show the wide diffusion of the conceit. Thus Fischart refers to it in *Gargantua*, Lessing in his *Vade-mecum für Herrn Lange*, and Le Sage depicts a bottle-imp in the first chapter of his *Diable Boiteux*. Goethe's Homunculus is a blending of the two conceptions, and rests therefore, no less than Helena or Mephistopheles himself, upon objective data of tradition. His clairvoyant powers are but a phase of that knowingness which pertains to all homunculi; while his classical sympathies, his hatred of medievalism, are natural in view of his humanistic origin. What Goethe superadds is the little man's imperious longing to 'commence existence.'

The problem of abiogenesia, or the artificial production of life from matter not alive, was once a very real problem, and has continued, in one form or another, to interest scientific men down to our own day. The possibility was seriously maintained by an eccentric contemporary of Goethe named J. J. Wagner (1775–1841), who was some time professor at Würzburg, and has left to an indifferent posterity a number of quasi-philosophical books. This Wagner is said to have predicted in his lectures (see Düntzer's larger Faust-Commentary, II, 119) that chemistry would yet succeed in producing men by crystallization. This particular whimsy does not appear in any published work of his, but in his treatise on *The State* (Würzburg, 1815) he describes an electrical experiment whereof he remarks: 'If the experiment succeeds, the result will be an organic product; for life is everywhere, needing only to be awakened.' (Cf. *Archiv für Litteraturgeschichte*, VI, 561.) It is quite possible that J. J. Wagner may have furnished a hint for the man-making Wagner of *Faust*. But it is all good-natured fun and not bitter-solemn satire. The sudden success of the abiogenetic experiment is of course Mephisto's work (ll. 6684 and 7004). Goethe was at one time in doubt whether he had made this point sufficiently clear (cf. Eckermann under date of Dec. 16, 1829).

6818+. **weitläufige,** 'straggling,' 'scattered.'

6819. The bell of a neighboring church strikes the hour at which Wagner has calculated that the contents of his retort should give signs of life. The loud clang is 'awful' to him, because it announces the fateful moment.

6823. **Finsternisse**; the plu. in the sense of the sing., as again in l. 10758.

6832. **Stern** = **Glück**; for other examples see Sanders Wb.

6837. **Rauchloch,** 'smoke-vent'; i.e., the chimney of the alchemist's 'hearth' (l. 6818+).

6842. **sich . . . zeichnen,** 'to delineate itself,' i.e., to copy the parent-form.

6852. **verlutiren,** 'seal up' with clay (*lutum*).

6860. **krystallisiren lassen,** 'produce by crystallization,' in contrast with nature's 'organic' or biologic process.

6864. 'Crystallized people' seems to mean fixed, stationary people, — old fogies, Bourbons.

6883-4. Homunculus is not Goethe, as Taylor curiously opines, but he does here give expression to a favorite idea of Goethe's. Cf. the well-known sonnet, Natur und Kunst, *Werke*, H. 3, 105.

6885. **Vetter.** Said Goethe to Eckermann, Dec. 16, 1829: "Moreover he calls him 'cousin,' for such spiritual beings as Homunculus, which are not yet darkened and narrowed by a complete assumption of human nature, were counted with the demons; whence a sort of relationship between the two."

6903-20. Faust is dreaming of Leda and the Swan. Homunculus redes his dream.

6924. **Im . . geworden,** 'born in the dark ages.' For other examples of jung werden = geboren werden see Grimm Wb. — The devil-myth as we know it *is* essentially medieval, but it begins much farther back.

6927. The unrimed line in a rimed context is probably the result of inadvertence. Schröer proposes for the missing verse:

In gotischer Häuser enger Klause.

6935. **der bequemste,** 'the most adaptable'; here used actively = der sich am leichtesten bequemende.

6937-9. The logic is: Take each person to the place of his dreams, fulfil his characteristic longing; then everything will be 'all right' (abgemacht).

6947. **classisch . . . sein,** 'it has to be classical,' i.e., it must have a classical counterpart.

6949. **antikische** = antike *plus* a tinge of contemptuous humor.

6952. **Peneios**; the river Penēus in Thessaly. Goethe here uses a genuine Greek form (Πηνειός), but just below the Latin Pharsalus instead of Pharsalos.

6955. alt und neu. Ancient Pharsālus consisted of two parts — an 'old' and a 'new.' In its territory, called Pharsalia, Cæsar and Pompey fought the great battle which decided the fate of Rome.

6956 ff. Homunculus has just spoken as if Mephistopheles must feel something of the tourist's passion for famous old battle-fields. The devil disabuses him: they are mementoes of human folly, of slavery to blind passion (cf. l. 7015).

6961. Asmodeus; here in the broad sense of a demon of strife; specifically an Eheteufel in l. 5378.

6970. Brockenstückchen means 'adventure' or 'piece of fun' in the style of the Brocken, i.e., of the Northern Walpurgis-Night. The sense is: A lark *à la* Brocken on classical ground might present some tolerable phases, but I'm not at home there. I shall find the heathen gates bolted.

6976. blöde, 'squeamish.'

6977. thessalischen Hexen. In the sixth book of the *Pharsalia* Lucan dilates at length upon the witches of Thessaly, ascribing to them all sorts of sinister powers and practices.

6994. Tüpfchen. 'The dot over the *i*' is proverbial for the final touch needed to make a thing just what it should be. For Homunculus it is a body to go with his mind. For this he must travel. But the game is worth the candle, for when he becomes a man it will be easy to get a number of nice things which men enjoy.

Classische Walpurgisnacht.

Pharsalische Felder.

Cf. Intr. pp. xxv ff. and p. li. — The idea of a specter-haunted battlefield, where the ghosts of the slain re-assemble each year on the anniversary of the fight and renew their conflict in the air, is found in the folk-lore of many peoples (see Grimm, D.M. II, 784 ff.). Goethe imagines such a *rendez-vous* on the field of Pharsalia (the battle took place June 6, B.C. 48), and then amplifies it into a general conclave of classical spooks of all kinds. The motive of the gathering is simply festivity. There is no over-lord corresponding to the Satan of the Brocken (l. 3959), sitting upon his throne and receiving the homage of his minions; wherefore Goethe remarked to Eckermann that the Classical Walpurgis-Night is democratic, while the Northern is monarchical. The choice of Pharsalia (rather than, say, Marathon or Chæronea) for this fantastic fiction grew out of Faust's need of a 'Thessalian witch.' As a matter of fact the battle-ground was some twenty or thirty miles remote from the river Peneus, but Goethe locates it roughly on the 'Pharsalian plain,' conceived as stretching away from the town northwestward to the river. The scene opens on the plain not far from the stream, and then changes, l. 7249, to the stream itself. Thence we follow Faust and Chiron down through the Vale of Tempe to the base of Olympus, and then return, l. 7495, to our starting-point on the 'upper Peneus.' The last scene takes us to the Ægean sea at the mouth of the river.

7006. **Erichtho.** The weird festival is opened (in classical iambic trimeters) by the witch Erichtho, who, according to Lucan's *Pharsalia* (VI, 507), was consulted on the eve of the battle by Sextus Pompeius, son of Magnus. Lucan has a long description of her horrible appearance and hideous practices.

7010. **grauer Zelten.** Until the moon comes out (l. 7033) the vale presents an illusion of spectral tents.

7020–1. Erichtho speaks as a partisan of Pompey, identifying his cause with that of Roman freedom. But we need not, with Schröer, see in this a serious expression of Goethe's own views; no more than in the attitude of Mephistopheles, who says in effect (ll. 6956 ff.): 'A plague on both your houses!' Pompey's cause was really that of the senate and the aristocracy.

7022. **träumte.** The seventh book of the *Pharsalia* opens with a picture of Pompey dreaming, on the eve of the battle, of his youthful triumphs in Rome.

7023. **schwanken Zünglein,** the 'swaying tongue' of Destiny's balance.

7025. **spendende;** *metri gratia* for spendend Inflection of an appositional adj. or pple. is common in the older language. Cf. ll. 7648–9, 8777, etc.

7034. **Meteor**; the luminous bottle of Homunculus, who precedes (l. 6987) and lights up the 'corporeal ball' consisting of Faust and Mephistopheles wrapped up in the magic mantle (l. 6985).

7036–7. According to Lucan, Erichtho avoided the haunts of men and lived in the tombs of the dead.

7040. **Schwebe**; supply ich. Homunculus, who is in charge, proposes to reconnoitre a little before alighting.

7044. **durch's alte Fenster.** The devil identifies himself with Wodan, who, from his dwelling on high, looks down *through a window* upon earth. See Grimm D.M., I, 112.

7056. **sie**; Helena, not Erichtho. Faust recovers consciousness.

7071–3. **Wär's nicht,** 'though it may not be.' Helena did not live in Thessaly, — but Thessaly is Greece.

7077. **Antäus**; the Libyan giant who got his strength from contact with mother earth. So Faust's soul is invigorated as his feet touch the soil of Greece.

7078. **find' ich** = indem ich finde; cf. seh' ich in l. 7044. 'Finding here the strangest things, I will investigate,' etc.

7081. **entfremdet,** 'alienated,' 'repelled.' Although really familiar with worse things at home, Mephistopheles facetiously identifies himself with the puritans of the North and pretends to be shocked by classical nudity. It occurs to him that the naked figures should be 'taken hold of according to the newest ideas and variously plastered over to a condition of fashionable decency,' i.e., treated like antique statues in a modern museum.

7092–3; unrimed lines. It has been conjectured that Goethe meant to write Niemand wird es preisen instead of Niemand hört es gern.

7093 ff. One of a group of Griffins (fabulous monsters with a bird's head and a lion's body) growls out an objection to Mephisto's greeting, on the ground that Greis is etymologically related to a family of disagreeable words beginning with *gr*. Mephistopheles observes that the preferred title Greif also begins with *gr*, and is promptly informed that *that* has nothing to do with the despised family, but is connected with the lucky greifen. The Griffin's arbitrary etymologizing, which is quite in the style of the pre-scientific masters, contains a touch of satire at the expense of the 'science où les voyelles ne font rien, et les consonnes fort peu de chose,' as Voltaire called it.

7097. **gleicherweise stimmig**, 'in like manner expressive,' i.e., of kindred meaning. Stimmig seems not to occur elsewhere except in compounds.

7098. **Verstimmen uns.** The cited words of like *meaning* are all *mean* words that put one out of humor. — **nicht abzuschweifen**, 'not to digress' — from this matter of etymology.

7103+. **Ameisen.** Herodotus 4, 27, and Pliny, *Hist. Nat.* 11, 31, tell of a race of gold-gathering ants of the size of foxes, that lived in central Asia and threw out gold-dust in making their burrows.

7106. **Arimaspen.** The Arimaspians (see Herodotus 4, 27) were a one-eyed race living in northern Scythia and engaged in feud with the gold-guarding griffins, whose treasure they had tried to steal. Milton refers to the myth in *Paradise Lost* II, 943 ff.

7109–11. The Walpurgis-Night is a time of truce; so the Arimaspians hope to succeed in 'running through' with their plunder before it can be taken away from them.

7111+. **zwischen die Sphinxe.** We have to do with *two* Sphinxes, the allusions referring now to the Egyptian Sphinx and again to the Theban Sphinx, whose riddle was guessed by Œdipus. Both are given the conventional form — a woman's head and bust, with the body of a lion.

7113. **Mann für Mann**, 'one after the other,' 'every one of them.'

7114–6. A Sphinx explains how it is that he understands them. They utter their characteristic 'spirit-tones' (snarling, squeaking, grunting, as the case may be), and he 'embodies' these sounds, i.e., gives them the form of the speech to which he is accustomed.

7123. **old Iniquity.** By a lapse of memory, it would seem, Goethe identifies the Iniquity, or Vice, of the English Moralities, with the Devil. In reality the Vice accompanied the Devil, beating him 'with dagger of lath, in his rage and his wrath' (Shakespeare, *Twelfth Night* IV, 2). Cf. also *Richard the Third* III, 1, where Gloucester likens himself (for using ambiguous language) to the 'formal Vice, Iniquity.' If the adjective 'old' is lacking in these passages, it is found in Ben Jonson's *The Devil is an Ass*, Prologue, l. 49, where the Vice calls himself 'true *Vetus*

Iniquitas.' Goethe is known to have busied himself with Ben Jonson in 1799. Cf. the note by Max Koch in G.-J. V, 320.

7130. **Hinauf . . . versteigen,** 'to mount upward,' i.e., to bother one's head about the stars, — when there is such a chance for amusement right at hand in guessing the riddles of an expert riddle-maker.

7133. **dich . . . aufzulösen,** 'to analyze your inward essence.'

7135. **Plastron;** the padded jacket used by fencers. The devil is for the 'pious man' an object on which to practice his ascetic rapier-thrusts.

7137. **Zeus zu amusiren.** Cf. the lines of Matthew Arnold:

> The gods laugh in their sleeve
> To watch man doubt and fear.

7144. **thust . . . Gute,** 'think yourself of some importance.'

7152. The Sirens — half woman and half bird of prey — balance themselves in the branches of the poplars that line the banks of the Peneus. Opitz also uses hinwiegen = aufwiegen.

7154. **Gewahrt euch** = wahrt euch, hütet euch.

7172–7. Mephistopheles, facetiously laying claim to a heart, criticises the new-fangled (romantic) song, which is all jingle and melody, but without deep feeling. The devil is not to be taken in by sirens.

7181 ff. Faust, who has been wandering about elsewhere since the separation of l. 7079+, now comes upon the scene. As moon-struck Philhellene he is delighted to find the true signs of the classical, 'grand and powerful features,' even in forms that are repulsive. This assures him that he is on the right track and quickens his hope of success, as he recalls the heroic memories suggested by what he sees.

7197–8. The meaning is: We are too old to have known her, the last of our race having been killed by Hercules, who lived before her time (but this is Goethe's invention). — **Reichen hinauf,** 'reach up,' i.e., 'forward.' *We* should say 'reach *down*.'

7199. **Chiron.** Chiron, the Centaur, is recommended on account of his wide acquaintance with the heroes of Helena's time. Cf. ll. 7337 ff. and notes.

7202. **Sollte . . . fehlen,** 'you surely should not miss it either,' — to visit us in our Ægean home. The Sirens hold out a hope that he may learn something of Helena from what Ulysses told them.

7210. **Statt . . . ließ**; a pregnant construction = anstatt dich binden zu lassen, wie Ulyß sich binden ließ. The Sphinx advises Faust not to be beguiled into attempting the perilous rôle of Ulysses, but instead to look up old Chiron.

7220. **Stymphaliden**; the monstrous Stymphalian birds, with beak and talons of iron, which were killed by Hercules (Alcides).

7227. Hercules killed the Lernæan Hydra by cutting off its many heads, which at first renewed themselves two for one until Iolaus came to his aid with fire-brands.

7234. **begrüßt manch**, 'greet many,' i.e., there will be many for you to greet. Cf. l. 6970.

7235. **Lamien.** Hederich writes thus of the Lamiæ: 'They are described as ghosts with an appetite for human flesh and blood, wherefore they tried to entice young people to them with all sorts of lures. To this end they assumed the form of beautiful women, who showed their white breasts to passers-by.' He adds that they were given to transforming themselves into different shapes (cf. ll. 7769 ff.). — **Lust-feine Dirnen** = feine Lustdirnen, 'elegant *filles de joie.*'

7240. **luftigen**, 'volatile.'

7241 ff. The general sense is: We are the very emblem of impassive stability; no danger of *our* changing our position. Ll. 7243–4, with the emphatic so, probably refer to a theory propounded in Creuzer's *Symbolik* (a work which is still to be found among Goethe's books), to the effect that the lines of sphinxes in front of the Egyptian pyramids had symbolic reference to the summer solstice (the sun between Leo and Virgo), and that the pyramids themselves were constructed with reference to astronomical calculations. Thus the sphinxes would be the regulators of the lapse of time, the changeless observers of changing events.

7246. **Hochgericht.** The 'high doom' of the nations is their fate as determined by the lapse of time. The following nouns are in apposition.

(Classische Walpurgisnacht.)

Peneios.

7249–56. The slumbering river-god Peneus is suddenly awakened by a sensation of trembling (the first signs of the coming earthquake) and calls upon the murmuring sedge and reeds, the willows and poplars, to lull him to sleep again.

7252. **Pappelzitterzweige** = zitternde Pappelzweige.

7256. **Aus . . . Ruh,** 'from my rest in the gently-flowing stream.'

7273. **Wie . . . schickt,** 'as my eye sends them yonder,' i.e., locates them in the distance. The expression sounds strange, but is scientifically correct. Loeper quotes from Helmholtz: Wir sehen die Sonne, die Sterne, an d e n Himmel, nicht an d e m Himmel.

7276. **Schon einmal**; cf. ll. 6904 ff. The dream of Leda and the Swan is here realized, — as it seems to Faust.

7300. **Wie . . . regt,** 'in the motion of head and bill'; a modal clause defining selbstgefällig.

7305. **Welle . . . wellend,** 'himself a wave tossing upon waves'; wellend = sich wie eine Welle bewegend.

7317. **dieser Nacht**; probably dat. with zugebracht, Nacht meaning the Walpurgis-Night. But Sprenger, *Zeits. f. d. Ph.*, 23, 453, insists that it is an adverbial gen. = in dieser Nacht.

7325. **Reuter**; archaic for Reiter.

7337. **Pädagog.** Says Hederich, under 'Chiron': 'He was a Centaur, that is, half man and half horse, but at the same time such a good physician, musician, and astronomer, that he instructed Hercules, Æsculapius, Jason, Achilles, and nearly all the young princes of his time, in the sciences needful to them.'

7342. **Pallas, Mentor.** According to the *Odyssey*, Pallas Athena gave advice to Telemachus in his dealings with the suitors, and then accompanied him as Mentor in his quest of tidings concerning his father. But Homer nowhere implies that Telemachus disgraced his teacher. In saying that Pallas reaped no honor from her mentorship, Chiron means only that her pupil turned out very much like other men who had not had the goddess of wisdom for a counsellor.

7365 ff. The lines name and characterize the more famous Argonautic heroes: the Dioscuri (Castor and Pollux), symbols of youthful strength and beauty; the Boreades (Zetes and Calais), who had charge of the oarsmen and delivered Phineus from the Harpies; Jason, the pensive, reasonable commander; Orpheus, the ship-musician, as Hederich calls him; and Lynceus, the lynx-eyed pilot, who could see through earth, sea, and sky.

7379. Gesellig . . . erproben, 'only in company can danger be tested,' is an indirect way of saying that a joint enterprise which offers a field for different kinds of ability is the best test of a hero's powers.

7389. Bruder. Hercules performed his labors at the bidding of his half-brother Eurystheus.

7390. Fraun; in allusion to the hero's service of Omphale, Queen of Lydia.

7391. Gäa, the earth; Gr. *γαία*.

7392. Hebe. Hebe became the wife of Hercules after his apotheosis.

7393–4. Song and sculpture are alike impotent to portray him.

7403. sich . . . selig, 'blest in its own esteem,' i.e., proud. Like Walther von der Vogelweide in his poem *Herzeliebes frouwelin*, Chiron prefers lively 'winsomeness' to statuesque 'beauty.'

7415 ff. The story was that Helena was carried away from Sparta by Theseus and Pirithous, and placed in charge of Aphidnus in Attica, whence she was rescued by her brothers Castor and Pollux. Chiron's part in the affair is an invention of Goethe.

7426. Philologen. After giving the story of the first abduction of Helena, Hederich adds: 'Some say she was only seven, or at the most ten years old, when she was carried off by Theseus.' Further on he discusses her age at the time of her abduction by Paris, quoting ancient authorities who took the question very seriously. Such pedantry concerning a 'mythological lady' amused Goethe. Cf. note to l. 8850.

7435. Pherä. Says Hederich, quoting the authority of Pausanias and Ptolemy Hephæstus: 'Also she is said to have married Achilles on the island of Leuce after her death, and to have borne to him Euphorion. He had loved her already in his life-time.' Why Goethe should have written 'Pheræ' (the name of a town in Thessaly) instead of 'Leuce' is not clear; probably a mere lapse of memory.

7450. **Manto.** Greek tradition tells of a soothsayer Manto who was a daughter of the blind seer Teiresias. Goethe makes her instead the daughter of the divine physician Æsculapius (Gk. 'Ασκληπιός), and imputes to her a humane, philanthropic character in sharp contrast with that of the horrible 'Thessalian witches' described by the poets.

7459. **mein Sinn ist mächtig** = ich bin des Sinnes mächtig, — *compos mentis*.

7461. **Heil der edlen Quelle** = edle Heilquelle, 'noble fountain of health,' i.e., Manto herself.

7465–8. The lines allude to the battle of Pydna (168 B.C.), in which the Macedonian king Perseus was defeated by the Romans under L. Æmilius Paulus. In reality Pydna is some thirty or forty miles north of the Peneus.

7483. **strudelnd hierhergebracht,** 'whirled hither.' The 'ill-famed night' is conceived under the image of a boisterous torrent.

7487. **Asklepischer,** 'Æsculapian,' 'medical.'

7490. **Persephoneia** transcribes the Gr. form Περσεφόνεια. The more usual form is Persephone (Περσεφόνη), in Lat. Proserpina. The fiction is that the goddess is herself a reluctant prisoner in Hades and is willing to give secret audience to any one who brings her greetings from the upper air.

7494. **Benutz' es besser.** Orpheus lost Eurydice by forgetting his promise not to look back. Faust is admonished to observe better the conditions imposed upon him.

7494+. **Sie steigen hinab.** Jan. 15, 1827, Goethe spoke to Eckermann concerning the poetic difficulties of the Classical Walpurgis-Night, "which then existed only as a sketch showing the 'what,' but not the 'how.' 'Consider,' he said among other things, 'the plea of Faust to Proserpine for the release of Helena. What a speech that must be, whereby Proserpine herself is moved to tears!'" A Paralipomenon has been found (No. 157) containing a sketch of the proposed scene, under the title of 'Prologue to the Third Act.' According to this the difficult plea is given to Manto, who reminds the goddess of her own earthly life. At sight of the goddess unveiled Faust falls into an ecstasy, from which he is recalled by Manto, who explains to him the conditions upon which his request has been granted. Finally the 'induction' was to be left to Manto, that is, *she* was to be the 'Thessalian sibyl' who should produce the 'phantasmagory' of the third act. But this, in view of the rôle given to Phorkyas, would be a needless and bewildering complication; which fact may have furnished another reason, in addition to those assigned in Intr. p. xxxvi, for the dropping of the entire scene.

(Classische Walpurgisnacht.)

Am oberen Peneios wie zuvor.

The *scenarium* is repeated, because, while no change of scene has been indicated since l. 7248+, the spectator is supposed to have accompanied Faust and Chiron to the base of Olympus.

7498. **Dem . . . Volk,** 'the wretched people' are such as live on land.

7500. **hellem Heere,** 'goodly band'; heller Haufe being a stereotyped formula = tüchtiger Haufe. So in l. 10737.

7510. **seeisch heitern Feste** = heitern Seefeste.

7518+. **Seismos,** 'Earthquake,' is personified by Goethe as one of the race of primeval giants, who pushes his way up from the earth, thus forming a volcanic mountain.

7524. **Wittern,** 'commotion of the air,' 'reverberation.'

7533. **Insel Delos.** The genuine Greek myth was that Leto, being with child by Zeus, was persecuted by the jealous Hera, who vowed that the pregnant goddess should have no place that the sun had ever shone upon in which to give birth to her offspring. To evade this vow Poseidon was instigated by Zeus to bring up the island of Delos, which had hitherto lain beneath the water. Here Leto gave birth to Apollo and Artemis. Goethe makes the island the result of a volcanic upheaval produced by Seismos.

7545. **Karyatide.** The huge giant with half his body still in the earth and bearing a mountain on his head and shoulders, is likened to a caryatid, the name given in architecture to a supporting column in the form of a woman.

7549. The Sphinxes see the eruption close at hand, but are confident it will not come near enough to disturb them in the position they have taken. Nothing ever disturbs them in their Egyptian passivity.

7550 ff. The lines allude to the great geological controversy between the Plutonists and the Neptunists. The latter believed that all rocks were of aqueous or sedimentary origin; while the former contended that volcanic eruption has played a certain part in the sculpturing of the earth's crust. As a student of geology Goethe was an ardent Neptunian; but one should not look in *Faust* for a didactic or partisan presentation of his views. *Faust* is poetry, not science. In the Classical Walpurgis-Night, and further on in the fourth act, both sides are fairly represented by competent champions. Here, very naturally, Seismos speaks for the Plutonists.

7557. **mahlerisch-entzückter** = mahlerisch-entzückender, 'picturesquely ravishing.'

7561. **Pelion und Ossa.** The Greek myth was that the Giants piled Pelion and Ossa upon Olympus in order to scale heaven. But Goethe makes them pile the two mountains, in a spirit of wanton sport, upon Parnassus, thus giving rise to the familiar 'double-peaked Parnassus' with its two summits of Tithorēa and Lycorēa. — **Ballen** instead of the more usual Bällen. A variant has: Mit Pelion und Ossa Ball gespielt.

7568–9. Seismos claims to have produced Olympus too.

7575. **Emporgebürgte** = Emporgebaute, 'built up' like a **Burg.** Grimm Wb. observes that Emporgeburgte would be more correct.

7579. **bewegt,** 'in commotion.' The building of the mountain by eruption is still in progress.

7580. **Ein Sphinx.** The gender is surprising in view of l. 7195 (cf. also l. 7146). The Egyptian sphinx was male, the Greek female.

7582 ff. The gold-guarding Griffins command their servants, the Ants, to gather the gold which they see gleaming in the crevices of the new-made mountain.

7588. **Zappelfüßigen,** 'nimble sprawlers.'

7598. **Allemsig,** 'very industrious'; a neologism, perhaps with intended play upon Imsen (l. 7634).

7601. **Berg,** 'rock.' Der Berg, or das Berg, is used by miners for worthless rock that contains no ore.

7602. **Herein.** The Ants begin to 'come in,' i.e., to return to where the Griffins are, with their pickings.

7605+. **Pygmäen.** The Homeric Pygmies, who dwelt on the banks of Oceanos and engaged in yearly feud with the Cranes, are here identified with the busy mountain-folk of Germanic mythology.

7621+. **Daktyle.** The Dactyls were a race of fabulous metal-workers living on Mount Ida. Their name, 'Fingers,' was variously accounted for by the Greeks, but they were not regarded as dwarfs. Goethe, however, identifies them with the shrewd little 'thumblings' (minute kobolds) of German folk-lore. Cf. l. 7875.

7625. **Finden auch Ihresgleichen,** 'they too will find their kind,' i.e., will not lack society. Finden indic., with sie referring to Daktyle as subject.

7626 ff. The Pygmy-Elders, as council of state, order weapons forged for the army, their policy being, 'In time of peace prepare for war.'

7634. **Imsen;** dialectic for Ameisen.

7635. **Rührig im Schwalle,** 'in busy commotion.'

7642. **Heimliche Flammen.** The layers of wood burning with 'smothered flames' produce charcoal for the smiths.

7644 ff. The Generalissimo of the Pygmies orders a campaign against the Herons (kinsmen and near allies of their natural enemies, the Cranes), in order that they may have plumes for their helmets.

7650. **Auf einen Ruck** = mit einem Male, 'all at once,' 'all of them together.' Construe with schießt.

7654 ff. The peaceable Ants and Dactyls are reluctant to serve the bloody ends of the Pygmies, but dare not refuse obedience.

7660 ff. The Cranes of Ibycus, flying high in air, see the wanton assault upon their kin, the Herons, and summon their more immediate kin, the cranes of the sea, to a campaign of vengeance. The story was that the poet Ibycus, beset by assassins near Corinth, cried out to a flock of passing cranes to avenge his death. Later, as the Corinthians were gathered in the theater, the cranes appeared, and one of the murderers who was present exclaimed, 'Lo, the avengers of Ibycus!' which led to a detection of the criminals.

7666. Mißgestaltete Begierde, 'monstrous cupidity,' for 'the cupidity of monsters.'

7671. Reihenwanderer, 'serried wanderers.'

7677. just = geheuer; 'I don't get to feel at ease.'

7679. zumal; as in l. 5801.

7680. Frau Ilse. Cf. n. to l. 3968 and Heine's well-known poem beginning:

Ich bin die Prinzessin Ilse
Und wohne im Ilsenstein.

7681. A ledge of rock on the Brocken is known as 'Heinrichshöhe,' and saga connects a Saxon Emperor Heinrich with Princess Ilse. See Heine's poem just referred to.

7682. The logic of **zwar** seems to be: To be sure, strange things go on even there. — For **Die Schnarcher** cf. n. to l. 3880; for **Elend,** n. to l. 3834+.

7683. gethan, 'fixed,' 'ordained.' There are no sudden upheavals on the Brocken. It's all permanent, and you know where you are.

7691. Abentheuer, 'strange scene'; not the coming adventure with the Lamiæ.

7710. Mannsen, 'men' = Mannspersonen. The word is a corruption of Mannsname, and occurs only in coarse or rough speech.

7711. Hansen, 'Jacks'; cynical for 'men.' Mephistopheles, an easy victim of female wiles, identifies himself with men.

7715. Cf. n. to l. 7235.

7719. Luder, 'vile jades'; properly the word means a 'bait of raw flesh,' then 'carrion,' and so anything disgusting. Goethe was in doubt whether to use the gross word.

7727+. The missing rime has been variously supplied by the commentators.

7731+. Empuse. Says Hederich of the 'spook' (Gespenst) Empusa: 'It is said to have two feet, one of them of iron, or, according to others, an ass's foot. It is also said to be able to change itself into all sorts of forms, as a plant, cow, snake, stone, fly, beautiful woman,' etc. This capacity of metamorphosis justifies the poet in regarding Empusa as kith and kin of the Lamiæ; but the ass's head (l. 7747) is Goethe's invention.

7736. Mühmichen; archaic for Mühmchen (l. 7756), 'auntie.'

7774. Lacerte, 'lizard.' The Lamia becomes a slippery saurian.

7777. Thyrsusstange; the Bacchic wand, wreathed with vine-leaves and terminating in a pine-cone.

7782. quammig, quappig. Both words mean 'fat and flabby.' Cf. Sanders Wb. under Quabbe.

7783. Orientalen. Goethe seems to have read somewhere that the sultan prefers fat beauties for his harem.

7785 ff. The Lamiæ take the form of horrible black bats that flutter about the interloper's head with 'noiseless pinions.'

7802. Graus, 'horror,' abomination'; not 'stone-heap,' as Schröer thinks. See *Zeits. f. d. Ph.*, 23, 454.

7809–10. The thought is: It's quick work riding to the Brocken here, where you can bring your mountain with you, i.e., produce it where you want it.

7811 ff. An Oread, or mountain-spirit, accosts the devil from a 'natural rock,' i.e., a rock not due to the recent upheaval, and protests against his hasty conclusion that everything about him is new or ephemeral.

7817. Gebild des Wahns; the new mountain.

7827. Wie . . . muß, 'how (strangely) it all comes about'; müssen of an existing fact, as in l. 4203.

7846. The philosophers' Gespenster are Hirngespinste, or 'phantoms of the brain.'

7850+. Anaxagoras und Thales; two ancient philosophers who here represent opposing views of nature's *modus operandi.* Thales of Miletus, who believed in water as a first principle, appears as a Neptunist, exalting the importance of water and of slow and gradual processes generally. Anaxagoras of Clazomenæ, who explained earthquakes as due to the violent escape of imprisoned gases, is introduced as Plutonist, insisting upon the reality and importance of sudden and violent upheavals.

7853–4. Die Welle . . . fern. 'The wave (from which I naturally take my cue) yields readily to every wind (of rational argument), but keeps aloof (i.e., can only recoil helplessly) from the steep rock (of prejudice like yours).' At least this seems to be the meaning, but the comparison can not be called very apt.

7855. Feuerdunst, 'igneous vapor,' 'flaming gas.'

7866. Äolischer, 'Æolic,' i.e., imprisoned and eager to escape, like the winds in the cave of Æolus.

7869. Was . . . fortgesetzt, 'what can be furthered by it?' Thales means that the volcanic mountain, though a fact, is a useless, isolated fact which can lead to nothing. It is outside the chain of natural development.

7872. The thought is: Only the very patient will follow the leaders in such a fruitless discussion.

7873. Myrmidonen, 'Myrmidons.' Ancient writers connected the name with *μύρμηξ*, 'ant.' Says Hederich: 'They had their name from Myrmex, not as having actually sprung from ants, but because they were no less industrious and saving than ants, and like ants burrowed in the ground and lived upon its products.'

7887. krallen, 'taloned'; but no such adj. occurs elsewhere. The first print has Krallen-Beinen, 'claw-legs,' which seems a better reading.

7897. Reiherstrahl; arrow plumed with heron-feathers.

7900 ff. Wishing to protect the mountain-folk from the vengeful Cranes, Anaxagoras implores the triune Luna for a natural darkness. A meteorite falls upon the mountain, giving it a pointed summit and crushing its inhabitants. Anaxagoras falls upon his face in terror, believing that he has conjured the moon from the sky. — The real Anaxagoras was a scientific rationalist, eminent in mathematics and astronomy. He explained eclipses as due to natural causes, and undertook to predict how long it would take a stone to fall from the sun. These views led to his arrest as an enemy of the popular religion. So Goethe makes him pray to the moon for an eclipse *without magic*. But the awful result is such as to shake his rationalism and convince him that the old story of the moon being conjured down from the sky by Thessalian witches (see n. to l. 7920) may have been after all true.

7903. Dreinamig-Dreigestaltete. Says Hederich, under 'Hecate,' quoting Servius as authority: 'In heaven she is said to be called Luna, on earth Diana, and in hell Hecate or Proserpina; wherefore three heads are attributed to her, from which she is called Tergemina, Triformis,' etc.

7907. gewaltsam=innige; about equivalent to 'passionate,' as im=Tiefsten=sinnige is to 'pensive.'

7920 ff. In describing the horrors of Thessalian witchcraft, Lucan writes, *Pharsalia* VI, as follows (we quote Rowe's translation):

Magic the starry lamps from heaven can tear,
And shoot them gleaming through the dusky air;
Can blot fair Cynthia's countenance serene,
And poison with foul spells the silver queen:
Now pale the ghastly goddess shrinks with dread,
And now black smoky fires involve her head;
As when Earth's envious interposing shade
Cuts off her beamy brother from her aid;
Held by the charming song she strives in vain,
And labours with the long-pursuing pain;
Till down and downward still, compelled to come,
On hallowed herbs she sheds her fatal foam.

7927. Windgethüm, 'wind-monster,' 'hurricane'; coined after the analogy of Ungethüm.

7928. Supply ich werfe mich. The 'steps of the throne' are the base of the mountain on which, as Anaxagoras thinks, the reluctant Luna has descended.

7946. nur gedacht; i.e., it was an illusion, like everything else in the Walpurgis-Night.

7959 ff. A Dryad, or tree-spirit, calls out to the devil from a venerable oak, and chides him for a narrow-minded tourist who visits a foreign land only to make odious and cynical comparisons.

7967. Phorkyaden, 'daughters of Phorkys,' called also Graiai. Their names and number are variously given, but usually as Pephredo, Enyo and Deino. Says Hederich, *sub voce* 'Grææ': 'They were gray old women. . . . They had one tooth and one eye in common, which they gave to each other by turns when they wished to eat or to see something. . . . The tooth was larger than the tusk of the strongest wild boar, and they had brazen hands. Furthermore, they dwelt in a place which neither sun nor moon shone upon, and never needed their eye except when they left their dwelling-place.'

7972. Alraune; cf. n. to l. 4979.

7990. des Chaos. Goethe does not follow Hesiod's theogony

closely, but regards the Fates, the Phorkyads, and the medieval Devil, all of them manifestations of the ugly, as children of Chaos (the primeval Ugliness).

7991. **gestern;** viz., at the Masquerade.

8006. **im Doppelschritt,** 'double quick,' — with a touch of satire on the rapid multiplication of (modern) heroes in marble.

(Classische Walpurgisnacht.)

Felsbuchten des ägäischen Meers.

8035. **Dich;** Luna. Cf. n. to l. 7920 ff.

8043+. **als Meerwunder;** i.e., with body half human and half that of a fish, as they are represented by artists both ancient and modern.

8046. **Volk;** object of ruft, the Sirens being addressed.

8050 ff. The Nereids are represented in ancient works of art with an abundance of jewels and other precious ornaments. Hederich, *sub voce* 'Nereides,' speaks of a Herculanean painting in which a Nereid is portrayed with pearls in her ears, golden bracelets and a golden girdle. It is Goethe's poetic fiction that the ornaments have been drawn up from sunken ships by the spell of the Sirens' song.

8055. **scheiternd,** 'in shipwreck.'

8058–63. The Sirens demand proof that the Nereids are something 'more than fishes'; i.e., that they are not vain, frivolous creatures with no thought of higher things. Says Hederich of the Nereids: 'Sonst bestund ihr Thun in nichts als daß sie sich auf dem Wasser lustig macheten, tanzeten und spieleten.'

8074. **Kabiren.** By way of proving their seriousness the Nereids and Tritons set out for the neighboring Samothrace to bring the mighty Kabiri — *θεοὶ δυνατοί* — to the festival. Of these mysterious Samothracian deities very little is known accurately. The vague and contradictory notices concerning their names, number, origin, and symbolism, gave rise even in ancient times to endless theorizing. Goethe's persiflage was more directly suggested, however, by Schelling's *Die Gottheiten von Samothrace*, published in 1815 (cf. Eckermann for Feb.

17, 1831). In this pamphlet Schelling absurdly exaggerates the importance of the Kabiri and their cult, and evolves, out of nothing, all sorts of deep-diving and unintelligible conclusions regarding them.

8076. **sich . . . erzeugen.** Schelling attempts to prove (p. 25) that the four Kabiri, viz. Axieros, Axiokersa, Axiokersos, and Kadmilos form a 'living progressive series' (lebendig fortschreitende), Kadmilos being superior to the other three. He then adds: 'With this god (Kadmilos) begins incontestably a new series of revelations whereby the series of personalities mounts to seven and eight.'

8082. **Nereus.** Says Hederich: 'He was one of the most important sea-gods, likewise in particular a renowned soothsayer. He foretold to Paris all the misfortune which his abduction of Helena would bring upon his country. He had his abode in the Ægean sea, and there the Nereids who surrounded him delighted him with song and dance. . . . He was able to transform himself into all sorts of shapes. . . . He is also praised as having been truthful, gentle, and just.' Instead of 'gentle' Goethe makes him a peevish old curmudgeon, soured by long experience of advising men and seeing them neglect his advice.

8108. **sich . . . gescholten,** 'has proved its own terrible accuser,' i.e., has turned out badly.

8116. **rhythmisch festgebannt,** 'held fast in rhythmic spell,' i.e., immortalized in the verse of Homer.

8121. **Des Pindus Adlern;** 'the eagles of Pindus' are the Greeks.

8124. **Zaudern.** The 'lingering' of Ulysses seems to allude to his detention by Calypso (*Odyssey* 5).

8127. **gastlich Ufer;** the land of the Phæacians, by whom Ulysses was entertained and conveyed home (*Odyssey* 6–13).

8137. **Doriden.** Hederich quotes ancient authority for distinguishing between the Dorides, daughters of Nereus and Doris, and the Nereids, daughters of Nereus by some other wife.

8146. **abgekehrt.** Aphrodite (Kypris, Venus) was born of the sea-foam, but her cult is essentially that of a land-goddess. Hence she is said to have 'deserted' her kindred of the sea; and Galatea, the fairest of the Dorids, is imagined as her successor in the famous Paphian cult. Cf. n. to l. 8379 ff.

8152. **Proteus.** Since Homunculus must pass through a long series of Protean changes on his way to 'existence,' he is referred by the impatient Nereus to Proteus himself, the great expert in metamorphosis.

8162. **als wie** = wie wenn, 'as if.'

8165. **Verklärte,** 'transfigured' by the proud consciousness of their dignity as escorts of the Kabiri.

8170. **Chelonens;** the name of a nymph who was changed by Hermes into a tortoise (*χελώνη*). The Nereids ride on a chariot of tortoise-shell.

8171. **ein streng Gebilde,** 'an austere group'; of the four Kabiri taken collectively.

8174–7. According to Herodotus, III, 37 (quoted by Hederich), the Kabiri-idols were the 'representation of a pigmy man.' Greek writers refer to them as *θεοὶ δυνατοί*, 'mighty gods,' *θεοὶ μεγάλοι*, 'great gods,' etc. In the pamphlet cited above, Schelling speaks of the Kabiri-cult as the 'oldest in all Greece,' and as 'bound up with all that is most venerable and glorious' in the earliest traditions. He also refers to the universal belief that 'these gods were especially helpful and propitious to seafarers.'

8182–5. The Sirens, themselves the enemies of the sailor, admit that their power is inferior to that of the Kabiri.

8186–9. See above, n. to l. 8076.

8194 ff. After developing his theory of ascending potences among the Kabiri (three of the first power ruled by a fourth, then three more of the second power, making seven, corresponding to the seven planets), Schelling evolves an eighth who is the over-lord of all the rest, and is therefore 'the supra-mundane god, the Demiurgus, or, in the highest sense, Zeus' (p. 27).

8198. **weſ't;** from archaic weſen, 'exist,' 'have one's being.'

8201. **fertig,** 'ready' — to travel. This is the etymological sense of the word (from Fahrt).

8204. **Hungerleider.** Schelling attempts (p. 11) to derive the names of the Kabiri from a Phœnician root meaning 'to long,' 'to be hungry.'

8206–9. The Sirens seem to mean that it pays to respect divinity wherever it may be enthroned; but the relevancy of the thought is not very obvious.

8213. **Ermangeln des Ruhms,** 'come short of glory.' The phrase is biblical (Rom. iii, 23).

8216. **Ihr die Kabiren** = wenn ihr aber die Kabiren erlangt habt. The glory of capturing the Golden Fleece pales before that of capturing the Kabiri.

8218. **Wir! ihr!** The Nereids say wir, the Sirens ihr.

8220. **Töpfe.** Homunculus sees straight. The gods about whom all the ado has been made are little, rude, pot-like idols of baked clay. — Creuzer had imputed to the Kabiri the form of pots (Krüge), and these Topfgötter had then been dilated upon sarcastically by Voss in his *Anti-Symbolik.*

8233. **wo . . . stockt** = wo auch und in welcher Gestalt er auch stockt, 'wherever and in whatever form he lurks.'

8240. **auf . . . Füßen** = auf zwei Füßen, wie ein Mensch.

8250. **greiflich Tüchtighaften,** 'tangibly substantial.' Tüchtighaft is new coinage.

8258. **So . . . schicken,** 'directly on his arrival (in the deep sea) it will adjust itself.' His being sexless, or rather bisexual, will make it only the easier for him to begin among the lowest forms of aquatic life.

8266. **Es grunelt,** 'there's a fragrant freshness.' In the *Divan* Goethe uses the same verb to denote the fresh smell of the grass or foliage after a shower.

8274. **Dreifach** goes logically with Geister in the sense of drei. 'Three remarkable spirits on the move.'

8274+. **Telchinen.** The Telchines of Rhodes, sons of Thalassa (the sea), were a family of dæmonic artisans in brass and iron. Their myth makes them the teachers of Poseidon (Neptune) and the forgers of his trident; also the first to have formed statues of the gods. — **Hippokampen;** sea-monsters with the fore-part of a horse and the tail of a dolphin.

8283. **Weßhalb;** viz., because the stormy sea is so dangerous.

8285. **dem Helios Geweihten.** Without ancient authority Goethe conceives the Telchines as ministers of the Rhodian Helios, or sun-god, who was represented in the famous Colossus.

8287. **bewegt,** 'astir' with life.

8295 ff. Rhodes was famed for its delightful climate, its clear sky, and its many statues.

8311. Erdestoß. The Colossus of Rhodes was destroyed by an earthquake in 224 B.C.

8327. geistig, 'as spirit'; this being all there is at present of Homunculus.

8332. völlig aus, 'all up.' The estate of man forms the *end* of the metamorphic progression. In a letter of 1810 Goethe writes: 'All literature is like the formation in water of molluscs, polyps, etc., until *finally* a man comes into being.'

8335 ff. Proteus admits that it may after all be worth while to be a man — of the kind that lives on after he is dead.

8348. Mondhof, 'ring around the moon.'

8355–8. Thales is opposed to the rationalization of lovely myths which embalm a holy religious sentiment and keep the heart warm. He prefers to believe that the filmy appearance in the sky is really the sacred doves of Aphrodite, and not an 'atmospheric phenomenon.'

8358+. Psyllen und Marsen. The Psylli were a race of immortal snake-charmers, magic healers, etc., who dwelt in Libya (see Lucan's *Pharsalia* IX). The Marsi were an Italian people who were popularly credited with healing snake-bites by magic (cf. Vergil, *Æneid* VII, 758). They are mentioned together by the elder Pliny, *Natural History* XXVIII, 3, 30: 'Psylli Marsique et qui Ophiogenes vocantur in insula Cypro,' i.e., 'the Psylli and Marsi and they who in the island of Cyprus are called Ophiogenes (snake-born).' It seems to have been simply a misunderstanding or a careless reading of Pliny's text that led Goethe to connect the Psylli and Marsi with Cyprus. He conceives them as the ancient dæmonic inhabitants of the island, as ministers of the sea-born Aphrodite, and hence as themselves denizens of the sea.

8368 ff. They cherish the old cult, disregarding and disregarded by the 'new race' of Romans (the eagle), Venetians (the winged lion), Christians and Mohammedans, who have at various times conquered and overrun the island.

8369. lieblichste Tochter; addressed to Nereus.

8374. wegt und regt, 'moves and stirs'; a formula like **regen und rühren** in l. 4684.

8379 ff. The description shows the influence here and there of the Galatea-frescos of Raphael and the Caraccis, engravings of which are still to be found in Goethe's collection at Weimar. They are referred to in an essay of his, *Werke*, H. 28, 302, in which he describes a picture of Galatea and Cyclops by Philostratus. In this picture the nymph is drawn over the waves in a shell-chariot by dolphins which are guided by Tritons. — Other hints were obtained from Calderon's *No Magic like Love*, with which Goethe became acquainted from A. W. Schlegel's translation in 1803. The play deals with the story of Circe and Ulysses, and has its climax when the hero is released from thralldom by the appearance of Galatea. Circe causes fire to come from the water, but the flaming sea is powerless against Galatea's love. Cf. Max Koch in G.-J., V, 319.

8388. Würdiger Unsterblichkeit = würdig der Unsterblichkeit.

8411. Was . . . kann; viz., immortality.

8433. blühend. The meaning seems to be: 'How my joy bursts into full bloom,' 'culminates.' The momentary glimpse of Galatea's ravishing beauty draws from old Thales a rapturous pæan to the water.

8445 ff. Galatea and her convoy circle ceremoniously about Nereus at a distance, and before they come near again the scene closes.

8465. offengebahren = offenbaren.

8470 ff. Under the spell of Love and Beauty Homunculus sees that here is the place for him to commence existence. His glass house begins to glow and groan with the intensity of his longing to enter upon the course which will make him like in form to what he sees. He dashes his cage in pieces against Galatea's throne, his flame suffuses the water, and he is 'wed to the Ocean.'

8479. Eros. Hesiod makes Eros, Love, the oldest of the gods; the one who first brought order and beauty into the chaotic world.

8483+. All Alle, 'altogether,' 'grand chorus'; an emphatic reduplication, as in Bürger's all überall. The chorus is a pæan to the four elements, — fire, water, air, and earth; represented by the flaming sea, the mild zephyrs above, and the mysterious grottos below.

Vor dem Palaste des Menelas
zu Sparta.

Cf. Intr. pp. xi ff. pp. xxii ff., and pp. liii ff. — The first part of the third act, as far as l. 9127, is conceived in the style of a Greek tragedy, but it is a free rendering of the spirit of the Greek tragic poets rather than a close imitation of their technique in matters of detail. In his later years Goethe was much interested in Euripides, of whom he came to have a higher opinion than he had held in his youth. Traces of Euripidean influence are quite numerous in the *Helena*. Reminiscences of Æschylus also appear here and there; of Sophocles less frequently. On this subject consult Morsch, *Goethe und die griechischen Bühnendichter*, Berlin, 1888; also the essay by Niejahr in the journal *Euphorion*, I, 81. The following notes will point out some of these classical reminiscences, but without attempting to exhaust the subject.

The meter of the dialogue is mainly the so-called iambic trimeter of the Greeks. This is a verse consisting normally of six iambic feet in three dipodies. The adaptation of it to German poetry requires before all things the avoidance of a pause after the third foot; otherwise it becomes simply an unrimed Alexandrine. Goethe's first experiment with the trimeter seems to have been made in the *Helena* of 1800 (cf. Harnack's essay *Über den Gebrauch des Trimeters bei Goethe*, V.L., V, 113). The result was somewhat monotonous, owing to a too exclusive use of the normal iambic foot, for which the Greek poets had a variety of substitutes (anapæst, tribrach, dactyl, spondee). In the final revision of the fragment of 1800, accordingly, he converted a large number of iambics into feet of three syllables, which are usually to be construed as anapæsts, sometimes as tribrachs. Thus, in ll. 8490–1, Der Wo'ge schau'kelndem' was changed into Des Gewo'ges reg'samem'; vom phry'gischem' Gefild' into vom phry'gischem Blach'gefild'. In l. 8495 den tap'fersten' der Krie'ger gave place to den tap'fersten sei'ner Krie'ger. As would be expected, the newer portions of the third act (those written in 1827) show also a pretty free use of trisyllabic substitutes for the iambic foot. But the Greek rules regulating the admissibility of these substitutes were not very strictly followed. The poet's principle was to reproduce the *effect* of the Greek measure, but to avoid metrical pedantry in adapting it to the German language.

The Doric form '**Menelas,**' familiar to Goethe in the French poets, is metrically more convenient than the Homeric 'Menelaos.' — **Panthalis** is mentioned by Pausanias as one of the attendants of Helena. Cf. Goethe's essay, *Polygnots Gemälde*, in *Werke*, H. 28, 245.

8488. The heroine announces first her repute and then her name, just as does Aphrodite at the beginning of the *Hyppolytus* of Euripides.

8491. **Blachgefild,** 'plain,' — the plain of Troy.

8492. **sträubig,** 'reluctant' rather than 'bristling.'

8494. **Dort unten;** on the sea-shore, at the mouth of the Eurotas. So too in the *Orestes* of Euripides, ll. 53 ff., Helena explains that she has been sent ahead by her husband, who has lately landed.

8496. **hohes Haus.** Thus, too, in the *Orestes*, ll. 356 ff., the returning Menelaus greets his ancestral home, and bethinks him of all that he has suffered since he left it.

8498. **Pallas Hügel;** the hill on which the so-called 'brazen house' of Athena was situated. — **Wiederkehrend;** viz., from his exile in Ætolia.

8499. **schwesterlich,** 'in sisterly companionship'; adv. with **wuchs.**

8503. **Weiteröffnen,** 'wider opening' than usual; *both* wings of the double door having been opened on so great an occasion.

8511. **Cytherens Tempel;** the temple of Artemis (Diana) on the island of Cythera, off Laconia. Says Hederich, *sub voce* 'Helena,' quoting Dares Phrygius as authority: 'Some say, however, that he (Paris) landed with his fleet upon the island of Cythera, whither Helena came out of curiosity to see him; and that she was there offering sacrifice to Diana when Paris carried her off from the temple, and after a hard fight with the inhabitants of said island, succeeded in getting away with her.'

8516 ff. The first three choruses present some analogy to the strophe, antistrophe, and epode of the Greek poets. Metrical schemes are unnecessary. Let the verses be read somewhat slowly with strong stress where the word-accent naturally falls, and the rhythm will take care of itself.

8528. Opfer. Says Hederich, quoting the authority of Pausanias: 'Some say he (Menelaus) was minded, upon the surrender of Troy, to kill her along with the others.' Cf. Intr. p. xvi, last foot-note.

8532. Zweideutig. Her supreme gift of beauty has not been an unmixed good, since it has brought trouble to herself and others, and the end is not yet in sight. Wherefore her 'fame and fate' are said to have been decreed 'ambiguously.' Begleiter in apposition with Ruf und Schicksal.

8537. gegen mir = mir gegenüber.

8538. Buchtgestad; the shore of the Bay of Laconia, at the mouth of the Eurotas.

8540. vom Gott, 'by *the* god,' — Zeus.

8544. Ufer; a forced use of the dat., but the meaning is clear. Dem Ufer aufziehen stands for auf dem Ufer hinaufziehen.

8570 ff. Tripods were used at sacrifices for the burning of incense, sometimes also in lieu of an altar. The vessels of water would be needed for the priest's ablutions; the other vessels, to catch the victim's blood and to contain the wine and barley-meal which were strewn upon the parts destined for burning.

8573. das flache Rund, 'the round plate' (Lat. *patera*).

8580. zeichnet = bezeichnet.

8588. erdgebeugten. The victim's head was drawn down in case of sacrifice to the gods of the lower world or to the dead; otherwise it was drawn up. But Goethe was hardly thinking of this distinction; he uses the word broadly in the sense of 'doomed.' The passage seems to have been suggested by such stories as that of Iphigenia, though in this case the victim was not an animal.

8607. ich weiß nicht wie. A phantom herself, Helena has only a phantom-memory of the recent past.

8614. Helenens; here, as in l. 7484, with stress, Hele'nens.

8621. Götter. The 'home-bringing deities' were especially Zeus (Ζεὺς εὐάνεμος, Jupiter redux), Castor and Pollux, Poseidon, and Fortune (Fortuna redux).

8624. wenn, 'albeit.'

8637. Angefrischt, 'with quickened memory.

8647. Tochter Zeus; cf. l. 8497. Tyndareos was her nominal father

The myth makes Clytemnestra and Castor the legitimate children of Leda; Helena and Pollux the result of her connection with Zeus.

8650. **Urbeginn,** 'primeval chaos.' The old cosmogonies make Night the daughter of Chaos and the mother of many monsters. — **Noch** seems to have additive rather than temporal force; 'multiform moreover like clouds of volcanic smoke.'

8653. **die Stygischen,** 'the Stygian — the hateful — gods.'

8676. **welch** = **irgend welches,** 'some sort of.'

8685. **Thalamos,** 'sleeping-chamber.'

8687. **Wunder;** here = 'monster.'

8691–2. That words can not paint forms successfully is one of the main theses of Lessing's *Laokoon*.

8697. **ich.** The Greek choruses often speak as one person, using the pronoun 'I.'

8700. **Ilios;** the usual form in Homer, as 'Ilion' is in prose and in the tragic poets.

8703–5. The 'terrible shouting of the gods' recalls passages in the *Iliad*, such as 5, 785, where Hera takes the form of the 'brazen-voiced (χαλκεοφώνῳ) Stentor,' whose shout was like that of fifty men; or 5, 769, where the wounded Ares utters a yell like that of a thousand men. — **Zwietracht** translates the Homeric Ἔρις, 'Strife,' who appears as goddess in *Iliad* 4, 440, 11, 73, etc. Goethe imputes to *her* the brazen voice of Stentor.

8732. **graugebornen.** Says Hederich, *sub voce* 'Grææ' (cf. n. to l. 7967): 'They have their name from γραῦς, an old woman, because they are said to have been gray old women from birth.'

8747–8. **Den . . . macht,** 'which the Detestable, the Eternal-wretched, excites in the lovers of beauty.'

8754. **Alt ist das Wort.** The commonplace that modesty and beauty seldom go together can be found, e.g., in Juvenal 10, 297: 'Rara est adeo concordia formae atque pudicitiae.'

8772. **Mänadisch wild,** 'like wild mænads' (bacchantes).

8784. **gegenwarts,** 'in presence of'; an adv. from **Gegenwart.** Cf. Thomas's *German Grammar*, § 374, *a*.

8792. **sich . . . bleibt,** 'looks out for himself.'

8803. nun Anerkannte; *metri gratia* for nun anerkannt. But adverb and noun go awkwardly together.

8808. deiner . . . Schwan, 'the swan of thy beauty,' for 'thy swan-like beauty.'

8811+. Choretiden, 'members of the chorus'; properly Choritiden, Gr. χορίτιδες.

8812 ff. Phorkyas and the chorus revile each other in classical billingsgate, thrust on thrust (so-called stichomythy), each trying to outdo the other in suggestions of ugly ancestry and associations.

8813. leiblich . . . Geschwisterkind, 'your bodily kith and kin,' literally 'cousin.' The monster Scylla had twelve feet and six heads.

8817. Tiresias; the old blind seer of Thebes, whom Odysseus meets in the lower world. The implication is that only such as he would care for their amorous advances.

8818. Orion; the ancient giant famed for his beauty, his stature, and his prowess in hunting. His 'nurse' does not figure in Greek mythology, but she must have been older than Orion himself, and if she was the great-great-granddaughter of Phorkyas, then Phorkyas must be very, very old.

8819. Harpyen, 'Harpies'; properly Harpyien, Gr. Ἅρπυιαι, monstrous, filthy birds, that befouled whatever they came near. Cf. Vergil's *Æneid* 3, 216.

8821. Blute. Homer, *Odyssey* 11, 228, ascribes to the shades in Hades an eager longing to drink the blood of the sheep slain by Odysseus. The implication of course is that the choretids belong in Hades.

8822. Leichen. Lucan's *Pharsalia* ascribes to Erichtho a hideous fondness for corpses. For the choretids Phorkyas is a horrible Thessalian witch. Cf. l. 9963.

8829. unterschworner, 'festering underneath'; from schwären. Discord among servants is likened to a sore festering beneath the skin.

8840. Traum- und Schreckbild = schreckliches Traumbild, 'horrible phantom.'

8850. zehenjährig. Goethe first wrote zehenjährig, and then, in deference to Göttling's mythological wisdom, changed it for the first print to siebenjährig. Later he changed his mind and authorized a return to the first reading. See Eckermann for March 17, 1830, and n. to l. 7426.

8851. **Aphidnus**; see n. to l. 7415 ff.

8853. **Heldenschaar**; dat. of the agent, — a bold construction even for the Second Part of *Faust*.

8854. **stille Gunst.** Helena's secret preference for Patroclus seems to be an invention of Goethe.

8860. **Creta's Erbe.** Says Hederich, *sub voce* 'Menelaus,' quoting Dictys Cretensis as authority: 'When now his mother's father, Creteus, died in Crete, he went with others of his co-heirs to the said island, in order to share with them his inheritance from Creteus.'

8864. **Creterin.** The fiction that Phorkyas was a free-born Cretan woman enslaved by Menelaus and then placed in charge of his palace accounts for a stewardess unknown to Helena, who was carried away during her husband's absence in Crete.

8872. **doppelhaft Gebild.** This alludes to the story, duly chronicled by Hederich, that it was not the real Helena, but only a phantom resembling her, that Paris carried off to Troy, the real Helena having been spirited away by Hermes to Egypt, where she was afterward restored to Menelaus.

8876–8. Cf. n. to l. 7435.

8879. **Idol,** 'phantom,' 'eidolon'; Gr. *εἴδωλον*.

8880. **ein Traum.** Says Hederich, on authority of Tzetes: 'Having seen her (Helena) once on the wall of Troy, he (Achilles) was so inflamed by her that he had no peace. He accordingly begged his mother, Thetis, to invent some means whereby he might enjoy her love. So Thetis, in order to satisfy him, counterfeited her form for him in a dream, and thus assuaged his passion a little.'

8889–90. **des dreiköpfigen Hundes**; i.e., Cerberus.

8894. **Tiefauflauerndes,** 'deep-lurking.'

8897. **auf** goes with **regest.** 'Thou dost stir up the worst of all the past,' etc.

8909 ff. The meter changes to a lightly-moving trochaic rhythm, which extends as far as l. 8930.

8913. **Tret' ich = indem ich trete.** Cf. l. 7078.

8929. **Wie . . . Drosseln.** The simile is borrowed from the *Odyssey* 22, 468 ff., where Telemachus hangs the wanton serving-maids. The passage runs, in Bryant's translation:

As when a flock
Of broad-winged thrushes or wild pigeons strike
A net within a thicket . . . .
So hung the women, with their heads a-row,
And cords about their necks . . . .
A little while,
And but a little, quivered their loose feet
In air.

8936+. **Zwerggestalten.** Here the illusion of the antique begins to dissolve and northern *diablerie* to assert itself once more. The rotund dwarfs are minions of destruction that wait upon Mephistopheles, who has here taken up the rôle of ballet-master (cf. Gruppe and erstarrten Bildern above).

8946. **aber doch** connects getrennten Haupts with anständig würdig. Though her head will be cut off, she is nevertheless to have decent, seemly burial.

8957 ff. Being in terror of a return to Hades, the choretids adopt a politer tone toward Phorkyas, addressing her no longer in forms suggestive of ugliness, but of wisdom and power.

8958. **Tag;** i.e., 'life,' instead of the night of Hades.

8978. **Richte,** 'limit,' 'border-line'; *die grenze, schranke, nach der man sich zu richten, die man innezuhalten hat,* says Grimm Wb.

8987. **starrt,** 'abounds.'

8994. **Thal-Gebirg** = Gebirgthäler. The reference is to the Arcadian highlands.

8996. **Taygetos im Rücken,** 'with Taygĕtus at its back' (acc. absolute). The point of view is not Sparta, where the speakers now are, but Arcadia, from which the high peaks of Taygetus (the range separating Laconia from Messenia) rise *behind* the nearer mountains to south-eastward.

9000. **cimmerischer Nacht,** 'Cimmerian night,' i.e., the far-away, unknown North.

9009. **Freigeschenken,** 'free gifts.' Tacitus, *Germania* 15, states that the Germani were wont to honor their chiefs with gifts of cattle and corn. Later, in feudal times, these voluntary gifts *pro honore* became an exacted tribute.

9015. **menschenfresserisch,** 'anthropophagous.' The allusion is to

Iliad 22, 346, where Achilles says that he could wish his fury prompted him to cut up the flesh of Hector and devour it raw.

9019. **mir nichts dir nichts,** 'regardlessly.'

9020. **Cyklopish;** in allusion to the so-called Cyclopean masonry of early Greek history. It consisted of huge irregular masses of rock, roughly hewn and put together without mortar.

9029. **Galerien . . . ein,** 'galleries to look out and in,' i.e., external and internal galleries.

9030. **Wappen.** Coats of arms, in the technical, heraldic sense, were unknown to the ancients, heraldry being of medieval origin. Phorkyas explains the word, therefore, by referring to the shield-devices of the Greek heroes.

9031. **Geschlungene Schlang'.** An antique vase at Weimar, in which Goethe was specially interested, has a figure of Ajax with a coiled dragon upon his shield.

9032. **Sieben vor Theben.** In the *Seven against Thebes* of Æschylus, l. 377 ff., we read that Tydeus had upon his shield a representation of the moon and starry sky; Polyneices, the goddess of justice (Dike); Eteocles, a hero scaling a wall by means of a ladder; Capaneus, a man with a torch, etc.

9038. **seinen**; a mere inadvertence for **ihren.** An earlier form for the preceding line shows:

Und solch Gebild führt hier ein jeder Heldensohn.

In changing from ein jeder Heldensohn to auch unsre Heldenschaar the incongruous possessive was overlooked.

9054. **Deiphobus.** Says Hederich, *sub voce* 'Deiphobus': 'After the death of Paris he took Helena for himself; wherefore . . . when Menelaus got hold of him he first had his ears cut off, then his arms, his nose, and finally all his external members.'

9060. **Um jenes willen,** 'on his account,' 'because of him' (Deiphobus).

9072. **Widerdämon,** 'evil genius'; Gr. *κακοδαίμων*.

9103. **auch.** The singing of the swan portends its *own* death; the chorus hope that it may not *also* portend theirs.

9117. **Hermes;** i.e., Hermes Psychopompos, the 'conductor of souls to Hades. To Hermes in this capacity was attributed a 'golden wand' (*ῥάβδον χρυσείην*, *Odyssey* 24, 2).

9118. **wieder zurück.** The members of the chorus *know*, then, that they are shades who have once been escorted to Hades. Cf. l. 9962.

9119. **grautagenden,** 'gray-lighted,' 'dismal.' The Hades of the *Odyssey* is far away on the confines of Oceanos; a land of 'eternal cloud and darkness.'

9120. **Ungreifbarer,** 'impalpable,' 'unsubstantial.' Cf. *Odyssey* 11, 206, where Odysseus tries to embrace the shade of his mother, but the form passes through his arms 'like a shadow or a dream.'

9123. **dunkelgräulich**; to be taken factitively. The clouds that have enveloped them float away, disclosing a dark-gray mass, as of dingy masonry, which presently becomes distinct as a medieval castle.

9126+. **Innerer Burghof.** Imagine a rambling but not inharmonious medieval castle, situated far to the north of Sparta in the Arcadian highlands. Ruins of 'Frankish' castles exist at various points in the Peloponnesus, and Goethe had read descriptions of them (cf. Intr. p. xxiii, foot-note); but there is no evidence that he borrowed any local details for his conception of Faust's castle. Helena and her attendants are set down by Phorkyas in the inner court, at one end of which rises a flight of steps adown which comes the procession of pages followed by Faust.

9135. **Pythonissa,** 'prophetess,' 'pythoness.' As Phorkyas has not told her name, Helena calls her 'Pythonissa' on account of her prophetic gift and wonder-working powers. There is no Gr. form *Πυθώνισσα* meaning 'prophetess,' although Plutarch, 2, 214 E, states that ventriloquists were called *Πύθωνες* and *Πυθώνισσαι*. Goethe seems to have got the form by taking the familiar Fr. *pythonesse* and treating it as if it were Greek.

9146. **aus vielen einsgewordnen,** 'made one out of many parts.' This *e pluribus unum* character is seen in many a medieval castle.

9156. **gereiht . . . früh,** 'formed in line and under discipline so early;' i.e., so early in life, when they are too young to be soldiers. The chorus has never before seen a procession of marching pages.

9164. **mit Asche**; in allusion to the apples of Sodom. The chorus suspect that the handsome boys are only illusory forms, like themselves.

9172. **Über überwallt er.** The repetition of über is a case of emphatic reduplication. It pictures vividly the process by which the filmy canopy gradually comes into its place, just over the queen's head, forming an appearance of cloud-wreaths.

9178. **Stufe für Stufe,** 'step after step.' The chorus are to occupy the steps of the throne in dignified order.

9180. **Würdig;** adj., not adv. 'Let it be blessed as worthy,' i.e., gratefully pronounced worthy.

9191 ff. Faust speaks in the (modern) iambic pentameter.

9195. **mir . . . entwand,** 'filched duty from me,' i.e., caused me to be recreant in my duty.

9217+. **Lynceus.** Here, as also in the fifth act, the warden of the castle is given the name of the 'lynx-eyed' pilot of the Argonauts, who could see through earth, sea, and sky, by night as well as by day. He defends himself in rimed stanzas, — something that is new to Helena.

9235. **Zinne? Thurm?** The meaning is: Could I think of my immediate, prosaic surroundings?

9239. **Sog ich an,** 'drank in,' an going with the verb. Sog ich ein would be more natural.

9243. **das beschworne Horn,** 'the sworn horn' for 'the sworn duty of blowing the horn.'

9252. In connection with **Halbgötter** think of Theseus; with **Helden,** of Paris; with **Götter,** of Hermes; with **Dämonen,** of Phorkyas.

9254-5. **Einfach** refers to the 'simple' or 'first' estate in which she caused the Trojan war; **doppelt,** to her return from Hades as *eidolon;* **dreifach,** to her recent return to Sparta; **vierfach,** to her present appearance in Arcadia.

9273 ff. Lynceus gives expression to the chivalrous beauty-worship of the Middle Ages, and at the same time identifies himself with the invading 'barbarians' of an earlier period.

9280. **prallt zurück.** Lynceus means that his occupation is gone, since the sharpest eyes are dazzled by the throne of beauty.

9287. **hundertfach gestärkt,** 'reinforced by hundreds.'

9300. **gedörrtes Gras,** 'withered grass,' as a symbol of the common and worthless.

9307. **Nun . . . allein.** The correct reading is nun, not nur, as most editions have it. The sense is apparently: 'Now the emerald (which I lately thought priceless for its own sake) deserves alone (i.e., has no other merit than) to adorn thy bosom.' Nun in contrast with an implied bisher; Smaragd, the name of a particular precious stone as representative of its class. The Weimar editor and Düntzer, however, understand the sense to be: 'Now the emerald (of all gems) alone deserves to adorn thee, rubies being paled by the blush of thy cheeks.' But why this unique distinction for the emerald? There are other gems besides emeralds and rubies, and Lynceus himself expects that his pearls will be used for ear-rings. It may be added that emeralds were thought to exert a refreshing, sanative influence upon the eye. Cf. *Wahlverwandtschaften* I, 6: Wenn der Smaragd durch seine herrliche Farbe dem Gesicht wohl thut, ja sogar einige Heilkraft an diesem edlen Sinn ausübt, u.s.w.

9310. **Tropfenei,** 'oval pearl.'

9319. **Erlaube mich** = dulde mich; 'permit me in thy train,' i.e., take me for one of thy vassals.

9326. **lose**; to be taken with das alles in contrast with fest, hence = abgelöst von mir, 'detached from its owner,' 'alienated.'

9327. **baar,** 'of cash value.'

9341. **lebelosem Leben.** We are to think of decorations representing green verdure, with statues of nymphs, gods, etc.

9347. **es ist gespielt**; it is mere child's play, inadequate to honor the Queen of Beauty sufficiently.

9349. **Übermuth,** 'exuberance'; to be understood in a good sense.

9359. **knieend.** The unattached pple. is poetic if not grammatical. Construe: Erst laß die treue Widmung, die ich dir knieend darbringe, dir gefallen, hohe Frau.

9363. **Gränzunbewußten,** 'unconscious of a limit,' i.e., 'limitless.' Her realm is the realm of beauty.

9368 ff. Helena is curious about the rimed speech of Lynceus — something she has never heard. Faust replies by giving her a lesson in riming.

9378. **von Herzen.** Classical poetry, so Schiller thought, is prevailingly 'naive' or objective; the romantic, 'sentimental' or subjective. To acquire the romantic tone, therefore, Helena has first of all to learn to speak 'from the heart.' Cf. Eckermann, March 21, 1830.

9376. **Wechselrede.** Cf. *Divan* VIII, 36:

> Behramgur, sagt man, hat den Reim erfunden,
> Er sprach entzückt aus reiner Seele Drang;
> Dilaram schnell, die Freundin seiner Stunden,
> Erwiderte mit gleichem Wort und Klang.

9410. **Offenbarsein** = Offenbarung, 'manifestation.'

9411. **so fern, so nah**; so 'far' as belonging to the antique world, so 'near,' as feeling the strange ecstasy of romantic love. Observe that the lines 9411–18 have both final and medial rime.

9415. **verlebt,** 'lived out'; i.e., as one whose life has been lived in the past.

9418. **Dasein ist Pflicht,** 'existence is duty.' The context shows the meaning to be: It is a duty to surrender one's self to a present joy, without trying to explain it.

9432. **leichte Waare**; the chorus, in distinction from Helena (Dieser). Cf. l. 8929.

9441+. **Explosionen**; probably of gunpowder, in spite of the anachronism. But Loeper understands bursts of martial music.

9443. **ungetrennten,** 'united.'

9446. **mit . . . Wüthen,** 'with bated, quiet fury,' i.e., with martial ardor duly held in check by discipline. Faust proceeds to harangue his generals, reminding them of their past deeds of valor, and promising each a Peloponnesian dukedom. The verb, treten auf, comes in the next strophe.

9454. **Pylos**; a seaport of Messenia, famed in heroic times as the home of wise old Nestor. Faust and his men arrive by sea, and since the old race of heroes is dead, they make quick work of the petty chieftains that oppose them.

9466. **Germane.** Goethe seems to have regarded Germanus as the name of a single tribe, and hence as on a par with Goth, Frank, Saxon and Norman, all of whom are really Germani. — The passage recalls, and is meant to recall, actual history. Early in the 13th century the Morea was conquered by French knights under the leadership of Champlitte and Villehardouin, who created the principality of Achaia or Morea. The feudal system was established by the building of castles, the creation of baronial fiefs, etc. This 'Frankish' occupancy continued for two centuries, and its architectural remains are still to be seen at various points.

9476–7. Faust decrees that the over-lordship of his feudal domain shall belong to Sparta, that being the ancestral home of his queen. In reality the Frankish Princes of Morea had their court at Nikli, the ancient Tegea; but they possessed a strong fortress at Mistra, near the site of Sparta.

9493. **sich verband**, 'formed alliances.'

9512. **Nichtinsel**; a fanciful substitute for Halbinsel, 'peninsula,' i.e., almost-island. The Peloponnesus is 'attached by a light chain of hills (the Isthmus of Corinth) to the last (i. e., the most southerly) mountain-spur of Europe.'

9514. **Das Land . . . Sonnen**, 'the land of all lands'; the 'land's sun' being a metaphor for the land itself. The ensuing description of Arcadia, the fabled home of love and poetry, is mainly imaginative, for Goethe had never been in Greece; but some hints were got from the accounts of modern travellers. In Castellan's *Briefe über Morea*, a book which Goethe drew from the court-library in July, 1825, we read, p. 189: 'The ancients compared their Elysium with this heavenly region; and their descriptions of it are still apt. It is the attribute of nature only never to grow old; Arcadia seems to have been her cradle: she is here ever young and blooming' (cf. ll. 9550–65). There follows then a detailed description, from which we quote a few sentences: 'About us, in the far distance, the view was shut in by mountain-chains. . . . Among the nearer and lower mountains, which were mostly covered with trees, we observed ever-green valleys. Brooks lost themselves among the trees, to re-appear in the meadows. . . . On another side we saw bare mountains, their notches punctured with caverns which, our guide said, were still occupied by hermits. A number of huts could be seen in the most happy locations,' etc.

9518–21. The fiction is that the swan's egg from which Helena came was hatched among the whispering sedge of the Eurotas. — Connect the als-clause with hinaufgeblickt in spite of the period.

9521. **überstach**, 'dazzled.'

9526–9. The thought is that while the jagged snow-clad summits endure (i.e., hold out against) the cold rays of the spring sun, the rocks lower down already show signs of verdure. — **Angegrünt,** 'tinged with green.'

9538. **Lebensnymphen,** 'enlivening nymphs,' — nymphs that give life to the scene.

9541. **zweighaft,** 'branch-abounding'; = mit vielen Zweigen.

9542. **starret mächtig,** 'stands forth in its might.'

9546–7. **mütterlich quillt Milch** = Muttermilch quillt.

9551. **heitert,** 'expresses serenity.'

9552. **unsterblich;** because the race, living under ideal conditions, remains the same from age to age, the father perpetuating himself in the son.

9558. **zugestaltet,** 'made like in form,' 'identified with.' In his youth Apollo kept the herds of Admetus in Thessaly.

9561. **ergreifen sich,** 'take hold of one another,' 'interblend'; the gods becoming as men, the best men becoming as gods.

9567–8. **zirkt für uns** = umzirkt uns, 'forms a domain about us.'

9578. **Ihr Bärtigen,** 'ye long-beards'; addressed to the sedate and skeptical men of learning (cf. l. 6705) among the spectators. Cf. n. to l. 10038+.

9579. **Lösung;** here in the sense of 'outcome.'

9603 ff. On the character and symbolism of Euphorion, cf. Intr. pp. xxiii ff. For the aureole (ll. 9623–4) see n. to l. 9902+.

9644. **Sohne der Maja;** Hermes, whose wonderful babyhood the chorus proceeds to set over against that of Euphorion. The description versifies Hederich's article 'Mercurius': 'Scarce born he stole the trident of Neptune, the sword of Mars from its sheath, from Apollo his bow and arrows, from Jupiter even his scepter; and if he had not been afraid of the fire he would have stolen from him his lightning. On the very day of his birth he challenged Cupid to a wrestling-match, and by tripping him up vanquished him; and when Venus, pleased with the feat, took him in her lap, he stole her girdle.'

9648. **Strenget,** 'wraps,' 'confines.' Goethe seems to have had in mind the verb strängen, 'to harness' (with Stränge).

9664. **Vortheilsuchenden.** This too is in Hederich, who says of Mercury: 'He invented the art of buying and selling, and in connection with this, that of gaining one's advantage by clever deception (seinen Vortheil durch einen geschickten Betrug zu machen).'

9696. **Gleich . . . Scherz,** 'it is forthwith your own play'; that is, the parents feel the child to be a part of themselves. His gayety is infectious and at once becomes theirs.

9707. **vieler Jahre.** The boy is the emblem of a wedded happiness that has lasted for years. As in the first scene of the Second Part, we have a symbolic lapse of time. Den Poeten bindet keine Zeit.

9713. **Zu allen Lüften,** 'to the great ether.'

9741. **Ländlich im Stillen** = im Ländlichstillen, 'in rural quiet.'

9745. **Leichter.** The comparative is to be taken absolutely in the sense of 'lightsome.'

9763. **dein Ziel erreicht.** The poetry of motion in the rhythmic dance completes his charm.

9774. **behende,** 'vehement.'

9782. **widert mir;** archaic for widert mich an, 'is repugnant to me.'

9784. **schier,** 'altogether,' 'completely'; = gerade or ganz.

9787. **Hörnerblasen;** of the mimic winding of huntsmen's horns.

9798. **widerwärtigen;** here = 'reluctant.'

9800. **Hülle,** 'visible envelope,' 'form.'

9804. **Glaubst . . . Gedränge,** 'dost think thou hast me in a strait?' Gedränge = Noth, Verlegenheit.

9813. **was . . . mir,** 'what should the confinement be to me?' 'why should I be confined?'

9832. **Apfelgold,** 'the gold of apples,' 'golden apples.' But Goethe may have had in mind the pomegranate, *pomum aurantium*.

9843–50. One of the most perplexing passages in *Faust*, owing to the uncertainty of the text. The MS. and the first print, of 1827, have Den instead of Dem in l. 9847. In the print of 1831–2, published under the supervision of Riemer and Eckermann, ll. 9847–8 were made to read: Mit nicht zu dämpfendem, Heiligem Sinn. This looks like an unwarranted making-over of the text, but as the emendation was published in Goethe's lifetime, it may possibly have had his approval. The sense would be: 'To the patriot sons of Greece, with their invincible spirit, may it (my coming) bring gain.' The Weimar editor condemns Riemer's emendation, but thinks the original reading unintelligible; he accordingly changes Den to Dem and revises the punctuation so as to give (presumably) the sense: 'To the patriot sons of Greece, to the spirit of stern resolution, to all fighters, may it bring gain.' For consistency's sake we have followed the Weimar edition, but it seems probable that Den is after all the right reading, the acc. being intended to anticipate Gewinn. The sense would be: To the patriot sons of Greece may it bring the spirit of stern resolution, to all fighters gain (the gain being the quickening of the patriotic spirit). Düntzer, reading Dem with comma after Bluts, would connect the dat. with gebar—'whom Greece has borne *for* patriotism.' The 'antecedent' of Welche is den Kämpfenden. Alle takes the place of allen, though the form is not common except after a prep. or in the nom.; cf. Thomas's *German Grammar*, § 317, 1.

9856. **sich selbst bewußt,** 'conscious of himself,' = 'relying upon himself.'

9861–2. In Castellan's *Briefe über Morea* (Weimar, 1809), a book known to have been read by Goethe (cf. n. to l. 9514), we read, p. 114, as follows: 'Often in the war with the Turks, their implacable enemies, the Mainotes are under arms continually. The boys are taught to handle the sword before they can plow; yes, even the women, in case of menacing danger, mix with the soldiers in the field and support and cheer their husbands and sons.' Also, p. 117: 'They (the Mainote women) learn likewise the use of weapons, and many of them have been known, when they could get no arms, to offer their shoulders as a rest for the gun of a brother or husband.'

9866. **Fern . . . fern,** 'far and thus farther still.' The form recedes even while the words are uttered.

9873. **gethan,** 'done deeds'—and thus proved his manhood.

9884. **donnern;** the thunder of the war between Menelaus and the vassals of Faust.

9897. **Doch!** = 'danger avaunt!'

9901. **Ikarus.** Euphorion's disastrous attempt to fly reminds the antique chorus of the similar case of Icarus, who flew too near the sun, so that his wax-fastened wings were melted off and he fell into the sea.

9902+. **eine bekannte Gestalt;** that of Byron. Said Goethe to Eckermann, July 5, 1827: 'As a representative of the newest era in poetry

I could use no one but him who is to be regarded without doubt as the greatest talent of the century. And then Byron is not antique and not romantic, but like the present day itself. Such a one I had to have. Moreover he suited my purpose completely on account of his unsatisfied temperament and his warlike tendency, which led to his death at Missolonghi.' — An 'aureole' is given Euphorion (cf. ll. 9623–4) as the symbol of supernatural genius.

9907–38. The choral dirge is, incidentally, Goethe's tribute to Lord Byron. 'Have you noticed,' said Goethe to Eckermann, July 5, 1827, 'that in the dirge the chorus falls quite out of its rôle. Up to this point it has been held throughout to the antique tone and never belies its maiden character; but here it suddenly becomes serious and deeply ratiocinative, and utters things of which it has never thought and can not have thought.' In the same conversation, after wondering what the German critics would make of the scene, Goethe goes on to observe that the 'fancy has its own laws,' and that 'if it did not produce things which must remain forever problematical to the understanding it would not be worth much.'

9920. **Mitsinn jedem** = Mitgefühl für jeden.

9924. **in's willenlose Netz,** 'the will-less,' i.e., passive, blameless 'net' of unnecessary complications. The allusion is to Byron's quarrel with society and general Freigeisterei der Leidenschaft.

9927. **zuletzt das höchste Sinnen;** the resolution to help in the Greek struggle for independence. In Stanhope's *Greece in 1823 and 1824*, a work read by Goethe in 1825, occurs the following passage in a letter of Trelawney to Stanhope (p. 323): 'From the moment he (Byron) left Genoa, though twice driven back, his ruling passion became ambition of a name, or rather, by one great effort to wipe out the memory of those deeds which his enemies had begun to rather freely descant on in the public prints, and to make his name as great and glorious in acts as it already was by his writings.'

9930. **gelang dir nicht.** Byron set out from Genoa in July, 1823, but found the Greeks disunited and without plans. After a vexatious delay of months he reached Missolonghi in December. Here he was presently given command of an expedition against Lepanto, but died April 19, 1824, before he had been able to strike a blow for the cause he had at heart.

9932. **sich vermummt**, 'masks itself,' i.e., wraps itself in mysterious silence.

9933–4. The lines allude to the fall of Missolonghi, April 22, 1826, after a two years' heroic resistance by the Greeks, — an event which saddened the hearts of Philhellenes all over Europe.

9935. **erfrischet**, 'create afresh.'

9938+. **Völlige Pause.** This is the pause referred to in the *scenarium* after l. 9678. It marks the end of the operatic Euphorion-scene.

9939. **Ein altes Wort**, 'an old truth.' That Goethe was not thinking of a particular proverb seems to be indicated by the fact that the expression of the desired thought as he finally shaped it in l. 9940 was reached only after much experimentation. The MSS. give the substance of the line in eleven different versions; a fact which is significant as showing the care and labor with which our poet wrought in his later years.

9941. **Des Lebens wie der Liebe**; cf. Intr. p. xxiv.

9954+. **Exuvien**, *exuviæ*, i.e., 'spoils,' 'mementos.'

9957. **um die Welt**, 'on the world's account.' The thought is: I do not pity the world.

9963. **alt-thessalischen Vettel**, 'old Thessalian hag.' This contradicts the fiction that Phorkyas is a Cretan; but can hardly refer to Manto, as Zarncke suggests. Panthalis calls the witch in whose power they have all been so long a Thessalian, because Thessaly was the land of witches.

9975. **Asphodelos**, 'asphodel,' the pale flower of Hades. Cf. *Odyssey* 11, 573.

9979. **Fledermausgleich zu piepsen.** In the *Odyssey* 24, 6, the shades are represented as 'twittering (τρίζουσαι) like bats.' Shakespeare makes the ghosts 'squeak and gibber.'

9981 ff. Panthalis decides that the nameless choretids, who do not feel the noble sentiment of loyalty to their queen, but think only of the inanity of their own existence in Hades, are not fit to retain their personality, but should be identified with nature's 'elements.' Accordingly they divide into four groups, the first becoming dryads, the second echo-nymphs, the third brook-nymphs, the fourth spirits of the vine. — It was a serious conviction of Goethe that a man's chance of personal immortality rests upon his amounting to something in this life; on his showing steadfastness and fidelity (letter to Knebel, Dec. 3, 1781), or on his being a 'great entelechy' (Eckermann, Sept. 21, 1829).

9992 ff. The dryads are conceived as directing the life-process of the trees, coaxing up the sap from the roots, putting forth the leaves and branches, and finally, for their good work, receiving the homage of the mortals who come to gather the ripe fruit.

10000. Schmiegen; supply uns.

10004 ff. The echo-nymphs are thought of as nestling in the waters of the lake close against the rocky wall.

10007. mäandrisch wallend, 'meandering.'

10009. bezeichnen's. The es refers to a distant house surrounded by cypresses which rise above the landscape, the winding shore, and the surface of the water. But Sprenger, *Zeits. f. d. Ph.* 23, 455, would refer it to the course of the water generally (der ganze Lauf des Gewässers wird von Cypressen eingefaßt).

10016. förderſamſt, 'most effectively,' 'to best advantage.'

10026. Tragebutten; tubs made to be carried on the back.

10029. widerlich zerquetſcht, 'crushed to an unsightly mass.'

10030. Becken, 'cymbals'; not really different from the preceding Cymbeln. — Here begins the description of a bacchanal, or Dionysiac orgy.

10033. öhrig Thier; the ass, whose loud braying frightened the giants and thus put the gods under obligation to Silenus.

10038+. von den Kothurnen, 'from the tragic buskins,' the effect of which was to give the ancient actor an appearance of colossal stature. The language is hardly to be taken as implying that Mephistopheles as Phorkyas has worn the buskins throughout the entire third act, for this is not easily thinkable (cf. Niejahr, *Euphorion* I, 103). We are rather to suppose that he suddenly assumes them, by way of indicating his responsibility for the phantasmagory, and then puts them off with the rest of his Phorkyas-mask, to show that his rôle as antique witch is now ended. As appended to the separately published *Helena* of 1827, this indication of the identity of Phorkyas and Mephistopheles was needed; but after the second act was written it became superfluous, and might very well have been omitted. — As to the 'epilogue' which is left to the discretion of Mephistopheles, there is no evidence that Goethe ever intended to write one. There is, however, a paralipomenon (No. 176) in which Phorkyas explains to the spectators what is *about to happen*, with humorous comments upon the suddenness of Euphorion's birth, the strangeness of his conduct, etc., and then declares that she is no longer needed. The ghostly drama is to spin itself out to a tragic conclusion without her bodily presence. She accordingly retires with an Auf Wiedersehen. But these rejected verses were clearly intended to come in at l. 9579. The poet changed his plan, decided to keep Phorkyas on the stage to the end, and then, being reluctant to give up the idea of a Mephistophelean comment on the piece, he provided for a *discretionary* epilogue at the close.

Hochgebirg.

Cf. Intr. p. xliii and p. lvi. — If one must think of a definite locality, let it be of some point in the Tyrolese Alps. It is worth remarking that the legendary Doctor Faust also makes the acquaintance of high mountain-peaks in the course of his aerial journeys. See the first Faust-book, chap. xxvii.

10039–66. Faust speaks, with the spell of the antique still upon him, in iambic trimeters.

10061. Aurorens . . . Schwung, 'the morning-time's love, its buoyant soaring.' The reference is to Gretchen; though the mood of the whole monologue, with its sadly transfigured memories of vanished joy, tells of the poet's own experiences.

10066+. tappt auf, 'comes stalking up.'

10067. endlich, 'quickly,' = rasch or behende; a common meaning of endlich in early modern German.

10075 ff. Goethe here reverts to the great geological controversy touched upon in the 'Walpurgis-Night' (cf. n. to ll. 7550 ff.). Mephistopheles, very naturally, speaks as Vulcanist, arguing that the mountain-top on which they have alighted was thrown up by a long-past explosion which he proceeds to account for. The first lines allude to the revolt of Lucifer and the rebel angels.

10077. **centralisch,** 'at the center,' viz., of the earth.—**Um und um** = **ringsherum.** Cf. *Paradise Lost* I, 61:

> A dungeon horrible on all sides round
> As one great furnace flamed.

10079. **Hellung.** Instead of Mephisto's 'excessive illumination,' Milton gives us

> No light, but rather darkness visible.

10087. **an ... Zipfel,** 'by another tag.' The meaning seems to be simply: We have things turned around.

10090. **Das ... kehren,** 'to turn things topsy-turvy.' For a succinct account of Goethe's geological views, which throws much light on this part of *Faust*, consult the concluding pages of his *Zur Mineralogie, Werke*, H. 33, 469. He was an ardent disciple of Werner, regarded granite as the primitive foundation of the earth's crust, and the crust itself as having been formed by crystallization and deposition from a primordial 'chaotic crystalline infusion.' When, therefore, De Beaumont, Von Buch, Von Humboldt, and other geologists began to claim a large rôle for Vulcanism, and to point to volcanic rocks which must have lain lower than the granite, this was turning things topsy-turvy. He deals with the subject in a number of his 'Tame Xenia,' one of which concludes:

> Denn Plutos Gabel drohet schon
> Dem Urgrund Revolution;
> Basalt, der schwarze Teufels-Mohr
> Aus tiefster Hölle bricht hervor,
> Zerspaltet Fels, Gestein und Erden,
> Omega muß nun Alpha werden.
> Und so wäre denn die liebe Welt,
> Geognostisch auf den Kopf gestellt.

The new views seemed to Goethe a return to the theory of Father Kircher, a seventeenth-century writer who explained earthquakes by the assumption of a fiery reservoir (*pyrophylacium*) at the center of the earth.

10092. **Übermaß,** 'superabundance,' in comparison with the previous confinement. For the devil as 'prince of the power of the air' see

Eph. ii, 2. In Eph. vi, 12, where our King James Bible has: 'For we wrestle . . . against the rulers of the darkness of this world, against spiritual wickedness in high places,' Luther has, more correctly: Herrn der Welt, die in der Finsterniß dieser Welt herrschen mit den bösen Geistern unter dem Himmel.

10095. **edel=stumm,** 'nobly-mute,' 'mysterious.' Cf. Goethe's saying in *Meisters Wanderjahre*, (*Werke*, H. 18, 262): Die Gebirge sind stumme Meister und machen schweigsame Schüler.

10097. **sich in sich selbst.** Cf. *Zur Mineralogie*, *Werke*, H. 33, 470, where Goethe says: 'According to my view the earth built itself out of itself; here (in the new theories) it appears everywhere burst, and the crevasses to have been filled up from unknown depths below.'

10098. **rein,** 'neatly' — with distinct outlines.

10102. **gemildet,** 'sloped gently,' 'prolonged in easy declivity.'

10109. **Moloch,** the biblical 'god of the Ammonites,' is introduced by Klopstock (*Messias* II, 351) as a rebellious devil who throws up mountains to defend himself against Jehovah. Goethe gives him a hammer which suggests that of Thor.

10111. **starrt;** used as in l. 8987. — **Von fremden Centnermassen** alludes to the so-called 'erratic' boulders, in which Goethe was deeply interested. In an essay of the year 1829 (see *Werke*, H. 33, 465) he explained those of North Germany as having been deposited by a primeval glacier, and thus became a pioneer in the new glacial geology. Here, however, the devil ascribes the 'erratics' to his primeval explosion, and commends the wisdom of the common people who, in their ordinary nomenclature, give the name of the devil to strange things that they do not understand (cf., in English, Devil's Gulch, Devil's Slide, Devil's Basin, etc.).

10127. **Zeichen.** The 'sign' is the mountain itself with its erratic boulders.

10129. **unsrer Oberfläche.** Like the tempter of Christ, the devil here speaks as if the world and the fulness thereof belonged to him. Cf. Matt. iv, 8, 9.

10137. **Bürger=Nahrungs=Graus,** 'the horror of burgher-nourishment,' i.e., of the market. — **Im Kerne,** 'in the centre,' 'at the heart.'

10145. **anzumaßen,** 'broad streets (wherein) to take on a grand appearance'; i.e., to parade, put on style.

10148. Rollekutschen. Grimm Wb. defines the word as a 'light, quickly-moving carriage.' Schröer refers Rolle to the bells of the horses.

10159. The sense requires one to supply after Und something like 'after all,' 'nevertheless.'

10160. mir . . . bewußt, 'in proud self-consciousness.'

10165. Schnurwege, 'roads straight as a string.'

10168. steigt es; viz., the main column of water.

10172. A syllable is lacking between da and gränzenlose; perhaps die.

10176. modern, 'in the newest style,' — that of the kings of France and the German princelings who imitated them. Faust has no wish to be such a modern Sardanapalus.

10192. Von allem = von alle dem, was ich meine, — my desire of large activity for its own sake.

10202. wie der Übermuth. The conduct of the sea affected him like arrogance and injustice on the part of a rational being.

10223. schmiegt . . . vorbei, 'creeps past,' i. e., can not get over. This line, with l. 10225, suggests the idea of dykes, l. 10226 that of drains.

10252–9. Faust gives expression to the political ideal of the benevolent despotism.

10272–3. Faust has no need to hear the story out, but knowing how it must have gone with the empire, he proceeds to describe the course of affairs, using the metaphor of a drunken man.

10285. das; getting up an insurrection ostensibly in the interest of public order, but really for selfish ends.

10294. Einmal . . . male, 'saved once is saved for a thousand times,' i.e., 'for good.' Cf. *Werke*, H. 2, 324:

> Nur heute, heute nur laß dich nicht fangen,
> Da bist du hundertmal entgangen.

10314–5. The thought is: Leave things to your staff (Mephisto and the Mighty Men), and your reputation as Field-Marshal will be secure.

10315. Kriegsunrath, 'war's evil,' put for Kriegsunheil for the sake of the pun with Kriegsrath, 'council of war'; perhaps with the subaudition 'war's lack of counsel.'

10321. Peter Squenz. The name is that of Shakespeare's Peter

Quince, as popularized in Germany by Gryphius in his *Absurda Comica, oder Herr Peter Squentz, Schimpff-Spiel.*

10322. **Vom . . . Quintessenz,** 'the quintessence of the whole crowd.' In the *Midsummer Night's Dream* Quince has a 'scroll of every man's name which is thought fit, through all Athens, to play in our interlude before the duke and duchess.' From this 'eligible list' he chooses his actors. Thus the selection finally made represents the quintessence, or refined extract, of the whole crowd. So Mephistopheles, instead of enlisting the mountain-folk as a whole, calls to his aid a concentrated extract of soldier-qualities in the shape of three 'mighty men,' like those who helped David against the Philistines. The Hebrew names Adino, Eleazar and Shammah are replaced by the allegorical names Fight-hard, Get-quick, and Hold-fast. In their make-up the Mighty Men represent Youth, Manhood, and Age.

10327. **jetzt.** The time really referred to is the hey-day of romanticism. Mephistopheles means: Medieval knights are now in high favor; and if mine are allegorical, so much the better, since allegorical knights are quite in the spirit of the middle ages. Or, perhaps the meaning is: Such fellows are more pleasing in allegory than in real life.

Auf dem Vorgebirg.

Legend makes Doctor Faust claim the credit of winning battles for Karl V. Thus the general idea of a victory won by magic rests upon popular tradition, but the particular expedients resorted to by Mephistopheles — the empty suits of rattling armor, the counterfeit water and fire borrowed from the undines and the mountain-folk — are inventions of Goethe. They are, however, quite in the spirit of magical folk-lore. Thus the Middle Age had its rain-making magicians who practiced their art against besieging armies. Cf. Loeper II, 259 ff.

10348. **die Wahl,** 'the choice,' viz., of a position. — **Uns glückt,** 'will bring us luck.'

10353. **allzu gänglich,** 'all too passable.' Although the hill is not steep it is rugged and difficult of ascent.

10360. **den Phalanx.** The noun is usually feminine, as in l. 10595.

10366. **zu trennen.** The Commander-in-chief hopes that the solid phalanx in the center, fighting on level ground, will be able to break the center of the advancing enemy.

10389. **viele** refers to individual princes or leaders; the following **Schaar** to bands of troops.

10395. **ihr.** The Emperor apostrophizes the disloyal leaders, who have 'excused their inactivity' by pleading the turbulent and dangerous condition of affairs. — **Wenn . . . voll,** 'when your account is complete'; i.e., when the measure of your guilt is full and the day of reckoning comes. But Loeper understands: Though your *own* account is correct (has no 'hole' in it), it will do you no good, for you will go down in the general ruin.

10402. **ein neuer Kaiser.** We are to understand that the Emperor took the field against a revolt of his subjects, and now learns for the first time that the insurgents have elected a 'new emperor.'

10409. **nur als Soldat,** 'only as a soldier'; i.e., only because I was taking the field in a military capacity, not because I expected to fight in person.

10412. **mir fehlte.** The sense is: Nothing was missed (the festival was perfect in all other respects, but) *I* was always shielded from danger.

10413. **Wie ihr auch seid,** 'however you are,' seems to mean 'however good your intentions may be.' — **Ringspiel** refers to the comparatively safe 'carousel' in which the mounted knights tilted at a ring, instead of at each other as in the old joust (Turnier).

10417. **besiegelt,** 'stamped with the seal' of the hero, hence 'called to heroic deeds.' The occasion alluded to is the Masquerade, though in ll. 5988 ff. the Emperor refers to his experience with the sham fire as if it had been only an amusing jest. Here he recalls it as a hero's ordeal. Cf. n. to l. 5998.

10423. **ungescholten;** supply aufzutreten. 'We come and hope we are welcome.'

10424. **hat . . . gegolten,** 'has come well in play' (on former occasions, as if oft were understood). The meaning is: Do not despise our aid, though you may not now feel the need of it.

10425. **simulirt,** 'ponders,' 'cogitates.' So used in popular dialect.

10426. **Felsenschrift.** The 'writing of the rocks' does not, as Grimm Wb. thinks, refer to runic inscriptions, but to the rocks themselves, conceived as a mysterious book in which the mountain-folk are able to read.

10434. **durchsichtige Gestalten** = crystals. Cf. n. to l. 880.

10439. **Nekromant von Norcia.** In the appendix to his *Benvenuto Cellini*, cap. xii, Goethe speaks of the uncanny reputation borne from of old by the mountains of Norcia. 'The earlier romancers,' he says, 'used this locality in order to take their heroes through the most wonderful happenings, and increased the popular faith in those magic beings whose forms had first been outlined by saga.' He then goes on to say that the local tradition of the place still preserves the memory of Master Cecco of Ascoli, who was burned at Florence as a necromancer in 1327. Finally he adds, with reference to a passage of the preceding biography, that Cellini's attention was at one time drawn to this region by a Sicilian who promised him treasures and other good things in the name of the spirits. Our fiction is, then, that a Sabine wizard, who had been condemned to death by the Roman clergy, was pardoned by the Emperor on the day of his coronation, and has ever since had his Majesty's welfare at heart. He has now sent Faust and Mephistopheles to offer the aid of the mountain-folk. The object of the invention is to break the force of any reluctance the Emperor might have to profit by the aid of magic. He is only reaping the proper reward of his former goodness of heart.

10467. **Selbst ist der Mann;** der Mann in the sense of der tüchtige Mann (cf. n. to l. 1759). 'A man who is a man is himself,' i.e., relies upon himself. The Emperor does not reject the proffered aid, is glad of the loyalty it betokens, but thinks he should fight out the issue alone with his rival.

10473. **Wie . . . sei,** 'however it may be,' i.e., though you may intend.

10475. The implication is: Does not the very adornment of the helmet bear witness to the value of the head it protects? The importance of the head is then further elaborated.

10484. **Lenkt ab,** 'parries.'—**Wiederholt,** 'gives back,' 'returns.'

10488. **Schemeltritt,** 'footstool,' with allusion to Ps. cx, 1: '... until I make thine enemies thy footstool' (in German, zum Schemel deiner Füße).

10497. **ist's geschehn;** viz., the rejection of the challenge.

10513. **schlapp** = schlaff, 'limp.'

10514. **graß** = gräßlich, 'horrible.'

10530+. **Eilebeute.** The name occurs in the German Bible, Is. viii, 1, where it translates *Mahershalal-hash-baz*, i.e., 'hasten the booty, rush on the prey.'

10533. **Herbst;** here = its etymological cognate 'harvest.'

10547 ff. Mephistopheles, who descended with the Mighty Men at the end of the preceding scene, now reappears from above and explains to the 'knowing ones' among the spectators the real nature of the noisy army with which he has suddenly covered the mountain. It is a little singular that he does not greet the Emperor, and that his arrival is taken as a matter of course.

10573. **rother ... Schein.** Riding under fire at the battle of Valmy (1792), to see what 'cannon-fever' was like, Goethe found the earth assuming 'a sort of reddish brown tint,' in which everything seemed to be 'swallowed up' (ll. 10575–6). Cf. *Werke*, H. 25, 59.

10576. **mischt sich ein,** i.e., becomes red too.

10584 ff. The illusion of Fighthard's many hands is explained as a mirage.

10594. **blitzen.** The gleam is caused by corposants, or St. Elmo's fires, such as are seen at night on the masts or yard-arms of ships. A pair of them are called Castor and Pollux (the Dioscuri).

10624–5. The eagle symbolizes the Emperor, the griffin his rival.

10655. **verfänglich** = 'in jeopardy.'

10664. **Raben.** Cf. n. to l. 2491.

10672. **folgerecht,** 'right for following,' i.e., 'wise,' 'sound.'

10689. **Geduld ... Knoten,** (we need) 'patience and cunning for the final difficulty.'

10737. **hellen Haufen.** Cf. n. to l. 7500.

10742. **Meister;** the Sabine wizard.

10749. **Wie ... hegt,** 'such as they (the dwarfs) cherish in their deep minds.'

10751. **Blickschnelles** = blitzschnelles, 'quick as a flash.'

10760. **Irrfunken-Blick,** 'the flash of wandering scintillations.'

10774. **wöhnlich** = heimisch; 'at home in their hereditary temper.' The empty suits of armor, once worn by warring Guelphs and Ghibellines, renew the old fight as if it came natural to them.

10780. **wider-widerwärtig** = äußerst widerwärtig; an emphatic reduplication, as in l. 5012, l. 8483+, and l. 9172.

Des Gegenkaisers Zelt.

On the passage in Alexandrines (ll. 10849 ff.), see Intr. p. xlv. Goethe's mild satire is a free parody of the famous Golden Bull of 1356, which described the relations, duties, and privileges of imperial dignitaries and officers of the court, and had much to say of ceremony and etiquette. Thus, when the Emperor wished to wash his hands, the Arch-chamberlain, the Elector of Brandenburg, had to hand him two silver basins of water and a fine towel. The Arch-dapifer, the Elector Palatine, had to place his Majesty's food before him in four silver dishes. And so forth.

10791. **Morgenstern;** a club with iron spikes.

10796. **ihn;** the adversary, whoever he may be.

10808. **Kreuz** = Rücken, 'back.'

10811. **zum Schoß hinein,** 'into my apron.'

10816+. **unsres Kaisers;** i.e., the Emperor of the drama, in distinction from the pretender.

10827–8. The meaning is: *Your* idea of honesty is to keep everything to yourself and levy contributions upon the people.

10830. **Handwerksgruß;** the formula with which journeymen were required to greet the members of their guild. Getquick's sign-vocal is 'Fork over.'

10832. **Gast.** For other examples of the singular form with plural meaning see Grimm Wb.

10851. **verrätherischer Schatz** = des Verräthers Schatz.

10858. **uns gefochten,** 'fought for our side' uns dat. rather than acc. But sich fechten occurs in l. 54.

10866. **Herr Gott, dich loben wir.** Cf. Goethe's poem of March 2, 1815 (*Werke*, H. 3, 284), apropos of the Holy Alliance, which had beaten the devil (Napoleon) by devilish means and was piously praising God for the victory:

> Sie sollten sich keineswegs genieren
> Sich auch einmal als Teufel gerieren,
> Auf jede Weise den Sieg erringen
> Und hierauf das Tedeum singen.

10868. **zur eignen Brust.** The pious Emperor thinks that he can not better praise God than by humbly showing his gratitude to the great men who have been the instruments of heaven's favor. He accordingly proceeds to decorate his four faithful 'generals' with 'arch'-dignities that have nothing to do with fighting or with the welfare of the state, but only with the ceremonial order of the palace, — in short, with his own personal pleasure. They accept the promotions gratefully and think only of shining at the approaching festival of victory.

10873. **o Fürst;** addressed to the Obergeneral, who is called a Fürst in l. 10502. — **Schichtung** is used in the general sense of 'disposition.'

10874. **Richtung** = 'movement' (in the military sense). The Emperor ascribes the victory to the general plan of attack ordered by his Commander-in-chief (ll. 10503 ff.). This was the 'main issue' (Hauptmoment), the unholy magic being a mere incident.

10876. **Erzmarschall,** 'Arch-steward' rather than 'Arch-marshal,' since the dignity has to do with court-ceremony and not with war (cf. n. to l. 4851+). Still Taylor is perhaps justified in translating 'Arch-marshal' in order to keep 'Arch-steward' for the Erztruchseß of l. 10899. The title Erzmarschall was at one time actually borne by the Duke of Saxony.

10881. **ich's.** The es refers to the sword — the symbol of the speaker's new dignity.

10898. **fördert** (not fordert). The festal mood 'promotes,' i.e., facilitates the Emperor's 'joyous procedure' of rewarding his friends.

10899. **Erztruchseß,** 'Arch-dapifer,' or, say, Lord High Dish-bearer.

10900. **Jagd, Geflügel-Hof und Vorwerk,** 'game-preserves, poultry-yard, and manor-farm.' Vorwerk denotes a small outlying farm belonging to a large estate.

10907. **Dich reizt nicht.** Logic seems to require a connective like obwohl or zwar.

10921. **venedisch,** 'Venetian'; *metri gratia* for venezianisch.

10942. **Anfall,** 'heirship'; 'succession' by hereditary right.

10947. **Beth',** 'tribute. Bethe, Bete, in the more usual Low-German form Bede, is a law-term denoting a tribute which was at first 'asked for' (bitten), then demanded as a right. Grimm Wb. renders it by *petitio, rogatio.* — **Geleit,** 'safe conduct,' i.e., the money paid to a sovereign prince for safe conduct through his territory.

10948. **Berg=, Salz= und Münzregal;** the royalty derived from mines, salt-works, and money-coining.

10957. **seiner Zeit,** 'in time.' Cf. Thomas's *German Grammar*, § 307, 2, *a*.

10965. **bethätigt;** here, apparently, = 'ordained.'

10987. **zur höchsten Zeit,** 'at the great festival'; used like M.H.G. *hōchzīt*, or *hōchgezīt*, which means a festival of any kind.

11020. **Schluß und Formalität,** 'the concluding formality' of the written conveyance.

11035–6. **Es ward . . . verliehn.** Cf. Intr. p. xlv. The verses there alluded to are printed in an appendix by the Weimar editor, under the heading Belehnung Fausts, though they describe in reality not a Belehnung, but a Ritterschlag. They are as follows:

Der Canzler lies't.

Sodann ist auch vor unserm Thron erschienen
Faustus, mit Recht der Glückliche genannt,
Denn ihm gelingt wozu er sich ermannt,
Schon längst bestrebsam uns zu dienen,
Schon längst als klug und tüchtig uns bekannt.

Auch heut am Tage glückt's ihm hohe Kräfte
Wie sie der Berg verschließt hervorzurufen,
Erleichternd uns die blutigen Geschäfte.
Er trete näher den geweihten Stufen,
Den Ehrenschlag empfang' er.

Faust kniet.

Kaiser.

Nimm ihn hin!

Duld' ihn von keinem andern.

Offene Gegend.

Cf. Intr. pp. xxxviii ff. — The story of Philemon and Baucis, which is treated by Ovid, *Metamorphoses* 8, 620 ff., is thus related by Hederich *sub voce* 'Baucis': 'An old woman in Phrygia, who made shift with her husband Philemon in a wretched hut, but in her poverty led a very peaceful and contented life. As now Jupiter and Mercury were traveling through the land in disguise in order to see how the people lived, there was no one but these two who was willing to receive them. These entertained them as best they could, and perceived finally that their guests must be gods, because the wine placed before them did not diminish in quantity. At last they (the gods) made themselves known, and commanded the old people to follow them, as a great misfortune was threatening the land. They did so, and climbed with the two gods a mountain from which at last they saw how the whole country below was covered with water, except only their hut, which however had been converted into a splendid marble temple. When now Jupiter commanded them to ask some favor, they asked that they might be priests in the new temple, and that neither of them might survive the other's death. Their wish was granted, and as they were once relating to the people the story of the submerged land they were both changed into trees, Philemon into an oak, Baucis into a linden, which trees stood before the aforesaid temple and were long held in honor.'

One sees here at a glance a number of the essential features of Goethe's picture: The little hut upon a hill; the pious old couple, happy in their poverty, attached to their home and to each other; the temple, the priesthood, the linden-trees. But the *story* is entirely different. Said Goethe to Eckermann, June 6, 1831: 'My Philemon and Baucis have nothing to do with that famous pair of antiquity or the saga relating to them. I gave them those names merely to elevate the characters. As the personages and the conditions are similar, the similar names produce a thoroughly favorable effect.'

11054. **jener Tage**; gen. of time. A lapse of years must be imagined between the shipwreck and the present time.

11059. **Kömmling,** = Ankömmling, hardly occurs, except here, in modern German.

11064. **zu empfahn.** The inf. construction is elliptical. 'Is it even you, still alive to receive my thanks,' etc.

11071–2. **Flammen, Silberlaut.** Supply something like ich denke an. Philemon had lighted an alarm-fire on the hill and rung his chapel bell, when he saw the ship in danger; wherefore the 'outcome of the adventure' is said to have been 'placed in his hands' (by Providence).

11087. **Älter;** the absolute comparative with the sense of a causal clause. 'Being rather old I was not present,' etc.

11104. **Erst;** to be joined with in der Weite. The word heightens the intended contrast. At the time of the shipwreck the sea came up close to the hill; now it is only seen in the far horizon.

11121. **Zelte, Hütten;** those occupied by Faust's workmen, who began their operations (faßten den ersten Fuß) not far from the hill.

11122. **Richtet;** here, as often in speaking of a building, = 'raise.'

11123–30. Baucis thinks that the bustle of workmen during the day was mere feigning which accomplished nothing, the real work having been done at night by evil spirits. She has even heard, and in her prejudice against the new lord is ready to believe, that human lives were sacrificed to the evil spirit by whose aid the work must have been done.

11133–4. The meaning is: We are expected to submit humbly to our neighbor's domineering ways.

Palast.

The palace is at a distance from the sea, but is led up to by a canal large enough for merchant-ships. The Faust of this scene, so Goethe said to Eckermann, June 6, 1831, is to be thought of as a hundred years old. He has a fleet of ships out, in command of Mephistopheles as skipper, the return of which is expected and is to be celebrated by a festival. The name Lynceus, as in the case of Philemon and Baucis, is used to 'elevate the character' into the sphere of pure poetry. On the meaning of the name cf. n. to l. 9217+. But the warder here is not to be identified with the phantom Lynceus of the third act.

11149. **Zu dir;** addressed to Faust, but as an apostrophe.

11150. **zur höchsten Zeit.** Cf. n. to l. 10987.

11156. **Hochbesitz,** 'grand possession'; **rein** in the sense of 'free from blemish,' the property of the old people being the blemish, because it is an eyesore to him. The temper and conduct of Faust with regard to Philemon and Baucis are hardly what we should expect from a man who will be dreaming presently of 'standing with a *free* people on a free soil' (l. 11580).

11160. **fremdem Schatten;** shade owned by others.

11169. **Glückan,** 'good-morrow.' Glück an, as if Glück ans Land, is properly a greeting *to* those who disembark from a ship, as Glückauf to those who ascend from a mine. But it is here used *by* those who disembark, as a greeting to Faust.

11186. **Ich müßte . . . kennen;** = a conditional sentence: 'If I know anything of marine matters.'

11189 ff. We are to understand that Faust makes a wry face over Mephisto's defense of piracy. There is an old proverb, Stank für Dank, of like meaning with Hohn für Lohn.

11202. **für die Langeweil,** 'for fun,' i.e., it can not count as a final distribution.

11213–4. **Er sich . . . läßt,** 'he will not be stingy.'

11217. **Die bunten Vögel.** The 'gay birds' are probably the gaudily dressed wenches who will lend interest to the festival for the sailors. But some understand the ships with their gay streamers (cf. l. 11163), others still the sailors.

11222. **Das Ufer . . . versöhnt,** 'the shore is reconciled to the sea'; i.e., the old battle of land and tide (ll. 10199 ff.), with its ever-changing fortunes, is at an end.

11225. **So sprich daß,** 'so speak (and it will be true) that,' i.e., 'you have the right to say that.'

11249. **Bethätigend** = durch die That verwirklichend, hence nearly = 'creating.'

11255. **Kür,** 'authority,' 'power' (Willens Kür not = Willkür).

11262. **widrig.** The medieval devil is the enemy of church-bells Cf. Grimm, D.M.. II, 854.

11263. **Bim=Baum=Bimmel,** ‘ding-dong-bell’; a word of Goethean coinage.

11266. **ersten Bad;** the infant's baptism in church (Bad der Taufe, Tit. iii, 5).

11268. **verschollner Traum,** ‘forgotten dream,’ i.e., a mere nothing. The obstreperous bell seems (to the devil) to say that that part of life which intervenes between the ‘dings and the dongs’ is of no importance.

11272. **gerecht;** seemingly a reminiscence of *King Lear* III, 5: ‘How malicious is my fortune that I must repent to be just.’

11274. **Mußt . . . colonisiren,** ‘have you not long since had to plant colonies?’ The implication is: Why then not make colonists of the old people?

11285. **Ein flottes Fest.** Say a ‘fleet’ festival for the pun's sake.

Tiefe Nacht.

11290. **Dem Thurme geschworen,** ‘sworn to the tower,’ i.e., bound by oath to the duty of a warder. Cf. n. to l. 9243.

11298. **gefallen;** supply hat. The meaning is: I have loved my vocation for the beauty that it has permitted me to see.

11301–3. The words recall a line from Goethe's poem *Der Bräutigam* (1829):

Wie es auch sei, Das Leben, es ist gut.

11309. **Doppelnacht.** The ‘deep night’ is doubly dark in the shadow of the lindens.

11337. **Mit Jahrhunderten** = Jahrhunderte lang.

11339. **zu spat;** to be taken with both clauses. ‘The word and the tone (of lamentation) are here too late.’ Faust sees that the damage by fire is past remedy, but he does not yet know the worst.

11358. **geschicht;** archaic for geschieht.

11374. **Das . . . erschallt** = das alte Sprichwort lautet. According to Düntzer, the proverb alluded to is: Gewalt geht vor Recht, i.e., ‘might makes right.' The chorus, i.e., the trio, receive Faust's angry rebuke with cool indifference. A bold servant risks everything in the service of a powerful master. The consequences are not his affair. Or perhaps the implication is that he gets no thanks for it.

11379. **lodert klein,** 'blazes feebly.'

11383. **Was schwebet . . . heran?** The smoke of the burned cottage, wafted toward Faust by the night-breeze, takes the form of the four phantom hags that appear in the next scene.

Mitternacht.

Cf. Intr. p. xxxviii. — At first Faust continues to stand on the balcony, while the four phantoms approach on the ground below. Their words are not addressed to him, but are dimly overheard by him. As he sees three of the four vanish he enters the palace from the balcony (the door which is 'locked,' l. 11386, is the main entrance below). The four old hags, Want, Debt, Worry, and Distress, are allegorical personifications of four great tormentors of human kind. It is their office to stalk abroad in the night-time (when the mind is prone to all sorts of doleful misgivings), and wherever they can find a possible victim, to afflict him with thoughts of gloom and desperation. The three who can not get into the rich man's house, viz., Want, Debt, and Distress, are introduced only for picturesque effect — as sisters of Frau Sorge, who is conceived as the spirit of worry, the enemy of all joy and buoyancy of of spirit. Cf. ll. 644–51.

11384. **Die Schuld.** Düntzer is no doubt right in insisting that Schuld is not to be taken in the moral sense of 'guilt.' There would be no reason for excluding Guilt from the rich man's house, especially from Faust's house after what has happened.

11403. **in's Freie.** 'Freedom' is here the state of free self-determination. Faust feels himself still somewhat under the dominion of the spirits to whom his magic has introduced him. They beset his path at every turn, afflicting him with causeless dread and superstitious alarms. What he does is not his own free act, and yet free action seems to him now to constitute the whole worth of life. Therefore he would fain be rid of the magic which he had once resorted to so eagerly (l. 377) as to a gate of higher spiritual knowledge.

11406–7. Contrast these lines, as evidence of the clearing-up promised in the Prologue, with those passages in Part First in which Faust gives expression to his transcendental yearnings — his desire to be something *more* than a man; e.g., ll. 392–7, 614–22, 1074 ff., 1770–5.

11408. **im Düstern**; in magic.

11409. **verfluchte**; cf. ll. 1587 ff.

11414–9. Faust here speaks the language of the modern man who has put away superstitions from his mind, but still has them in his blood. He returns in a buoyant mood from a morning walk, and the sudden croak of a raven disturbs him. The commonest occurrences become signs, portents and omens (l. 11417). — **Es eignet sich** = es ereignet sich.

11433. **nur**; to be taken with gerannt. 'I have simply rushed through the world' (cf. ll. 1750–9 and 1766–75). This can only refer to the time subsequent to the compact. Before that he was a brooding self-tormentor.

11443. **blinzelnd**, 'blinking,' — dazzled by the glories of an imaginary heaven, with angels and seraphs and just men made perfect (Seinesgleichen) beyond the clouds. The lines are by no means to be taken as an agnostic expression of disbelief in personal immortality (cf. Intr. p. lxxii), but as a condemnation of Jenseitigkeit, — of the doctrine that the goodness of this life depends upon issues that lie beyond death.

11448. The thought is that what he knows (i.e., can know) is within his reach on earth.

11456. The meaning is that the victim of worry becomes dead to the aspects of nature.

11481. **Rollen**, 'rolling,' denotes a mechanical, un-human course of life, which is no longer freely self-determined.

11482. **Lassen** = fahren lassen, 'letting go,' 'quitting.' Giving up is painful, and 'ought' (i.e., the voice of duty) disagreeable.

11492. **Das geistig-strenge Band** = das strenge Geisterband, 'the strenuous spirit-tie' that binds a man to the spirits he has once invoked.

11497–8. These rather mysterious lines seem to mean: Most men are (spiritually) blind all their lives; you, Faust, have not been so; it is therefore your turn now in old age.

11499. **tiefer tief** has the effect of a superlative (tiefste Nacht). The phrase occurs in the *Urfaust*, l. 166.

Großer Vorhof des Palasts.

Mephistopheles as overseer, working as usual in the night (cf. l. 11125), summons to his aid a band of Lemurs. Nominally they are workmen ordered out to dig a trench in furtherance of Faust's plans; but in reality they are grave-diggers, for Mephistopheles foresees that the end is at hand. The ancient Roman Lemŭres were spirits of the *wicked* dead (hence here minions of the devil). Goethe conceives them as loose-jointed, shambling skeletons, half-and-half creatures patched together out of ligaments, sinews and bones. They have a short, uncertain memory. In an essay of the year 1812, *Der Tänzerin Grab*, *Werke*, H. 28, 403, Goethe speaks of the 'doleful Lemurs that retain enough of muscles and sinews so that they can make wretched shift to move about, do not appear altogether as transparent skeletons and do not collapse.'

11531–8. The stanzas are a free adaptation of the Gravediggers' song in *Hamlet* (the Clown personating the corpse):

In youth when I did love, did love,
Methought it was very sweet,
To contract, O, the time for, ah, my behove,
O, methought there was nothing meet.

But age, with his stealing steps,
Hath clawed me in his clutch,
And hath shipped me into the land,
As if I had never been such.

Shakespeare borrowed the verses from an earlier poem attributed to Lord Vaux, whose text runs:

I loth that I did love,
In youth that I thought swete,
As time requires; for my behove
Methinks they are not mete.

For Age with steling steps
Hath clawde me with his crowch;
And lusty Youthe awaye he leapes,
As there had bene none such.

Goethe's **Mit seiner Krücke getroffen** shows a knowledge of the earlier version, which he may have had from Percy's *Reliques*.

11547. **Wasserteufel.** As paganism gave way to Christianity the old gods and goddesses became devils and witches.

11566–7. **Sogleich, Gleich.** The adverbs both mean 'directly,' 'forthwith,' one going with behaglich, the other with angesiedelt. — **An des Hügels Kraft,** 'along the mighty hill,' that is, the dyke; 'mighty' with reference to its power to resist the sea.

11572. **Gemeindrang,** 'common impulse,' — public spirit become instinct. A fine word coined by Goethe.

11576. **erobern,** 'conquer,' 'make one's own by struggle.' The thought of this famous passage is that ethical merit lies only in constantly renewed effort. The man who accepts freedom, or life itself, as something to be passively enjoyed, without trying to make good his title by energetic activity of his own, is not worthy of the boon he enjoys. Cf. ll. 682–3.

11578. **tüchtig**; here = 'busy,' 'filled with activity.'

11581. **dürft' ich sagen,** 'I *might* say.' Observe the potential form of the statement. Faust does not speak the fateful words (l. 1700) to the *passing* moment, as one whose cup of happiness is already full, but as one who is dreaming of a future moment when his great plans shall be realized. It is a matter of Vorgefühl.

11589. **leeren Augenblick.** The 'highest moment' for Faust has proved to be the moment of his death, which must be understood as ensuing in a natural way. But he is not ready to go — he has still further use for life. When, therefore, he sinks back upon the ground, perhaps gasping for breath, Mephistopheles comments cynically upon his insatiate desire to live on; upon his eager clinging to the 'last, vile, empty moment' of dissolution, when life has really nothing more to offer.

11593–4. **Die Uhr steht still, Der Zeiger fällt.** Cf. n to l. 1705. Since that note was written, E. Schulte has published an article, *Zeitschrift für deutsche Sprache* 8, 441 ff., in which he argues with much plausibility that these expressions are to be understood with reference to the old, medieval water-clocks, which were so constructed that the hour-pointer (Zeiger) would rise steadily for twenty-four hours and then drop back to the starting-point. The 'falling of the hand' would thus be a natural symbol for the completion of a period.

11595–603. Mephistopheles takes umbrage, from the devil's point of view, at the suggestion of the Lemurs that death is *the end*. If it were, what would be the sense of creation with its constant toil and moil? Better the eternal-empty to begin with!

11600. **Was . . . lesen,** 'what is to be read in it?' i.e., 'what does it mean?'

Grabelegung.

The long speech of Mephistopheles over the dead body of Faust contains much that was evidently suggested to Goethe by pictures that he had seen. Among these, so far as yet identified, the most important place must be assigned to Lasinio's reproductions of the Campo Santo frescos at Pisa, a publication with which Goethe is known to have been familiar. See the interesting essay by G. Dehio, and the accompanying reproductions, in the seventh volume of the *Goethe-Jahrbuch*. In the enthusiasm of discovery Dehio went perhaps a little too far in his attempt to establish correspondences between the pictures and Goethe's text. Some of his combinations are slightly fanciful. Still it must be admitted that the Pisan frescos form a helpful, even an indispensable, commentary to this portion of *Faust*. We therefore reproduce the pertinent ones, not, however from Lasinio's engravings, but from recent photographs which exhibit the old paintings in their present somewhat damaged condition.

In the first, the 'Triumph of Death,' of which we reproduce one half, Death is seen sweeping over the earth with her scythe (*Morte*, 'death,' is feminine in Italian). At the left are the wicked and careless, above them is their destination, hell, represented as a mountain with several openings (viele, viele Rachen), from which issue smoke and flame. At the right are the pious, for whom Death has no terrors; above them, the way to heaven. Beneath the figure of Death are those that have just succumbed to her scythe. Their souls are escaping from their mouths in the form of little naked sprites, which are forthwith taken possession of either by angels or by devils. In some cases, however, the right to the soul is not determined without a battle, a pulling and hauling such as we see depicted in the air above *la Morte*.

The second picture represents 'Hell' — presumably the interior of the mountain just spoken of. Here we see the place of torment divided into compartments (nach Stand und Würden), and the tortures of the damned are portrayed by the artist with a wealth of horrible detail which lets us into the spirit of the lines:

> In Winkeln bleibt noch vieles zu entdecken,
> So viel Erschrecklichstes im engsten Raum.

Everywhere devils, with straight or crooked horns, are prodding their victims. Above at the right appears the open maw of the 'colossal hyena,' with its gruesome tusks (Eckzähne klaffen). Below is the fiery pool, with spirits of the damned trying to swim ashore, but ever driven back by the spears of the devils. Conspicuous in the foreground sits the monstrous Prince of Hell himself.

11604–7. These lines recall the third stanza of the Gravediggers' song in *Hamlet*:

> A pickaxe and a spade, a spade,
> For — and a shrouding sheet;
> Oh, a pit of clay for to be made
> For such a guest is meet.

Goethe divides the stanza into a solo (the soloist speaking in the name of the dead man) and a responsive chorus.

11610. Es; i.e., 'your (the dead man's) furniture.' His earthly possessions were never really *his*, but only loaned to him for a season.

They now belong to the living, who are his 'creditors' in the sense that they and they only have a claim upon the property.

11613. **Titel**; here in the sense of the Eng. 'title,' i.e., 'legal claim,' 'documentary right.'

11614. **jetzt**; viz., in these days of spreading universalism. Cf. l. 2509.

11623. **sie**; the soul. The old artists represent the soul as escaping from the mouth at death, its form being that of a little winged sprite. Cf. the Pisan fresco *Trionfo della Morte*.

11625–9. Mephistopheles means that the moderns no longer accept the cessation of breathing as a sure sign of death. The soul may linger until decomposition sets in.

11633. **Das Ob**, 'the whether'; i.e., whether the person is really dead, whether it is not a case of apparent death.

11635+. **flügelmännische**. Mephistopheles makes vehement motions with arms and legs, — motions like those of a fugleman or file-leader.

11638. **Von altem . . . Korne**, 'of the ancient diabolic cut and metal.' The metaphor is from the mint, Schrot being the 'clip' from the bar. Strehlke thinks the form of address expressive of gratitude for long and faithful service. Cf., however, the following note.

11639. **Bringt . . . mit**, 'at the same time bring along the jaws of hell'; a bit of cynical irony, on the part of the poet, to account for the fact that the jaws of hell open in Faust's front yard. Instead of taking the dead man's soul away to a remote hell, the devils are to bring their hell with them so as to have it handy. So, in l. 7810, the classical spooks 'bring their Blocksberg with them,' i.e., produce it where they want it.

11640. **Rachen viele, viele**. Mephistopheles, who is too much of a rationalist not to be alive to the humor of the situation he is creating, excuses himself for seeming to imply that hell has but one maw, whereas it has (or used to have) several, intended for different orders of sinners. He therefore slyly intimates (perhaps with a wink *ad spectatores*) that henceforth, democracy being the new order of things, people will expect equality to prevail 'in this last great game also' (in death as well as in life). They will not insist critically upon the 'many maws,' but be content with one, the important thing being after all not the entrance but the interior.

11643+. Höllenrachen. Cf. Is. iv, 14: 'Therefore hell hath . . . . opened her mouth without measure.' Goethe's conception, following the old artists, is that of a huge monster with yawning jaws, adown which Mephistopheles descries the whole medieval Inferno (details suggested by Dante and the Pisan frescos).

11644. Eckzähne klaffen, 'tusks yawn'—a bold but easily understood use of language.

11647. Flammenstadt. For the infernal city of Dis, with its mosques

Vermilion as if issuing from the fire,

cf. Dante, *Inferno* 8, 72 (Longfellow's translation).

11650. Die Hyäne. The name 'hyena' may have been suggested by the monstrous head (called by Dehio a Krokodilskopf) which appears above and at the right in the Pisan fresco *L' Inferno.* But Goethe's 'hyena' is not a monster *in* hell, but the monster whose jaws constitute the Höllenrachen. The damned, swimming in the fiery lake, think to escape, but the monster closes its jaws, devouring them afresh and forcing them to 'renew their agonizing hot career.'

11654–5. Here again Mephistopheles drops into the rôle of the cynical rationalist. He says to his devils: Your arrangements for frightening sinners are good, but the sinners no longer believe in your terrors.

11655+. Dickteufeln. The two orders of devils (cf. l. 11669+), distinguished by the the thickness of their bodies and the shape of their horns, were no doubt suggested by pictures.

11657. vom Höllenschwefel; to be taken with feist. 'Your fatness has the true glisten of the sulphur-diet.'

11659. Hier unten; referring to the lower part of the dead man's body.—The supposed phosphorescent gleam of incipient decomposition is identified by Mephistopheles with the escaping soul, which the Greeks conceived in the form of a butterfly (psyche).

11661. Die . . . aus; to be taken conditionally as a warning to the devils to handle the soul carefully. 'If you pluck out *them* (the wings) the psyche becomes a vile worm.' The wings with which it mounts upward are the real essence of the *animula, vagula blandula;* without them it would not be worth fighting for.

11662. Stempel; in allusion to the apocalyptic 'mark of the beast' (χάραγμα). See Rev. xvi, 2, xix, 20, and xx, 4.

11663. **Feuer-Wirbel-Sturm,** 'the whirling tempest of fire,' is the 'lake of fire burning with brimstone' of Rev. xix, 20.

11664–9. The fat devils with the straight horn do not at first obey orders, but fix their attention upon the dead man's mouth. Mephistopheles accordingly repeats his command to keep an eye on 'the lower regions' — the region of the navel. The idea that the 'bowels' are the seat of psychic life, especially of tender and sympathetic emotions, is perfectly familiar from the Bible; see, for example, Jer. xxxi, 20; Lam. i, 20; 1 John iii, 17. It is, therefore, a little far-fetched to suppose, with Düntzer, that we have here an allusion to the claim of the clairvoyants to a special organ of vision located in the navel. Goethe was interested at one time in the scientific problem of locating the psychic organ; cf. *Werke*, H. 27, 37, where he speaks of having read and pondered over Sömmering's *Versuch dem eigentlichen Sitz der Seele nachzuspüren.* It may be added that the Gr. *φρήν*, *φρένες*, means first the diaphragm, then the parts about the heart, the breast, then the heart itself, and finally the mind. When now we remember that *πνεῦμα*, *spiritus*, *anima*, are simply the breath, that escapes from the mouth, we see that Mephistopheles has reason enough for his uncertainty as to the precise point where the elusive psyche may make its exit.

11669. **Nehmt es**; es = das, was ich euch sage.

11670. **Firlefanze,** 'clowns,' 'jackanapes'; usually said of clownish *conduct.* — The tall, gaunt devils are bidden to thrash and comb the air with their claws in order that they may be sure to catch the soul should it escape the vigilance of their fat comrades, and, in accordance with its nature, try to mount upward.

11675. **das Genie,** 'the sprite.'

11676. **Folget.** The angels address each other, proclaiming their divine office as bringers of forgiveness, life (resurrection from the dead), and love.

11679. **vergeben;** best taken as an inf. of purpose with folget. But Düntzer would supply es sei.

11682. **Freundliche Spuren,** 'tokens of affection,' i.e., 'loving emotions.' It is the office of the angels to 'cause' or 'effect' these (wirket = bewirket) in all living creatures.

11686. **Tag;** in allusion to the 'glory' that invests the angels

11687. **Gestümper.** Mephistopheles means to criticise the music as like the bungling work of school-children.

11689. **tiefverruchten Stunden,** 'hours of deep depravity.' For the conspiracy of Satan and his minions against the 'new race called man,' cf. *Paradise Lost* 2, 348 ff.

11695. **unsern eignen Waffen;** viz., hypocrisy.

11698+. **Rosen.** In the Pisan fresco the angels fight with crosses. Goethe gives to his angels a different symbol of divine love, namely, the rose. We learn further on, l. 11942, that the angels have received them from holy penitent women.

11691. **Das Schändlichste;** viz., the worst sins. The meaning is that the vilest sinners just suit the pious rescuers. No allusion to Faust.

11703. **beflügelte;** to be understood with Rosen, Zweiglein being used as if the two words formed a compound, Zweiglein-beflügelt, 'winged with little branches.'

11704. **Knospen entsiegelte,** 'unsealed,' i.e., just opened, 'from the buds.'

11712. **Gauch;** here = 'gawk,' 'fool.'

11715. **Das;** namely, the roses.

11716. **Püstriche,** 'puffers.' For the devils as mighty puffers cf. ll. 10082 ff. According to Grimm Wb. the Saxons had at one time a god (Abgott) who was called Püster, or Püsterich, because he had inflated cheeks and blew fire from his mouth.

11717. **Broden;** a form preferred by Goethe to the more usual Brodem. It is used here of the foul breath of the devils.

11718 ff. Instead of shriveling up, the roses are converted into stinging flames, by which the devils are enervated. That is, the symbols of pure celestial love become in *this* atmosphere the stimuli of 'voluptuous heat' (Schmeichelgluth).

11730. **Herz wie es mag** = wie es das Herz mag, 'such as the heart desires.'

11731-4. The sense seems to be: 'Our true words (the message of love that we bring) prepare (repeat bereiten) infinite day for the eternal hosts in the bright ether.'—**Äther im Klaren** (better perhaps klaren), = im klaren Äther. The lines are obscure at best, and have been variously explained.

11741. **Du!** addressed to one in particular of the fluttering roses which he tries to seize.

11742. **Gallert-Quark,** 'sticky filth.' The meaning is: If I catch that radiant light of yours, there'll soon be nothing left of you — nothing but a grease-spot.

11745. **Was . . . angehört;** viz., the soul.

11747. **Was . . . stört;** the message of love.

11749. **ein;** i.e., euch in's Herz ein.

11756. **ihr;** addressed to the devils who, from the maw of hell into which they have tumbled helter-skelter (l. 11738), look back languishingly toward the angels.

11759. **Auch mir**, sc. geht es so.

11761. **feindlich scharf,** 'keenly repulsive.'

11767. **Wetterbuben,** 'cunning reprobates.' Wetterbube, like Blitzbube, Blitzkerl, etc., is used in the sense of 'shrewd fellow,' and also in that of 'scamp,' 'reprobate.' Here spoken half in amorous endearment, half in reproach.

11784. **Ist . . . Liebeselement.** The meaning is: Is this the time and place for amorous sensations?

11811. **wenn . . . durchschaut,** 'when he looks himself through and through' — and sees that the love-magic has only affected his skin.

11822. **preis't,** 'sing praises'; here intransitive.

11828. The sense is: *That* was the object of their amorous wiles. Naschen in the sense of 'to play the wanton.'

11840. **kindisch . . . Ding** refers to absurde Liebschaft, — hardly to the bringing together of Faust and Gretchen, as Loeper thinks.

Bergschluchten.

Cf. Intr. p. xli. — As for the conception of the holy mountain, there seems no room for doubt that our poet's imagination was stimulated first and foremost by what he had read of Montserrat, near Barcelona. On this mountain there formerly existed a Benedictine convent, connected with which were a number of hermit-cells perched high up on the rocks and accessible in part only by bridges and ladders. Here the young hermits lodged, but with advancing years they moved into more comfortable habitations lower down. In the interest of his symbolism Goethe reverses this, making the highest cells the holiest and converting the whole into an ascending scale of spirituality. In the year 1800 he received from W. von Humboldt, who had lately visited the spot, an extended description of Montserrat. Humboldt wrote feelingly of the impression produced on him by the grand scenery of the place, its deep solitude and atmosphere of seclusion from the world. Cf. Bratranek, *Goethe's Briefwechsel mit den Gebrüdern von Humboldt*, p. 166.

In the *Deutsche Rundschau* for 1881, L. Friedländer first drew attention to the Pisan fresco, 'Anchorites in the Thebaid,' as the probable source of Goethe's scenery in this portion of *Faust*. Cf. also G.-J., 7, 264. This picture, which we have not thought it worth while to reproduce, shows the Nile with rocks and trees rising terrace-like. Holy hermits are ensconced here and there and engaged in various occupations. At the left Zosimus is giving the last eucharist to Mary of Egypt (cf. l. 12053). In the centre, above, lions are digging the grave of a dead anchorite. At the right a holy man is being beaten with bludgeons by two devils. Close study will show, however, that Goethe's specific indebtedness to this picture is very slight indeed, — much less than has been claimed. What is most important is, as Dehio says, the *Stimmung* that pervades it.

The opening chorus is so eloquent of pictorial suggestion that the editor of this edition was induced to look through Goethe's collection of engravings in the hope of finding some more plausible 'original' for our holy landscape than had previously been noted. The search was not altogether disappointing. From one of the poet's Italian portfolios we reproduce a (so-called) Titian, representing St. Jerome in the wilderness, of which verses 11844–53 read like a poetic description. The waving forest, the heavy-lying rocks, the clambering roots, the thick-crowding tree-trunks, the dashing waves, the protecting hollow, the friendly creeping lions — all are there.

11843+. **Chor und Echo.** The chorus is to be thought of as consisting of holy anchorites, but not necessarily of the four *patres* introduced by name. The singers need not be definitely located by the imagination. Their song is a diffused music which, blending with the mountain-echoes, makes vocal, so to speak, the genius of the entire locality.

11844. **heran.** The tree-tops swayed by the wind seem to approach. But the following dran and hinan show that there is no very definite point of view.

11849. **die tiefste.** A deep hollow in the rocks protects from the dashing water. But Schröer, who locates the singers high up the mountain, gives to die tiefste the meaning of 'far below.'

11850. **Löwen.** The harmless lions of the holy mountain recall Is. lxv, 25.

11853. **Liebeshort,** 'refuge of love.' The spirit of love which pervades the scene creates an asylum which even the lions respect.

11853+. **Pater ecstaticus.** According to Loeper, several of the early Christian mystics, e.g. Ruysbroek (1293–1381) received the name 'Ecstaticus.' But Goethe probably used the distinctive name in a generic sense, as in the case of the other *patres;* i.e., to suggest a type of saint rather than a particular individual. Our 'ecstatic father' is a holy man whom mortification of the flesh, the destruction of the gross earthly part, has made superior to the force of gravity. Such saintly buoyancy is ascribed in hagiologic lore to Philip of Neri. See Goethe's *Italienische Reise*, under date of May 26, 1787.

11854–7. The nouns are not to be taken as vocatives, but as a rapturous description of the ecstatic state in which the pain of the body is felt as a divine bliss. The saint therefore courts a further castigation of his mortal frame, until there shall remain nothing but the 'kernel of everlasting love.'

11865+. **profundus.** This name was given to Bernard of Clairvaux, who was called even in his youth 'marvellously cogitative' (*mire cogitativus*), and later became distinguished for his excessive self-abnegation. He was also an ardent lover of nature.

11866. **Wie,** 'in that.' The modal particle means that the precipice, the brooks converging to a cascade, the high-towering tree, as they severally manifest themselves, are all phases of God.

11882. **Sind;** namely, the thunder, the rain and the lightning.

11886–7. The bodily senses are felt as a galling fetter.

11889+. **Seraphicus.** The name was given to St. Francis of Assisi.

11892. **im Innern**; sc. des Wölkchens.

11898. **Mitternachts Geborne**; in allusion to the superstition that infants born at midnight do not live long. The 'blessed boys' are the spirits of children who died before they had known sin.

11902. **Liebender**; the *pater* himself.

11906 ff. Swedenborg, in whom Goethe early became interested, claimed to converse with spirits who entered into this or that part of his body in order to be able to see earthly things. The 'blessed boys' having died before their senses were developed, the *pater* loans them his and tells them the names of the things they see.

11911. **abestürzt**; abe is archaic for ab.

11936–7. The quotation-marks are found in the MS., penciled in by Goethe himself. But the lines are not really quoted. The marks were meant to have the effect of underscoring. On the importance attached by Goethe to the thought of these verses, cf. Eckermann, under June 6, 1831.

11956. **wär' er von Asbest** is a way of saying: Had it passed through fire and flame.

11959. **Die Elemente**; the 'elements' of mortality. When the soul has once allied itself with gross matter, only divine love can break up the union and cause the soul to appear in perfect purity.

11984. **Englisches Unterpfand**; a pledge or token of trust on the part of the angels.

11985. **Flocken**; used loosely, it would seem, in the sense of 'dross,' — the clinging remains of mortality (cf. l. 11954). The whole matter is at best somewhat unimaginable, but Schröer is surely wrong in thinking of Flocken as a garment which is to be taken off.

11988+. **Doctor Marianus.** That the fourth saint is called 'doctor' instead of 'pater' is not especially significant. Goethe first wrote 'pater.' The epithet 'Marianus' marks him as especially devoted to the Virgin Mary.

11994. **Im Sternenkranze,** 'with starry halo.'

12020–3. The meaning is that the *privilege* of showing grace to women who have sinned is not taken from the Holy Virgin, is not made foreign to her nature, by the fact that she is herself immaculate. The construction of **Dir** with **benommen** implies not only that the penitents have the right to approach her, but that she is eager to pardon.

12029. **Schiefem, glattem Boden,** 'the steep, slippery ground' of carnal temptation.

12052+. **Maria Aegyptiaca.** Like the other two penitents with whom Gretchen is here associated, Mary Magdalen and the Samarian woman, Mary of Egypt is one whose sins on earth had been sins of sensuality. For seventeen years, according to the *Acta Sanctorum* (see under April 2), she led an abandoned life. Coming to Jerusalem at the festival of the Elevation of the Cross, she was about to enter the church when an invisible hand thrust her back. Smitten with remorse over her own unworthiness, she prayed to the Virgin, was then lifted and borne miraculously into the church, where she heard a voice bidding her go beyond the Jordan and find peace. Acting on the command she spent forty-eight years of penance in the desert, and, as she was about to die, wrote in the sand a message for the monk Socinius, requesting that he bury her body and pray for her soul.

12077. **mächtigen Gliedern**; the members of the new spiritual body (1 Cor. xv, 44), which has developed rapidly under the tutelage of the child-angels (cf. l. 11987).

12104–11. **Chorus mysticus.** Taylor has the following excellent comment upon the closing lines: 'Love is the all-uplifting and all-redeeming power on Earth and in Heaven; and to Man it is revealed in its more pure and perfect form through Woman. Thus, in the transitory life of Earth, it is only a symbol of its diviner being; the possibilities of Love, which Earth can never fulfil, become realities in the higher life which follows; the Spirit, which Woman interprets to us here, still draws us upward (as Margaret draws the soul of Faust) there.'

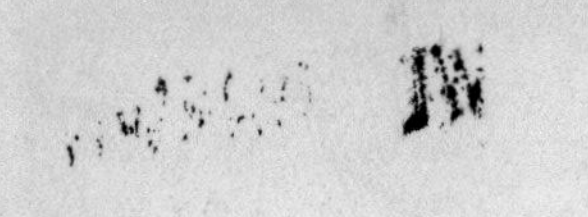